The Forgotten Compass

Biblical Performance Criticism Series
Orality, Memory, Translation, Rhetoric, Discourse

David Rhoads and Kelly R. Iverson, Series Editors

The ancient societies of the Bible were overwhelmingly oral. People originally experienced the traditions now in the Bible as oral performances. Focusing on the ancient performance of biblical traditions enables us to shift academic work on the Bible from the mentality of a modern print culture to that of an oral/scribal culture. Conceived broadly, biblical performance criticism embraces many methods as means to reframe the biblical materials in the context of traditional oral cultures, construct scenarios of ancient performances, learn from contemporary performances of these materials, and reinterpret biblical writings accordingly. The result is a foundational paradigm shift that reconfigures traditional disciplines and employs fresh biblical methodologies such as theater studies, speech-act theory, and performance studies. The emerging research of many scholars in this field of study, the development of working groups in scholarly societies, and the appearance of conferences on orality and literacy make it timely to inaugurate this series. For further information on biblical performance criticism, go to www.biblicalperformancecriticism.org.

Books in the Series

Holly E. Hearon & Philip Ruge-Jones, eds.
The Bible in Ancient and Modern Media

James A. Maxey
From Orality to Orality: A New Paradigm for Contextual Translation of the Bible

Antoinette Clark Wire
The Case for Mark Composed in Performance

Robert D. Miller II, SFO
Oral Tradition in Ancient Israel

Pieter J. J. Botha
Orality and Literacy in Early Christianity

James A. Maxey & Ernst R. Wendland, eds.
Translating Scripture for Sound and Performance

J. A. (Bobby) Loubser
Oral and Manuscript Culture in the Bible

Joanna Dewey
The Oral Ethos of the Early Church

Richard A. Horsley
Text and Tradition in Performance and Writing

Kelley R. Iverson, ed.
From Text to Performance: Narrative and Performance Criticisms in Dialogue and Debate

Annette Weissenrieder & Robert B. Coote, eds.
The Interface of Orality and Writing: Speaking, Seeing, Writing in the Shaping of New Genres

Thomas E. Boomershine
The Messiah of Peace: A Performance-Criticism Commentary on Mark's Passion-Resurrection Narrative

Terry Giles & William J. Doan
The Naomi Story—The Book of Ruth: From Gender to Politics

Bernhard Oestreich
Performance Criticism of the Pauline Letters

Marcel Jousse, Edgard Sienaert, ed.
Memory, Memorization, and Memorizers: The Galilean Oral-Style Tradition and Its Traditionists

Margaret E. Lee
Sound Matters

Thomas E. Broomershine
First-Century Gospel Storytellers and Audiences

Margaret E. Lee and Bernard Brandon Scott
Sound Mapping the New Testament, Second Edition

"Experience the excitement of discovery—of an author whose work may well change your way of looking at the Bible. This book lets Marcel Jousse speak for himself, but also allows us the privilege of accompanying major scholars as they step out of their routine to engage critically and enthusiastically with Jousse. Unsurprisingly, Jousse taught in Paris. Perhaps surprisingly, he was a Jesuit priest."

—BERNHARD LANG, University of Paderborn

"This excellent introduction to the French ethnographer Marcel Jousse's pioneering and groundbreaking work on orality and memory within the Palestinian Jewish milieu of Jesus enables readers to (re)discover his contributions to the study of the New Testament and modern intellectual history. Combining two of Jousse's lectures with an introduction and critical assessments, the book indicates his avant-garde ideas and their relevance for contemporary scholarship."

—CATHERINE HEZSER, SOAS University of London

"What a joy this volume is for anyone interested in orality! Though focused on biblical studies, it equally appeals to communication or media-ecology scholars by its introduction of the work of the anthropologist Marcel Jousse to new generations. Seeing and hearing Jousse in the context of his work makes him come alive and opens up additional ways of thinking about how people interact with their communication environments."

—PAUL A. SOUKUP, SJ, Santa Clara University

"*The Forgotten Compass* points the way to a paradigm more fully suited to the Aramaic Targumic world of Rabbi Jeshua of Nazareth. A global anthropologist and contemporary of Rudolf Bultmann, Jousse offers a robust, full-bodied approach to the Scriptures, at once very old and very new. Jousse is a treasure trove indeed for younger scholars especially who seek alternative pathways to discovery."

—RANDOLPH F. LUMPP, Regis University, emeritus

"Jousse used an argument from the astronomer Laplace: great discoveries occur when previously distant concepts finally meet. *The Forgotten Compass* is one of those rare events. This magnificent collection constitutes a true reencounter, where Gospel studies come again face to face with the investigation of the traditions of oral style. The intellectual gestures of both sides will create a current able to irrigate the unified field of biblical studies and oral traditions."

—Gabriel Bourdin, Institute of Anthropological Research

"Marcel Jousse was well known for his groundbreaking study of oral tradition and memory. To celebrate this work and to probe further its significance and ongoing relevance for biblical studies and Jesus research, editors Werner Kelber and Bruce Chilton have assembled an impressive roster of scholars who assess Joussean thought. Rich with insight, these essays move forward in positive ways the study of orality."

—Craig A. Evans, Houston Baptist University

The Forgotten Compass
Marcel Jousse and the Exploration of the Oral World

Edited by
WERNER H. KELBER
& BRUCE D. CHILTON

CASCADE *Books* · Eugene, Oregon

THE FORGOTTEN COMPASS
Marcel Jousse and the Exploration of the Oral World

Biblical Performance Criticism Series 19

Copyright © 2022 Wipf and Stock Publishers. All rights reserved. Except for brief quotations in critical publications or reviews, no part of this book may be reproduced in any manner without prior written permission from the publisher. Write: Permissions, Wipf and Stock Publishers, 199 W. 8th Ave., Suite 3, Eugene, OR 97401.

Cascade Books
An Imprint of Wipf and Stock Publishers
199 W. 8th Ave., Suite 3
Eugene, OR 97401

www.wipfandstock.com

PAPERBACK ISBN: 978-1-7252-7833-2
HARDCOVER ISBN: 978-1-7252-7834-9
EBOOK ISBN: 978-1-7252-7835-6

Cataloguing-in-Publication data:

Names: Kelber, Werner H., editor. | Chilton, Bruce D., editor.

Title: The forgotten compass : Marcel Jousse and the exploration of the oral world / edited by Werner H. Kelber and Bruce D. Chilton.

Description: Eugene, OR: Cascade Books, 2022. | Biblical Performance Criticism Series 19. | Includes bibliographical references and index.

Identifiers: ISBN 978-1-7252-7833-2 (paperback). | ISBN 978-1-7252-7834-9 (hardcover). | ISBN 978-1-7252-7835-6 (epub).

Subjects: LSCH: Jousse, Marcel, 1886–1961. | Oral tradition. | Bible. Criticism, interpretation, etc. | Folklore—Performance. | Mnemonics. | Anthropology.

Classification: BS2555.52 F67 2022 (print). | BS2555.52 (epub).

A Scripture quotation in Chapter 4, marked is taken from the Amplified® Bible (AMPC), Copyright © 1954, 1958, 1962, 1964, 1965, 1987 by The Lockman Foundation Used by permission. www.lockman.org.

Contents

Preface | *ix*

List of Contributors | *xiii*

1. The Work of Marcel Jousse in Context | *Werner H. Kelber* | 1
2. Mimism and the Ancient Biblical Recitatives | *Marcel Jousse* | 54
3. The Anthropology of Mimism, of Memory, and of the Invisible | *Edgard Sienaert* | 71
4. An Oral Perspective on Proverbs 31:10–31 | *Mark Timothy Lloyd Holt* | 104
5. What Use is Jousse? Oral Form as a Mnemonic Device in the Hodayot | *Shem Miller* | 127
6. Sound, Memory, and the Oral Style | *Margaret E. Lee* | 150
7. Jousse, Oral Composition, and the Gospel of Mark | *Joanna Dewey* | 180
8. Origin and Techniques of the Biblical Recitations | *Marcel Jousse* | 198
9. The Au/Orality of the Aramaic Gospel | *Bruce Chilton* 211
10. Marcel Jousse, the Synoptic Problem, and the Past and Future of Gospel Studies | *Matthew D. C. Larsen* | 234
11. Conclusion: Implications of the Work of Marcel Jousse | *Werner H. Kelber* | 258

Index | *291*

Preface

THE PURPOSE OF THIS book is to provide a general introduction to the oeuvre of Marcel Jousse (1886–1961), and especially to develop some implications for the study of the New Testament and for biblical scholarship generally sixty years after his death. This French scholar and self-described anthropologist was a pioneering figure in the study of formulaic oral style and of the role of memorizing processes in human culture. His claim to continued recognition is intimately linked to his groundbreaking study *Le Style Oral*, a wide-ranging exploration of the oral-memorial components in human culture. Equally, if not more, significant are some one thousand lectures that he delivered for twenty-six years, from 1931 to 1957, at various academic institutions, including the École des Hautes Études, the École d'anthropologie, the Laboratoire de Rythmo-Pédagogie, as well as at the Sorbonne. When *Le Style Oral* was published in 1925, it was greeted with considerable admiration but also with expressions of skepticism.

Among those whose imagination was fired up by the book was the young North American classicist Milman Parry. Jousse's Paris lectures on oral style and tradition greatly affected Parry's exploration of the oral, formulaic language of the Homeric epics. As far as the posthumous legacies of these two founding figures in the areas of orality and memory are concerned, they could not have been more different. Parry's ideas were already during his lifetime discussed by colleagues both inside and outside the discipline of classical philology, and his work has received a steadily growing recognition following his early death. His approach was further continued and vastly extended by Albert Lord into what came to be known as the *Parry-Lord Thesis*, which by now has impacted over one hundred language areas. By contrast, the oeuvre of Marcel Jousse has remained largely unacknowledged in the human and social sciences, and it has never been given an adequate presence in biblical scholarship. It is the purpose of *The Forgotten Compass* to remedy this situation.

The idea for the book has grown out of a Society of Biblical Literature seminar session on November 26, 2019, that was devoted to the legacy of Marcel Jousse. The positive reception of the papers encouraged the panelists to consider publication. All six Seminar panelists agreed to the proposal, and all of them have contributed their revised works to the volume. Other colleagues have actively helped by means of consultation and direct contributions. It was also decided to include two representative samples of Jousse's public lectures in order to offer readers an experience of his oral style of presentation.

The chapters of this book have been arranged in an order designed to successively bring readers into the world of Jousse while conveying a great many implications of his work. Following Kelber's broadly designed introduction, Jousse's first essay provides an initial introduction to his principal themes with a focus on the mimetic topic. The subsequent essay by Sienaert traces the interaction of Jousse's biography with his thinking and further develops the anthropological law of mimism. The next four chapters cover critical insights that have arisen from an appreciative reading of Jousse's *Le Style Oral,* proceeding in chronological order of the texts dealt with: Holt (Hebrew Bible), Miller (Dead Sea Scrolls), Lee (Sermon on the Mount), and Dewey (Mark). Jousse's second essay takes readers deep into the intricacies of his work on rhythm, gesture, pearl-lessons, and clamp-words. Next comes Chilton's essay, which illuminates Jousse's biographical background in an oral French culture, and additionally reflects on Jousse's principal theme of targumic connections with gospel traditions. Larsen's essay thematizes the so-called Synoptic problem in the context of an emerging gospel tradition, and directs its gaze toward the future, contemplating what gospel studies might look like under the impact of a Joussean reading. Kelber's conclusion summarizes implications with particular emphasis on the gospel tradition.

As far as Bible citations are concerned, three contributors have chosen to use their own translations: Bruce Chilton, Werner Kelber, and Marcel Jousse.

By far the most important role in the making of this book has been played by Edgard Sienaert. Born and educated in Belgium, he received academic training in early medieval French literature. Holding degrees in Romance languages and literatures, he published "Les lais de Marie de France: Du conte merveilleux à la nouvelle psychologique" (1978). At that point in his life Sienaert had no idea what oral tradition meant. After he had accepted an appointment at the University of Natal (now Kwa-Zulu-Natal), South Africa, he began making connections between the living oral tradition as he experienced it around him in Zulu country and the writings of Marie de France. What the poetess had heard and put in writing was now taking on new meaning: "the dead letter became voiced." Researching everything he could find on oral tradition, he discovered Marcel Jousse, whom he judged to be "the only author who truly understood what orality entailed." In 1988 Sienaert founded the Center for the Study of Oral Tradition and started his career as translator of Jousse's oeuvre.

Beginning with his translation (made together with Richard Whitaker) of *Le Style Oral* into English (1990), he has continued editing and translating Jousse's lectures, essays, and stenographic materials, and writing extensively about his thought over a period of more than forty years. That Jousse's work is beginning to appear in English translations is almost entirely due to the efforts of Sienaert. By now he ranks as the most distinguished translator and foremost interpreter of the French anthropologist. If it were not for Sienaert's more than four decades of tireless work, the name and thought of Marcel Jousse would still be largely unknown in English-speaking countries. The editors express their heartfelt thanks to Sienaert for his unflagging and selfless work as translator, editor, and interpreter of the work of Marcel Jousse.

In 1986 the Association Marcel Jousse was founded for the purpose of publicizing and advancing his anthropological research, especially in the areas of orality and pedagogy. Edgard Sienaert currently serves as chair of the association. In the interest of making the Marcel Jousse archive conveniently accessible to researchers, the association has recently agreed to have it located in the library of the Institut Catholique de Paris. The association's active website is *www.marceljousse.com*, which can be viewed in French, English, and Spanish, including a Jousse lecture re-enacted by the French actor Gérard Rouzier. The electronic version of Jousse's lectures can be ordered via the website. The association has a strong following in Spain as well as in Latin American countries, and a Spanish translation of *Le Style Oral* has recently appeared.

The Editors

List of Contributors

Marcel Jousse (1886–1961) pioneered dynamic anthropology as the study of the *anthropos* living in continuous, fluid interaction with his physical and social environment. Born in the rural Sarthe region southwest of Paris, he unwaveringly held on to the three defining values of his maternal hearth: his social status as a member of the peasant society, his religious status as a Christian, and his linguistic status as a Sarthois speaker. Ordained in 1912, he entered the Jesuit order in 1913. In 1918, after three years of serving in the trenches of World War I, he was sent to the US as an artillery captain to train American officers. While in the US, he familiarized himself with the Amerindians, whose sign language confirmed his intuition that the human expression did not start with language but with mimage, whole-body gestures. On his return to France, he pursued formal studies in psychology, anthropology, ethnology, phonetics, and various speech pathologies. The year 1925 saw the publication of *Le Style Oral*, which marked the beginnings of a successful teaching career with appointments at the Sorbonne (1931–1957), the École d'Anthropologie (1932–1950), and the École des Hautes Études (1933–1945). While apart from his book his written publications came to no more than twelve essays, the recordings of his lectures come to more than twenty thousand pages. From 1950 onwards failing health forced him to discontinue most of his lecturing activities. He died on August 14, 1961.

Bruce Chilton is the Bernard Iddings Bell Professor of Philosophy and Religion at Bard College. He wrote the first critical translation of the Aramaic version of Isaiah with commentary (*The Isaiah Targum*, 1987), as well as analyses of Jesus in his Judaic context (*A Galilean Rabbi and His Bible*, 1984; *The Temple of Jesus*, 1992; *Pure Kingdom*, 1996; *Rabbi Jesus*,

2000). Recent work includes *Resurrection Logic: How Jesus' First Followers Believed God Raised Him from the Dead* (2019), and *The Herods: Murder, Politics, and the Art of Succession* (2021).

Joanna Dewey is the Harvey H. Guthrie Jr. Professor Emerita of Biblical Studies at Episcopal Divinity School, Cambridge, Massachusetts. Her work has focused on the Gospel of Mark, oral composition and transmission, and feminist criticism of the New Testament. Her publications include *The Oral Ethos of the Early Church: Speaking, Writing, and the Gospel of Mark* (Cascade Books, 2013) and *Mark as Story: An Introduction to the Narrative of a Gospel* with David Rhoads and Donald Michie (1999, 2012).

Mark Holt is a college administrator in Darwin, Australia. His Education doctoral research was on orality and literacy with a Mon Khmer language group in Northern Thailand. He has been working towards a Master of Theology with Laidlaw College in New Zealand and continues to be exposed to the oral milieu through indigenous participation in local church life.

Werner H. Kelber is the Isla Carroll and Percy E. Turner Professor Emeritus of Biblical Studies at Rice University. His work has focused on gospel narrativity, oral tradition, biblical hermeneutics, the historical Jesus, media studies, memory, rhetoric, text criticism, and the history of biblical scholarship. Among his publications are *The Oral and the Written Gospel: The Hermeneutics of Speaking and Writing in the Synoptic Tradition, Mark, Paul, and Q* (1983; 1997); *Jesus in Memory: Traditions in Oral and Scribal Perspectives* (2009; coedited with Samuel Byrskog); and *Imprints, Voiceprints, and Footprints of Memory* (2013).

Matthew D. C. Larsen is Associate Professor at the University of Copenhagen. He is the author of *Gospels before the Book* (2018). Forthcoming books are *Ancient Mediterranean Incarceration* (coauthored with Mark Letteney); and *Early Christians and Incarceration: A Cultural History*.

Margaret E. Lee is retired as Assistant Professor of Humanities at Tulsa Community College. She is the author of "Sound Mapping" in *The Dictionary of the Bible in Ancient Media* (2017) and numerous articles on sound mapping, especially in the Gospel of Matthew. She is the editor of *Sound Matters: New Testament Studies in Sound Mapping* (Cascade

Books, 2018), and coauthor with Bernard Brandon Scott of *Sound Mapping the New Testament*, 2nd ed. (Cascade Books, 2022), and coauthor of *Reading New Testament Greek: Complete Word Lists and Reader's Guide* (1993).

Shem Miller is an instructional associate professor at the University of Mississippi (Oxford) and a research fellow at the University of the Free State (Blomfontein, Republic of South Africa). His work focuses on orality studies, performance criticism, memory studies, and media criticism of the Dead Sea Scrolls and the Jewish literature in the Second Temple period. He is the author of *Dead Sea Media: Orality, Textuality, and Memory in the Scrolls from the Judean Desert* (2019), and of several articles on orality and oral tradition in the Dead Sea Scrolls.

Edgard Sienaert is honorary research associate in the Centre for Gender and Africa Studies at the University of the Free State in Blomfontein, South Africa. Holding degrees in Romance languages and literatures, he published "Les lais de Marie de France: Du conte merveilleux à la nouvelle psychologique" (1978), and co-translated Marcel Jousse's seminal work: *The Oral Style* (1990). Recent publications are: *In Search of Coherence: Introducing Marcel Jousse's Anthropology of Mimism* (Pickwick Publications, 2016), and the editing and translation of a number of Jousse's essays in *Memory, Memorization, and Memorizers: The Galilean Oral-Style Tradition and Its Traditionists* (Cascade Books, 2018).

1

The Work of Marcel Jousse in Context

WERNER H. KELBER

The Oral Style

Je vous apprends comment
trouver ce que je n'ai pas pu trouver
moi-meme.
I am teaching you to find what I have found
myself to be unable to find.
—Marcel Jousse, SJ
École d'Anthropologie, January 3, 1949

Je suis inclassable. On n'a jamais pu
me classer dans la vie.
I am unclassifiable. No one has ever managed to
classify me in life.
—Marcel Jousse, SJ
Sorbonne, November 26, 1951

Je ne prends jamais de références, mais j'ais une
mémoire qui est dans mes doigts.
I never take any notes, but I have a memory
which is in my fingers.
—Marcel Jousse, SJ
Sorbonne, February 1, 1934

2 *The Forgotten Compass*

Editorial and Formatting Motivations

It is fitting to commence this book with an overview and appraisal of *The Oral Style*, Marcel Jousse's principal written work. Characterized by his assistant, Gabrielle Baron, as "the single, primary, major work in Marcel Jousse's oeuvre and the very foundation of his whole scientific career,"[1] described by Edgard Sienaert as "a work of fundamental importance in the field of orality-literacy studies,"[2] and introduced by John M. Foley as "a cornerstone of modern studies of oral tradition,"[3] it seems ideally suited to serve as entrée into the intellectual world of the French anthropologist. To the extent that Jousse is known at all, his claim to fame has been closely linked with this book.

It should be acknowledged at the outset that *The Oral Style* provides not only the most important, but also an exceptionally difficult gateway into Jousse's thinking. Both in terms of content and organization it is a highly unconventional work that confronts readers with an array of serious challenges. Quite possibly, the book's puzzling content and organizational logic, and its bewildering terminology, have contributed to Jousse's lack of recognition for much of the twentieth century. Readers who approach the book with expectations of a single, magisterial author, a coherently developing narrative, and a discernible progression toward a thematic point of culmination, will be disappointed and perhaps turn away in frustration.

Instead of the expected authorial presence of Jousse, readers are confronted with a steady stream of citations from altogether 176 different authors. As Jousse himself emphasized, "My book is made up almost entirely of quotations."[4] The majority of the studies cited were either written in or translated into French, originating mainly from the last decades of the nineteenth century and the early decades of the twentieth century. As Jousse described the genesis of the bibliography, it was the result of a lengthy and complex selection process. It began with some five thousand books that were rigorously trimmed down to a list of some five hundred books. From them he collected those books for the bibliography from which he had extracted the assortment of citations that make up the bulk of *The Oral Style*.

1. Jousse, *The Oral Style*, xiii.
2. Jousse, *The Oral Style*, xi.
3. Jousse, *The Oral Style*, viii.
4. Jousse, *The Oral Style*, xv.

Jousse himself contributed a fair number of augmenting segments, explanatory comments, and complementary notes that served as links and introductions to the cited pieces, generating the semblance of a connective framework over the whole book. As a rule, his own writings closely interact and blend in with his chosen quotations. Seeking to assist readers' comprehension, Jousse places these in quotation marks, and additionally lists the names of their individual authors in brackets at the conclusion of each quotation. At times, however, the formatting arrangement is puzzling and difficult to follow. Occasionally it is unclear where opening quotation marks are being closed, and it is not always easy to differentiate Jousse's voice from those of other authors.

There is also the issue of terminology. Not only is Jousse's own style impregnated with oral discourse, but he introduces a set of terms that are bound to leave readers clueless. What, for instance, is one to make of "intussesception," of "rhythmo-typography," of "dynamogeny," or of "transfer formulas," to mention just a few?

Then there is, last but not least, the issue of the book's general organization. Apart from the steady succession of quotations, *The Oral Style* is evenly divided into two parts. Part 1 is titled "The Anthropological Foundations of Oral Style," and Part 2 is called "The Oral Style." Inevitably, this raises the question: Why did Jousse choose to commence his study on oral style with the topic of anthropology, defining it as foundational for the conceptualization of oral style? This is not a customary manner of approaching matters of orality. In sum, *The Oral Style* is a perplexing entrée into Jousse's difficult lifework.[5]

It is undoubtedly atypical for an academic review to make an issue of the bibliography. But as the product of a prolonged selection process, Jousse's bibliography is bound to hold a key to his project. At the very least, a closer look at the deliberately constructed bibliography will give us initial insights into some of Jousse's editorial motivations.

What is immediately noticeable is the strong representation of the disciplines of ethnology, linguistics, philosophy, psychology, and biblical scholarship. Ethnology is represented by a remarkably large number of studies on subjects such as the laws of the Qur'an's poetic language, Muslim rhetoric, ancient festivals and songs of China, Arabian metrics,

---

5. There are limitations to the way a book of this kind can be adequately reviewed. It could well be judged to be a primer in the new genre of antibooks that seek to overcome the conventional book technology consisting of author-pages-paragraphs and chapters.

a grammar of Tamachek (a Berber language spoken by North African tribes), popular songs among the Afghans, expressions of wishes among the Chinese, and Egyptian hieroglyphics. In the area of linguistics, one encounters studies on comparative Semitic languages, phonetics, metrics, rhythm, the cognitive function of deaf-mutes, memory, and imagination. Philosophy makes its appearance with subjects such as scholastic philosophy, metaphysics, cognition, and aesthetics. Under the rubric of psychology, one discovers such topics as child psychology, psychology of reasoning, linguistic psychology, scientific theory of sensibilities, and spiritual energy. Biblical scholarship is conspicuous in items about the Hebrew Bible, Hebrew grammar, the history of Hebrew poetry, Isaiah, Jeremiah, the Sermon on the Mount, Jesus, Paul, archaeology, and the Aramaic origins of the Fourth Gospel. Add to this baffling bibliographical miscellany books on French literature, poetry, Greek literature, Homer and the Homeric question, the Babylonian Talmud, Assyrian and Babylonian religions, astronomy, the language of music, gestures, and dance—and one will have gained a fair impression of the scope and variability of Jousse's bibliography. But what, one is bound to ask, is the purpose of this mélange of seemingly disconnected items? No less surprising is the fact that this rich and variegated assortment of disciplines and subjects is subordinated under the conceptual umbrella of oral style. What bearing does the bibliography have on Jousse's project of *The Oral Style*?

Whatever Jousse intended the label *oral style* to convey, his bibliography strongly suggests that he had something rather different in mind from what in our time generally falls under the heading *oral tradition*. As far as theoretical designations are concerned, it is not always recognized that during Jousse's lifetime terms such as *oral-traditional literature*, *orality-literacy studies*, *oral hermeneutics*, *secondary orality*, and the like were virtually nonexistent in the humanities and social sciences. Jousse's theories antedated two seminal studies that conceptualized the modern communications theory, Marshall McLuhan's *The Gutenberg Galaxy*,[6] and Walter Ong's *Ramus, Method, and the Decay of Dialogue*[7] by more than three decades. There was no widely agreed-upon term that would cover what today in a very generalized sense carries the label *media ecology*. The one term that was in current use was *oral tradition*, and it was noticeably this term, and not *oral style*, that under the auspices of form

---

6. McLuhan, *The Gutenberg Galaxy*.
7. Ong, *Ramus*.

criticism became the favorite in biblical scholarship. Deliberations on these two designations are nor inconsequential wordplay, because Jousse was aware of the concept of oral tradition, and he understood that there was "an essential difference between oral tradition and oral style tradition" (*il y une différence essentielle entre la tradition oral et la tradition de style oral*).[8] That is to say, he intentionally opted for *oral style* as opposed to *oral tradition*. Since there is no known evidence of the term *oral style* prior to Jousse, Sienaert has concluded that "as far as I know, Jousse was the first to call oral tradition, oral-style tradition, i.e., to attach the notion of style to the notion of tradition."[9] Hence, not only was the designation "oral style" Jousse's deliberate choice, but it was, as far as we know, also a term of his own making. Given the relevance of these two terms, both for Jousse's work and for biblical scholarship, it seems reasonable to examine both with the aim of clarifying Jousse's very particular concept of oral style.

Oral Tradition in Form Criticism[10]

While oral tradition had for some time served biblical scholarship as a useful explanatory category, it was form criticism that elevated oral tradition to conceptual status. The discipline was singularly devoted to the exploration of oral tradition. In reviewing the concept of oral tradition as it was programmatically introduced by form critics, it is well recognized that the discipline has undergone significant changes since its arrival in New Testament studies over one hundred years ago. Nonetheless, a comparison with Jousse's conceptualization is historically relevant because the three leading New Testament form critics were contemporaries of Jousse. In fact, each of the foundational works by Karl L. Schmidt,[11] Martin Dibelius,[12] and Rudolf Bultmann[13] concerned itself with the gospel tradition, and all antedated Jousse's *Oral Style* by a few years. Moreover, traces of basic form-critical assumptions have found their way deep into current studies of the gospel narratives and their tradition.

8. Jousse, lecture at the Sorbonne, February 16, 1956.
9. Sienaert, private correspondence with the author.
10. For the following section on form criticism, see Kelber, *Imprints*, 454–63.
11. Schmidt, *Der Rahmen*.
12. Dibelius, *Die Formgeschichte*.
13. Bultmann, *Die Geschichte*.

The following nine principles may be said to be constitutive of conventional form criticism; none of them would meet with Jousse's approval. *One*, the review must begin with the discipline's formal designation. Form is a visually based concept that imagines speech as something assimilable to the spatial surfaces of printed pages. In selecting form as its foundational category, the discipline was inevitably drifting toward visualizable language. Beginning with its conventional classification, therefore, form criticism was fated to move toward a literary paradigm. *Two*, from an early point on, the form critics were inclined to define and practice the new discipline as a methodology in service of the *quest for the historical Jesus*. It was rapidly welcomed as an instrument ideally suited to recover Jesus' sayings and parables with methodological precision. Eventually, form criticism viewed itself alongside historical, literary, and redaction criticism as a component of the basic methodological apparatus of New Testament studies.

Three, there was broad agreement among the early form critics that the aim of the new discipline was to recover the original form of a dominical saying, parable, or narrative unit. By pruning away what were perceived ornamentations and secondary additions from textual units one expected to arrive at the original form. While most form critics were fully aware of the technical difficulties involved in the process of the original reconstruction, what was missing was a clear voice cautioning that in oral tradition "the original form" was an alien proposition to begin with. *Four*, form critics across the board advocated the principle of detachable speech. It was and continues to be a favored form-critical procedure to identify and isolate segments from their textual environment, and to scrutinize their assumed oral identity. Once again, a cautionary voice was required to explain that texts and textual extracts are not equivalent to spoken words.

Five, implied in the concept of detachable speech is the notion that speech is operational, and hence identifiable, in isolation. Spoken words are assumed to be self-explanatory because they occur in contexts exclusively of words. Yet, word power is actualized not by the delivery of words alone but by multiple interactions with social contextuality. One finds only limited form-critical awareness that oral verbalizations, perhaps more than written words, live in and from social context as fish swim in water. Missing, once again, was a clear understanding that vocalized language was intricately interwoven with its surroundings to the point where social context can be said to function as a coproducer of meaning. *Six*, a specific allowance form critics made for social setting was the conjecture that a predictable correlation existed between characteristic speech forms and distinct social settings. Put another way, it was assumed that definable oral genres were drawn to, or generated by, definable "settings in life." But the coexistence and indeed interaction of orally verbalized words with socially contextualized speakers or audiences is a world apart from the form critics' rigidly formalized correspondence pattern between speech and life settings. There is no known theorem in orality studies to support the form-critical correspondences between speech and life settings.

Seven, form criticism typically conceptualized oral tradition along the lines of linear transmission processes. Moreover, the linearity of tradition was frequently understood in evolutionary terms. It was a widely accepted contention that the dominant trend of the tradition was from smaller to larger, and from simple to more complex units. What was lost sight of was the fundamental linguistic fact that speech exists in time, and never in space, and that living speech and dialogue is unimaginable on the spatial model of directionality, let alone on evolutionary directionality. *Eight*, all form-critical principles elaborated above appear to be derived from a text-centered thinking that is ultimately rooted in print technology. The form-critical exploration of oral tradition, therefore, gives every appearance of treating it as a derivation from or adjunct to textuality. It is one of the great ironies that the discipline dedicated to recovering oral tradition has desensitized biblical scholarship to the core values of oral tradition: the world of sound, mnemotechnical style, the nature of living words, performance (rather than form), repetition, and recitation, word power, and many more qualities. But nothing seems more baffling than the virtual absence of memory and remembering from the form-critical model of tradition. Patently, oral tradition and memory exist in cohabitation, and a model of oral tradition without reference to memory is unfathomable. In sum, form criticism barely raised a curtain on the oral factor only to rapidly drop it again. *Nine*, one looks in vain for an awareness, let alone a differentiated treatment, of the psychodynamics of speech vis-à-vis papyrological writings, and living words versus chirographically crafted manuscripts. Bultmann's famous assertion that it was "immaterial (*nebensächlich*) whether the oral or written tradition has been responsible; there exists no difference in principle,"[14] for all intents and purposes aborted the project of crafting a concept of oral tradition.

14. Bultmann, *The History*, 87.

It must be acknowledged: this kind of trivialization of the linguistic and sensory differentiation of oral versus scribal media dynamics leaves little room for orality-scribality studies and the fashioning of an oral hermeneutic. The form critics' terms and criteria of observation were those bequeathed to them by the textual-typographic media. Form criticism, one is bound to conclude, has remained captive to text-centered modes of thinking.

Corporeal and Global Anthropology

Against the background of form criticism's treatment of oral tradition, we can now bring out more fully and cogently Jousse's concept of the oral style. Setting these two projects side by side, it is patent that they are worlds apart. The citational arrangement, the bibliographical selection, and the organizational disposition of Jousse's seminal work strongly suggest that his concept of oral style was unrelated to form criticism's thematization of oral tradition. It appears to be Jousse's sui generis formulation.

Understanding Jousse's thought begins with anthropology, and specifically with his very own conceptualization of the discipline. To sense what is at stake here, one needs to reinforce this point: anthropology is the single most important key to *The Oral Style* and to Jousse's oeuvre generally. Not literacy, not even Jousse's valorization of orality and memory, nor language itself, but anthropology facilitates initial access to Jousse's mode of thinking. Put differently, all verbal and nonverbal attributes cited, discussed, and described in *The Oral Style* are first and foremost rooted in anthropology, and not in communications history or media theory. At the same time, however, we need to discard the conventional identity of anthropology as the science of ancient life forms rooted in a millennial geological history. From Jousse's point of view, anthropology's task was to ascertain the laws that govern human interactions with the surrounding world, both in small matters and in large ones. A principal question that guided his explorations was how human beings communicate both by interiorizing and responding to their environment, and by assimilating and reacting to the world around them.

At this point it seems appropriate to lay aside the massive world of textuality and literary theory, and to direct attention to nontextual human practices, experiences, and customs—in short to the human lifeworld. Not unlike conventional anthropology, so also Joussean anthropology thematized the human body. The difference was that Jousse centered on living, not on dead humans. He was not favorably disposed toward what he referred to as skeletology, the study of bones, skulls, and desiccated bodies; above all, he was interested in living and breathing, gesturing, and speaking human bodies. This brings us to the first principle of Jousse's anthropology, which states that all human interactions—verbal, mimetic, gestural, and cognitive—are corporeally grounded. While, to my knowledge, Jousse did himself not use the term "corporeal cognition," Gabrielle Baron has articulated the concept perfectly by stating that Jousse was "putting the whole body at the disposal of thought."[15] Jousse himself included a citation in *The Oral Style* that strongly favored this concept: "We think with our hands as well as with our brain, we think with our stomach, we think with everything; we should not separate one part from the other."[16]

There is therefore every reason to conclude that the title of the first part of Jousse's seminal book, "The Anthropological Foundations of Oral Style," was the result of a programmatic, carefully deliberated choice. It encapsulated an essential feature of his program.

Jousse's foundational positioning of *The Oral Style* in corporeal anthropology entails implications that take us to the second principle of his work. Once anthropology has been declared foundational, linguistic, ethnic, and national identities have lost their explanatory power. To be precise, they are of preliminary, but not of ultimate significance. Attention is bound to be focused on humankind, the human inhabitants of the earth, whether considered individually or collectively.

By way of example, Jousse's *Oral Style* has detailed the attributes and qualities distinctive to many international cultures, just as it has described many characteristics that were intrinsically linked with Islamic traditions. There is above all Israel's targumic tradition, which, we shall see, occupied pride of place in Jousse's work, and has received exceptional recognition. It is in fact a principal rationale of *The Oral Style* to convey a distinct impression of the wealth and profusion of local and ethnic customs, experiences, voices, cognitive operations, mechanisms of thought, modes of verbalization, rhythmic arrangements, and so forth. But as Jousse understood the citational information he had collected, all of it was an expression of one and the same human organism, and all of it

---

15. Jousse, *The Oral Style*, xiv.

16. Jousse, *The Oral Style*, 34; citation from Pierre Janet, typed lecture notes from the Collège de France, 1923–1924.

conformed to the overriding laws of catholicity, understood in the sense of universality.

Philosophically, the citational assemblage, while set forth in detail and fully acknowledged, was subordinate to universals. In Jousse's own words, "Oral style is only a particular form of global style."[17] Therefore, the second principle of Jousse's anthropology states that oral style is a global manifestation of humanity. To Jousse the global nature of his project seemed to be so utterly rational and commonsensical a matter that it required neither defense nor affirmation: "The term *globalism*, in fact, has no meaning at all (*n'a absolument aucun sens*), it is a tautology. Man cannot be but a global being."[18]

In the light of the second anthropological principle, Jousse's biographical selection loses much of its apparent strangeness. Once he was committed to the globality of "oral style," it followed that his bibliography would be modeled accordingly, covering ethnic milieux worldwide, collecting samples from an all-inclusive laboratory, and encompassing conventions and laws from across the globe. Based on the commonality of all humans, and in principle applicable to languages, peoples, and verbalizations across the board, *The Oral Style* enacted a theory of universal implications. In current parlance, *The Oral Style* is representative of an early example of cultural studies that concentrated upon oral communications culture.

Locating the oral style in a global anthropology marks a development of theological consequence. Is it possible to conceive of a biblical hermeneutic and a Christian theology intrinsically founded in and responsive to the human condition? Can we imagine a New Testament interpretation whose origins lie not in the historical-critical paradigm or in prior textuality, not in Greco-Roman rhetoric nor even fully in the Jewish tradition, but ultimately in criteria and principles derived from and related to the human experience? What if one were to formulate a biblical theology that was motivated not by the drive to systematize theological virtues and christological principles but by a close attentiveness to the human sensorium—sense perception and sensibilities? Could one conceivably approve of Jousse's description of Yeshua as "our model for all, regardless of our confessions, whether you are Catholics, whether you are Jews, Muslims, fetishists, or whether you are nothing at all" (*notre modèle*

---

17. Jousse, *In Search*, 57.
18. Jousse, lecture at the Laboratoire de rythmo-pédagogie, March 11, 1936.

à tous, quelles que soient nos confessions, que vous soyez catholiques, que vous soyez juifs, musulmans, fétishistes, ou que vous soyez rien-du-toutistes)?[19] Last but not least, are recent developments in cultural studies moving us, or interested in moving us, toward a global anthropology?

The Jousse Project

Having established the anthropological rationale of Jousse's project, I will explore more fully the relevance of the title *The Oral Style*. In the most general terms, the book intended to give an account of what Jousse has called *verbomotors*, namely cultures that managed life verbally, interactively, and personally, in other words orally. He was by no means the first person to deal with issues of oral style and tradition, to identify and explain aspects of oral composition, and to inquire into the formalities of special, dedicated language. In fact, his bibliographical collection of citations bears testimony to a multidisciplinary, scholarly awareness of orality's omnipresence in human culture. All the voices sounded, references documented, and dynamics illustrated had been in place prior to Jousse. It is therefore somewhat misleading to suggest that he was the discoverer of oral style and oral tradition. More to the point, what Jousse accomplished was to collect a vast amount of evidence, to let the gathered testimonies speak for themselves, and, above all, to imagine and work toward a synthesis of the data. The aim of the project was to make a case for the authenticity of oral-style cultures as phenomena different from anything classical, textual scholarship had imagined. The singular achievement of *The Oral Style* was to advocate the paradigmatic significance of verbomotoric traditions and to elevate them to the status of a civilization distinct from writing culture and in need of a comprehensive examination. Jousse's lifework constitutes the most developed, complex, and nuanced theory of oral-memorial dynamics to date.

It is indeed possible that in addition to the observed difficulties associated with *The Oral Style*, the nature of the project itself has discouraged readers from attending to and delving into the intrinsic logic and mechanisms of oral-style cultures amply displayed in Jousse's book. Presumably, the exclusive identification of the chirographic and typographic media world with Western civilization may well blind us to oral styletraditions, even though the latter have for a very long time antedated the

---

19. Jousse, lecture at the Sorbonne, January 19, 1956.

history of writing and print, have coexisted and interacted with it, and have remained a viable force until our own time. It is also possible that the assumed stability of the textual medium has instilled in us an inclination to distrust an oral tradition that has seemed forever in the making so that it became acceptable, at best, in textually based terms. Was this not the case of form criticism that it sought to render oral tradition intelligible by filtering it through textual and typographic media sensibilities? To a humanistic scholarship that has for more than five centuries heavily relied on documentary evidence, and that has accessed its ancient sources and published its own results in print, knowledge could well appear to be synonymous with textualized knowledge. Add to this the fact that the oral medium, unlike textuality, exists in virtuality, inaccessible to our measuring controls and below our threshold of visual awareness. Given all these obstacles that have littered the path toward a thematization of orality, is it realistic and warranted to devote a whole book to oral style perceived as a civilization sui generis?

John Miles Foley has challenged what he has called "the ideologically driven textual ecology,"[20] and raised the issue of a "default notion of history" that was, he argues, born out of a "media chauvinism."[21] We do well to heed his reminder that "letters and pages and books didn't always have the upper hand . . . They didn't always represent the trump technology, the medium through which all other media had to be interpreted."[22] Prompted by Foley's reminder that writing "is in fact a very recent invention,"[23] I will briefly call to mind some relevant data of the media history.[24]

If we plot the entire history of *Homo sapiens* over a calendrical period of twelve months, focusing not on geological but on media developments, we observe the emergence of the first written characters and the oldest script some 346 days into the year. What this suggests is that roughly 95 percent of human history elapsed before writing made its presence known. Late November or early December in the species year is the earliest possible date for tentative and isolated scribal stirrings—scribblings, scrawls, and scratches that may, or may not, qualify as

20. Foley, *Oral Tradition*, 253.
21. Foley, *Oral Tradition*, 113.
22. Foley, *Oral Tradition*, 50.
23. Foley, *Oral Tradition*, 113.
24. For the basic data concerning media history, I am indebted to Foley, *Oral Tradition*, 50–51, 113–15.

writing. Another way to put it is that the life experience of *Homo sapiens* for the most part has depended wholly on alternative technologies to the chirographic and typographic media, namely, on oral communication. For most of human history oral discourse served as the principal means of communication. To sum up, writing systems have existed for less than three weeks of the species year, Gutenberg's printing press was invented on December 27, and the internet on December 31. "OT [Oral Tradition] alone has stood the test of time as a medium we have used continuously since the beginning."[25]

In the global context, the textual ideology represents a very recent invention whereas humanity's oral legacy turns out to be the silenced majority today, and the rationality of Jousse's project conspicuously leaps into relevance. His intention is to take issue with a "default notion of history" and to develop an alternative perspective that is not based on spatialized, linearized, and visualized knowledge.

Mnemotechnics

The challenge before us now is to get to the core of *The Oral Style* and to explore the relevance of the volume's subtitle, *Rhythmic and Mnemotechnical Oral Style among the Verbomotors*. Attention will be directed to the authorial citations and an attempt will be made to summarize their principal affirmations. To that end, I will be surfing through the citational evidence and seek to distill from the plethora of quotations the three anthropological laws of parallelism, rhythm, and formulism that seem to be broadly representative of *The Oral Style*. All three are closely interrelated and in their aggregate, or rather in their interactive dynamic, may give us a reasonable impression of the substance and intention of *The Oral Style*.[26]

The law of parallelism or of balancing parallels, is "so natural that we come across it in all recitations from one end of the world to the other."[27] Binary parallelism occurs in the form of antithetical balancing and synchronic balancing—the former designating contrast or reversal, and the latter equivalence or consequence. The rabbinic saying "The things that were passed on in writing you will not be allowed to pass on orally,"

25. Foley, *Oral Tradition*, 115.

26. For the sake of simplicity, we will footnote the citations in reference to the Jousse volume without acknowledging the numerous individual authors. Readers who wish to verify individual authors are referred to Jousse's book.

27. Jousse, *The Oral Style*, 98.

would be a case of the former, and the Turkish aphorism "He glides like a serpent and he stings like a scorpion" is a case of the latter. It is characteristic of all features of oral style (parallelism included) that they never function just linguistically. Flowing from human bilateralism, parallelism is unmistakably based on corporeal anthropology. At the same time, it comes into play by way of motor mechanisms consisting "entirely of innate or acquired capacities."[28] First and foremost, therefore, parallelism is a psychophysiological, and not a semantic, law. It would be a mistake to view parallelism merely as an ornamental device contrived to embellish the rhetoric of poetry. Nor would it be entirely satisfactory to reduce it to its pragmatic effects on our memory and memorizing faculties. Some citational witnesses have taken "the law of universal oscillation" one step further, describing it as an essential component of oral thought processes.[29] It follows that oral style does not use parallel structures for merely rhetorical or memorial purposes, but thinks in binary terms. Anthropologically grounded, psychophysiologically functioning, and cognitively interacting, parallelism is a phenomenon of universal validity. "One can say without any exaggeration, that it plays as vital a role in the world of thought and human memory as does gravitation in the physical universe."[30]

Intrinsically linked to the parallel balancing constructions is the law of rhythm. Broadly speaking, rhythm may be described as the power that energizes oral recitations. As the authorial citations in *The Oral Style* make abundantly clear, the nature and operations of rhythm are "as complex as life,"[31] and by no means less elaborate than textual hermeneutics. But just as an understanding of literacy necessarily depends on pertinent hermeneutical tools, so oral style requires that we acknowledge and implement fitting approaches. Repeatedly the authors caution their readers "to abandon our typographical conventions,"[32] and to recognize the inadequacy of "our tame little bookish theories of rhythm."[33] Phonetics and linguistic psychology, rather than literary criticism, appear to be preferred auxiliary instruments suitable for coming to terms with the

---

28. Jousse, *The Oral Style*, 97.
29. Jousse, *The Oral Style*, 99.
30. Jousse, *The Oral Style*, 95.
31. Jousse, *The Oral Style*, 102.
32. Jousse, *The Oral Style*, 195.
33. Jousse, *The Oral Style*, 192.

phenomenology of rhythm. Among the issues relevant for rhythm is the large subject of vocality or the quality of sound, including long and short vowels, closed and open syllables, and the exploration of stress, duration, tone, and pitch in oral recitations. In the discourse on rhythm a general distinction is made between rhythmists and metricians. Rhythmists are those who perform speech as a habitual social activity, "which all, or nearly all, can and must practice in certain circumstances,"[34] whereas metricians are inclined toward professionalism—deliberate rhetorical expertise that shows a tendency toward nascent writing. More than once readers are discouraged from interpreting rhythmic style through the existing categories of a particular rhetoric, a given metrical system, or established poetic versification. It is only by dissociation from textually rooted oral categories that the universal laws of rhythm will emerge. Since the invention of printing, most aspects of rhythm have "been banned from the domain of historical, scientific and moral thought,"[35] because they have become useless in typographic culture. In the words of Foley, "the long journey into silence" was well on its way, and it amounted to a "radical reduction at almost every stage."[36]

Closely tied to the laws of parallelism and rhythm is the law of propositional clichés or formulism. Many authors observe what they variously refer to with terms such as "oral clichés,"[37] "stereotyped oral formulas,"[38] "formulas echoed again and again,"[39] and "traditional clichés," and many other such terms.[40] The opinion that "this language of 'clichés' is a universal one,"[41] and far from being an isolated feature, appears to be widely shared by the authors cited in *The Oral Style*. For those of us who are conversant in matters of orality, the occurrence of clichés is an established commonplace of oral style, but in the nineteenth century and the early twentieth century the temptation was to view the data as a disease rather than as a symptom. If repetition and stereotype, principal attributes associated with clichés, were seriously considered at all, they

---

34. Jousse, *The Oral Style*, 145.
35. Jousse, *The Oral Style*, 132.
36. Foley, *Oral Tradition*, 139.
37. Jousse, *The Oral Style*, 62.
38. Jousse., *The Oral Style*, 63.
39. Jousse, *The Oral Style*, 64.
40. Jousse, *The Oral Style*, 65.
41. Jousse, *The Oral Style*, 62.

were frequently judged as evidence of inadequately or incompetently developed literary skills. Or, if one was thinking in oral terms, the question was, Why did the performer not exercise better control over his material? Even in those rare cases where the clichés were appreciated as a stylistic mode of knowing, the challenge remained to not exclusively view them as linguistic occurrences but to explore both their verbal and nonverbal operation. Again and again, *The Oral Style* lets readers know that there is no oral discourse and no knowledge communicated orally, that is not linked with affective, gestural, and social features. There is no such thing as cerebral knowledge by itself, a singularly verbal representation, or a pure act of thinking. Nor were the clichés wholly spontaneous, ad hoc compositions. The oral reciter/composer was speaking, thinking, and remembering "with the gestural clichés of his social milieu built into him,"[42] enacting traditional, ready-made schemas that had been in circulation "long before they were uttered by the oral composers themselves,"[43] and communicating formulaic diction with the partial assistance of "choreographic gestures,"[44] such as facial expressions, bodily swaying, and manual gesticulations.

In his foundational study *The Oral Style* Jousse has brought the issue of an oral phenomenology to the forefront. Concepts such as the original form, a linearly conceived oral tradition, detachable speech, and other form-critical conjectures are nowhere to be found. It is tempting to imagine how well *The Oral Style*, a publication contemporaneous with the rise of form criticism, could have served as a viable alternative to it. The book's uniqueness stems not only from the way it is prominently thematizing orality but from its explicating oral style in the broadest possible terms—covering a very large canvas of linguistic and paralinguistic facets, corporeal and cognitive functions, and social and psychological components. Last but not least, the book solidifies orality's grounding in anthropology and history. This whole profusion of attributes and sensibilities is brought under the unifying umbrella of *The Oral Style*.

I have, in the interest of analysis and representation, singled out what I think are the three representative laws of parallelism, rhythm, and cliché. In speaking actuality, however, we will have to think of them as dynamic and interactive processes serving multiple purposes. As the

---

42. Jousse, *The Oral Style*, 63.
43. Jousse, *The Oral Style*, 65.
44. Jousse, *The Oral Style*, 102.

book's subtitle suggests, Jousse thought of this vast assortment of oral features as primarily empowered to serve the mnemotechnical needs of a verbomotoric culture. Hence, memory is the largely hidden force and deep stimulus lurking in the background of everything that is being said in *The Oral Style*. Jousse, we shall see, will locate memory in central position and weave an elaborate and intricate phenomenology around it.

The Memory Discourse

> Memory may well be more reliable than written documents.
> —Marcel Jousse, *Memory, Memorization, and Memorizers*, 122

> At present, we are but at the very first dawn of a science of memory.
> —Marcel Jousse, *Memory, Memorization, and Memorizers*, 129

Memory in Myth and History

According to ancient mythology, Mnemosyne/Memoria, at once the goddess of memory and imagination, bore Zeus nine daughters, the Muses, who represented different branches of the arts and sciences. As mother of the Muses and as memory personified, Mnemosyne was viewed as the wellspring of civilization and the matrix of all artistic and scientific labors. The ancient myth announced, in less mythological language, the privileged status and the supremacy of memory in human affairs. In addition to being celebrated in the ancient myth, memory enjoyed a productive and influential history and was continuously acknowledged throughout ancient and medieval times.[45] Variously invoked and honored as one of the five canons of rhetoric, one of the three powers of the soul, one of the three aspects of prudence, the treasure house of eloquence, the storehouse for countless images, the esteemed custodian of rhetoric, and the deep space of the human mind, Memoria was widely viewed as a mainstay of civilization.

---

45. Carruthers, *The Book of Memory*; Coleman, *Ancient and Medieval Memories*.

Yet at the same time, the high culture of medieval learning benefitted from a rapidly expanding chirographic landscape, and the steady extension of the textual base tended toward an erosion of the recitational style and memorial design of writings. Ideas enshrined in an ever-growing number of manuscripts began to assume a semblance of authorial stability, irrespective of their continued oral functioning. And yet, Mary Carruthers merits close attention when she announces that "it is my contention that medieval culture was fundamentally memorial, to the same profound degree that modern culture in the West is documentary."[46] While the theologians of the High Scholasticism of the thirteenth and fourteenth centuries excelled in formulating intricate philosophical, theological and linguistic theories with a signal keenness of intellect, many of them retained memorial faculties that may seem implausible to the typographic mindset of the modern West. Yet by way of example, Thomas Aquinas's entire *Summa Theologica*, the pinnacle of Scholastic theology and philosophy, was fundamentally a work of memory: it was mentally composed and much of it dictated, sometimes to more than one secretary and on different topics simultaneously.[47]

Against the background of memory's impressive sovereignty in ancient and medieval history, the changing fortunes of memory and the decline of oral-memorial sensibilities in modernity are strikingly obvious. The development was particularly noticeable in biblical exegesis and hermeneutics, which marginalized the role of memory, leading to its near extinction as far as the scholarly interpretation of the Bible was concerned. The leading cause of the demise of memorial faculties, of the decline of memory's authority, and of what Walter J. Ong has called "the decay of dialogue" can be determined with a fair degree of accuracy. In his classic book on Pierre de la Ramée Ong has described how in the wake of the Gutenberg revolution an educational reform captured the French academic system and rapidly spread across large parts of Europe. At its core it was designed to dismantle the five-part structure of rhetoric, the center of the medieval knowledge base, and in the process to facilitate a restructuring of the human sensorium. In short, it disengaged knowledge from the memorially grounded, vocally competent world of medieval disputations toward the space-bound world of silent words on paper.[48]

---

46. Carruthers, *The Book of Memory*, 5.
47. Carruthers, *The Book of Memory*, 2–7, 169, 203.
48. Ong, *Ramus*; Kelber, "The 'Gutenberg Galaxy,'" 1–16.

More than any other event, it was the advent and advance of the "high-tech" typographic medium in the fifteenth century that ushered in a sweeping transformation of all personal, social, and institutional arrangements in Western history.[49] "The printing press as an agent of change," to cite the title of Elizabeth Eisenstein's two-volume set,[50] was deeply implicated in and partly precipitated Renaissance humanism, the Reformation, and the rise of the modern sciences, and it can justly be viewed as one of the principal forces that ushered in and helped shape modern society and the modern mindset. But what exactly was the connection between the typographic medium and the demise of memory?

The answer lies in what was one of the defining features of the print medium, namely, its ability to construct a technologized language that thoroughly transformed book production into a series of mechanical processes. Put differently, the capacity of typographic technology to generate all-encompassing rationalization processes rendered the role of memory superfluous. Hence, in a communications culture that had been radically technologized, memory was bound to lose the vital dimension of its raison d'etre. From the perspective of a media conscious historiography, it could well be argued that the world of premodernism and modernity asserted itself at the expense of and to the detriment of the ancient and medieval world of oral-memorial dynamics and sensibilities, not unlike the way that the post-Gutenbergian digital era is about to undermine and deconstruct five centuries of typographic logic.

With this foray into the media history of typographic technology as background, we should not be surprised that modern historical scholarship of the Bible, operating in the shadow of the Gutenberg galaxy, has been locked into what I have called a typographic captivity. It is a consequence of this condition that modern biblical scholarship until recently has been suffering from a consequential diminution of memorial and oral sensibilities. On the whole, the discipline has shown only limited and narrowly confined interest in memory. Both the cause of and the broad range of implications of the memorial decline have seldom been acknowledged, let alone discussed in depth. If any allowance is made for memorial functions, the inclination has been to reduce memory to the power of individual mental faculties, and to highlight exceptional feats of memorial prowess. Inasmuch as gospel studies allowed for memory,

---

49. McLuhan, *The Gutenberg Galaxy*.
50. Eisenstein, *The Printing Press*.

the focus until recently was likely to have been on storage and preservative functions. Memorial abilities were preferably viewed as a vehicle for securing the stability and historical reliability of the tradition. Memory, in other words, if recognized at all, was taken to be a conservative more than a constructive or cognitive force.

Until very recently, memory has enjoyed very little welcome in any of the major subdisciplines of modern biblical scholarship: historical criticism, redaction criticism, literary criticism, the New Criticism, text criticism, and structuralism. Those causal rationales that were acknowledged in the Gutenbergian scholarship of the Bible as playing a principal role in the formation of tradition and gospel were predominantly of a historical and textual kind, and not of a memorial and oral kind. Perhaps the most conspicuous case of a *damnatio memoriae* is evidenced by form criticism. Ironically, the very discipline that served as the dominant methodological approach in twentieth-century biblical studies and for some time rose to become the favorite child of historical criticism, and whose very mission had been to explore the oral components of the tradition, approached the subject matter with little or no recognition of the role of memory.[51]

It is worth keeping in mind both memory's preeminence in history and its steep decline in the post-Gutenberg era in order to adequately assess its startling reemergence in the work of Marcel Jousse and others in modernity. When thus viewed in the broader context of media history, Jousse's objective to make memory the center of attention was an unforeseen proposal, in open conflict more than in continuity with memory's typographically induced amnesia in the Gutenberg galaxy. This may well be another reason for the lack of interest and outright rejection Jousse's work has encountered. Not only did Jousse's rehabilitation of memory run counter to the academic conventions of his time, but it signaled the privileging of a *topos* that seemed to belong to a distant past now superseded by modernity's typographical, literary imagination. In the period following the death of Jousse, biblical scholarship continued until recently to move in directions predominantly of the text-centered kind. In Freudian terms, one might suggest that Jousse's centering on oral-memorial media realities marks a return of what had been repressed by the print medium's tight grip on much of our historical work.

---

51. Memory (*Gedächtnis*) is an expendable category in Bultmann's *History of the Synoptic Tradition*, and it is nonexistent in the index of his acclaimed book.

It is of interest to observe that just as Jousse's rediscovery of oral style and culture roughly concurred with Parry's studies of Homer's formulaic language, so was Jousse's reconceptualization of memory partially contemporaneous with a second pioneering figure, namely, Maurice Halbwachs (1877–1945). While Jousse, we shall see, interpreted memory in broadly conceived anthropological terms, Halbwachs, the student of Henri Bergson and Émile Durkheim, approached memory strictly from a sociological point of view. But Jousse and Halbwachs were united behind the objective of highlighting the *topos* of memory, and of elevating it to a central position both with respect to antiquity (Jousse) and in reference to modern times (Halbwachs). Moreover, Halbwachs published his famed *Les cadres sociaux de la Mémoire*[52] in 1925, the same year that saw the publication of Jousse's seminal *Le Style Oral*, as noted above. There exists no confirmation, however, that the intellectual projects of the two authorities on memory were ever connected analogously to the way that Jousse and Parry were interacting and commenting on each other's work. Nonetheless, it is worth noting that the Parisian academic careers of Jousse and Halbwachs overlapped for approximately nine years. Jousse, as mentioned above, was teaching from 1931 to 1957 at a several Parisian academic institutions. Halbwachs taught from 1935 to 1944 at the Sorbonne, until in 1944 he was detained by the Gestapo and transferred to the concentration camp Buchenwald where he perished in February 1945.

On the one hand, interest in the work of Halbwachs, and in Parry's work too, has surged dramatically, making an impact on cultural and intellectual history, whereas Jousse, on the other hand, cannot get a mainstream hearing and has remained largely unacknowledged and unexamined. And yet, it should once again be noted that the 1930s and 1940s were consequential decades in the academic life of Paris, where the ground was prepared, and the seeds were sown for a revival of sensibilities that had been suppressed or marginalized by the rise of historical, typographically grounded scholarly consciousness.[53]

Today it is widely assumed that the modern memory discourse was principally initiated by the sociologist Halbwachs. Jousse, the "anthropologist of memory," as he called himself, has remained excluded from

52. Halbwachs, *Les Cadres Sociaux*.

53. This sketch of academic life in Paris from the 1930s to 1940s is narrowly focused on the modern rediscovery of orality and memory. It is not here the place to delineate a fuller picture of Parisian intellectual culture.

our reconceptualization of the history of memory studies. As for Halbwachs, four interrelated premises characterized his concept of memory. His sociology of memory proceeded from the premise that memory is of the past, and over time recedes into an ever more remote temporal distance. It follows, firstly, that the past is never directly accessible and cannot be retrieved in direct, unmediated fashion. Secondly, for the past to be recovered in the present, a mediation through social frameworks, the so-called *cadres sociaux*, is indispensable. Thirdly, what is remembered, therefore, is not the past as "pure" past, but select memories couched in social frames of reference. This suggests, fourthly, that the work of memory is not primarily fed by needs for preservation or historical reliability but by the desire to make the past intelligible and serviceable to the present. In brief, it was Halbwachs's achievement to discover the past as a remembered and socially constructed past whose objective it was to define and consolidate present group identities.

The legacy of Halbwachs lay dormant for a period of about forty years until it experienced an unexpected boom chiefly generated by the work of Jan Assmann and Aleida Assmann.[54] Deliberately relying on Halbwachs's model and consciously in the spirit of the French scholar, the Assmanns, along with a growing number of colleagues representing diverse disciplines, explored how cultures sustained communal identities across the vicissitudes of history through variously constructed remembrances of their past. Entirely in Halbwachs's sense and frequently citing him by name, they interpreted memory dynamically and closely tied to the formation of group identity. Currently, this social concept of memory goes under the name *cultural memory*. Vigorously promoted and widely publicized by academics, journalists, politicians, and artists, cultural memory has permeated the postmodern consciousness of Europe, and it plays a major role especially in German academia.[55]

It is one of the ironies of the orality-memory discourse that Parry and Halbwachs, who helped initiate our perception of oral style and social memory, subjects that were central to Jousse's oeuvre, today are widely acknowledged as founding personalities of a new paradigm in cultural studies, whereas Jousse, a giant in the study of orality and memory,

---

54. Jan Assmann, *Das kulturelle Gedächtnis*; Aleida Assmann, *Erinnerungsräume*.

55. It is not by accident that it was in postwar Germany that the modern memory discourse was launched and taken to a level of public awareness. For obvious reasons, remembering in that country is an onerous obligation, and remembrance of the not-so-distant past a deadly serious matter and inextricably tied to national identity.

has largely been forgotten. The anthropologist who insisted that "everything needs to be understood in terms of memory,"[56] has fallen victim to academic amnesia.

The Anthropology of Memory

What did Jousse have in mind when he frequently referred to himself as an "anthropologist of memory"?[57] Obviously, he was using this self-designation to convey the idea that memory was central to his concept of anthropology. But in the context of his work both terms—*anthropology* and *memory*—need further explanation. As for *anthropology*, Jousse used the designation not in the sense of prehistory or paleontology, but in the broad sense of human nature and the human species. As for *memory*, he extended its meaning far beyond the conventional designations such as faculties of recall or functions of the mind. Memory, we shall see, was for him a multifaceted reality. Conceived as an anthropological category, it constituted not merely a specific attribute of the individual person but the human person in his and her relation to their environment. Nor was memory for Jousse merely a matter of how we retrieve or reconstruct the past; it was more an issue of how we cope with and interact with the world around us. Thus, both *anthropology* and *memory* were substantially broadened and universalized.

In keeping with the distinctive character of his anthropology, Jousse chose the Greek term *anthropos* to designate the human person conceived as both the carrier and the embodiment of memory. *Anthropos* as memory defined the human person above all as a memorially empowered, living organism endowed with communicative and interactive capabilities. Concretely, *anthropos* was understood to be the individual who was facing the world, acting, being acted upon, and reacting, as well as absorbing, replaying, and responding to events and experiences, small and large. The idea of *anthropos* as Memory represented a conceptual understanding that is unknown in this comprehensive cultural fashion in the oeuvres of either Parry or Halbwachs, and in fact unprecedented in modern biblical hermeneutics.[58]

---

56. Jousse, *Memory*, 19.

57. Jousse, *Memory*, 21, 39, 45, 143, 146, *passim*.

58. The notion of memory as the way of the mind encountering and interacting with the world is by no means a foreign idea in patristic hermeneutics. See, for example, Hochschild, *Memory*. But it is not here the place to explore ways Jousse's

The anthropology of memory that Jousse has placed before his hearers is first and foremost a corporeally based phenomenon, and only secondarily a cerebrally empowered faculty. This must be appreciated: a corporeal memory discourse, while by no means absent in antiquity, and still entirely viable in Scholastic theology, is a feature unthinkable in modernity's exegetical and hermeneutical approach to the Bible. Jousse's oral-memorial paradigm time and again had recourse to starkly corporeal features. By way of example, he reminisced that what he had learned from his mother in childhood, was "embedded forever in my muscles."[59] Similarly, he observed that "our mother tongue is the only language we truly know, because it informed our entire musculature with all its semantic compartments."[60] As far as the ancient Palestinian milieu was concerned, the people were living by the Torah in their native Aramaic that had been "indefatigably buccalized and memorized from childhood."[61] The mouth of the speaker experienced how the oral recitation "vibrates in his musculature,"[62] while the meturgeman-translator carried the oral-style tradition "'in his mouth,' so to speak,"[63] possessing it as "a memory in waiting."[64] Still, Jousse is very clear that "mere muscular buccalization and . . . 'parroting' without comprehension"[65] was entirely insufficient for living in and out of the tradition. Ancient people were expected to "eat and drink the lesson with the gestes of an intellectual gourmet."[66] In fact, Jousse described the absorption and comprehension of the Aramaic formulaic tradition as a process of ingestion, "a manducation and bibition," "an eating and drinking."[67] What is conventionally called the tradition, he could refer to as a "'manducation-memorization,'" formulaically molded so as to be "meticulously gustative."[68] But we modern people, he lamented, "bookishly insensitive"[69] by training and by habit as we are,

anthropology of memory is replaying items of the ancient memory discourse.

59. Jousse, *Memory*, 272.
60. Jousse, *Memory*, 192.
61. Jousse, *Memory*, 214.
62. Jousse, *Memory*, 385.
63. Jousse, *Memory*, 105.
64. Jousse, *Memory*, 61.
65. Jousse, *Memory*, 289.
66. Jousse, *Memory*, 289.
67. Jousse, *Memory*, 277.
68. Jousse, *Memory*, 335.
69. Jousse, *Memory*, 79.

have lost all sense of how oral performance resonates "in the reciting laryngo-buccal muscles,"[70] and how it operates by exhaling through "the lungs and the throats of living people."[71] Methodologically, oral-style research should, therefore, not be done visually on paper, but by way of reliving the oral impact on the "laryngo-buccal muscles of the reciter."[72]

Jousse's neologisms "laryngo-buccal" muscles and "buccalization" require a word of explication. These are anatomical terms referring to organs centrally involved in inhaling and exhaling air for purposes of breathing and vocalization. The larynx is the voice box that houses the vocal cords and is engaged in respiratory functions and the production of sound. The buccinator, a facial muscle forming the anterior wall of the cheek, is of special interest to speech therapists; it facilitates the expelling of air, for example when whistling or playing a wind instrument. Jousse's pointedly anatomical nomenclature leaves no doubt that, in his view, memorial functions are tied to, stored in, and exercised by the body.

Let me reiterate: this notion of corporeality as seat of memory introduced an understanding of language, remembering, and cognition that is scarcely imaginable in historical criticism,[73] and different from anything modernity's biblical hermeneutics has been used to or is comfortable with. It is, however, worth reminding ourselves that the concept of the somatic nature of thought, and of the sensory, indeed somatic processes of perception are integral features of Aristotelian philosophy and Thomistic theology.

The corporeal strand represents but one aspect of Jousse's anthropology of memory. Formulism is another feature that is intimately coupled with memory. While the pervasive influence of formulism in the Palestinian targumic tradition, including in the language of Jesus, is the topic of the following segment, the focus here is on formulism's synergistic relations with memory. Jousse expressed the matter as follows: "*Memory* and *formulism* support each other in supple collaboration."[74] Formulism and memory correlate with one another, and they are mutually dependent on each other. It "lives for the memory and in the memory."[75] Pre-

---

70. Jousse, *Memory*, 135.
71. Jousse, *Memory*, 77.
72. Jousse, *Memory*, 45.
73. A very noteworthy exception is Hezser, *Rabbinic Body Language*.
74. Jousse, *Memory*, 47 (italics original).
75. Jousse, *Memory.*, 46.

cisely, what was the nature of the connectedness, and in what manner did memory and formulism support each other? The answer was developed from a wealth of observations Jousse had accumulated about Palestinian, targumic diction, demonstrating the extent to which such diction was interwoven with rhythmic components, sound and echo effects, parallelisms, antithetical and iterative constructions, and dualisms of various kinds. Rhythm, he observed about Palestine's generally proverbial style, "is an element consubstantial with the thought and logic";[76] similarly, "rhythm and logic coincide."[77]

Jousse's elaboration of a host of formulaic attributes and interaction with somatic bilateralism is a world removed from form criticism's awkward treatment of oral tradition, and it ranks as a masterly conceptualization of oral-mnemonic style. By way of example, let us remember his exceedingly nuanced discernment of the phenomenology of rhythm. As far as rhythm was concerned, he identifies four different types: "the rhythm of intensity, the rhythm of duration, the rhythm of pitch and the rhythm of timbre."[78] He clearly recognizes that the net impact of the rhythmic orchestration of formulaic language was in conformity with the structure of the human mind. What, in his view, significantly corroborated the mnemonic attractiveness of Palestinian formulism was its heavy reliance on bilateral structures, the very features that corresponded to and cooperated with "the human bilateral body."[79] Thus, the key to the operational synergism between the targumic Palestinian language and memory lay for Jousse in oral-style patterning generally and bilateral structuring specifically. Based on this correspondence, he viewed the formulaic diction as a strategy for achieving interiorization in the human brain, and in this manner for facilitating memorization. As he would phrase it, "our *reception* of the formulas is essentially memorization."[80] Closely akin to and yet distinct from the corporeal strand, we might call this function of Jousse's anthropology of memory the mnemotechnical strand.[81]

---

76. Jousse, *Memory*, 237.

77. Jousse, *Memory*, 264; see also Jousse, *The Parallel Rhythmic Recitatives*, 11.

78. Jousse, *In Search*, 243.

79. Jousse, *In Search*, 59.

80. Jousse, *Memory*, 368 (italics original).

81. Jousse himself has used the term *mnemotechnical* frequently in reference to formulism, see *Memory*, 64–68, 115, *passim*.

Related to the interiorizing function of formulism is its ability to stabilize the flow of life. *Anthropos* as Memory, we saw, represents the individual who is continuously interfacing with the world, ingesting and replaying bits of information, actions, and voices as these incessantly invade consciousness, or who is knowingly inviting external influences into the mind. This understanding is based on an interactive model of individual and social fluidity.

However, it stands to reason that in a linguistic and social world of unlimited fluidity, the work of memory will inevitably come to grief. An uninterrupted stream of consciousness and a mode of perpetual flux are ill-equipped to capture memories in any kind of holding pattern. A model of unrelieved linguistic mobility would generate an informational and sensory overload and result in memorial dysfunction and ultimately amnesia. As Jousse explains this matter, "Any memory attempting to carry an undivided burden in bulk would be inefficient and incapable of understanding the detail of the treasure it carries."[82] To secure memory's efficient workings, a measure of ordering, dividing, and structuring is required such as linguistic partitioning into memorially comprehensible components, and arrangement of words into manageable speech units. To be sure, Jousse exercises great care in characterizing oral traditionists not as mindless stabilizers but rather as competent utilizers, even improvisers, and in making the point that formulas are not to be mistaken for lifeless invariants: "memory is not mechanical repetition."[83] In a blatant affront to textual hermeneutics, he claims, as stated in the second epigraph to this segment, that "memory may well be more reliable than written documents."[84] This is the case, in his view, not in terms of preservation per se, but precisely because the memorially empowered tradition allowed reality to remain in play, and memory to stay actively involved in the flux of life—and for this reason memory continued to be directly relevant to the human existence. And yet, in Jousse's overall model of memory, formulism is a device designed to control the flow of life so as to make it memorably attainable and usable. Thus, formulaic phrasing amounts to a compression of the vagaries and often chaotic conditions of life into linguistic units that are "stylized for easy memorization."[85] "All

---

82. Jousse, *Memory*, 20.
83. Jousse, *Memory*, 47.
84. Jousse, *Memory*, 122.
85. Jousse, *Memory*, 235.

flows,' says the mechanism of fluidity. 'All needs to come to a halt, when rest is needed,' says formulism."[86] By way of comparison, one may say that what for Halbwachs were *les cadres sociaux*, for Jousse was formulism, steadying features that facilitated remembering and allowed aspects of the past to be rescued into the present. In the context of Jousse's anthropology of memory we will call this aspect of formulism the stabilizing strand.

Anthropos as memory does not live all by himself in a void. Jousse's particular interest, we will see, is directed toward the *anthropos* who flourished in the social environment of the Palestinian cultural milieu. It seems that Jousse could not state nearly enough that the mnemonic culture he was describing was rooted in and distinctly the product of the Palestinian, dominantly oral domain. To be precise, he identified two types of ethnic, linguistic milieus, "a double Palestinian oral-style tradition that had always existed: the scholastic oral-style tradition, in scholastic Hebrew, and the peasant oral-style tradition, in targumic Aramaic."[87] But it must not be ignored that the reference to the Palestinian double tradition was accompanied by the qualifying remark that "the only living oral-style tradition was obviously the peasant oral-style tradition."[88] Additionally, he singled out two social institutions of central importance in the cultivation of the Hebraic-Aramaic double tradition: the paternal home and the house of the assembly, the synagogue. In both social settings the Hebraic Torah was implemented and reactivated, albeit provided with explanatory modifications and translated in the Aramaic language. As for the home setting, Jousse declared himself unequivocally: "The paternal house is the primordial milieu of the Palestinian tradition."[89] The abba-father of the family was in charge of the daily teaching of the Torah, and his instruction-memorization activities proceeded from the centrally positioned scroll of the Torah.

What may appear to be a straightforward matter involved complexities that must not be overlooked. Given the bilingual, and indeed multilingual, culture, the sefer-scroll was not an authority sufficient unto itself. Communicating the Hebrew text, therefore, called for the engagement of elaborate operations. Since Aramaic rather than Hebrew was the

86. Jousse, *In Search*, 22.
87. Jousse, *Memory*, 36–37.
88. Jousse, *Memory*, 37.
89. Jousse, *Memory*, 226.

widely familial language, the Hebrew text first had to be recited before it could be orally translated into an Aramaic version. The recitation of the Hebrew itself, far from being a simple reading exercise, necessitated special knowledge about the vowelized intonation of the strictly consonantal text. The Aramaic translations themselves covered a wide variety of options, ranging from word-for-word repetition, substitution of words and clauses, all the way to what may be called midrashic expositions. As for the second social institution, the synagogue, the objective was essentially the same: recitation of the Hebraic Torah and targumization into the "real living Torah of the people of Israel."[90] Over time, the Targum was subject to both ritualization and codification: it was integrated into the synagogal liturgy, and gradually found its place in the writing culture. In this manner, the Hebraic-Aramaic Torah, domesticated in the paternal home and institutionalized in the synagogue, came to play a key role in the people's religious and cultural identity formation. We may call this aspect of Jousse's memory paradigm the social strand. In the next segment I shall return to this central act of targumization and examine it strictly from the angle of media perspectives.

Yet another, and arguably the most important, feature of the anthropology of memory was *mimism*, a term derived from the Greek and adopted by Jousse. Broadly, it connotes the deeply ingrained human style of imitation, and it characterizes what in his view was constitutive of the *anthropos*. "Man is a natural mimer,"[91] he asserted, paraphrasing Aristotle's observation that "Of all animals, Man is the greatest mimer, and it is through mimism that he acquires all his knowledge" (*Poetics* IV,2).[92] Prompted by this conviction, Jousse entertained a lifelong professional interest in the study of children's behavior and development. For children, he observed, are boundlessly curious, make unceasing inquiries, and learn by imitation, thus amply demonstrating Aristotle's premise that mimism was a congenital condition of *Anthropos*. As Jousse put it memorably: "In the beginning was mimism."[93] Following childhood, *anthropos* continues to live in the mimetic mode, processing the world by way of appropriation and response. Underlying this mimetic approach to the world one recognizes once again one of the principal epistemological

---

90. Jousse, *Memory*, 255.

91. Jousse, *In Search*, 25.

92. Jousse, *In Search*, 15.

93. Jousse, *In Search*, 4.

maxims of Thomistic philosophy: the *adequatio mentis* (or *intellectus*) *et rei*, which suggests the mind's capacity to correspond to realities in the world—or, in different words, the compatibility between mind and reality.[94] It stands to reason that if it is through mimesis that *anthropos* is confronting and coping with life, is interfacing with the environment and bringing to consciousness what has remained beneath the level of conscious thought, then knowledge itself is a mimetic catalyst: "Mimism is our sole means to acquire knowledge," and "our only true way to know."[95] Call it what you will, "*attention, intelligence, thought, memory, association of ideas*,"[96] it is in fact congenital mimism and as such continues to be the driving force in the constitution of Anthropos. In a manner suitable to his paradigm of memory, Jousse described the mnemonic activities of *Anthropos* as the "mimodrama of memory."[97] As custodian of and principal agent in the mimodrama, *Anthropos* both embodies and actualizes what Jousse called the mimemes.

When Jousse defines memory as "the sum of our mimemes"[98] he is confronting us with the "immense complexity of the memorizing operation."[99] Since we are here at the heart of his anthropology of memory, it is fitting to probe more deeply into the nature and distinctiveness of mimism. Precisely how are we to understand the mimemes, and what role do they play in the mimodrama? Are they identifiable parts of the human body, related perhaps to the laryngobuccal muscular system? Are they external to the human body, existing in virtual reality? Or ought we to imagine them strictly as components of language, much like style or rhythm? Are the mimemes visible or invisible? Do they consist in units of information or patterns of connectivity? Do we have to think of them as physical, spiritual, ideational, or as a combination of all these attributes? On these questions, as on virtually all issues concerning Jousse's work, Edgard Sienaert points the way toward understanding. Sienaert's programmatic statement that "Jousse's anthropology of mimism is a dynamic anthropology, the science of a supple human in a fluid universe,"[100] lets

---

94. Jousse, *In Search*, 37–38, 80, *passim*.
95. Jousse, *In Search*, 36.
96. Jousse, *In Search*, 126 (italics original).
97. Jousse, *Memory*, 143.
98. Jousse, *In Search*, 17.
99. Jousse, *Memory*, 106.
100. Jousse, *In Search*, 35.

us know that mimemes and the mimetic enterprise are viable and solely knowable in contextuality and interactivity, corporeal, mnemotechnical, stabilizing, social and textual fluidity. It may be for this reason that Jousse again and again revisited the mimodrama, approaching the mimetic operations from different angles and redescribing them in manifold ways. By way of example, he could refer to the mimemes as something invading our bodies from without, "playing in our ocular mechanisms, playing in our auricular mechanisms, playing in our laryngo-buccal mechanisms."[101] While he viewed mimemes as something that "we have in us,"[102] he also understood *Anthropos* as "an amplifying exteriorizer" who "plays outside his inside mechanism."[103] Then again, Jousse chose to name mimemes the "first and primary tool"[104] of *Anthropos*, defining it as an "expressive tool, mounted in him previously, pressing out what had been pressed in."[105] These and numerous other mimetic dynamics show the mimemes to be functioning in real time and under conditions where "interaction is the all-important element."[106] It is by dint of interaction with the corporeal, mnemotechnical, social, and stabilizing functions of memory that *Anthropos* can be said to be "constructing his self, mimeme by mimeme."[107]

Since all these multifunctional, mimetic activities are engaged in action (in other words, operational in process), they are ill-defined in the status of stability and are objectively indefinable "in the way of artificial words of a dictionary."[108] This being the case, Jousse was confronted with the challenge of coming to terms with "a quasi-inextricable complexus of interactions"[109] that was both congenital and environmental; *semper in motu* and, however fleetingly, *in situ*; an overlap of exteriorization and interiorization; simultaneously reception and expression; and, last but not least, an efficient synergism between bilateral diction and the structure of the human brain.

---

101. Jousse, *In Search*, 18.
102. Jousse, *In Search*, 17.
103. Jousse, *In Search*, 33.
104. Jousse, *In Search*, 19.
105. Jousse, *In Search*, 230.
106. Jousse, *In Search*, 17.
107. Jousse, *In Search*, 63.
108. Jousse, *In Search*, 227.
109. Jousse, *In Search*, 34.

A further complication arises from Jousse's statement that "we will never grasp the essence of the object, never grasp the object in itself."[110] As Sienaert explains, Jousse viewed the input of knowledge "not [as] a passive reception but an adjustment of the external real to my internal real."[111] In different words, "one could *know* the real only insofar as one *replayed* the real."[112] The word "replay" is a favorite in Jousse's vocabulary, and it is not to be confused with the typographically administered processes of reprinting. By way of analogy, just as the body has to metabolize substances in order to sustain its existence, in like manner so does *anthropos* have to reprocess the memorial input to render it suitable for usage. Memory, from this perspective, is not a storage facility any more than it is a mental-psychological faculty, but it is rather a metabolizing organism. Now, if all mimetic interactions entail metabolizing processes, one can posit a metamorphosing of externalities into interiority, or, in Jousse's language, a translation of "a phenomenon into a mimeme, un *phénomène* en mimème,"[113] this phrasing once again reminding us of Halbwachs's premise that there cannot be unmediated remembering of the past. This is the reason why Jousse could rightly express the view that "in truth, mimism is metaphor,"[114] reinforcing his claim that "we can know only through metaphor."[115]

The preceding differentiations between memory's corporeal, mnemotechnical, stabilizing, social, and mimetic operations are the result of a strictly analytical approach. The analysis displays the innate and acquired mechanisms of memory's behavior, and it raises our awareness of the rich complexities of the memorial operations. In the process we also observed Jousse struggling with the formidable problem of nomenclature, his efforts to apprehend and describe transactional processes, his unceasing rehearsing of the formulaic orchestration of targumic language, and his ambitious striving to fathom the memorial identity of *Anthropos*, while all along seeking to penetrate the "inmost anthropological depths" of memory.[116] Notwithstanding our analysis by way of definition and divi-

---

110. Jousse, *In Search*, 37.
111. Jousse, *In Search*, 78.
112. Jousse, *In Search*, 37 (italics original).
113. Jousse, *In Search*, 35 (italics original).
114. Jousse, *In Search*, 35.
115. Jousse, *In Search*, 37.
116. Jousse, *In Search*, 51.

sion, we must not lose sight of the fact that Jousse's own rhetorical style and manner of reasoning are relational and synthetic rather than dialectical and analytic. As for the multiple memorial operations that we have isolated, Jousse was always reckoning with memory's workings in real time. He has integrated the memorial attributes and activities, interconnecting and blending them into a single, unified memory model that is organic rather than distributed, broadly epistemological rather than narrowly analytical.

It may well rank as one of Jousse's greatest accomplishments that he made memory the centerpiece of his whole paradigm. The sheer scope, vast complexity, and nuanced exposition of his memory discourse surpasses any treatment or theory of memory we have seen in biblical scholarship during the last five centuries of the Gutenberg era. If mainstream biblical scholarship assigned a role to memory at all, it was disposed to espouse a narrow focus, preferably accentuating its cognitive, preservative, and archival role, and associating it with oral tradition. By Jousse's standards, memory is definitely a catalyst of oral-style tradition, but a memorial confinement strictly to oral tradition is entirely out of step with his thinking. The narrow focus belies the broad sweep of memorial potentials, and thereby obscures memory's composite character and intricate involvements in human affairs. Crucial to Jousse's memory theory is the fact that it plays out its role as a multifaceted phenomenon and a multifunctional organism. This will, we shall see, have implications for our perception of gospels and tradition. Whether Jousse accents memory as tool or operation, as organism or activity, as internalization or externalization, as mimism or interaction, as formulaic synergism or somatic bipolarity, as power or intelligence, or as a combination of any or all of these features, he views it as a fundamentally anthropological category. "Memory is the whole of Man and the whole of Man is Memory."[117] Be it as *Homo faber*, constructing and replaying traditions, as a creature encountering and metabolizing the environment, or as mime and responder, *Anthropos* is the embodiment and actualization of principally memorial processes. What, one may ask, would be the implications of the centrality, variability, and anthropologically grounded force of memory for a scholarship that assigned the guiding rationale for the gospel tradition to a logic heavily shaped by chirographic textualism and typographical formatting techniques?

---

117. Jousse, lecture at the Sorbonne, February 28, 1957.

Galilean Yeshuaism and the Aramaic Targum

> At the time of Rabbi Yeshua, the real living Torah of the people of Israel was the Aramaic translated oral targum.
> —Marcel Jousse, *Memory, Memorization and Memorizers*, 255.

> The synagogue would never have allowed the use of a written text for the targumization.
> —Marcel Jousse, *Memory, Memorization, and Memorizers*, 36.

The Jewishness of Jesus

An appraisal of Jousse's understanding of the identity and objective of Jesus's mission begins and ends with a focus on his rootedness in Jewish culture. For many of us that may seem to be a commonplace proposition. And yet, to fully grasp Jousse's thesis of the Jewishness of Jesus, one has to take into consideration and fully be cognizant of the historical circumstance in which Jousse was living and pursuing his work. His teaching career in Paris, which covered the period from March 1931 to March 1957, partially overlapped with the rise of Nazism and the radicalization of anti-Judaism in Germany.[118] Manifestly, Jousse was keenly aware of the political developments.[119] From 1933 to 1945 most German institutions, professions, and civil society generally were affected by and frequently committed to anti-Judaizing sentiments and policies. In biblical scholarship, a primary objective of a growing number of exegetes and theologians was to purge from the Bible its perceived Jewish liabilities and encumbrances.[120] What is more, anti-Judaism was not confined to

---

118. Because the term *anti-Semitism* is a misnomer, implying discrimination against all Semitic peoples, the historically pertinent term *anti-Judaism* is preferable.

119. With Hitler's rise to power in 1933, attacks against Jewish citizens accelerated across Germany. In 1935, the Reichstag unanimously passed the Nuremberg Laws, which stripped Jews of civil and citizenship rights. In 1938, in the so-called Crystal Night (*Reichskristallnacht*), Jewish communities in Germany, Austria, and the Sudetenland (bordering on Czechoslovakia) suffered a pogrom of massive proportions which was publicized on radio stations and in newspapers across the world.

120. Lorenz, *Ein Jesusbild*. For a notorious example of the reconstruction of a Jesus robbed of his Jewishness, see Grundmann, *Jesus der Galiläer*. The author was

German political extremism, but it has been shown to be an ideology that is thoroughly intertwined with the Western tradition.[121] As David Nirenberg has expertly shown, the catastrophe of the twentieth century was the culmination of centuries of pathological fantasies that scapegoated Jews for the ills of society. Seen in this context, Jousse's unshakable insistence on Jesus's Jewishness can in part a least be interpreted as an act of defiance in the face of fascism and deeply ingrained anti-Jewishness in Western discourse. His passionate advocacy of the Jewish origins of Christianity, the Galilean setting of Yeshuanism, the Aramaic identity of Jesus, and the targumic form of his message cannot be viewed simply as a matter of historical commonsense, let alone sentimental romanticism. Given the calamitous developments in Germany and the precarious conditions in Europe generally, Jousse's Jewish thesis was bound to be a high-risk provocation in the political environment in which it was being introduced and developed. In his own words, to lecture on the Galilean, Aramaic, Jewish identity of Jesus at a number of prestigious academic Parisian institutions "during the German and anti-Jewish occupation, and as a Frenchman" required a considerable portion of "elementary courage."[122] This was the case all the more so since the Jewishness of Jesus was, in his view, not an accidental social circumstance but the quintessential core of Jesus' identity. Minimize or disclaim his Jewishness, and you have a Jesus uprooted from his tradition and ill understood.

There has been a strong inclination in biblical scholarship to associate Jesus with the scribal, educated class and its devotion to the close study of scrolls. Since, according to received understanding of the Gospels, Jesus cited Scripture, interpreted Scripture, challenged scribal teachings, and accused opponents of being ignorant about Scripture, the assumption that Scripture played an indispensable role in his life, and that he therefore must have been a scribal literate and deeply immersed in the reading and studying of the Hebrew Scriptures, seems glaringly obvious.[123]

---

the theological director of the Institut zur Erforschung und Beseitigung des jüdischen Einflusses auf das deutsche kirchliche Leben (1939–1945). It was the stated purpose of the Institut to purge theology and church, and German society generally, of all Jewish influences. After the war, Grundmann pursued a celebrated career in theology, church, and academia, while amnesia was relegating Jousse to oblivion.

121. The authoritative study on the subject is David Nirenberg, *Anti-Judaism*.

122. Jousse, *Memory*, 388.

123. Keith, *Jesus' Literacy*. The author argues that Jesus was not a representative of scribal literacy, although he refrains from interpreting Jesus in the context of an orally dominated communications culture.

Yet scriptural learning must not necessarily flow from poring over and intensely studying the scrolls. One of the key ideas Jousse proposed was that in first-century Galilee, as in all dominantly oral cultures, alphabetic literacy was by no means a prerequisite for scriptural competence and knowledge. In his view, a mastery of Scripture, orally apprehended and memorially internalized, was commonplace in a society that managed life for the most part verbally, communally, and interactively. Jesus, Jousse argued, rather than acquiring his scriptural proficiency from the scribal establishment, drew on and benefited directly from the oral-style tradition as a participating member of the "peasant university."[124] A paysan himself, Jesus was drawing from, participating in, and contributing to the living Israelite tradition that was cultivated primarily in the paternal home, as was pointed out above.

The Aramaic, tragumic tradition that nourished Jesus, Jousse further proposed, was "a gigantic millennial mechanism, developed by thousands of successive and memorizing geniuses."[125] Tradition, as Jousse imagined it, was a phenomenon of profound diachronic depth. Nothing could be further from the truth than to picture Jesus as the solitary inventor of his proclamation. Jousse strenuously objected to theories that postulated a Jesus who fashioned his message apart from, let alone in conflict with, his Jewish legacy. This would presuppose notions of individuality, subjectivity, and personhood that have defined the modern concept of historical authorship. For Jousse, Jesus was not an authorial genius but an oral, memorial one. The Lord's Prayer, Jesus' quintessential prayer, may serve well to illustrate Jousse's notion of traditional, as over against authorial, compositional mechanisms. All the individual elements of the prayer are demonstrably existent in the Aramaic tradition, like "'living targumic dominoes.'"[126] The speaker created from tradition, whereby "the pieces of the game remain the same, but their combinations are quasi-indefinitely renewed."[127] In other words, compositional creativity in the oral, memorial environment is greatly the result of innovative employments of tradition: "The formula is old and the whole is new."[128]

---

124. Jousse, *Memory*, 35–36.
125. Jousse, *Memory*, 19.
126. Jousse, *Memory*, 382–85.
127. Jousse, *Memory*, 382.
128. Jousse, *Memory*, 392.

As far as Jousse's peasant thesis is concerned, we once again have to take note of the unconventionality of his thinking. Whereas standard treatments of Judaism in Hellenistic and Roman Palestine have put the spotlight on the literary and political elite such as the Hasmonean dynasty, the Herodian client kings, the Roman governors, the high priestly aristocracy, and the Pharisaic scribal scholars, only few biblical scholars, such as Norman Gottwald[129] and Richard Horsley,[130] have centered on peasant society as a distinct sociological category worthy of academic scrutiny.[131] This seems all the more justifiable since "the peasantry comprised 90 percent or more of the population" of Roman Palestine.[132] Unlike Gottwald and Horsley, however, Jousse did not develop the political implications deriving from Jesus' close association with peasant society, although he knew, of course, that "Palestine [was] under the yoke of the Romans,"[133] and he contemptuously referred to "the terrifying scorched-earth tactics"[134] that were "caused by the same Roman 'civilizers,'"[135] and he was also aware of "the antagonism between the 'intellectual' Judahites from Jerusalem and its environs, and the 'ignorant' Galileans."[136]

The Aramaic Issue

In the academic study of the New Testament, the subject of the Targums and the Aramaic tradition has been pursued by a very small number of experts, and never rose to the level of priority in theological and religious education. The disciplinary discourse has shown scant awareness of the historical significance of the Aramaic targums in Second Temple Judaism, let alone with respect to the early Jesus tradition. Even though the targumic process constitutes a linguistic and interpretive phenomenon par excellence, it has not been part of the hermeneutical discussion surrounding the texts of the New Testament, and it has not played a notable role in the quest of the historical Jesus. Nor has there been an appreciable

---

129. Gottwald, *The Tribes of Yahweh*.
130. Horsley, *Bandits, Prophets and Messiahs*.
131. Scott, "Protest and Profanation"; Scott, *Weapons of the Weak*.
132. Horsley, *Bandits, Prophets and Messiahs*, xii.
133. Jousse, *Memory*, 292.
134. Jousse, *Memory*, 20.
135. Jousse, *Memory*, 359.
136. Jousse, *Memory*, 241.

recognition of the targumic presence over a remarkably lengthy period in Jewish history, extending deep into the Middle Ages.

In part, the scholarly inattention to the Aramaic language is due to the linguistic identity of the biblical texts, which assigned priority to the Hebrew and Greek languages as a matter of historical commonsense and propriety. Moreover, the Greek version of the Gospels, we will further develop below, conditioned scholars to divert attention away from Jewish and toward Hellenistic cultural priorities. Added to that, the targumic tradition is widely considered a late tradition that could not be expected to have much relevance for casting fresh light on the history of first-century CE Jewish culture. Last but not least, there is the additional fact that the extant Aramaic targumim constitute a subject matter of substantial historical and linguistic complexity that call for Aramaic and Hebrew expertise, proficiency in the history of Second Temple Judaism, and, I should like to add, keen media sensibilities.

Among the few scholars who have addressed the Aramaic question in relation to the gospel tradition are Charles F. Burney[137] and Charles C. Torrey,[138] who were seeking to make a case for Aramaic originals underlying the canonical Gospels. More recently Matthew Black focused on what he perceived to be "un-Greek" syntax, grammar, vocabulary, and word order in the Gospels and Acts as evidence of translations from Aramaic.[139] Maurice Casey endeavored to identify first-century Aramaic substrata underlying Mark and the sayings source Q.[140] In the English-speaking world the standard work on the targumic tradition is Paul Flesher's and Bruce Chilton's study on *The Targums*.[141] To this day it remains basic to any in-depth consideration of the history, interpretation, and value of the targumic tradition. Jousse's approach differs in two respects. One, he notably prioritized the targums and the Aramaic tradition, making it a centerpiece of the understanding of Jesus and the gospel tradition. Two, he interpreted the targums in an exclusively oral and memorial mode of communication. So central is the targumic issue to Jousse's work that an appreciation of his paradigm remains deficient without extensive knowledge of the targumic tradition and practices.

137. Burney, *The Aramaic Origin*.

138. Torrey, *Translated Gospels*.

139. Black, *An Aramaic Approach*.

140. Casey, *Aramaic Sources*; Casey, *Aramaic Approach*.

141. Flesher and Chilton, *The Targums*. See also Chilton et al., eds., *Comparative Handbook*.

The Targum in the Jewish Context

In view of the scarce recognition of the Aramaic language in New Testament studies, the perceived inapplicability of the targum, and the noted strangeness of Jousse's paradigm, I will approach the Targum first by reestablishing the communications context in which the targumic transactions were taking place. Rather than focusing directly on the targumic act, I propose to probe initially the communications conditions as they obtained in ancient and rabbinic Judaism, Qumran and Galilee, in the gospel and Hellenistic school traditions, paying particular attention to the history of the Aramaic language and the targumic culture generally, and to specific facets such as scribality and the oral register, reading, writing, and compositioning processes, as well as memory formations. After I have staked out the macroenvironment I will secondarily explicate the targumic act within its appropriate communications setting. My hope is that the contextual approach will make the targumic phenomenon more readily accessible, and remove much of the perceived strangeness from Jousse's paradigm altogether.

As far as Aramaic is concerned, it is recognized as one of the world's oldest continuously spoken languages, and it is assumed to have first appeared as a distinct language in the eleventh century BCE. It became the official language of the Assyrian Empire (911–605 BCE), the Babylonian Empire (605–539 BCE), and the Persian Empire (550–330 BCE), and eventually evolved into the lingua franca of large parts in the ancient Near East. A widely held view states that Aramaic gradually became the primary medium in postexilic Israel, while Hebrew was in the process of developing into the preferred language of the scribal and priestly elite. This is a picture sketched in broad outline, which is, however, frequently contested, qualified, and updated. On closer inspection, complexities of various kinds are manifest.[142] For example, the existence of a significant portion of Hebrew materials both among the Dead Sea Scrolls and the Bar Kokhba documents raised the question whether the usage of Hebrew was more widespread than is often assumed. Moreover, bilingual features, especially in urban settings, were not uncommon: Jews proficient in Aramaic and in Hebrew, Aramaisms present in Hebrew and Hebraisms present in Aramaic, Greek loanwords present in Hebrew and Semitisms present in Greek. Further, Aramaic was differentiated into

---

142. See especially Wise, *Language and Literacy*.

various dialects: "Virtually all Galileans spoke one dialect or another of Aramaic."[143] Turbulent political conditions, manifested above all by Palestine's existence in the shadow of Hellenistic dynasties and under the impact of the "scorched-earth" policy of imperial Rome,[144] further complicated social and ethnic identities. Depending on whether Jews assimilated to Greek *paideia* or rose to the threat posed by Greco-Roman imperialism, their cultural and political preferences did have an impact on the kind of medium and language they decided to converse in, or not to converse in.

Galilee in the first century CE was a predominantly agrarian society.[145] Economic self-sufficiency was the guiding principle that governed daily life. Trade relations existed primarily on the local and regional levels, and principal trade routes for the most part bypassed Galilee. The Roman road system, which is often identified as evidence for an expansive trading network, may have been constructed mainly for military and not primarily for economic purposes, and it was in any case largely developed during the second century CE. Hellenization is recognized to have been primarily an urban phenomenon that did not penetrate deeply into the Galilean countryside.[146] Nazareth was an insignificant hamlet that is never mentioned in the Hebrew Bible or in rabbinic literature; hence the slogan "Can anything good come out of Nazareth?" (John 1:46). Of the four major Galilean towns, Scythopolis and Tiberias were more thoroughly Hellenized than Sepphoris and Caesarea Maritima, but Jesus is not reported to have set foot in any one of them. Exegetes often refer to Caesarea Philippi as the locale of "Peter's confession," missing the point that Mark and Matthew position the event outside the town, deliberately, it seems, keeping Jesus away from the urban center (Matt 16:13; Mark 8:27).[147] Capernaum, the locale Jesus is most directly associated with, was a fishing village that had little to show in terms of Hellenistic architecture. Jousse's understanding of Jesus is wholly based on the premise that he was raised in and conversed in Aramaic, the lingua franca of the rural population of Galileans. It is a viewpoint widely shared by scholars. In addition to making the case for Jesus the native Aramaic speaker,

---

143. Wise, *Language and Literacy*, 331.

144. Jousse, *Memory*, 359.

145. On the following, see especially Horsley, *Galilee*; and Horsley, *Archaeology*.

146. Chancey, *The Myth*.

147. Luke does not mention Caesarea Philippi at all in connection with Peter's confession (Luke 9:18).

Jousse made much of the sociological difference between urban and rural settings. Jesus, he argued, was a representative not of the scribal guild but rather of the peasant society. The peasant milieu, the oral style of communication, the Aramaic language, and the targumic tradition were of paramount importance in Jousse's understanding of Jesus.[148]

On the matter of the targumic tradition, the two most influential and broadly sanctioned renditions were Targum Onqelos of the Pentateuch and Targum Jonathan of the Prophets. In addition to Onqelos, three more Pentateuchal targums have come down to us: Pseudo-Jonathan (also known as Targum Yerushalmi in medieval times), Fragmentary Targum (collections of select targumic materials), and Neofiti (discovered in 1949 in the Vatican library). The rabbinic literature of the Mishnah, Tosefta, and the Palestinian and Babylonian Talmuds, dated roughly from 70 to circa 600 CE, evidences a relatively sparse amount of targumic references and citations, although the existence of major targumim was known both in Palestinian and in Babylonian Judaism of that period. Since rabbinic Judaism focused its attention on the talmudic tradition, and the Babylonian Talmud was in the process of becoming "the crowning document of rabbinic Judaism,"[149] the rabbis, understandably, were not of one mind about the status of Aramaic renderings of the Hebraic Scripture. To ask the question simply, was the targumic project an extension of or a separate addition to the Hebraic Torah? Typically, rabbinic Judaism was inclined to view the targumim "not as a substitute for Scripture but as a mediating accompaniment," and "as being close to but still less than . . . Scripture."[150] Over time, rabbinic aspirations inclined toward authorizing the exact wording and thus standardizing the targumic texts, while the Babylonian rabbinate eventually favored and secured the primacy of Onqelos.

Two historic discoveries of Jewish manuscripts, one relatively little known and the other widely publicized, have significantly advanced and refined our perception of ancient and medieval Judaism. These findings also amplified our collection of Aramaic and specifically targumic materials. Toward the end of the nineteenth century a trove of some four hundred thousand Jewish manuscripts, mostly in fragmentary form, was discovered in the genizah (storeroom) of the Ben Ezra Synagogue in the

---

148. Of the countless reconstructions of the historical Jesus, the one developed by Richard Horsley in many of his publications comes closest to Jousse's understanding.

149. Flesher and Chilton, *The Targums*, 139.

150. Fraade, "Rabbinic Views," esp. 282.

old city of Cairo. They have opened a window into a period of a thousand years of Jewish and Middle Eastern history. Many of the manuscripts were written in Aramaic, among them a number of targums to the Pentateuch, and others that were selected for special use at festivals.[151] The Aramaic scrolls have been dated to a time ranging from the eighth to the fourteenth centuries.[152] Paul Kahle, orientalist and pioneer in the study of the Genizah Targums, was of the view that they carried traditions that reached back to the first century and were crucial to understanding Jesus' language and the hermeneutics of the early gospel tradition.[153] However, one needs to recall that the dating of ancient manuscripts is intricate business, and the dating of the targumic materials notoriously so. Dating the targums, we shall see, requires considerable text-critical circumspection and analytical nuance. At the very least, however, the targumic findings at the Cairo Genizah have demonstrated that throughout the Middle Ages the targums were extensively copied and distributed, suggesting the likelihood of continuing targumic activities.[154]

As is well known, the Dead Sea Scrolls take us much further back to a period roughly from the second century BCE to the first century CE. About 17 percent of the Scrolls are in Aramaic, among them two translations of Job, 4QtgJob and 1QtgJob, and one of Leviticus, 4QtgLev.[155] However, the targumic identity of these renderings has been debated because they manifest less interpretive engagement than later targumim. A characteristic feature of Qumran's Aramaic materials worthy of attention is that "nearly all of them can be seen to depend on or relate to the Hebrew Scriptures in some way."[156] The phenomenon of "rewritten Scripture"—including literal and modified translations, expansions and abridgements, and the pesher method of interpretation—is amply confirmed by the Scrolls, although it may complicate the process of securing definitional clarity about what precisely constitutes a targumic version.

It is worth noting that the point is debated to what degree the Scrolls, while clearly reflecting the community's ethos and ritual practices, were also representative of the broader communications landscape of Jewish

---

151. Klein, *Genizah Manuscripts,* has identified thirty-eight Palestinian Targums.
152. Flesher and Chilton, *The Targums,* 76.
153. Kahle, *Cairo Geniza.*
154. Flesher and Chilton, *The Targums,* 77.
155. Via private correspondence with Shem Miller.
156. Machiela, "The Aramaic Dead Sea Scrolls," especially 250.

life in Roman Palestine. Still more pertinent is the media question and a consideration of the Scrolls' oral-memorial implementation. For the most part Qumran scholarship has reconstructed the world of the Scrolls in a dominantly textual image, introducing the label "the ancient library of Qumran," fixing attention on textual hermeneutics and until recently heightening the profile of textual stability while underplaying the plurality of the scriptural tradition. In this regard it cannot go unmentioned that Jousse himself succumbed to the textual lure of the Scrolls, suggesting that they "belong outside a truly real and living oral milieu," and comparing their operation to the use of "dead Latin" in a monastery.[157] But could it be, as Richard Horsley has suggested, that the Scrolls were appropriated "by collective recitation and other performance,"[158] and that they were but the "visible tips of icebergs with their far larger bases invisible, floating in a vast sea of oral culture"?[159]

The Targumim in the Ancient Communications Context

In an exhaustive study of Jewish literacy in Roman Palestine, Catherine Hezser has subjected the concept of Judaism as a quintessentially textual religion to a critical review.[160] The "book religion" model, while powerfully attractive, especially in Protestant circles, "is insufficient as a description of post-exilic Judaism."[161] Throughout Jewish antiquity, she argues, education was voluntary and primarily a parental obligation. Only in Amoraic times, from the third century onwards, were schools and teachers becoming more widely available, although education was, almost without exception, administered orally, in the form of dialogue and disputation. While Torah centered, it was orally communicated, hence not text centered. As far as the general population was concerned, knowledge of reading and writing cannot therefore be assumed to have been widespread. The rabbinic tradition, while generating a textual body of vast dimensions, was heavily oral in composition and implementation, and centered on the rabbinic sage (Jousse's meturgeman), who served as embodiment and mediator of the tradition. Memory played a paramount

---

157. Jousse, *Memory*, 37.

158. Horsley, *Text and Tradition*, xv.

159. Horsley, *Text and Tradition*, 49. See also the crucially important work by Miller, *Dead Sea Media*.

160. Hezser, *Jewish Literacy*.

161. Hezser, *Jewish Literacy*, 208.

role in composing, organizing, and reciting the tradition.[162] Manuscript variants were often a "natural consequence" of ancient (Jewish) communication practices of re-copying manuscripts multiple times. In point of fact, "the modern category of one 'original' or 'Urtext' . . . never existed in antiquity."[163]

In a brief but highly consequential article, "The Ancient Israelite Scribe as Performer,"[164] Raymond Person dispels the idea that Jewish scribes were mere copyists. He singles out a variety of "scribal interventions"[165] that demonstrate active scribal engagement in the composition of manuscript, and the engagement is partially of a textual nature but often of an unmistakably oral kind. In many instances, he argues, it was the scribes' oral, memorial mentality that allowed for the so-called variants. In these instances, the so-called variants are better explained as performative writings or deliberate alternative readings, rather than as derivations from presumed originals. "Even though Israelite scribes were among the most literate in their society, they were nevertheless influenced significantly by the primarily oral culture in which they lived."[166] Person's study is an urgent appeal to begin understanding Israelite literature from "the perspective of the aesthetics of an oral tradition."[167]

In *Memory and the Jesus Tradition* Alan Kirk manages an uncommonly masterly grasp of the ancient communications culture.[168] Drawing on social, linguistic, and cognitive studies, the book has contributed immeasurably to raising memory to paradigmatic significance with regard to the Jesus tradition. Kirk defines the early Jesus tradition as "the artefact of memory,"[169] functioning as a dynamic and versatile system, empowered by memorial dynamics, and as a carrier of conventionally patterned schemata (Jousse's formulaic units). The patterned schemata were the result of a "massive reduction of detail essential to memory formation"[170] that was achieved at the expense of the very information highly prized by the historian. The memorially efficient items were both culturally acquired

162. Hezser, *Jewish Literacy*, 204.
163. Hezser, *Jewish Literacy*, 434.
164. Person, "The Ancient Israelite Scribe."
165. Person, "The Ancient Israelite Scribe," 607.
166. Person, "The Ancient Israelite Scribe," 608.
167. Person, "The Ancient Israelite Scribe," 603.
168. Kirk, *Memory*.
169. Kirk, *Memory*, 47.
170. Kirk, *Memory*, 66.

and cognitively wired. Objecting to viewing memory's constructive and selective operations as the outcome of weak and defective faculties, Kirk argues that "this large-scale 'forgetting' of particulars is in fact an expression of memory's efficiency."[171] Finally, to account for the rise of the gospel genre, he adopts Jan Assmann's concept of *Traditionsbruch* (rupture in the tradition).[172] When as a result of the fading of the foundational memories "a crisis of memory" ensued "at approximately the forty-year threshold,"[173] the early Jesus tradition underwent a medium shift facilitating a rememorization in chirographic form.

In "Memory and Tradition in the Hellenistic Schools" Loveday Alexander examines the comparative relevance of the *apomnemoneumata* (*memorabilia*) genre with respect to the early gospel tradition.[174] She proceeds from the observation that many of the genre's items bear similarities to materials encountered in the Gospels: dialogues, anecdotes, aphorisms, apothegms (short instructive sayings), gnomic wisdom sayings, *chreiai* (concise statements in narrative form), and so forth. While the prevailing approach of classical and biblical scholarship has been to treat the *apomnemoneumata* "as a purely literary phenomenon,"[175] Alexander views it as "an oral performance culture that took pride in verbal craftsmanship."[176] Transmitted to us as a written genre but meant to be "endlessly re-oralized," the genre of the *apomnemoneumata* was "perched on the cusp between orality and writing."[177] Particularly relevant for the gospel genre is Alexander's conclusion that the genre does not manifest an innate quasi-evolutionary drive toward biographical narrative: "there were a thousand and one other things you could do with anecdotes."[178] Frequently existing in the form of compilations, the genre served as a "cultural databank"[179] that played a role in diverse fields such as education, entertainment, polemics, gossip, and others.

---

171. Kirk, *Memory*, 107.

172. Kirk, *Memory*, 204–5, 254; also see Jan Assmann, *Das kulturelle Gedächtnis*, 101, 278, 300. For Assmann, the changes from oral tradition to the chirographic medium enact a shift from communicative to cultural memory.

173. Kirk, *Memory* 205.

174. Alexander, "Memory and Tradition."

175. Alexander, "Memory and Tradition," 132.

176. Alexander, "Memory and Tradition," 122.

177. Alexander, "Memory and Tradition," 122.

178. Alexander, "Memory and Tradition," 125–26.

179. Alexander, "Memory and Tradition," 124.

Richard Horsley is one of a small number of New Testament scholars of his generation who has seriously grappled with the issue of the Greek version of the gospels versus the Aramaic language used by Jesus. In "The Language(s) of the Kingdom: From Aramaic to Greek and Galilee to Syria"[180] he makes the case for "an Aramaic substratum"[181] beneath parts of Q. What distinguished his study is the implementation of five exceedingly pertinent research topics: biblical scholarship's entrenchment in the print medium, the issue of limited literacy and the dominance of oral communication, the pluriformity of "scriptural" scrolls and the absence of standard editions, the concept of a "little tradition" (in rural regions) vis-à-vis the "great tradition" (in scribal circles), and ancient linguistic diversity and the primacy of spoken Aramaic in Galilee. Synthesizing advancements in these areas, Horsley postulates an Aramaic Israelite popular tradition underlying Q/Luke 7:18–35. In part, his argument is built on an analysis of the oral, performative nature of Q,[182] on Aramaisms discernible even in the transliterated Greek, and on the identification of a distinctly local coloring of words and phrases. Central to his argument is the observation that the allusion/citation to the tradition in Q/Luke 7:22 and 7:27 does not correspond closely with either the Septuagint or the Masoretic Text. Rather than assuming reliance on written standard editions, Horsley submits that Q, at this point, represents a popular reactivation of the "great" scriptural tradition.

This contextual review of the communications culture carries considerable explanatory implications for understanding Jousse's targumic project. We encountered media attributes and properties that appear to be foundational and associated with a representative body of Jewish, early Christian, and Hellenistic traditions. Among them are the multifunctionality of oral diction, oral-scribal interfaces, performative operations by scribes, and memorial composition and apperception that emerged as high-profile features.[183] As for the oral medium, it dominated and oftentimes monopolized ancient communications to a degree virtually impossible to imagine within the modern typographic mindset. In the words of Horsley, oral dynamics interpenetrated every single piece of

---

180. Horsley, *Text and Tradition*, 198–219.

181. Horsley, *Text and Tradition*, 207.

182. Horsley with Draper, *Whoever Hears You.*

183. As far as our chirographic evidence is concerned, orality appears inseparable from scribality. However, the only way to come to terms with ancient intermediality is to analyze the nature of oral versus scribal mediality separately.

ancient scribality: "I am becoming convinced that virtually any example of or reference to writing in ancient Judean texts is intricately related to and embedded in oral communication."[184] In large measure, oral verbalization was the medium through which knowledge and information was transmitted and interpreted.

Words in that environment functioned not as lexical items but predominantly in an exercise of power for the benefit of hearers. "Scriptural" traditions were frequently multiform, rooted in rhythmic psychodynamics, and predisposed to auditory sense perception. There was no single Ur-saying, nor for that reason could "variants" be conceived as a divergence from or aberration of an "original." Can we, children of a culture habituated to typographic fixity, imagine a world that was well functioning in the absence of a single, standard edition and thriving in scribal pluriformity? What mattered was often not the oldest rendition, but the most recent one! As far as the chirographic medium was concerned, we will need to dishabituate ourselves from the conventional image of scribes strictly as rote copyists, and familiarize ourselves with an expanded identity for scribes as curators of their people's cultural legacy, intent on maintaining, modifying, and updating tradition. In view of the cost and labor-intensity involved in the scribal production, recurrent updating (*Fortschreibung*) of existing manuscripts was by no means an uncommon practice.

Written artifacts were not necessarily calculated to be finite products such as printed copies, with securely fixed boundaries and definitive meanings firmly in place, but more likely existed on hold and in waiting to be orally reactivated or upgraded. On the whole handwritings were pragmatically oriented and not (merely) bent on conservation, inclining toward memorial interiorization rather than aiming for literary perpetuity. In different words, scrolls were frequently designed to be authoritative in an oral way.

Memory, finally, loomed large. All five authors cited above (Hezser, Person, Kirk, Alexander, and Horsley) are agreed on this. Memory constituted front and center of the ancient (and medieval) media world in ways largely inconceivable after more than five hundred years of the now rapidly declining Gutenberg era. We need to understand the importance of this matter: it was memory, not manuscripts in and of themselves, that ultimately served as the brain of communicative processes, affecting the

---

184. Horsley, *Scribes*, 93.

work of scribes, and being instrumental in the recitation and reception of scrolls. Fact versus fiction was not the major issue in oral-scribal-memorial processes because the communicative intent was the actualization of tradition in the hearts and minds of hearers, and not the preservation of the past for the sake of the past.

Thus, when viewed in the context of the ancient media culture, the targumic tradition and indeed Jousse's project generally lose much of their assumed strangeness. Far from displaying an aberrant linguistic behavior, Jousse's paradigm bears a remarkable likeness to basic communicative features that were common in ancient and rabbinic Judaism, and it displays key features that are entirely comparable to those found both in the early gospel tradition and in the educational and entertainment practices current in Hellenistic culture. Rather than misdirecting us to a *terra incognita*, it now appears that Jousse was familiarizing us with a project that is substantially homologous with what may well be called the mainstream of the ancient communications world. Undoubtedly, there exist a myriad of linguistic, communicative, and social differences between the Qumran scrolls, the early Jesus tradition, the rabbinic tradition, and the Hellenistic school practices, as well as significant divergences between those four cultural legacies vis-à-vis the targumic tradition, just as there are a host of features that are strictly idiosyncratic to the targumim and not shared by other traditions. Nor do we close our eyes to the fact that writings such as for example Isaiah, Deuteronomy, or the Psalms were in the process of assuming authoritative significance, even though their special status did not exclude their continued multiformity. Nonetheless, when compared with the communications world dominated by the typographic medium, all these observed media characteristics, including the targumic one, constitute something of a congruent model. All are united in their emphatic cultivation of the verbal art, of a specialized (formulaic or dedicated) language, of massive oral-scribal interfacing, of scribal activism, of scribality's subservience to oral dynamics, and first and foremost of memory's centrality. These are essential, unitive features that warrant the designation of a single oral-scribal-memorial paradigm of transcultural significance, an alternative paradigm to the historical, documentary paradigm. By comparison, it is the historical-critical paradigm—representing a world of fixed texts reproducible in fully identical copies, methodically organized words confined to a spatialized, visualized, and linearly sequenced format, and assumed to be composed by individual authors—that gives every appearance of being aberrant and a stranger in a foreign land. The strangeness we perceive in Jousse's paradigm lies entirely in our expectations. If, however, we allow ourselves to be informed by Jousse's oral-scribal-memorial paradigm in the context of the ancient communications environment, we will be struck by the strangeness of our own typographically rooted historical-critical paradigm.

When the targumic material is thus viewed in context, it is apparent that approaching it with questions about dating, authorship, literary sources and dependencies would be tantamount to a category mistake. Jousse, we remember, has been asking us to reset our dominantly textual key to a different register altogether. Let me therefore return to the central act of targumization one more time and examine it strictly from the angle of oral-scribal-memorial sensibilities.

The Targumic Act

The targumic act did not simply entail a translation from Hebrew into Aramaic, although it did that, too. It did not merely process a transfer from the written to the oral medium, although in large part that is precisely what it did. Nor is targumization entirely reducible to a communication from reciter to receiver/translator and on to the people, although generally that is also what was occurring. To begin with, the Hebraic written Torah was the point of departure for the targumic process, but it was the Aramaic Torah, be it in the memories of people or in written form, that was going to take on a life of its own. Above all else, it was memory's thoroughgoing engagement in the targumic process that was apparent. With the Hebrew text being foundational, targumization enlisted memory full-time. The Hebraic recitation placed heavy demands on the mental-memorial faculties of the meturgeman-translator. Analytically, one may differentiate the Hebraic oral recitation, its memorial reception by the meturgeman, his Aramaic translation, and its oral delivery to the congregation. In performative actuality, however, Hebraic reception, Aramaic translation, and Aramaic translation's oral transmission are conceivable as a single process. In other words, reception and translation would have been accomplished in the single act of oral delivery. One may very well assume memorial knowledge of the Hebrew Torah on the part of the meturgeman, and it seems entirely plausible to postulate memorial knowledge of the Aramaic Torah among congregational members, many of whom will have carried parts of it in their memory since childhood. In terms of language, media, communication, and memory, the central act of targumization constituted an exquisitely complex transaction that in its entirety serves as an illustrious example of the oral-scribal-memorial paradigm.

It was in the rabbinic period that the targumim flourished and attained peak of development. Rabbinic authorities were instrumental in appropriating and solidifying the targumic materials in the written medium. To a large extent, it was in the standardized, chirographic form that the synagogal materials sustained their existence far into the Middle Ages—hence Chilton's statement that the targumim reflect "the extensive, dialectical interaction between synagogue and [the rabbinic] academy."[185] But we need to be mindful that apart from its written form the targum all along continued to occupy its designated place in the synagogue setting. Its paramount significance lay in the oral-scribal-memorial transaction, and not in its written codification per se. Keeping this synagogal worship context in mind, Jousse has sensibly assigned the targum to the category of liturgy, "as the synagogue would never have allowed the use of the written text for the targumization."[186] Likewise, Flesher and Chilton contend at the very outset of their magnum opus that "Targums belonged more to the liturgy than the academy."[187] Is it an overstatement to claim that the central feature of the synagogal service and the principal significance of the targum lay in the ritual of the transformation of the written form of the Hebraic Torah into the vernacular oral Aramaic?[188] What this ritual was meant to accomplish was the in-corporation into people's hearts and minds of what was sacred beyond all else, although it had remained an unaccustomed and barely understood language.

---

185. Chilton, *A Galilean Rabbi*, 40.

186. Jousse, *Memory*, 36.

187. Flesher and Chilton, *The Targums*, ix.

188. In reaction to an overly textual approach to the Targums, I am, in the spirit of Jousse's liturgical explication, inclined to assign sacramental significance to the targumic act proper. Would we be going too far in introducing the Catholic term *transubstantiation*? Jousse used the term in the traditional, religious sense with reference to the eucharistic rite (*In Search*, 52–53), and also broadly with regard to the transformative interiorization of knowledge and information (*In Search*, 68). However, he appears to have refrained from applying the term to the tagumic act.

Bibliography

Alexander, Loveday. "Memeory and Tradition in the Hellenistic Schools." In *Jesus in Memory: Traditions in Oral and Scribal Perspectives*, edited by Werner H. Kelber and Samuel Byrskog, 113–54. Waco: Baylor University Press, 2009.

Assmann, Aleida. *Cultural Memory and Western Civilization: Functions, Media, Archives*. New York: Cambridge University Press, 2011.

———. *Erinnerungsräume: Formen und Wandlungen des kulturellen Gedächtnisses*. C. H. Beck Kulturwissenschaft. Munich: Beck, 1999.

Assmann, Jan. *Cultural Memory and Early Civilization: Writing, Rembrance, and Political Imagination*. New York: Cambridge University Press, 2011.

———. *Das kulturelle Gedächtnis: Schrift, Erinnerung und politische Identität in frühen Hochkulturen*. C. H. Beck Kulturwissenschaft. Munich: Beck, 1992.

Black, Matthew. *An Aramaic Approach to the Gospels and Acts*. 3rd ed. Oxford: Clarendon, 1967.

Bultmann, Rudolf. *Die Geschichte der synoptischen Tradition*. 3rd ed. Forschungen zur Religion und Literatur des Alten und Neuen Testaments 29. Göttingen: Vandenhoeck & Ruprecht, 1957.

———. *The History of the Synoptic Tradition*. Translated by John Marsh. New York: Harper & Row, 1963.

Burney, C. F. *The Aramaic Origin of the Fourth Gospel*. Oxford: Clarendon, 1922.

Carruthers, Mary J. *The Book of Memory: A Study of Memory in Medieval Culture*. Cambridge Studies in Medieval Literature 10. Cambridge: Cambridge University Press, 1990.

Casey, Maurice. *An Aramaic Approach to Q: Sources for the Gospels of Matthew and Luke*. Society for New Testament Studies Monograph Series 122. Cambridge: Cambridge University Press, 2002.

———. *Aramaic Sources of Mark's Gospel*. Society of New Testament Studies Monograph Series 102. Cambridge: Cambridge University Press, 1998.

Chancey, Mark A. *The Myth of a Gentile Galilee*. Society for New Testament Studies Monograph Series 118. Cambridge: Cambridge University Press, 2002.

Chilton, Bruce. *A Galilean Rabbi and His Bible: Jesus' Use of the Interpreted Scripture of His Time*. Good News Studies 8. 1984. Reprint, Eugene, OR: Wipf & Stock, 2013.

Chilton, Bruce, et al., eds. *A Comparative Handbook to the Gospel of Mark*. The New Testament Gospels in Their Judaic Contexts 1. Leiden: Brill, 2009.

Coleman, Janet. *Ancient and Medieval Memories: Studies in the Reconstruction of the Past*. Cambridge: Cambridge University Press, 1992.

Dibelius, Martin. *Die Formgeschichte des Evangeliums*. Edited by Günther Bornkamm. 3rd ed. Tübingen: Mohr Siebeck, 1959;

———. *From Tradition to Gospel*. Translated by Bertram Lee Woolf. The Scribner Library. New York: Scribner, 1965.

Eisenstein, Elizabeth L. *The Printing Press as an Agent of Change: Communications and Cultural Transformations in Early Modern Europe*. 2 vols. Cambridge: Cambridge University Press, 1979.

Flesher, Paul V. M., and Bruce Chilton. *The Targums: A Critical Introduction*. Studies in Aramaic Interpretation of Scripture 12. Waco: Baylor University Press, 2011.

Foley, John Miles. *Oral Tradition and the Internet: Pathways of the Mind*. Urbana: University of Illinois Press, 2012.

Fraade, Steven D. "Rabbinic Views on the Practice of Targum, and Multilingualism in the Jewish Galilee of the Third–Sixth Centuries." In *The Galilee in Late Antiquity*, edited by Lee I. Levine, 253–86. New York: Jewish Theological Seminary of America, 1992.

Gottwald, Norman K. *The Tribes of Yahweh: A Sociology of the Religion of Liberated Israel, 1250–1050 BCE*. With a new preface. Biblical Seminar 66. Sheffield: Sheffield Academic, 1999.

Grundmann, Walter. *Jesus der Galiläer und das Judentum*. 2nd ed. Veröffentlichungen des Instituts zur Erforschung des jüdischen Einflusses auf das deutsche kirchliche Leben. Leipzig: Wiegand, 1941.

Halbwachs, Maurice. *Les cadres sociaux de la mémoire*. Travaux de l'Année sociologique. Paris: Alcán, 1925.

———. *On Collective Memory*. Edited, translated, and with an introduction by Lewis A. Coser. The Heritage of Sociology. Chicago: University of Chicago Press, 1992.

Hezser, Catherine. *Jewish Literacy in Roman Palestine*. Texts and Studies in Ancient Judaism 81. Tübingen: Mohr Siebeck, 2001.

———. *Rabbinic Body Language: Non-Verbal Communication in Palestinian Rabbinic Literature of Late Antiquity*. Supplements to the Journal for the Study of Judaism 179. Leiden: Brill, 2017.

Hochschild, Paige E. *Memory in Augustine's Theological Anthropology*. Oxford: Oxford University Press, 2012.

Horsley, Richard A. *Archaeology, History, and Society in Galilee: The Social Context of Jesus and the Rabbis*. Harrisburg, PA: Trinity, 1996.

———. *Galilee: History, Politics, People*. Harrisburg, PA: Trinity, 1995.

———. *Scribes, Visionaries, and the Politics of Second Temple Judea*. Louisville: Westminster John Knox, 2007.

———. *Text and Tradition in Performance and Writing*. Biblical Performance Criticism Series 9. Eugene, OR: Cascade Books, 2013.

Horsley, Richard A., with Jonathan A. Draper. *Whoever Hears You Hears Me: Prophets, Performance, and Tradition in Q*. Harrisburg, PA: Trinity, 1999.

Horsley, Richard A., with John S. Hanson. *Bandits, Prophets and Messiahs: Popular Movements in the Time of Jesus*. New Voices in Biblical Studies. Minneapolis: Winston, 1988. Reprint, Harrisburg, PA: Trinity, 1999.

Jousse, Marcel. *In Search of Coherence: Introducing Marcel Jousse's Anthropology of Mimism*. Edited and translated by Edgard Sienaert. Eugene, OR: Pickwick Publications, 2016.

———. *Memory, Memorization, and Memorizers: The Galilean Oral-Style Tradition and Its Traditionists*. Edited and translated by Edgard Sienaert. Biblical Performance Criticism Series 15. Eugene, OR: Cascade Books, 2018.

———. *The Oral Style*. Translated by Edgard Sienaert and Richard Whitaker. Albert Bates Lord Studies in Oral Tradition 6. New York: Garland, 1990.

———. *Le style oral rythmique et mnémotechnique chez les verbo-moteurs*. Paris: Beauchesne, 1925.

———. *The Parallel Rhythmic Recitatives of the Rabbis of Israel*. Translated with notes by Edgard Sienaert. Paris: Association Marcel Jousse. 2021.

Kahle, Paul. *The Cairo Geniza*. 2nd ed. Oxford: Blackwell, 1959.

Keith, Chris. *Jesus' Literacy. Scribal Culture and the Teacher from Galilee*. Library of New Testament Studies 413. London: Bloomsbury, 2011.

Kelber, Werner H. "The 'Gutenberg Galaxy' and the Historical Study of the New Testament." *Oral History Journal of South Africa* (2017) 1–16.

———. *Imprints, Voiceprints, and Footprints of Memory*. Resources for Biblical Study 14. Atlanta: Society of Biblical Literature, 2013.

Kelber, Werner H., and Samuel Byrskog, eds. *Jesus in Memory: Traditions in Oral and Scribal Perspectives*. Waco: Baylor University Press, 2009.

Kirk, Alan. *Memory and the Jesus Tradition. The Reception of Jesus in the First Three Centuries* 2. London: Bloomsbury T. & T. Clark, 2018.

Klein, Michael L. *Genizah Manuscripts of Palestinian Targum to the Pentateuch*. 2 vols. Cincinnati: Hebrew Union College Press, 1986.

Lorenz, Elisabeth. *Ein Jesusbild im Horizont des Nationalsozialismus*. Wissenschaftliche Untersuchungen zum Neuen Testament 2/440. Tübingen: Mohr Siebeck, 2017.

Machiela, Daniel A. "The Aramaic Dead Sea Scrolls: Coherence and Context in the Library of Qumran. In *The Dead Sea Scrolls at Qumran and the Concept of a Library*, edited by Sidnie White Crawford and Cecilia Wassen 244–58. Studies on the Texts of the Desert of Judah 116. Leiden: Brill, 2016.

McLuhan, Marshall. *The Gutenberg Galaxy: The Making of Typographic Man*. Toronto: University of Toronto Press, 1962.

Miller, Shem. *Dead Sea Media: Orality, Textuality, and Memory in the Scrolls from the Judean Desert*. Studies on the Texts of the Desert of Judah 129. Brill: Leiden, 2019.

Nirenberg, David. *Anti-Judaism: The Western Tradition*. New York: Norton, 2013.

Ong, Walter J. *Ramus, Method, and the Decay of Dialogue: From the Art of Discourse to the Art of Reason*. Cambridge: Harvard University Press, 1958.

Person, Raymond F. "The Ancient Israelite Scribe as Performer." *Journal of Biblical Literature* 117 (1998) 601–9.

Schmidt, Karl Ludwig. *The Framework of the Story of Jesus: Literary-Critical Investigations of the Earliest Jesus Tradition*. Translated by Byron R. McCane. Eugene, OR: Cascade Books, 2021.

———. *Der Rahmen der Geschichte Jesu: Literarkritische Untersuchungen zur ältesten Jesusüberlieferung*. Berlin: Trowitzsch, 1919.

Scott, James C. "Protest and Profanation: Agrarian Revolt and the Little Tradition." *Theory and Society* 4 (1977) 1–38.

———. *Weapons of the Weak. Everyday Forms of Peasant Resistance*. New Haven: Yale University Press, 1985.

Torrey, Charles Cutler. *Our Translated Gospels: Some of the Evidence*. London: Hodder & Stoughton, 1936.

Wise, Michael Owen. *Language and Literacy in Roman Judaea: A Study of the Bar Kokhba Documents*. Anchor Bible Reference Library. New Haven: Yale University Press, 2015.

2.

Mimism and the Ancient Biblical Recitatives[2]

MARCEL JOUSSE

Lecture

The ideal of modern science is to find a methodology applicable to every single specialized science. Envisaging an anthropology as a science of the *human mechanics*, the anthropology of gesture modeled itself on the methodology of the celestial mechanics. Human mechanics will no doubt be more flexible in its approach than celestial mechanics, but before developing a new and singularly complex science, it is best to look around and to find out if disciplines that faced similarly complex problems did not perhaps succeed to sort these problems and to reduce them to a single question mark.

Thus, having first worked on the problems of celestial mechanics and being more familiar with these problems than with those of other

---

1. Not prepared in writing, destined to be heard, not read, the "oral" lectures were performed orally and later typed out from stenographic recordings. The present translation is done with a reader in mind and therefore, for the purpose at hand, as translator, I braved the instruction of the Rabbis (Babylonian Talmud, Gittin 60b), which Jousse quotes a few times—not without relish:

The things that were passed on in writing you will not be allowed to pass on orally.
The things that were passed on orally, you will not be allowed to pass on in writing.

2. École des Hautes Études on 21 November 1933. Original title : *Le mimisme dans le style oral palestinien.*

disciplines, I tried to narrow down human mechanics to a number of laws, all of them based on *observation*. There are times, of course, when one is forced to knot two observations into one provisional knot, but as a matter of principle, there should be no discontinuity in the construction of a science.

The Stages of Human Expression

The recording apparatus we used to observe human mechanics revealed *three great laws*. I codified these as the three great stages of human expression: the stage of the *corporeal-manual style* or *global style*, the stage of the *oral style*, and the stage of the *written style*. All three are based on the one great law I dealt with at the School of Anthropology: *the law of human mimism*.

Human mechanics, like celestial mechanics, should not *invent* but *observe*. Therefore, when I attempted to set down a common, coordinated basis for the three great stages I had observed, I arrived at the following: in the course of uncountable millennia—counting is impossible, seeing the many questions raised by present-day science about the origin of Man—all ethnic milieus start off in corporeal-manual or global style, which lasts for a few thousand years; this stage then develops into an oral stage, and, later, in some other millennium, the written style stage is arrived at.

The length of time the various milieus remain in one or another stage might vary. Some remain for longer in one stage and for a much shorter time in another. It is for ethnography and prehistory to give us the relevant information based on the documents available in the various ethnic milieus. What is of greater interest to the anthropologist of gesture, however, is that—his methodology being a human one, an ethnic methodology—the three stages are bound to appear, and that when they do, they always follow each other, from a corporeal-manual style to an oral-style stage to a written style—this last possibility appearing later in one ethnic setting than in another.

In any case, when we find ourselves in an ethnic milieu comparable to that of Palestine[3] and at the stage when *writing* is known, it will not come as a surprise that the laws of the *oral style* and those of the *corporeal-manual* or *global style* coexist. The anthropologist finds himself here

---

3. Jousse understands by Palestine ancient Canaan, the cultural area the Romans called *Palestina*.

in a position similar to that of the experimental *phonetician*. A phonetician recording the articulations of French, for example, expects to come across a variety of gestural responses, because he knows that the articulations have passed from mouth to mouth, from the mouth of the mother to the mouth of the child, and so on. He knows that at some point, there will be a near total degradation of these articulations, as we will discover when we study them at the School of Anthropology. What this phonetician might then be able to establish is the history of these articulations, going back even as far as their very first uttering. This he could do either through written texts that reveal the "probable" state of an articulation at a given moment, or from inference from across a number of various *patois* milieus—*patois* incidentally, should be called more accurately a particular stage of language development. All this on the proviso, of course, that this phonetician *has all the documents possible at his disposal*.

In a study such as ours, it is advisable to use one method only, as long as this method carries sufficient promise, is sufficiently rich, is sufficiently informed about all the anthropological facts. In my case, I am backed up by all the experts in the relevant fields. My role here, as I told you earlier, is that of *liaison officer*; it is not to know everything, alas! Quite often, I am crushed by fatigue because of the amount of work that needs to be done and just yesterday, as I was to give my lecture at the School of Anthropology, I did indeed faint from tiredness and overwork.

To do science today is a frightful undertaking, and anyone wanting to contribute something to an experimental science has to subject himself to the martyrdom of observation. That it is a particularly harsh martyrdom many of you present here know all too well. Far then from me to come here before you with the naïve air of someone who knows it all. Quite the contrary, I am here before you as someone begging for collaboration.

Before me I have eminent men, men knowledgeable in the specialized techniques it is my task to knot together. I need not mention names; I only have to look at the faces before me to see experts in Assyriology, in psychology, in psychiatry—all of whom have asked themselves the difficult questions human mechanics pose in its multifold aspects. It would be an intriguing exercise to compile a sort of professional registry of all of you, seeing that with concerns so dissimilar, you have so similar an orientation.

What I want to study is this great law of human expression and its transmission, with the possibility of new laws manifesting at any moment, laws that will enable me to deal more effectively with the problems I am tackling. At present, psychiatrists such as my collaborator Dr. Morlaâs[4] use the problems I raise in the anthropology of language as the very basis of their research; Miss des Grées du Loû[5] uses lectures such as this one today, as the foundation for her rhythmopedagogy; still others use what I am saying to seek answers for the texts they are analyzing. Just the other day, my dear friend and young collaborator Fr. Follet[6] told me that to interpret the stele of Hammurabi, one needed to grasp fully the meaning *of the gestures* and *of the attitudes* depicted. I have everything to learn from Father Follet (he is a master Assyriologist), but what I already well knew is that all of us need to study *the great law of the gesture*, this perduring law that, until now, remained almost wholly neglected.

When, in 1925, after some twenty years of work, I said, "*In the beginning was the rhythmic gesture*; language was first *a corporeal-manual gesticulation* that was later transposed on the laryngobuccal muscles," I was regarded as an oddball, no less. But last Saturday, I went to a remarkable talk by a young professor and collaborator of Dr. Dumas. I could have given my stamp of approval to each of his sentences, which included a quotation thrown in from my first book, *The Oral Style*—and the listeners who attended with me did indeed quote my book, referring correctly to my definition: *Language is a mimic and significative gesticulation*. At the end of the lecture I saluted, noting that my work has left such deep marks already that the need was no longer felt to cite me as a source of the definition of language. Of this I received there and then incontrovertible evidence.

Palestinian Anthropology

Mimismological gesticulation finds nowadays its application not only in psychiatry but also in Palestinian anthropology. This Palestinian milieu is so *traditional* that it remains rooted in its tradition to this very day.

---

4. Joseph Morlaâs (1895–1981), psychiatrist, specialized in apraxia. He was a lifelong supporter of Jousse's global-gestural approach to medicine.

5. Gabrielle des Grées du Loû (1880–1955), Breton traditionist who was in charge of Jousse's rhythmopedagogical laboratory. She composed the melodies for gospel recitatives modeled on the Palestinian oral texts collected by the German theologian and Palestine ethnographer Gustaf Dalman (1855–1941).

6. René Follet (1902–1956), Assyriologist.

Some say that Israel remains a kind of mirage. The great genius Pascal[7] was perplexed by this Palestinian tradition that went all over the world with hardly a change. Why is this so? It is because we find life there, life we need to study in ever more depth, but life that has been ignored until now.

On the Greek milieu we have mountains of handbooks and psychology textbooks. But try to do Palestinian psychology and you will find naught. Yet, the Palestinian milieu has been for us an immense source of richness. It is within the Palestinian milieu that an anthropologist comes across the major problems of human mechanics, and where he finds things so admirably kept, because rites *are preserved*.

I am very happy to have a large number of priests before me today, as it should be when I deal with the great fundamental questions concerning our civilization and our religion. The problems I raise are formidable; a number of them I bring to resolution. These problems and their solutions, when posed and solved scientifically, should be known to those who every Sunday explain to us the texts of a Rabbi of Israel who was not an orator—not a Cicero, not a Demosthenes—but who was a *Rabbi* (seated) and a *catechist* swaying in accord with the formula uttered, as is still the case among the present-day Arabs: a catechizing Rabbi surrounded by talmids who sway and learn his recitatives by heart.

Jesus, Galilean Rabbi

This now is a wholly different notion of the teaching of Rabbi Yeshua. When the Sermon on the Mount is mentioned, we see some or other half dozen vague hieratic gestures. An anthropologist stands back from the Sermon on the Mount *as it is normally represented*.

Alfred Loisy[8] put the problem in all its frightful complexity when he said, "How could one, after forty years, and in another language, remember words heard by ignorant people who did perhaps not always

---

7. Blaise Pascal (1623–1662), *Pensées*, 620: "The Jewish people are distinguished both by their antiquity and their exceptional duration ... Their history enfolds in its duration all our histories and precedes our own history by a long time. The law that governs them is at once the most ancient law in the world, the most perfect, and the only one which has been always observed without any break."

8. Alfred Loisy (1857–1940), biblical scholar. Wrong method begets wrong science: Loisy's Graeco-Latinist philological approach to the biblical texts clashed with Jousse's ethnoanthropological method. It is Jousse's contention that Loisy's method inevitably led to the denial of the historicity of Jesus.

understand?"[9] As an anthropologist, I do not need to enter into any religious intricacies. I prefer to put the question altogether differently, and I say, "In Israel, teaching was done by the Rabbis." But try to find studies on the psychology of the Rabbi in Israel: you will find next to nothing. The single exception is the book I had published in 1930[10] and that has been admirably summarized and used by Professor Goguel, under whose aegis I teach here. Why is this so? Because the import of that book has not yet been understood. Scholars busy themselves glossing from Greek to French in the margins of the texts.

The Palestinian milieu is not, however, the Greek milieu. It is a derision to drag Jesus of Nazareth into Greek psychology and to turn him into some sort of Greek orator. One author even compared the eloquence of Rabbi Jesus of Nazareth with that of Demosthenes! How can one possibly not have sensed the formidable hiatus in this comparison!

Any anthropologist who is free of religious preoccupations and as researcher concerned only with the objective recording of cold facts, inevitably wonders if he will not find in the Palestinian milieu what he had previously found in the Ionian milieu: the law of the three stages of human expression. I discussed this at length with Mr. Victor Bérard,[11] before his premature death. Victor Bérard has written enthralling studies on Homer, and it is he who demonstrated, with gestures, how the *aiodos*[12] recited, making it all too clear how much the living Homer is diminished when he is reduced to no more than a written text, translated by dint of dictionaries.

Mimism and Liturgy

In the Palestinian milieu we find the major law of mimism at the ritual stage. I pointed out earlier that the present-day priest still carries out, unwittingly, this same mimismic replay. During most of the duration of the Mass the priest adopts a hieratic posture, hands extended, but at the (dare I say) most ritual part of the mass, he begins to mime *gesturally* while reciting the traditional words: he takes the wine, lifts his eyes, makes the age-old ritual gestures, and utters this sentence:

9. Here Jousse paraphrases Loisy from memory.
10. Jousse, *Les rabbis d'Israël. Les récitatifs rythmiques parallèles* (Paris: Spes, 1930).
11. Victor Bérard (1864–1931), classicist and archaeologist, specialized in Hellenistic and Homeric studies.
12. Traditional Greek singer of tales.

> Redo this as a memory-aid of me.[13]

How striking that, in a liturgy so algebrozed, so *read* from the missal, there would still be, at this most central, *most sacred* moment of the mimodrama we call the Mass, this *traditional mimismic gesticulation*. It is this, the might of the tradition, as it perdures among us, to this day. How interesting wouldn't it be to have film recordings going back, from century to century, all the way to that moment when the Rabbi himself made this primordial gesture! It may well be that we would not find that great a difference between the Rabbi consecrating the Bread and the Wine as his Flesh and as his Blood and the gestures of the present-day priest at Mass.

That then is the great power of the anthropology of gesture and how it positions itself. It is a *living* methodology which seizes the gesture in its evolution, and which, in its folly, hopes to see filing before it—as cinematography enables us to do now—the primordial gesture, from year to year, from century to century, and from millennium to millennium.

Until very recently, we were unable to fix the gesture. Now, the oral gesture was fixed by my dear master Rousselot[14] through his recording apparatus, and cinematographic equipment fixes the global gesture. These developments mean that a whole world is available to us, opening up the possibility of putting on record the last phases of things mimismological still alive in traditional ethnic milieus comparable to the Palestinian milieu of Jesus' time.

This altogether curious phenomenon was remarked upon by someone very much removed from my method, but whose hand was forced by observation and analysis of the facts: Father Buzy.[15] As pedagogues, you must have his books on your desk. In 1923, Father Buzy brought out a study, published by Gabalda, with the title *The Symbols of the Old Testament*. The title does not tell much. However, if you read this book after having initiated yourself in the methods of the anthropology of gesture, you will immediately see how the *global* gestural ritual phase persists in

---

13. "Redo this as a memory-aid of me": not "in memory of me," because the Consecration is a mimodrama, the *gestural* reenactment of a first enacting of the Palestinian mimemes of the manducation, the eating of the flesh and the drinking of the blood.

14. Jean-Pierre Rousselot (1846–1924), founder of experimental phonetics. Jousse dedicated his *The Oral Style* to him.

15. Denis Buzy (1883–1965), archaeologist and exegete; the extract is from *Les paraboles* (The parables) (2nd ed., Paris: Beauchesne, 1932), translated by Edgard Sienaert from Jousse's lecture; Jousse gives no reference.

an *oral*-style environment. Buzy confirms this in another book, from which I take this excerpt:

> In February 1912, the caravan arrived at the end of its journey to the Western shores of the Black Sea. Having visited Engadi, Masata, the Epelostounc (?), the caravan had made its way back to the mountainous region of the gorges of the Wadira. The last encampment was to be at the shores of the Pilyadma, at a short day's distance from Hebron [we find ourselves clearly in our Palestinian milieu]. To manifest their joy in the success of the caravan, the *mouks* or young men, *aikareng* or keepers of the tradition, performed for the travelers a show of chant and of pantomimes of their own. [This is a particularly intriguing passage for us who are anthropologically interested in the gestural stage, one that endures, as I said]. It was a completely dark, moonless night, and the brilliance of the beautiful stars of Palestine was frequently crossed by the wild chase of clouds galloping towards the deep Dead Sea basin. We were ringed all around the encampment by the sickening howls of packs of jackals. It is in this desert décor that the young peasants executed the various figurative tableaux of their epos. The epos was naturally the story of a razzia with the martial allures of a warrior song.[16]

I could delve deeper into this survival of the global style in the various present-day Palestinian milieus. I will return to this at a later stage, provided I have a few years before me still, before allowing my young successors to deal with this matter in more depth.

We have here a vast unexplored problem. It is one thing, *the dead text*; it is another, a wholly different thing, *the immense law of the human mechanics* that arises, and that we are able to capture with our recording devices. This is why I am not at all surprised to see this same Buzy surprised by a problem he poses himself: "They are extraordinary, those mimes, those pantomimes that we come across throughout the Palestinian tradition. Yet, they are not savages, these Palestinians, but still, what they do is somewhat akin to the mimicry of the pantomimes of savages."[17]

There you have then, as always, the inescapable personal equation. Other people's rhythmics, when they differ from our own square

---

16. Buzy, *Les paraboles*, translated by Edgard Sienaert from Jousse's lecture; Jousse gives no reference.

17. Again Jousse quotes Buzy without a reference; the quote comes directly from Jousse's lecture as translated by Edgard Sienaert.

rhythmics, we do not deem normal. Mr. Spire,[18] who is honoring me here with his presence, knows how our organism, used as it is to a syllabic rhythm, struggles to get a feel for the flexible rhythm of sentences that balance to an analogous, but not identical rhythm.

These then are all matters that need our attention when we have before us the Rabbis of Israel and their catechism, and their mishnah, as in the balanced and splendidly traditional first recitations of Genesis, and, again, in the last recitations of the talmuds and of the midrashim.

Recovering Life

These mechanisms have never been studied, and I am very happy to see Israelites taking part in this research and collaborating in it. I hope that you will have the pleasure of reading in the next issue of the *Revue de Paris*, an article by Mr. Spire on this topic. There is among us, presently, a common desire to find life again. Life has been so mortified, adjusted, syllabized! Let us take life as it is. Let us record it. Let us not busy ourselves with knowing if syllables were counted, if stresses fell at rigorous intervals sprung up in echo as by magic, but let us try to grasp what is still real in Man, what was alive in his manual style, in his oral style. That is the important question.

The matter I bring to you is of a daunting complexity. I was told many a time about my own inadequacy, and I humbly admit to it as, indeed, I do not know everything. I need the help of coworkers to approach the problem with the laws I formulated, but from facts I borrowed from a host of observers. I say "borrowed" because, if you can muster the heroism to read my first book, you will find there a series of quotations drawn from five thousand authors. I did so because I believe that science today is so complex that no single person can see the whole picture.

---

18. André Spire (1868–1966), Jewish poet and rhythmician who regularly attended Jousse's lectures. He published a book with the very Joussean title *Plaisir poétique et plaisir musculaire: essai sur l'évolution des techniques poétiques* (New York: Vanni, 1949 = Poetic pleasure and muscular pleasure: An essay on the evolution of poetic technique).

Look at science, this is to say at the real, as a circle, and imagine a person who spent a lifetime adjusting himself to the real; then from here to there, you have this person's own peculiarities, but at one point he has touched the real. To seize the whole real in all its supple complexity, you have to rely on thousands upon thousands of observations by other people. You construct your own circle of the real from all their particular points of contact with the real as they have observed it. That is what my book attempted: I reconstructed the real, the circle of the real, by stringing together quotations from thousands of individuals who have each seen, fragmentarily but *profoundly*, one single point.

This then is my method, and I am happy that this method has immediately been understood and applied by the young master of French psychiatry, Dr. Morlaâs. I mention him often because, looking presently for support from all sides, it is my joy to find young researchers who say, "Yes, there lies the truth," and so you see how the fruits of your labor are carried into mine. Rhythmopedagogy is another very rich field for experimentation, and a number of educators have become aware of this. Rhythmicians too are looking at the problem. Mr. Spire is wont to say, "But why not return to these more supple rhythms that match in beauty our own hardened and stereotyped rhythms?" And I happily add that, when I read the rhythms of Mr. Spire, it feels to me as if it is his ancestors I am reading again, the Rabbis of Israel, so deeply is the entire unchanged tradition embedded in the very musculature of the Israelite.

Global-Oral Style

You understand now that, modest anthropologist that I am, my search is to find my anthropology among you. I need to gain my anthropology *from you*. Our École des hautes études does not have professors, there are only *directors of studies*. That is what I do: I give direction—I do not bring you work done, but work to be done, and I try to keep in line with the most highly scientific methods practiced at this school.

Concretely, let us see what problems there are and how we can revisit them anew, and so let us have a look at Buzy again. His study is set off by a question that expresses an immense stupefaction: How is it possible that in Israel we see mimism arise to such an extent? As an example, he borrows from the first book of Kings, chapter 2, verses 29–39:[19]

> At that time, Jeroboam had left Jerusalem
> > he met in his way the prophet Alijah the Shilonite
> > > clad in a new mantle.
> > > > They were both alone in the field.
>
> Alijah seized the new mantle he had on him
> > and tore it up in twelve pieces
> > > and he said to Jeroboam:
>
> Take ten pieces for yourself
> > for thus has spoken Yahweh, the God of Israel:
>
> "I will wrench the kingdom from the hands of Solomon
> > and I will give you ten tribes.
> And there will be one tribe because of my servant David
> > and because of Jerusalem,
> the city I chose among all the tribes of Israel."

Buzy now asks the question we expected him to ask—we, anthropologists who know that the global corporeal-manual style is bound to reappear everywhere: "Would it not have sufficed for the prophet Alijah to transmit orally to Jeroboam the message of Yahweh? It seems to me his brilliant promises would not have been less well received had Alijah been satisfied with telling the young pretender: the kingdom of Solomon will be divided during the reign of Jeroboam. Yahweh will leave one tribe only and leave you ten. And the prophet would have saved his new mantle."[20]

He would no doubt have avoided the loss of his new coat, but he would at the same time have lost the compellent strength borne by the human muscle expressing human thought. Why is it that a person who speaks carries more strength than a dead written page? Why is it that a living being carries more strength than someone who is reading? Because there is, there, what we are all looking for and will be looking for more and more in cinematography: Life and Gesture, and it is the gesture that, at present, seems to gain primacy over the written book. A recent survey carried out in our high schools revealed that a great number of young

---

19. In fact, he borrows from 1 Kings chapter 11, verses 29–36. The biblical quotation that follows is Jousse's own translation and comes directly from his lecture, as translated by Edgard Sienaert.

20. Edgard Sienaert translates this Buzy quote directly from Jousse as it appears in the lecture, without a citation.

scholars no longer read the great novels we used to read in our youth, novels such as Les Misérables, and many others, but that they went to see these novels mimed and played globally in the movie theater.

We are indeed, presently, in a phase where the replay of gestures seeks to regain its full strength. In this, the great traditional Palestinian civilization can provide us with a wealth of facts. What I am giving you today is a mere outline, and I hope to spend an entire year on this topic in the near future. The lectures listed in my program are no more than stepping-stones for a future series of lectures. If I am not able to complete the series, my young coworkers will.

All the traditional texts must be revisited; they need to be reexamined *gesture* by *gesture* to work out how they were transposed to the laryngobuccal muscles. Global gesture became oral gesture. In the Semitic milieu, and particularly in the Palestinian milieu, all the Hebraic and Aramaic *roots* are *concrete*: they are latent gestures. To truly understand the sentences of the Nabis and Rabbis, we need to *replay* their underlying gestures. It is here that rhythmopedagogy comes to the fore, as it has its very bases in the Palestinian milieu. We are often told, as Catholics, that there is a need for a catechism developed with children in mind, children being first and foremost miming beings, melodist beings, concrete beings. Yet, what are we giving them? Our catechism is a little theological treatise made by and for theologians—there is a priest here in the audience who knows the problem and who will confirm.

Rhythmopedagogy

Religious circles express surprise when children, upon turning eleven, "set themselves free from their communions," as we say in the Sarthe, and no longer bother about such things. But what are children expected to understand and to remember of what is as dead as those who are explaining it to them? What are they expected to remember of this Jesus, who is depicted to them as someone so hazy and so distant that some of those teachers—some of whom are not all that far from this chair, I may add—are tempted to think of him as a myth!

I was very small still when I heard the old illiterate grandmothers recite to us the traditional stories their own grandmothers had told them. I heard my mother, in the evening, melodize to me the recitatives of the gospel. She had not studied them through the unattractive blackboard techniques I am using here, but she had inserted them in her delicate and melodious laryngobuccal muscles. When I found myself later before Homer, I said: "But that is my mother's style . . ." And thinking about my mother's gospel recitations, I came to understand that those were *oral formulations* comparable to the oral formulations of the Sarthe. And when, from the age of thirteen, I started to work on the targumim, I immediately sensed that we had there a formidable problem that had escaped the savants whose bookishness had prevented them from grasping just how simple the problem really proved to be.

Where did I get the science that I bring to you, and that must be of some value, seeing that the great masters of science today make use of it? This science I received from the lips of illiterates, from the maternal lips, and from children's games.

We see Broca—I saw him again just a moment ago—holding for all eternity in his hand a skull he looks at and measures. I do not know if one day I will have my own statue, but if it is to be, please do not put a skull in my hands. No, put me discreetly, as discreetly as possible, unseen, and please not in bronze, but put me there with all around me young children playing pantomime, because they would have seen me here one day doing mime. It will be that: the life of Jousse, traditionally relived by children, and it will be my most cherished statue because it will explain the laws I discovered in the child.

What I bring you here is the child, the illiterate, the reciting mother, but with these, with these poor ununderstood things, how many problems will be solved! I studied much, and all those studies led me to simply go and observe the child and to observe the illiterate—not the imbecile—let there be no confusion! The peasant is all too often mistaken for an imbecile or for someone inferior. There is a world of difference between the ignorant and the illiterate, and the real *ignoramus* is often he who paled from spending a lifetime poring over thick manuscripts. That is how objective I am when I come across a problem, and that is how I go about finding a solution.

Today, I give you an overview of everything that will unfold in the coming years concerning the mimismic gesture. I am giving you this outline because I wanted to refer you to this book by Buzy that is required reading.[21] I could have chosen in there any of the many mimemes of those great Nabis from Israel. There is, for example, the Nabi who gets hold of a yoke and compares this yoke he carries to the yoke that those he

---

21. Buzy, *Les paraboles* (The parables).

is catechizing will have to carry; there is the breaking up of a kingdom, with the Nabi taking a jug, smashing it before his spectator-auditors and telling them, "That is the fate that awaits you." The pedagogy of a savage, you might think: it is pedagogy so much alive that it is the pedagogy of tomorrow.

The pedagogy of the Palestinian ethnic milieu is a miracle! In an article written for the journal *L'Univers israélite*, Monsieur Spire said that young Catholic children today should be educated through the old Palestinian pedagogy.[22] Indeed! It is a pedagogy very different from that of the Greeks, because it has preserved life to its fullest extent. It is our Greek-based pedagogy that has made us the victim of so many *pseudo-problems* concerning the Palestinian books. These books are traditional texts, but they were dealt with through the methods of the École des Chartes,[23] when they should have been *studied* through living anthropological methods. How many admirable and splendidly intelligent men ran aground on these pseudoproblems!

What Alfred Loisy said about the application of the oral tradition on the evangelical milieu is a matter for another day. We were far apart from each other in these problems. However, he had that rare quality: intellectual humility. The sentences that I will read out to you will show you what intellectual humility means in a savant, and I highly salute Mr. Alfred Loisy for this—and I am well aware of the import of what I am saying.[24] Such problems, however, need to be resolved with something altogether different from a ready-made, hardened and sclerosed judgment. When one has spent forty and sixty years in a vicious circle, one needs a great deal of flexibility to break that circle and to adjust to the facts, and that is difficult.

I have just given you an outline of what it is that we will attempt to do in this series of lectures. And now, in the ten minutes left, I would like to show you how the formulaic oral-style method applies to the gospel narratives.

In Israel, we are dealing with a milieu that is in essence catechized by recitation in echo. There are no orators in Israel, there is no Demosthenes,

---

22. Jousse mentions this article but gives no reference; he lectured without written notes and quotes (as in this case), from memory.

23. The École Nationale des Chartes is a college of palaeography and archival studies in Paris.

24. Alfred Loisy had been excommunicated *vitandus*, i.e., as someone with whom the faithful should not associate. See note 8, above.

there is no Bossuet. There are solely catechists, but catechists who know their trade admirably, which is why we need to relearn our own trade as instructors in accordance with a set of laws that were developed and that evolved over millennia.

Teaching there was not in Hebrew, as the Hebrew language from before the exile was no longer understood. Teaching was done in the oral Aramaic targumim that were put in writing centuries later. This is why it is so important to distinguish between oral composition and this same oral composition put in writing. I may not know *when* the Aramaic targumim were put in writing, but I know with certainty that this will have happened *well after* their oral composition. Everyone who studied Testament criticism will confirm that the Aramaic targumim are spread over centuries, and that some targumim that were certainly memorized *orally* at the time of Rabbi Jesus and *put in writing* only well after Rabbi Yeshua of Nazareth. But whether oral or in writing, their formulations remained identical, with, obviously, identifiable additions. It is these additions that were used, in a wholly antiscientific fashion, to date the texts.

Let us suppose that in a translation put in writing *after* Mohammed, the name Mohammed crops up or one of the characters from about the time of Mohammed—surely we would not conclude that the entire targum is exactly from Mohammed's time. It is the problem I touched upon last time concerning Homer. The *digamma* was used by Homer and his contemporaries, but it is absent from the written text tradition of Homer. This proves that the text was put in writing *after* its oral composition, and that, between the oral version and the written text, the digamma fell from the lips. It would not have fallen from the writings as no one would have scratched the Homeric texts to remove the digamma.

The problems posed by the targumim are similar, but nothing or next to nothing is done on the question of the targumim. If one of the apprehenders, one of the talmids of Jesus of Nazareth, Simon, for example, called "Kepha" (we will later look into the question of the proper names), this Rabbi Kepha could not himself put the life of his Rabbi in anything but the formulations of the targumim. It is this I ask our priests to study. In our seminaries we are made to learn the Latin of Cicero, to get a feeling of his written clauses, to translate the verse-lines of Virgil and for us, and, how wondrous, we discovered the dactyl:

$$- \cup \cup \ - \cup \cup \ - \cup \cup \ - \cup \cup \ - \cup \cup \ - \cup$$

Mimism and the Ancient Biblical Recitatives 69

My question now is, What did this bring about in our human organism? We have dactyls in our French language; we have anapests. Never has anyone made us feel an anapest in our admirable French rhythm, yet, we would have felt it so well and understood it so well:

> Et les fruits passeront la promesse des fleurs [25]

and the fruit will exceed the promise of the flowers

We would have felt this, and we would have felt this balancing in our dreams. But how could one have expected us to feel any rhythm when it was forgotten that we had a rhythming body? All problems were posed by dint of manuscripts, by dint of written sources, always relying on writing, with, as ideals, Cicero, Demosthenes, Homer, Virgil—but all of that written, *dead*.

It would have been altogether more educational to show us who those improvisors were we find everywhere and the what and how of their living rhythm. But, no, we had to be sclerosed into writing: "To be this or not to be."

Well, it is better not to be, because we will rebound to find life again.

Under those dead written texts there are jewels buried that a living breath could bring to life again. I am going to verify this before you, here and now: I will redo the oral work that Kepha would have done to transmit the gestures and sayings of his Rabbi. Using the formulaic system of his Palestinian milieu, he would recite as follows:

> And it happened that Jesus came down the mountain
>   and came to Him great multitudes

or: and came to Him his talmids

or: and He sat down

or: and them He was teaching

but "them he was teaching" means: them he was teaching as a Rabbi teaches, which is rhythmocatechistically, with his apprehenders, young and old, mirroring him and echoing him. And indeed, Kepha, in the formula that follows, sequences the gestures in all their phases: to speak, one

---

25. The verse-line is from François Malherbe (1555–1628) and known to all French scholars.

has to open one's mouth; to see, one needs to lift one's eyes; to take, one needs to extend one's hand.[26]

These are things I showed to Father Follet, who pointed out how mistaken are those who strive to serve us endless commentaries on such and such a Greek form, when it is a Rabbi Yeshua we are dealing with and who speaks in traditional Aramaic formulas so as to be understood, retained, and transmitted.

---

26. The sequence refers to the miracle of the healing of the leper: Kepha, a targumic memorizer-composer, witnessing the mimodrama of the healing, would instantaneously record this particular saying and deed of his Master with the appropriate rhythmomelodic formulas, which he draws from his treasure chest of traditional formulas. He would operate in the same way when recording in his memory the raising of the daughter of Jairus, the healing of the leper, and other historical narratives.

3

The Anthropology of Mimism, of Memory, and of the Invisible

EDGARD SIENAERT

> ... for unless sounds are held in the memory by Man, they perish, because they cannot be written down.
> —Isidore of Seville, *Etymologies* III, XV

The Itinerary of a Human Scientist

The story of my life is the story of my work,
the story of my work is the story of my life.[1]

An autoethnographer well before autoethnography became a fashionable research methodology, Jousse would use personal experience to illustrate and to make understood wider sociocultural facts and events, past and present. His research axiom is, "It is so much easier to invent than to observe"[2] or "To discover is to see that which exists; to invent is to con-

---

1. Marcel Jousse, "Du style oral breton," 27.
2. EA 28/11/32. The abbreviations refer to the lectures given by Jousse at the Sorbonne (S), at the École des hautes études (HE), at the École d'anthropologie (EA), at the École d'anthropo-biologie (EAB), and at the Laboratoire de rythmo-pédagogie: (Lab).

struct that which does not exist:"³ anthropological science has to stick to what is observable, recordable, and analyzable.

Observation is difficult, and self-observation even more so; the observatory therefore becomes a place of labor, a laboratory. The Laboratory of Rhythmopedagogy, which Jousse founded in 1932 has as its sole instrument the living human being: it is a laboratory of the self, by the self, on the self. Two years after the founding, in a lecture on "Scientific Discovery,"⁴ Jousse retraces his own scientific itinerary as a methodological case study of how his anthropology and his laboratory of awareness came about.

Milestones

Born in 1886 in the rural, oral, and poor Sarthe region of France, southwest of Paris, Jousse lived the strong peasant community life with its regular gatherings of peasants swopping stories and the village women reciting, or rather *rhythmomelodizing*, narratives and parables from the Bible, checking each other like hawks on accuracy. Later, he would pit the gibberish coming from the pulpit against the living gospel of his mother.

> My mother had an extraordinary memory. An orphan, she had been raised by her own illiterate grandmother who had taught her orally all she knew of the old cantilenas of the Sarthe. My mother never saw any of these cantilenas in writing. It is to the rocking of these old songs that I woke to consciousness and when I let go, it is these first rocking movements I experience again. It is altogether curious to see how these first rhythmizations could have influenced an entire life. It is obvious that I owe my hypersensitivity to everything rhythmic to this training that occurred well before I awoke to consciousness: those cantilenas that rocked me necessarily informed the entire infinitesimal system that is underpinned by all of our receptive fibers.⁵

Auguste-Francois Maunoury, a teacher of the classics, developed a method for the study of Greek, not through the words but through their Indo-European roots.⁶ These roots that invariably refer to concrete actions are what Jousse would later call *operational gestures*: there is first the

---

3. S 14/12/33.
4. S 01/02/34.
5. S 01/02/34.
6. Maunoury, *Anthologia micra*.

The Anthropology of Mimism, of Memory, and of the Invisible 73

real, the thing; then, the representation of the thing by the gesture—of the whole body, but especially of the hands; and finally, there is the oral, laryngobuccal gesture: the word.

> I started studying languages through a method based on roots and formulas. That was how I studied Homer in the Latin Firmin-Didot translation. I will show you just how beneficial such study of language through the roots and through the formulas proves to be. When, at the age of thirteen, I came across the targumim in Walton's polyglot,[7] I immediately made the connection with my previous experience. I had asked the vicar of my parish: 'What language did Jesus speak?' He answered: 'My teachers at the seminary were not too sure; some said that he had spoken Greek, others, following Renan, said it was Syro-Chaldaic.'—'What is Syro-Chaldaic?'—'It is something we have conserved in what is called the targumim.' From that moment on, the Walton polyglot ... was my preferred reading. I had compiled a small digest that I kept in my pocket throughout the war, and had you found me dead at the Battle of Verdun, you would have found an artillery officer with a digest of the targumim in his pocket.[8] I never ceased to work on these targumim as I tried to taste in my mouth the very words of Jesus. This Jesus of Nazareth has truly haunted me, scientifically.[9]

With the maternal rhythm, melody, and bilateral balancing, and the studying of language through the roots rather than through lists of discrete words in a dictionary, came the discovery of fixed and mute graphic signs that once must have been sounded on living lips.

> On Thursdays, my mother used to go to Le Mans, and when I had been a very good boy, she would take me with her. As I was keen to know everything, she took me to the museum where there was this mummy the schoolmaster had told us about. If you happen to be in Le Mans, go to the Préfecture museum, and there you will see my beloved. You enter a large room, then another to the left, and, in a large, rather unusual box, lies an

---

7. The Walton Polyglot, a collaborative edition of the Bible in nine languages—Hebrew, Aramaic, Samaritan, Syriac, Arabic, Persian, Ethiopic, Greek, and Latin—published from 1654 until 1657 under the direction of the Anglican priest, and later bishop, Brian Walton (1600–1661). The targum—Aramaic for translation—is the originally spoken translation of the Hebrew Bible texts by a professional translator-interpreter, a me*turg*eman.

8. HE 29/11/44.

9. S 01/02/34.

> Egyptian priestess, immobile, serene, neatly embalmed ... I would stand there for two hours maybe, motionless in front of this small dead face and small desiccated body, with the two hands crossed on the chest. The sight had an extraordinary effect on me, because there were small rigid drawings that formed a sort of miniature procession all around the sarcophagus. An idea came into my mind that was to haunt me subsequently, and continues to haunt me: all these little drawings painted all around, had they once been alive, like that little priestess lying there, all embalmed? Were they not all alive once, those frozen characters, as in the games children play? Was there not a complex game going on all around this stiff embalmed figure, involving people who gestured, as children do?
>
> The association haunted me: what we had there were dead signs that had once been alive, just as that little priestess was dead, but had once been alive. I have been truly haunted by that. The outcome of that meeting is obvious: if I am here, it is because of my beloved, that small Egyptian mummy.[10]

At age twenty-eight and an ordained Jesuit priest, Jousse spent three years in the trenches of World War I. At the beginning of 1918, now a much-decorated artillery captain and specialist of the seventy-five-millimeter field gun, he was sent to the United States to ready American officers for the war effort. Two seemingly unrelated experiences were to prove life-changing: his encounter with the American Indians on their reservations and the discovery of their sign language, together with his visit to the Mount Wilson astronomical observatory, then the largest telescope in the world.

> Celestial mechanics was the direction I had taken when I was twenty and that lead me to the Mount Wilson Observatory in California. There I found myself before one of the most beautiful spectacles any human can witness. Before these splendid mirrors that scour the nebulae, worlds are forming, worlds where perhaps in a few billion years beings will 'breathe' as we now breathe. And precisely there and then it came to me that there was a living mechanics that was not being studied, namely human mechanics. It was at that moment that I left the still inanimate nebulae to turn to the nebulae that were being disanimated. I have, ever since, tried to make understood the

---

10. S 01/02/34.

greatness of life and of the human gesture and of the human enterprise.[11]

The nebulae being disanimated were the American Indians he had met, and by association, all the peasant cultures, past and present, not least the rural culture of his own Sarthois childhood.

At the observatory, the director, George Ellery Hale, told him of the attempt by the physical sciences to find the center of gravity in the solar system, or if there was no center in this immense conglomerate of nebulae, then to at least find the simplest law possible that regulated them. Transferring this to the human sciences, Jousse wondered about finding such a unifying law that would explain all the erratic facts about language, writing, pedagogy, children's play, mental illnesses, and even the technical problems encountered by the then still young mechanics of cinematography: why not try to find a unifying law governing this dust cloud of human experimentations?

Publications

On his return to France at the beginning of 1920, Jousse formally studies behavioral psychology, experimental phonetics, psychology and psychiatry, ethnology and sociology. All these, his previous and continuing religious studies, and his life experiences coalesced in the 1925 publication *The Rhythmic and Mnemotechnical Oral Style of the Verbomotors*—or *The Oral Style*.

> What exactly was my book on *The Oral Style*? A cento, a sort of mosaic made only of texts borrowed from other people. At least, it appeared so. What did I do? I read some five thousand books from which I retained five hundred, and from these five hundred volumes I selected those sentences that would be the most tangent with my reality, the real as received by me *in my mimemes*. From each author I took a sentence that, at a given point, coincided with this circle of the real; they were what you call tangents. And so, with a tangent here, a tangent there, I came by means of about five hundred tangents to trace *my* circle of the real ... With formulas borrowed from five hundred authors, I succeeded in making a coherent whole: a circle of the real made with the tangents of other people.[12]

11. HE 23/04/41.
12. HE 45/02/07.

The quotations are strung together on the single theme of the existence of an *oral style*. "The oral style" is, first, a *style*, or a way of being and a way of expressing that being as closely to the real as possible; it is, second, an *oral* style, or a set of rules for effective facilitation of mnemonic composition, communication and transmission without reliance on support outside oneself and therefore an incarnated, an embodied style, hinging on a memory that remembers globally and expresses itself in whole-body mimodramatics; it is, finally, *the oral style*, as the book gives oral-style texts and composition worldwide and through time a properly defined common morphology: the oral style is rhythmic and mnemotechnical, which is to say, rhythm is expressed in balancing and in formulas that are measured and dense and therefore memorizable, portable, and faithfully transmittable.[13]

"One fine day, the Jousse mine exploded. It made a heck of a din!"[14] Indeed, if the book became a success in an environment wholly fixated on writing and for which what was not in writing did not exist, it was a *succès de scandale*; in many clerical circles Jousse would never be forgiven for having done away with, or at the very least having cast doubt on, entrenched written-text exegesis.

The publication, five years later, of *The Parallel Rhythmic Recitatives of the Rabbis of Israel: Genre of the Maxim*, is an illustration of how oral-style composition operates in the ethnic milieu of ancient Palestine.[15] Through the juxtaposition of one hundred recitatives—from various epochs and from the simplest of binaries and ternaries to more complex rhythmic schemas—and through the graphic bicolor layout of the texts on the page, Jousse shows how the mnemotechnical devices of traditional

---

13. Jousse's is an evolving and progressively sharpening terminology: in a 1931 lecture on "Globalism in psychology and in pedagogy," he states, "I have mentioned to you how in the last three years a few doctoral theses were presented on the oral style. We should focus more and more closely on global style as that is where, I think, the true solution lies. Before being oral, the gesture is global. Oral style is only a particular form of global style" (S 18/06/31).

14. Fr. Léonard, quoted in Baron, *Mémoire vivante* 65. The main contention was summarized in the title of a very short and skeptical notice in the newspaper *L'Intransigeant* of 30 June 1927: "Les paroles mêmes du Christ" [The very words of Christ]. That we have the literality of Yeshua's words is central to Jousse's biblical research: those who doubt or deny that we have Yeshua's very words are infected by the "virus," not of "philo*logy*," which is the love of language, but of "philo*graphy*," the love of writing (EA 28/11/38). See below.

15. By Palestine, Jousse understands ancient Canaan, the cultural area the Romans called *Palestina*.

mnemonic oral style create rhythm and balance, and how they function as memory aids. Importantly, he shows how someone fully knowledgeable of e.g., the targumim, could proceed to rearrange the old formulas into a new pedagogical, didactic counting-necklace.

Jousse's main publication, however, was not in print but in recorded word. Himself an oralist, a verbomotor with whole-body memory—one could call him hypermnesic—he would in twenty-five years give a thousand-odd lectures at four different institutes of higher learning in Paris, to audiences varying from preprimary schoolteachers to established scholars and writers. The lectures were composed and delivered without writing. Always moving, he spoke for an hour with memory as his only guide, bar a memory-aid card with a brief outline of the lecture. The record taken down by a stenographer was afterwards typed out and conserved in seventy-two letter-size volumes—some twenty thousand pages, now available in electronic form.

All posters advertising the lectures ended with the sentence: "The anthropological studies of M. Marcel Jousse aim at bringing together the disciplines of psychology, ethnology and pedagogy." The yearly programs, always grounded in anthropology, included art, rhythmics, linguistics, neurology, and biblical studies. The introduction to *The Oral Style* had concluded already that "Science has nowadays become so complex that in order to make an advance into any new sector, we must employ the method of warfare used on modern battlefields: the joining of forces."[16] Jousse's is in itself a comprehensive anthropology, joining many forces and indeed, "Joussism is not easy to understand because it is underpinned by the whole of human mechanics."[17]

At the invitation of Maurice Goguel, dean of the Protestant faculty of theology at the prestigious École des hautes études, Jousse gave, from November 1933 till November 1944 a total of three hundred lectures. There is a pattern as text is always set in context: the first series of lectures—1933–1934—is called: *The Psychophysiological Laws of Memory in the Palestinian Oral Style*, and it starts with a lecture sketching the sociocultural context: "The Psychology of the Ethnic Milieu: An Overview of Formulaic Transmission." The next series, on the *Psychology of*

---

16. Jousse, *The Oral Style*, 28.

17. EA 14/01/40. In this chapter, I will deal with Jousse's ethnoanthropology: his anthropology of mimism, and his ethnography of oral-style tradition in ancient Palestine—the latter an aspect of this complexus of human mechanics that was of special concern to him as a scientist and as a believer.

the Parable in the Palestinian Oral Style, sets out the broader context: "Concrete Pedagogy and Algebraic Pedagogy." Other lectures deal with "The Genres in the Palestinian Oral Style—Parable, Apocalypse, History, Maxim," or with specific mnemotechnical memory aids such as balancing, assonance, alliteration, mnemomelody, graphic abbreviations, recitational variants, and transfer-translation. For the use of his students Jousse published a dozen essays that crystallized a number of his lectures, such as "Father, Son, and Paraclete in the Palestinian Ethnic Milieu," "The Manducation of the Lesson in the Palestinian Ethnic Milieu," and "The Targumic Formulas of the Our Father in the Palestinian Ethnic Milieu."[18]

On the 21st of March 1957, Jousse gave what was to be, unwittingly, his last lecture at the Sorbonnne. Two years prior, he had begun to dictate notes to Gabrielle Baron, his assistant, as a preliminary to a synthesis of his anthropology. Ill-health prevented him from realizing this project, but after his death in August 1961, Gabrielle Baron bundled her notes in a file she labeled *Dernières dictées—Last Dictations*.[19] The notes deal mainly with three aspects of Palestinian orality: the Aramaic targumim, the Gospels as a mnemonic and mnemotechnical counter-necklace, and the transfer of the Aramaic-Galilean tradition into the Hellenistic milieu by the bilingual Aramaic-Greek interpreters.

The Anthropology of Mimism: A Dynamic Anthropology of the Living Human Being

In 1876, the physician and anatomist Paul Pierre de Broca founded the Paris School of Anthropology. After his death in 1880, the French anthropological society had a statue erected in his honor. The statue fell victim to the Occupation in 1941 and no longer exists, but from photographic evidence we see how the visitors to the School of Medicine were greeted at the entrance by Broca holding a calliper in his right hand, to measure size, while looking pensively at the human skull in his left hand. Anthropology then, as all sciences in their infancy, concerned itself mostly with establishing credence by collecting, listing, and categorizing data.

Marcel Jousse arrived a generation later, and while recognizing that he stood on the shoulders of giants, he nonetheless called the static

---

18. These lectures were never published, but since 2003 they have been available as *Les cours de Marcel Jousse (1931–1957)* on two compact discs through the Association Marcel Jousse in Paris.

19. The *Dictations* form the first part of Jousse, *Memory*. See the bibliography.

anthropology of his predecessors a skeletology, and the skeleton, however necessary, he saw as no more than the coat hanger of the human. Against such static anthropology he set a dynamic science of the living, breathing, and gesturalizing human, in live interaction with an environment in ceaseless movement. And against the all-pervasive metaphysical terminology of his time, Jousse defined the *anthropos* not as a body, not as a soul, but as an indivisible entity, a human compound, a global energetic whole that manifests itself, to itself and to the world outside, in energetic explosions called gestures.

By this globalist definition of the human, all our senses and all our faculties—memory, thought, will, and intelligence—are psychophysiological; all actions upon us and all reactions from us—all *im*-pressions and all *ex*-pressions, macroscopic or microscopic—necessarily engage our whole being. The *anthropos*'s unique function in the universe is to be reflective, to become conscious of himself and of his environment. If the universe is all movement or unconscious action in interaction, this movement in Man becomes conscious and is called gesture: "in us, all is gesture,"[20] "Man is a conscious gesture."[21]

Mimism, the Unifying Anthropological Law

> "At heart, what is it that the great geniuses of the astronomical world do? They reduce a countless number of phenomena to a single law."[22] "I gave the anthropological world a great law, one equal to the great law of universal gravity in the physical world."[23] "I found that on the basis of this law, we could see clear in the *anthropos*. The *anthropos* is not something dead; the *anthropos* is a living being. And whoever studies the dead *anthropos* should always remind himself that he is accountable for his work to Life."[24]
>
> The old celestial mechanics told us that bodies in the universe attract each other in direct proportion to their masses and in inverse proportion to the square of the distance between them. Which is the law of human mechanics? Could there not

---

20. Lab 11/03/36.
21. EA 07/11/32.
22. S 22/02/34.
23. S 20/12/34.
24. EA 21/01/35.

be in Man a mimismic force that drives him to *construct* his thought, his language, his memory and everything else?[25]

Long before developing static and exterior tools, Man had turned himself into his own best tool: being wise, he became maker—*Homo faber quia sapiens*—for what he saw and observed, he intelligized and wanted to re-create. He saw and observed the cosmos, his surrounding reality, and by *miming* it—mirroring and echoing it—he made it his own.

Two and a half millennia ago, Aristotle held that "Imitation distinguishes Man from the animals and it is through imitation that he acquires his earliest knowledge."[26] Jousse revives this postulation but expands "earliest" knowledge to "all" knowledge and "imitation"—which is voluntary—to "mimism"—which is spontaneous: "Mimism distinguishes Man from the animals, and it is through mimism that he acquires all his knowledge."[27] Man is *mimismic*; he is a born *mimer*: "The great anguish of my life has been to wonder: why do I play? Why does everyone play? Why do all little children play? I was haunted by what I have later called the law of mimism."[28]

"What is mimism? It is the universe facing a living mirror and this living mirror intussuscepts and replays the universe."[29] Mimism is a process of intussuscepting, memorizing, intelligizing, expressing.

The Mimismic Process, from Impression to Expression

Intussusception: "To intussuscept is to grasp the real, to grasp the whole real, to grasp the real wholly."[30] Things outside us we know in so far as they play inside us, and things inside us we know in so far as we play them out: "In truth, it is no more inside than outside. We have no more interior than we have exterior. We are wholly interior; we cannot escape this interiority, which is why I have used the word *intussusception*: 'to receive within.' What is it that we receive? The ambient real."[31]

25. EA 16/01/33.
26. EA 13/11/44.
27. Lab 06/02/35.
28. EA 09/03/39.
29. EA 14/03/49.
30. EA 13/11/44.
31. S 12/11/51.

The Anthropology of Mimism, of Memory, and of the Invisible 81

Memorization: With or without our knowledge, the cosmos presses itself upon us relentlessly, and we register this flux of the real in us. We are not mere reflecting mirrors, but mirrors that retain what they reflect. Whatever we mime (therefore all our mimismic gestures) leaves an energetic imprint, a trace, a mimeme. It is the sum of these mimemes that we call our memory: "The whole of Man is memory and memory is the whole of Man"[32]—"*Omnia mecum porto*: I carry everything in me."[33]

Intellection: Still more than a reflecting and retaining mirror, "I am the conscious mirror of the real."[34] "Intellection—*intus-legere*, reading inside—is what I call consciousness. Consciousness is human specific: I know that something came into me and that it remained there as a mimeme."[35] Human memory then does not remain a passive storehouse of discrete interactions, because awareness triggers memorization and rememoration, imbricating our mimemes in propositional clusters or mimodramas through causality, comparison, contrast, metaphor, and precedence in time as well as in space. Herein lies the beginning of knowledge, science and logic, when, from the macrocosm of stored impressions a mastered microcosm is made, a world of which I can make sense.

An Anthropology of the Memory: Traditioning with Every Fiber of Our Human Compound

Immediate experience, and memory as stored experience, tells us that we are transient, that the mimemes we construct ourselves with also break down even before our physical death. We withstand the flow of things and oblivion by solidifying and so conserve and to make last the things that pass, and to transmit what we incarnated in our global, intelligent musculature—hence our liturgies, which are transmissions of gestures; hence the projections of our mimemes on rock faces, on papyri, on any type of outside support; hence the force that we bring to bear in the establishing of the memory and of tradition, which is handed-down memory; hence, most importantly, our performance of all those acts in accordance with the innermost anthropological laws of expression that engage our

---

32. S 28/02/57.
33. S 14/01/54.
34. Labo 15/12/1937.
35. EA 13/11/44.

human compound as our main mnemotechnical tool in this ceaseless endeavor.

Traditioning in accordance with the Universal Laws of Human Expression

In one of his earlier lectures, Jousse posed a question and provided its answer:

> How does Man, placed at the heart of all the actions of the universe, set about to conserve these actions within him, and to transmit these actions from generation to generation?
> I think the problem is solved: with nothing but our mute muscles, mute but intelligent and capable of molding themselves to the shape of things, the *anthropos* managed to carry and to transmit the great human tradition ... It is the victory of thought over matter. Hence the interest of anthropology alongside psychology. For what we are dealing with is a wholly new opening up and expansion that has gestural language bursting forth from the muscles of miming *anthropos*. This, I believe, is now scientifically established.[36]

"The greater the number of gestural elements a psychophysiological state carries with it, the easier its reemergence will be."[37]

"The *anthropos* intussuscepts the exterior world through all the diversified fibers of his organism. Even if for any one reason, such as adaptation to evolving circumstances, this intussusception specializes in one or the other gesture of a particular organ, the mechanism as a whole will not be essentially altered."[38]

"If we were pure mirrors, the real would replay and there would be no error. It is this we call memory: the gestures that replay the real objectively."[39]

Human expression is determined by the human condition: we are bound by time, by space and by our transience. The psychophysiological laws that determine our expression can therefore be formulated as *rhythmism*, which is the sequencing of our gestures in time; as *bilateralism*, which is the distribution of our gestures according to our bilateral

---

36. EA 03/04/33.
37. S 12/01/33.
38. EA 01/02/39.
39. S 09/12/42.

structure—up and down, fore and aft, left and right; as *formulism* that compresses our expression for ease of composition, memorization, and transmission. It is by their conformity to these laws that Jousse defines civilizations, for it is this conformity that determines their degree of engagement with the real and their resultant style of expression of this real.

Traditioning in Mnemonic Global Style

"Man is a memory,"[40] and style is how memory is expressed. Jousse recalls and expands on Buffon's well-known aphorism "Style is the Man himself:"[41] "'Style is the Man himself' is the whole man giving himself wholly to the real, the whole man receiving and wholly replaying the real."[42]

"Where Buffon told you, 'Style is the Man', I dare add, 'Style is that Man who took in so much of the universe that he was able to encase this universe in a triphasic formula, replay it at will, and claim to all and sundry: I am the master of myself as I am of the universe. That I am, that I want to be.'"[43] For Jousse, "Style is first a matter of physiology";[44] "Style is the gesture";[45] "Style is Man's gesture."[46]

Style is Jousse's gauge of civilization, "from more or less spontaneous, to more or less algebrozed. That is how I see the *anthropos*, and it is that, the anthropology of mimism."[47] Thus, "Language is first and first of all, *mimage*":[48] the original *mimage* or global-manual mimodramatic style has the mimer experiencing and expressing the real with his whole being and with the hands, especially; *language* is secondary and reduces the global gesture to phonatory laryngobuccal or oral gesture, one less demanding of energy; in a third stage, language *written*—mimographic,

40. S 03/03/55.

41. Aphorism of the French naturalist and author Georges-Louis Leclerc, count of Buffon (1707–1788), in an address to the French Academy. Quoted by Jousse, i.a. in EA 09/01/45.

42. HE 12/02/41.

43. EA 09/01/45.

44. EA 01/03/37.

45. S 26/02/42.

46. HE 14/02/39.

47. EA 21/11/38.

48. S 01/02/34. "Mimage," or expression by gestures. Jousse created the term by analogy with "language," laryngobuccal expression, or speech.

first, then alphabetic—entrusts the expression to an outside support, thus further reducing the gesture and becoming progressively algebraic, with signs signifying whatever one chooses them to signify, without any direct reference to anything real, as witnessed by the evolution of our alphabet. There is a final, terminal stage: *algebrosis*: the morbid, necrosed algebra that signals the death of the gesture, as all connection with the real is now severed.

It is Jousse's contention that it is this latter stage our own civilization has reached: "We have lost the sense of the gesture."[49] "Our style is no longer corporeal; our style is no longer *us*; our style no longer conforms with our own equilibrium."[50] "Our style is no longer corporeal; our style is no longer *us*; our style no longer conforms with our own equilibrium."[51]

> What I am trying to do is to make my listeners aware of the formidable question of Man's behavior before the real, and this demands a first great conversion by all who are presently shaken by the immense cataclysm that is called a change of civilization. It is a conversion all of us need to *first* force upon ourselves, *each of us*. And before converting anyone else, I have tried to convert myself and it is my own human conversion you hear three times a week. And it is tragic, this conversion.[52]

An Anthropology of the Invisible: Choosing between Two Explanatory Systems

The Invisible is not a metaphysical invention but an anthropologically observable fact—one that has determined behaviors, shaped cultures and indeed defined humanness: "In whatever way Man is understood—as the normal, biologically normal outcome of the *anthropoid*, or, as is my deep belief, as a unique creature in the universe—Man is *tormented* by what we are going to study today: the *Invisible*. We find Man, everywhere, dissatisfied with the mountains, dissatisfied with the rivers, dissatisfied with the trees; yet, the real is beautiful and science is boundless. Man

---

49. EA 12/12/32.
50. HE 13/02/26.
51. HE 13/02/26.
52. HE 09/02/44.

is nonetheless dissatisfied with the visible and has found it necessary to explain the visible things by invisible things."[53]

All science is an attempt at explication and mastery, but all science is ephemeral and subject to the knowledge available at the time. Each milieu has its own explanatory science that must be understood from within, just as each milieu itself must be understood from within. Gods came and went, there were sciences of visions and of dreams, and now we have laboratories from which the invisible is banned. These laboratories that ban the invisible, Jousse held, only set us back where we started, with unknown powers—no longer gods or a God, but powers unknown, offering neither certainty nor protection. The very term *invisible* is testimony to the constraints of our human compound, as we cannot but define this power by what it is not: not visible, not touchable, not accessible; the invisible is what remains beyond the field of our senses, however much we enhance these mechanically, with microscopes or telescopes.

But to live under a law drafted by an unknown and deaf power that strikes blindly and inexorably is inhuman—hence throughout the history of humankind the attempts at naming the Invisible and at making the Invisible visible, accessible, and manageable.

Anthropology shows us just how contradictory the answers are Man has given in this search for the impossible explication, and how biased our civilization has become in favor of one vision, one by nature as ephemeral as any other.

> On the one hand there is the experimental Greek milieu; on the other there is the revelationary Palestinian milieu. Both equally claim to be dealing with the real, which is to say that they have the science. Through a curious vivisection, we have not carried our research in the direction of the Palestinians; from them we retained no more than an affective waft that we call faith, religion. What we inherited from the Greek milieu, however, we delved into and deepened ever more, and it is this science that we now consider to be the true science. From an anthropological point of view, this is a fundamental error, and I entreat the philosophy teachers who are present here: you cannot mutilate human science merely on the basis of your pseudo-classical training.[54]

---

53. HE 20/11/34.
54. HE 31/01/45.

"The problem is that you, like me, we were put immediately in the presence of Greek texts explained by Greek authors from the language point of view, or rather from the point of view of grammar or of semantics."[55]

As an experimental anthropologist who treats equally all science—that is, all explicative systems developed by humanity and known to him—Jousse opts for the ancient Palestinian revelational knowledge system, to him the most comprehensive and the most coherent: "*here* I am a Palestine anthropologist. I try to understand. True or false is of no concern to me. What I do know is that there is found a coherent human gestural attitude in itself."[56]

"Not all people are, fortunately, at our algebrozed and artificial stage. Only by observing the *anthropos* in some other ethnic milieus will we find what wells up from the very depths of spontaneous *anthropos*..., because among us, this spontaneous *anthropos* has all but disappeared."[57]

"When we find ourselves before such *anthropologically* pure beings, however, we are struck by the clarity of their vision and expression of things. Of this I had become aware of at a very early age as I lived in contact with the peasant milieu of the Sarthe."[58]

"We have lost the sense of the gesture" is the clarion call, in 1932, of a veteran of World War I who will see his conviction confirmed when France is defeated a few years later: the civilization and the religion that are his, are in their death throes. He repeats the call ten years later, in 1942, in the midst of the occupation of his land: "You saw what is meant by the fall of Western civilization and of religion! Religion fell a long time ago, and because the religion of that little peasant Yeshua fell, the civilization carried by this religion fell in turn. Would there be a way to save the civilization by restoring the fundamental bases of the religion?"[59]

The way is signposted in the title of this lecture: "Taking the Real Back in Our Hands"[60]—"We need to go back to the very bases of our

---

55. HE 24/01/1945.
56. S 20/01/38.
57. EA 27/01/36. Lecture on *Algebrosis and the death of civilizations*.
58. EA 23/01/33.
59. EA 24/03/42.
60. *Remise 'en mains' du réel*.

civilization, and we need to pose the problem: what is our civilization made of?"[61]

"The habit that I am wearing is a battle dress ... my role is to show the youth what direction to take."[62]

He identified and squared up against two sciences that had teamed up and sapped the foundations of the civilization and the religion: philosophical positivism, which would only deal with the visible, material world, and "Germanic philological methodology," which had become the basis of a "Greco-Latinicist exegesis"[63] that understood text only as writing and accordingly only studied written documents: what was not in writing did not exist. "Wrong method begets wrong science,"[64] and wrongly premised Greco-Latinist studies lead to Platonian, Greek, Latin and Cartesian readings.

"Twenty years ago, I asked myself the following all-important question: is it possible for anyone, in the heart of Paris, in a country like France, in a quasi-dead civilization, to muster the strength to introduce, if I dare say so, this vaccine of life into the very Palestinian milieu these people ["the old theologians"] had monopolized?"[65]

The battle lines are drawn: positivism negates the anthropologically obvious, viz. that the Invisible exists; as a method, Greco-Latinism is irreparably flawed.

Palestinian Anthropology: Finding and Applying "a Method Suited to the Milieu We Are Studying"[66]

Palestinism—Jousse's neologism for Palestinian anthropology—establishes the anthropological fact of the Invisible for certain societies that cannot be understood on the basis of one's own self-satisfied "positive" science exclusive of this Invisible. Equally, there is the ethnographical fact that there are societies where oral composition exists and that express themselves in oral style, mimodramatically and rhythmocatechistically, even when writing is available.

61. HE 07/03/45.
62. HE 07/05/40.
63. HE 30/05/45.
64. HE 10/11/43.
65. HE 02/04/40.
66. EA 22/01/34.

"Palestinism must first be a question of anthropological and ethnic science before being a question of religion":[67] "faith is scientific religious intelligence."[68] "Even if I were an unbeliever, an atheist anthropologist, when explaining these mechanisms, it would be my task to find out *of what they are made*. And do not, ever, come and tell me that it is poetry, that it is mythology: never! Never! They are different systems. Some are more solid, others are weaker, [but all, the Druids, the Greeks, the Romans], they all believed in their system. And that is what anthropology is about, to understand their system, and it is that, science."[69]

"I speak here not as a Catholic priest, not as a Christian, but as an anthropologist entirely rooted in the Palestinian milieu . . . You will never understand an ethnic milieu unless you insert yourself in all its living mechanisms."[70]

Diction and Scription:
"'Written, Written; Oral, Oral,' the Rabbis say."[71]

The peasant Jousse had firsthand experience with the worldview of a traditional society and of its mimodramatic oral-style expression; the scholar Jousse studied its textual tradition and in *The Oral Style* established for oral-style texts a global grammar, morphology, and syntax, which he would further define in his oral lectures, giving oral-style texts an appropriate methodology, terminology, and presentation on the page.

The first task of the Palestine anthropologist is to clear terrain cluttered by centuries of misreading of texts because of ignorance of their context: "There was no room at the inn for an Aramaic Yeshua"[72] because those who taught him were "totally ignorant of the pedagogy of the founder of their religion, which is quite simply monstrous."[73]

The study of Palestinian texts should begin with the understanding that they are pedagogical and utilitarian, not rhetorical or aesthetic; that Palestinian pedagogy is a pedagogy of an intelligent and comprehending memory in which all the elements are meticulously calibrated and structured to facilitate memorization by repetition (echoing); that the stylistic

67. S 28/02/57.
68. HE 26/05/43.
69. S 13/01/38.
70. HE 20/11/34.
71. HE 21/05/41.
72. S 25/02/54.
73. EA 01/03/43.

norms of oral composition are not those of writing; and that "there lies an abyss between scription and diction."[74] Even when an oral composition is put in writing—*scriptioned*—the text retains its oral stylistic characteristics. The text put in writing serves as a memory aid only, the writing is not for composition and transmission but for verification and, in times of danger, preservation.

"Science begins with precise language."[75]

We need to "pasteurize" our terminology: orally composed lessons are not homilies, sermons or discourses, but *rhythmocatechisms* as their teaching is done through mirrored and echoed movement—received through the ears and eyes, understood through the throat, and proffered through the mouth in rhythmomelodic formulas; their message is delivered in small portions, chewable mouthfuls that are *buccalized* and *manducated* by learners who are not disciples who listen passively, but *apprehenders* who *audition*: they hear and retain whole-bodily; these texts are not poetry in verses and stanzas, but *recitatives of blocked formulas*; they are not an amorphous "oral traditional" mass, but are in distinct genres—*proverbs or maxims, parables, apocalypses, histories*. These texts are formulaic and as the formulas are known to all, a single audition might suffice for a novel arrangement to be remembered there and then.

> It was repeated to me in every tone: "The apostles could not have retained the Sermon on the Mount after a single listening." But of course not. No one of your own faithful could possibly retain by heart any one of your sermons. What you call the Sermon on the Mount is not a sermon; it is a rhythmocatechism. And what was said was not said once, but had been repeated hundreds of times; it was a *mishnah*, a repetition. And it was put in the form of a didactic counting-necklace before being put in writing in a stable form.[76]

> The word *preaching* should be banned. There never was a predication of the gospel. Jesus never *preached*; he rhythmocatechized just as the Qur'an is taught to the children, but then without books. We should not speak of *sermons*. Ethnically, a *Sermon on the Mount* is a nonsense... There is in fact no preacher, there are no sermons, and there are no discourses: there is no Discourse

74. HE 11/11/42.
75. HE 22/03/44.
76. S 01/03/56.

after the Last Supper—no more than there is a Sermon on the Mountain. There are rhythmocatechisms made of crystallized pearls, easy to memorize.[77]

A Compensatory Rhythmotypography

The linear outlay of the biblical texts that came down to us in written-down versions obscures their orally composed origin. For the original oral structure and characteristics to reappear, a compensatory rhythmotypographic layout is needed that brings into relief the mnemotechnical devices of the text—the verbal linkages such as alliterations and consonances; the parallelisms, repetitions, wordplays, binary and ternary rhythmic patterns. It is an anthropological and ethnic revivification process whereby the written sentences are visually turned back into the original vocal propositions, reincarnated in living throats and mouths, on living lips—and reaching the eyes and ears of living "auditioners," who at once learn and memorize rhythmocatechistically.

The Worldview of Palestinian Anthropology: "The Invisible Mimed through the Visible"[78]

Ancient Palestinians, as members of a traditional society, did not make any clear-cut division between the visible and the Invisible. The Palestinian center of gravity was not the center of the world, but the center of the heavens, the center of the "World-from-above" and the "World-to-come," the Throne of glory of the Divinity, the Throne created before the world. Through earthly analogies, the Invisible is *hominized* (brought to live as a human being), *ethnicized* (situated in a particular time and space), *particularized*, (incarnated in a specific individual: "The Word that became flesh and lived among us"[79] is the Invisible become visible, and this visible one was a man, a Galilean peasant, called Yeshua, and he was the world-above incarnated, mirrored and echoed in the world-below, and sublimating this world-below. He was the divine gesture vibrating in our human gestures.

77. HE 08/11/44.
78. Title of lecture HE 20/11/34.
79. John 1:14.

The Anthropology of Mimism, of Memory, and of the Invisible 91

The Invisible needs to be visualized, ocularized, and it does this splendidly through the powerful anthropological agency of the mimodrama. So, we see that what is mimed in the World-above will be mimed in the World-below, and more exactly, the World-below mimes because the World-above has been miming first and set for it the prototype.[80]

The Palestinian tradition does indeed methodically implement the great law of global and oral mimism. It is the mishnaization, the repetition-in-echo, which is etymologically signified in the currently totally algebrozed Greek word: *catechization*. The Palestinian traditionists are mishnaists or tannaists, catechists, more exactly rhythmocatechists because rhythm mnemonically sustains this method, which is so deeply anchored in memory, but an intelligent and comprehending memory: "Learn and understand" is the golden rule of this tradition of which all the elements, large and small, are meticulously developed and structured for faithful repetition in echo. It is this total, gestural and recitational communication, from the "abba-father" to the "bera-son," that manifests the paternal love:

FIGURE 3.1

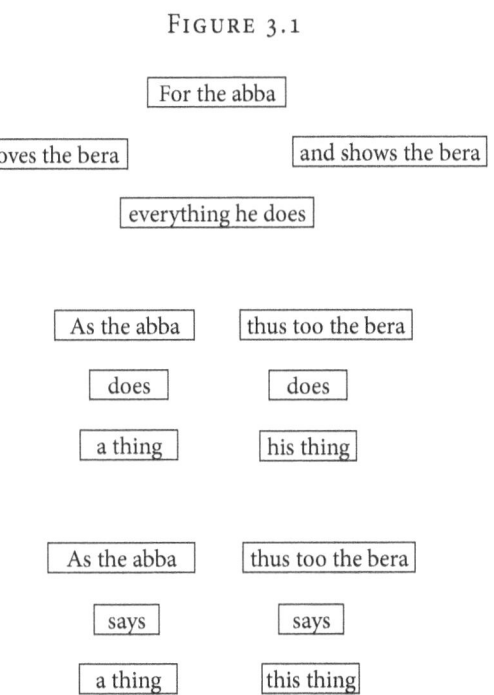

---

80. HE 13/11/37. All biblical references are Jousse's own, free translations.

> The abba shows his love visually and auditorily. On this mirrored and echoed reflection rests the whole of the Palestinian traditionist doctrine. Almost all the analogies, even the most transcendent, derive from this. There we encounter, beyond *human mimism*, what could be called *transcendental mimism*.[81]

Mimism, Memory and the Invisible: Mimodrama, Human and Divine

The term *mimism* appears for the first time, in the first of Jousse's recorded lectures.[82] The connection of mimism and the Invisible, however, is already profiled in *The Oral Style*, the last sentence of which reads, "If God allows me to realize the work that I project, I will return to each of the rather rough lines of [this] sketch and refine them in a series of specialized studies, in close cooperation with the learned discoveries of French and foreign technicians in experimental and scientific research on this mysterious human word, that frail and marvelous echo of the eternal and creative Word!"[83]

Jousse's anthropology of mimism is his attempt to explicate the "impossible explication." It is a synthesis that gradually unfolds, till, ever more probing, it defines itself as what it was from the beginning: "the formidable and universal law of mimism which goes from Man up to God."[84] In a lecture close to twenty years after the publication of *The Oral Style*,[85] Jousse discusses his progress in the work he had projected then and that became the anthropology of mimism and its application in the Palestinian context. In the introduction to the lecture, mimism and the Invisible are fused in two balancing lines:

> In the mimodrama of the Creation, divine mimism humanized Man.
> In the mimodrama of the Communion, human mimism divinized Man.[86]

---

81. Jousse, "Father, Son, and Paraclete in the Palestinian Ethnic Milieu." In *Memory*, 225–72 (232–33). The presentation of this short extract is an example of rhythmotypography as it suggests the traditional rhythmic balancing of the yoke (left-right) and the burden (lifting up and down).
82. S 05/03/31.
83. Jousse, *The Oral Style*, 284.
84. S12/02/53.
85. "French Anthropology and Its Discoveries," École des hautes études, November 10, 1943.
86. HE 10/11/43.

A traditional mimodramatic society, Palestine explains things in mimodramas—the great mimodrama of Genesis, the "mysteries" of the Trinity, of the incarnation, of the redemption, of the Eucharist, of the transubstantiation . . .

Yeshuanism: ". . . to eat and to drink the Teacher who will transform us into himself"[87]

In Jousse's mimism, two transubstantiations conjoin as mimodramas: in the mimodrama of the creation, the Creator hominizes the human animal by endowing him with consciousness, thus transubstantiating an unconscious into a conscious cosmos; in the mimodrama of the communion, Yeshua—"The Word became flesh that lived among us"—divinizes the conscious *anthropos* by allowing him to partake in the transubstantiation of the visible into the Invisible.

> Every morning at 5 o'clock, I feel the replay of this living tradition when I say what you call *Mass* and what I call *the Palestinian mimodrama of the Bread and the Wine*.[88]

> [Then] come to me, from the depths of the Palestinian milieu, the true explications of all that I say, of all that I do. From under every word that I speak, the Aramaean bursts forth. All the gestures that I do are the gestures that were traditional in Israel for how many thousands of years?[89]

> I take the dead matter of the bread and of the wine and I say: "This is my Flesh. This is my Blood." And what is most extraordinary is that I am perfectly convinced of the reality of this. Yet, I am not a simpleton. Think, if you like, that I am a residue of old dogmas, but, with all my intelligence, which is as sharp as yours, I can say, with my customary humility: "I believe, to the point of giving my flesh and my blood, that I am before a transubstantiation."[90]

> [It is] the formidable transubstantiation of the teaching Word that one eats while eating the Teacher.[91]

87. EA 20/12/48.
88. EA 12/12/49.
89. HE 15/01/35.
90. EAB 03/03/48.
91. EA 23/02/48.

To an outsider wholly *a*-logical, transubstantiation is, in the light of Palestinian ethnoanthropology, the pure gestural *ana*-logic of the mimodramatics of a pedagogue playing on the polysemantism of the Aramaic language.

> Through an imperceptible progression, the Palestinian can eat the bread of wheat, eat the bread of the lesson, eat the flesh of the teacher. Through a similar imperceptible progression, he can drink the wine from the grape, he can drink the wine of the lesson, he can drink the blood of the teacher. And following his logical thought, the teacher will make eat his bread, his lesson and his flesh and he will make drink his wine, his teaching and his blood. Extraethnically, this is untranslatable, but it is anthropologically explicable.[92]

Jousse invariably insists that the formula "Do this in memory of me" be changed to "Do this as a memory aid of me," because the Communion, being a mimodrama, it is a "global and oral and rhythmoformulaic"[93] performance of a verbalized gesture: "He did not say '*say* this again' . . . but 'redo, replay,' using the term in the Joussean sense: 'Replay this as a memory aid of me.'"[94]

As transubstantiation in the Communion is a contentious subject between Protestants and Catholics, Jousse calls on the authority of a Protestant anthropologist, Gerardus van der Leeuw,[95] to support his claim that transubstantiation is not a question of religion first, but an anthropological and ethnic reality. He quotes van der Leeuw: "To a Galilean peasant, the question of the real presence is undeniable. When the Galilean peasant Yeshua says to you: 'This is my body, this my blood,' for him, it is true." And he comments, "That is the question. You don't have to analyze this chemically; it is a question of anthropology. Did Yeshua's milieu believe in miracles? Or were they sure miracles took place? But absolutely! . . . If we want to understand, we are, all of us, you as well as I, forced into this method: 'What is it about in the Palestinian milieu of the beginning of our era?'"[96]

---

92. HE 10/11/43.
93. S 21/02/57.
94. EA 18/03/41.
95. Van der Leeuw, *L'Homme primitif.*
96. HE 09/02/44.

Having answered this question scientifically, Jousse performs at Mass, with Palestinian gestural logic, the gestures of Israel: this is the "coincidence from within, which is to simply redo the gestures of the ethnic milieu one is studying."[97]

> "This, every time you will redo it, you will redo it as a memory aid of me." ... Which is why I wanted to understand Aramaic in its utmost depths, to study as much as it is possible to study:
>
> As a memory-aid of me you will redo it.
> That is all I have been doing my whole life. And when you come here to listen to me, it is still all that I am doing: to try and understand what it is, this memory that makes it possible for people entrapped for two thousand years in a sclerosed liturgy, to replay the gestures of a Galilean peasant. That is memory, and, maybe human memory was made solely for this, to perpetuate this great consecrating gesture. I believe it was created only for this. All other gestures are but poor imitations.[98]

Yeshuanism: "Religion Is a Life and a Science"[99]

Today, "no one denies the power of science ... , but how many there are who deny the power of religion, which is what I call the science of the Invisible."[100] "The savant of our ethnic milieu poses the problem: 'Can science and faith be reconciled?' I, as anthropologist, say: 'The question is put wrongly. Do you understand what it is you are talking about?'"[101]

> A religion is a system of explanatory gestures. This is why, in the beginning, there was no separation between religion and science. The great builders of religions were all great constructors of explicative systems. Moses was a savant in his time. Confucius was a savant in his milieu and in his time, the Buddha was a savant in his milieu and in his time.[102]

---

97. S 16/12/37.
98. S 28/02/57.
99. EA 01/03/43.
100. Lab 19/01/38.
101. HE 31/01/45.
102. EA 24/02/44.

And what I am presently trying to save is the civilization of the Galilean peasant Yeshua.[103]

I have kept the Faith and I will bring it to others in the form of civilization. Later perhaps will it be possible to go beyond civilization.[104]

My position is not an easy one to hold because the theologist milieus always want to use our science to convert, but I am not made for that, I am made to be with you and like you: I search. Obviously, you'll say that I made a choice seeing that the habit I wear shows that my choice is made. *Yes, that choice is made,* but I do not satisfy myself with the little science that I have, which is why I continue to work, always, always, always to clarify for myself that great thing I spent my life on.[105]

"Like Shaul of Giscala, I will be able to say:

The good fight	I fought
the course	I staid
faithfulness	I defended[106]

One is generally of the religion of one's mother. One knows, in fact, the visible or the invisible world only through one's mother.[107]

I should like to repeat the well-known phrase: 'A little science distances from religion. A lot of science (does not bring you back to) but maintains you there.' Because I, I don't believe conversions are possible. One is born in a religion. And my studies consist solely in deepening what I received at the maternal hearth. What I am trying to do is to become conscious of the formidable mechanisms that are at work in the traditional teaching of my mother. And you are witness to what I personally do at the School of anthropology, before an audience of Muslims or Judaists or of anyone confession, because at heart, it is about

---

103. EA 13/12/43.

104. EA 10/03/42.

105. HE 06/02/40.

106. These words are inscribed on Jousse's tomb in the cemetery of Fresnay-sur-Sarthe.

107. S 19/01/56.

understanding how a mother transmits to her child a tradition that is beyond her.[108]

Invited at the École des hautes études to take over a series of lectures on the theme "the New Testament and primitive Christianism," Jousse on principle changed the title to "Old targumic Testament and Aramaic Christianism," because he understood Hellenic or Greco-Latinized Christianism to be secondary to Yeshuanism, the primary true primitive Christianism: there is not a Hebrew Old Testament and a Greek New Testament, but there is an oral-formulaic creation of "Christianism" by Yeshua. True Christianism is therefore *Yeshuanism before christo-graecism*,[109] as posed by the title of a lecture immediately preceded and followed by two titles that encapsulate the two contrary interpretations of the origin of Christianism: "The Bankruptcy of 'Papyrovorous' Criticism" and "The Rhythmocatechistic Civilizations."

Yeshuanism is the doctrine of the Meshiha, Meshianism—Meshianism having taken the meaning of "waiting for the Messiah" and not "the coming of the Messiah," Jousse creates the term "Yeshuanism": Rabbi Yeshua of Nazareth [is a] historical character, [an] anthropological phenomenon, with a human personality, with a milieu, with a pedagogy":[110] he is "the *anthropos Yeshua*, clearly belonging somewhere, *a Galilean* and a *peasant*,"[111] a popular Galilean peasant-rabbi and a traditional oral-style pedagogue, a teacher who lived and taught mimodramatically and rhythmocatechistically in Aramaic targumic formulas, in accordance with fundamental, spontaneous anthropological oral-style expression.

"A genius in memorization,"[112] finding himself facing "the frightening magma of the Hebraic Torah transferred in Aramaic after the Babylonian captivity,"[113] he so mastered this centuries-old memory of his people that he could organize this vast, fluid, and jumbled targumic tradition into a new, cohesive explicative system that would lay the foundation of a new civilization and religion.

True faith is to be true to *true* Christianism by establishing scientifically the words and deeds of its founder, Yeshua: "I preserved the

---

108. EAB 03/03/48.
109. HE 09/12/42.
110. HE 15/05/34.
111. HE 09/12/42.
112. HE 15/11/38.
113. S 03/03/38.

faithfulness to the Palestinian texts."[114] "I brought what is needed to restore Yeshua's rhythmocatechism in line with that of other peoples of traditional oral style."[115]

Haymanuta to the researcher in Palestinian oral-style tradition, as to the Palestinian, means exactness in the instruction received as in the instruction transmitted; exactness in the memorization by a trained and trusted memory in exact gestural and verbal recitation. "'Do we have Yeshua's very words?' But of course, because all the living tools, be they of the visible or of the invisible world, are *oriented* towards exactitude, so much so that even what is called *faith* is *haymanuta*, this is to say fidelity, stable fidelity."[116]

Turned into bookish amnesiacs by our own near-exclusive reliance on the outside memory of the book or any other recording device, we have forgotten the capacity of human memory, and we judge oral-style memory by our own lack of it. Jousse's injunction is, "He who does not believe in the memory does not enter in these milieus of oral style. There indeed, memory is stupefying. This is, among other reasons, why Yeshua the Palestinian has not written."[117]

Yeshua did not write: he calls on "this formidable mnemonic and mnemotechnically equipped and organized gestural corporeal-manual and oral pedagogy *to insert the Invisible in the human muscles*, and so we do not have all kinds of interior revelations, but we have the Invisible 'who became Flesh and who lived among us.'"[118] Yeshua fashions his message to be carried and transmitted in the intelligent musculatures of living human beings: he was no longer the Invisible become visible *among* them but *in* them.

> It is precisely because Yeshua has never written that we have exactly his *gesta*—his words and deeds."[119]

> He has not written, nor did he ask anyone to write for him, this in a country that knew writing. He did not say, "Here, this is my manuscript," or, "Write under my dictation and make whatever number of copies," like the Torah that could be found in every

---

114. HE 30/05/45.
115. EA 43/03/01.
116. HE 02/02/44.
117. HE 10/11/43.
118. Lab 26/04/35.
119. S 28/01 54.

synagogue. No, he said: "Go, teach all the Goyim as I myself have taught you." ... This poses a problem that has been with me my whole life, because it is the problem of the Invisible *among us*.[120]

To this anthropological and ethnic guarantee of authenticity, Jousse adds a historical if paradoxical argument: Yeshuanism's short lifespan. After the Master's disappearance, the chosen leader, Kepha, composed a traditional mnemonic recitational *seder-sefer*, an ordering and counting-necklace, on which he strung Yeshua's doctrinal pearl-lessons alternating with his own historical recitatives. This necklace the teaching envoys used and adapted, each according to his circumstances, and assisted by professional Aramaeo-Hellenist interpreters.

Because the writing-oriented Greek milieu did not know and did not depend on the oral-style laws of living memory, the Greek transfer-translations of the envoys' Aramaic catechisms were soon frozen in writing. However, "for anyone who knows the targumic formulas, the Greek is nothing more than a translucent veil"[121] under which the original formulas can be recovered through retrotranslation. It is an arduous task, but one that can and needs to be done[122] if the Gospels are to be understood on their own terms and in their own context.

> Having memorized the Aramaic targums from the age of thirteen, I felt that, in the Gospels, I was not confronted with original Greek but with a transfer in Greek. But transferring what? Aramaic formulas ... What I felt ever more forcefully playing in me was the Aramaic formulism ... And when I found myself before the *Our Father*, it was not the *Our Father* in Greek that played in me, but the *Our Father* in Aramaic ... Who now amongst you—and I do not know if I have priests present here—is capable of reciting by heart the immense Aramaic targums of the Hebraic Torah? Yet, this is what is needed if one is to understand the play of formulism ... And that, Yeshua knew so well that you find him squaring off in these terrible pilpuls with Satana or with one or the other Rabbis! Throw in a formula and another one responds; one formula arises, and right there another one follows suit! Here is where mastery of the ancient formulas reigns supreme and where unexpected

---

120. Lab 26/04/35.

121. HE 11/11/42.

122. As proof of such retrotransfer or retrotranslation, Jousse cites often the *Apocalypse of Esdras* in Aramaic targumic formulas by Gry, *Les dires prophétiques d'Esdras*.

> juxtapositions spawn new arrangements. It is that, the law of formulism. But how could poor philologists ever see what took an anthropologist, with an entire career focused on ethnic tradition, a life-time to resuscitate?[123]
>
> We travel all over the world trying to convert people to a Greco-Latinized Christianism, when true Christianism so dominates all ethnic particularism that it seems to well up from the very depths of anthropology.[124]

Spiraling Upward

Marcel Jousse wanted his anthropology to be "not a *system*, but an observation."[125] It could, accordingly, "only be a science in a dotted line."[126] One article on Jousse opens with the observation, "There is not a page of Marcel Jousse that does not make the reader lift his head,"[127] and a former student of his remarked, "What is striking with Fr. Jousse is that he makes you rethink everything."[128]

As the references in this chapter make clear, I treat the one thousand-odd lectures of Jousse as a single corpus, disregarding when, where and to whom they were taught: his is a synthesis unfolded to and fro, defined and refined, confirmed and contradicted. When asked, "But how did you arrive at this synthesis of the anthropology of gesture and rhythm?" Jousse answered: "It is rather difficult to go publicly into all the detail of the steps and countersteps that are necessary to elaborate something that holds together. But it might be interesting to see what someone who is in no way transcendent can achieve by dint of observation."[129]

> By the time I turned twenty, my work was done. I think discoverers discover when very young.[130]

---

123. EA 12/03/51.
124. S 03/03/55.
125. Lab 25/03/36.
126. EA 27/11/33.
127. Baillaud, "Sur la manducation," 67–71.
128. HE 11/06/41.
129. S 01/02/34.
130. EA 12/01/41.

True explicative mimodrama starts with a synthesis, first, but turns back later to confirm each gesture in detail. It is in this face-to-face phase that the verification is done.[131]

Where I come from, we have a type of hawk, the kestrel. At some moment, it feels as if the whole of nature is falling silent, the small birds stop calling. Look! There is a bird of genius: the hawk. He turns, he is circular. And then he centers and swoops on the small bird there, huddled on a branch of the apple tree. It is that, the genius, the specialist, circular and centered . . . But one must be able to do the inverse mechanism too. You start from the center. You go in a spiral and you find the universe![132]

I am a methodologist and that is why I say to you "Take," and not just "Read," but "Replay, play back within yourself."[133]

It is not in death that you will understand life; it is in you, yourself, replaying life, and then you will not only know "I think therefore I am," but "*I live, therefore I understand.*"[134]

Publications by Marcel Jousse

Dernières Dictées: Notes sur l'élaboration de la tradition de style oral galiléen et sur son émigration hellénistique. Edited by Edgard Sienaert. Paris: Association Marcel Jousse, 1999.
[Part One: Last Dictations. On the Elaboration and Emigration of the Palestinian Oral Style. In *Memory, Memorization, and Memorizers.* Eugene, OR: Cascade Books (2018) 15–147].
Les cours de Marcel Jousse (1931–1957). Available on two CDs. Paris: Association Marcel Jousse, 2003.
Du mimisme à la musique chez l'enfant. Paris: Geuthner, 1935.
["From Mimism to Music in the Child." In *In Search of Coherence.* Eugene, OR: Pickwick Publications (2016) 236–44.]
"Du style oral breton au style oral évangélique." Cahiers Marcel Jousse 8 (1996) 23–75.
Judahen, Judéen, Judaïste dans le milieu ethnique palestinien. Paris: Geuthner, 1946.
["Judahite, Judean, Judaist in the Palestinian Ethnic Milieu." In *Memory, Memorization, and Memorizers.* Eugene, OR: Cascade Books (2018) 207–24.]
La manducation de la leçon dans le milieu ethnique palestinien. Paris: Geuthner, 1950.
["The Manducation of the Lesson in the Palestinian Ethnic Milieu." In *Memory, Memorization, and Memorizers.* Eugene, OR: Cascade Books (2018) 274–345].

131. EA 17/02/36.
132. EAB 14/01/48.
133. S 10/02/55.
134. HE 05/12/33.

L'anthropologie du geste. Comité des Études Marcel Jousse. 3 vols. Paris : Gallimard, 1974–1978; new edition in one volume, 2008.
Le bilatéralisme humain et l'anthropologie du langage. Paris: Geuthner, 1940.
["Human Bilateralism and the Anthropology of Language." In *In Search of Coherence*. Eugene, OR: Pickwick Publications (2016) 260–91.]
Le mimisme humain et l'anthropologie du langage. Paris: Geuthner, 1936.
["Human Mimism and the Anthropology of Language." In *In Search of Coherence*. Eugene, OR: Pickwick Publications (2016) 223–35.]
Le style oral rythmique et mnémotechnique chez les verbo-moteurs. Paris: Beauchesne, 1925.
[*The Oral Style*. Translated by Edgard Sienaert and Richard Whitaker. Albert Bates Lord Studies in Oral Tradition, 6. New York: Garland,1990.]
Les formules targoumiques du "Pater" dans le milieu ethnique palestinien. Paris: Geuthner, 1944.
["The Targumic Formulas of the *Our Father* in the Palestinian Ethnic Milieu." In *Memory, Memorization, and Memorizers*. Eugene, OR: Cascade Books, (2018) 346–90.]
Les lois psycho-physiologiques du style oral vivant et leur utilisation philologique. Paris: Geuthner, 1931.
["The Psycho-Physiological Laws of Living Oral Style and Their Use in Philology." In *In Search of Coherence*. Eugene, OR: Pickwick Publications (2016) 245–59.]
Les outils gestuels de la mémoire dans le milieu ethnique palestinien: le formulisme araméen des récits évangéliques. Paris: Geuthner, 1935.
Les Rabbis d'Israël. Les récitatifs rythmiques parallèles. Vol. 1, *Genre de la maxime*. Paris: Spes, 1930.
[The Rabbis of Israel: The Parallel Rhythmic Recitatives. Vol. 1, Genre of the Maxim. Paris: Association Marcel Jousse, 2021.]
Mimisme humain et psychologie de la lecture. Travaux du Laboratoire de rythmo-pédagogie de Paris. Paris: Geuthner, 1935.
Mimisme humain et style manuel. Paris: Geuthner, 1926.
["Human Mimism and Manual Style." In *In Search of Coherence*. Eugene, OR: Pickwick Publications (2016) 206–22].
Père, Fils et Paraclet dans le milieu ethnique palestinien. Paris: Geuthner, 1941.
["Father, Son, and Paraclete in the Palestinian Ethnic Milieu." In *Memory, Memorization, and Memorizers*. Eugene, OR: Cascade Books (2018) 225–73].
Rythmo-mélodisme et rythmo-typographisme pour le style oral palestinien. Travaux du Laboratoire d'anthropologie rythmo-pédagogique. Paris: Geuthner, 1952.

References

Baillaud, Bernard. "Sur la manducation de la parole de Jean Paulhan par Marcel Jousse—et réciproquement—ou Par quel bout les prendre." *Nunc* 25 (2011) 67–71. [On the manducation of the word in Jean Paulhan by Marcel Jousse—and vice-versa—or where to start.]
Baron, Gabrielle. *Mémoire vivante: Vie et œuvre de Marcel Jousse*. Paris: Le Centurion, 1981. [Living Memory: Life and Work of Marcel Jousse].
Gry, Léon. *Les dires prophétiques d'Esdras, IVe Esdras*. Paris: Geuthner, 1938.
[The Prophetic Sayings of Esdras, Fourth Esdras].

Leeuw, Gerardus van der. *L'Homme primitif et la Religion: Étude anthropologique*. Paris : Alcan, 1940. [Primitive Man and Religion: An Anthropological Study].

Maunoury, Auguste-François. *Anthologia micra: Petite anthologie ou Recueil de fables, descriptions, épigrammes, pensées contenant les racines de la langue grecque*. Paris: Poussielgue, 1863.

[Anthologia Micra: A small anthology or collection of fables, descriptions, epigrams, thoughts comprising the roots of the Greek language].

Walton, Brian, ed. *Biblia sacra polyglotta: complectantia textus originales, Hebraicum cum Pentateucho Samaritano, Chaldaicum, Graecum: versionumque antiquarum, Samaritanae, Graecae LXXII interp., Chaldaicae, Syriacae, Arabicae, Aethiopicae, Persicae, Vulg. Lat. quicquid comparari poterat: cum textuum et versionum orientalium translationibus Latinis ex vetustissimis mss. undique conquisitis . . . : cum apparatu, appendicibus, tabulis, variis lectionibus, annotationibus, indicibus, etc.: opus totum in sex tomos tributum*. London: Roycroft, 1654–1657.

4

An Oral Perspective of Proverbs 31:10–31

MARK TIMOTHY LLOYD HOLT

> Les découvertes consistent en des rapprochements d'idées susceptibles de se joindre et qui étaient isolées jusqu'alors.
> Discoveries consist of bringing together ideas susceptible of being connected which were hitherto isolated. (Laplace)[1]

Introduction

So begins Marcel Jousse's multilingual book, *The Oral Style*. Proverbs 31:10–31 is a text that lends itself to such rapprochement. It brings together extended poetry that is usually perceived to be theological with oral sayings that are typical of daily life. The translated writings of Marcel Jousse make no comment on this particular text, but his approach facilitates fresh insights into a text which are usually ignored. This introduction will give a brief overview of some contemporary understanding of the text before Jousse's insights from the beginning of last century are introduced. The remaining sections use these insights to reexamine the conventional analysis of Prov 31:10–31.

---

1. Jousse, *The Oral Style*, 3.

Proverbs 31:10–31

Proverbs 31:10–31 is often viewed as a didactic poem describing the desirable traits of a good woman or wife. However, the proverbial form, the literary context, and the vocabulary employed suggest that it is the virtue of wisdom that is being described using the metaphor of a valiant woman. The metaphor works in both directions. If wisdom and strength are described by what the poet extols as feminine qualities, femininity is also being described as wisdom and strength.

Christine Roy Yoder gives a helpful metaphor of the book of Proverbs as a literary mosaic.[2] Each proverb is a "multivalent slice of truth."[3] She cites Gerhard von Rad's claim that the two parts of a one-line proverb require more participation and interaction than a developed didactic poem.[4] Beyond the single mosaic tile or proverbial line, the interactions between bordering pieces are also important. These bordering pieces can form poetic units of two or more proverbs through catchwords, wordplay, sound, inclusio, and repetition of key words.[5] This metaphor of a literary mosaic is especially helpful for Prov 31:10–31, which has the form of a didactic poem, but the diversity of a colorful mosaic.

The subject of the poem is אשת חיל. Yoder translates the term as "a woman of substance."[6] A better translation is Al Wolters's phrase "a valiant woman" because it reflects the wider scriptural use of the term.[7] Outside of the poem, the only other times חיל is used as an attribute of a woman are in Prov 12:4 (in contrast to one who brings shame) and Ruth 3:11 (whose reputation was clearly the virtue of valor, not wealth). While sometimes referring to wealth (e.g., Gen 34:29), the attribute of חיל is used more often attached to or standing for גבור meaning a strong man or warrior. Other translations (KJV: "virtuous"; NIV: "noble character"; RSV: "good") fail to bring out the warrior connotations of the word.

Lexical and thematic parallels link the poem strongly to the opening chapters of Proverbs (1–9) where wisdom is frequently personified as

---

2. Yoder, *Proverbs*, xxviii.
3. Yoder, *Proverbs*, 27.
4. Von Rad, *Wisdom*, 27.
5. Yoder, *Proverbs*, xxvii.
6. Yoder, *Proverbs*, 288–97.
7. Wolters, *The Song*.

feminine.[8] The lexical and thematic parallels of similarity described by Yoder are summarized in Table 4.1 below.[9]

TABLE 4.1:
PARALLELS BETWEEN PROV 31:10–31 AND PROV 1–9[10]

Attribute	Proverbs 31	Proverbs 1–9
is difficult to find	31:10	1:28; 8:17
is more precious than jewels	31:10	3:15; 8:11
has a household	31:15, 21, 27	9:1
has a staff of "servant girls"	31:15	9:3
provides food	31:14	9:5
provides security	31:11	1:33
does fruitful labor; yields valuable fruit	31:16, 31	8:19
works industriously to bring in revenue/profit	31:18	3:14
is known in city gates	31:23, 31	1:21; 8:3
gives and receives honor	31:25	3:16; 4:8
is strong	31:17, 25	8:14
loathes wickedness	31:12	8:13
stretches out hands to needy	31:20	1:24
laughs	31:25	1:26; 8:30
teaches	31:26	1:23, 25; 8:6–9, 14, 32–34
fears the Lord	31:30	1:29–30; 8:13

---

8. Yoder, *Proverbs*, 290.

9. Yoder, *Proverbs*, 290.

10. A similar analysis of parallels has been made between Prov 31:1–9 and Prov 31:10–31. See Hurowitz, "The Seventh Pillar."

The difference between the two sections of Proverbs under analysis here is that Prov 1–9 is clearly metaphorical while Prov 31:10–31 is usually (especially in modern times) interpreted literally. Even Yoder, after pointing out these parallels, goes on to exegete Prov 31:10–31 as describing an actual or idealized woman who can be critiqued for reinforcing patriarchal values and objectification.[11]

Al Wolters analyzes Prov 31:10–31 as a heroic hymn[12] and also proposes the existence of a pun played in v. 27 on the Hebrew of צפה "to look to" and the Greek σοφία "wisdom." This fits well with the suggestion on a broader literary level that the valiant woman is seen as the end bracket of the main content of Proverbs (Prov 10–30) matching the "wisdom as woman" poem in Prov 9:1–12.[13] An inclusion is also noted in vv. 21 and 30.[14]

A literary analysis of the text such as Yoder presents is problematic. The content appears as an alphabetized recipe for a good spouse. Yet lexical and thematic parallels suggest an alternative interpretation. Similarly, the kind of genre analysis Wolters presents explains the structure as that of a hymn. However, the content is oddly secular for a hymn, to the point that God is only mentioned in the penultimate line.

Marcel Jousse

Marcel Jousse (1886–1961) is best-known because of the influence of his book *The Oral Style*,[15] on theories of oral composition, most notably on Milman Parry's *Studies in the Epic Technique of Oral Verse Making* (1930) and on Albert Lord's *The Singer of Tales* (1960). Jousse linked Lowth's[16] description of Hebrew poetic parallelism to oral composition in general and, specifically, to recovering the original Aramaic sayings of Jesus. Jousse also claimed that this parallelism was rooted in the bilateral structure of human physical and mental composition. Three other works by Jousse expanding on these themes have also been translated

---

11. Yoder, *Proverbs*. 292–300.
12. Wolters, *The Song*, 3–14.
13. Camp, *Wisdom and the Feminine*, 179–208.
14. Waltke, *Proverbs*, 515.
15. Jousse, *The Oral Style*.
16. Bishop Robert Lowth was the eighteenth-century biblical scholar who introduced the idea of parallel clauses as the basic principle of Hebrew poetry.

into English. They are *In Search of Coherence*,[17] *Memory, Memorization, and Memorizers: The Galilean Oral-Style Tradition and Its Traditionists*,[18] and *The Parallel Rhythmic Recitatives of the Rabbis of Israel*.[19]

In Search of Coherence contains a more philosophical expression of Jousse's anthropology. *Memory, Memorization, and Memorizers* amplifies the connections Jousse makes between the oral style and the sayings of Jesus and his followers. *The Parallel Rhythmic Recitatives of the Rabbis of Israel* is an assortment of the didactic genre of maxims (aphoristic sayings) selected from various epochs of the rabbinic tradition.

However, it is *The Oral Style* that contains the foundation of Jousse's ideas. *The Oral Style*, published in French in 1925, contains nine chapters dealing in Part One with the anthropological foundation of oral style, balanced with nine chapters detailing how this oral style works in Part Two. In what follows I will focus on Part Two.

Part Two of *The Oral Style*, chapter 10, "The Automatic Repetition of a Propositional Gesture: Parallelism," begins with an extract from a 1931 paper of Jousse emphasizing the importance of Bishop Lowth's recognition of Hebrew poetry's "parallelism of clauses." Jousse states that this linguistic phenomenon "plays as vital a role in the world of human thought and human memory as does gravitation in the physical universe."[20] Jousse goes on to claim that thought is an automatic, instinctive reflex triggered by psychic stimuli, often continuing in a long chain.[21] These reflexes result in balanced (though not mathematically exact) "symmetrical, synonymous propositional gestures."[22] Thus, Jousse forms an anthropological (as opposed to literary) base to understand the parallel schema on which Prov 31:10–31 appears to be built.

Chapter 11, "Rhythmic Oral Styles," calls this propositional gesture a "'dance' on the laryngo-buccalic muscles of an improviser or reciter," which, for a certain number, becomes formulaic in accordance with rhythmic schemas.[23] Composition in this oral style consists of imitating these formulaic clichés, matching them with others of similar form,

17. Jousse, *In Search*.
18. Jousse, *Memory*.
19. Jousse, *The Parallel Rhythmic Recitatives*.
20. Jousse, *The Oral Style*, 95.
21. Jousse, *The Oral Style*, 97.
22. Jousse, *The Oral Style*, 99.
23. Jousse, *The Oral Style*, 109.

rhythm, and structure.²⁴ However, this is a living rhythm, not a mechanical meter.²⁵ According to Jousse, in order to be rhetorically effective, it is necessary that they should be composed in such a way that they can be easily recited by the performer.²⁶ This is an intuitively obvious but usually overlooked explanation for the poetic features that occur in Prov 31:10–31.

Chapter 12, "The Instinctive Mnemonic Employment of Rhythmic Schemas," elaborates on the mnemonic power of these schemas. This mnemotechnical purpose has been gradually replaced by the emphasis on pleasurable feelings created by rhythm when read from written poetry.²⁷ Yet Jousse claims that it is essential to memorize the Word of Yahweh in order to understand the "almost untranslatable, 'didactic metaphors,' traditional symbols, . . . and . . . Instruction passed *from mouth to mouth.*²⁸ Jousse even makes a literal translation for *pastor* as "he who makes eat" to signify "he who makes learn orally."²⁹ Memorization of Scripture is likened to eating or digesting.³⁰ Others have interpreted references to food in the Song of the Valiant Woman (31:14, 15, 17, 27, 31) in a similar way. These allegorical interpretations include Talmudic interpretations,³¹ and renderings from Origen,³² and Augustine.³³ It is significant that the break with allegorical interpretation came in the Reformation period.³⁴ Perhaps the coincidental invention of the printing press began to remove the association of consuming God's word with memorization and eating food. Chapter 13, "Oral Style, A Living Press," makes the distinction between the modern concept of aesthetic poetry for entertainment and the retentional, rhetorical, and memorial functions that rhythmic recitations had before the widespread use of writing. The statesmen and orators of these

24. Jousse, *The Oral Style*, 110.
25. Jousse, *The Oral Style*, 113. Jousse links the living rhythm of oral cultures with the free form poetry of the symbolists in French, and modernists such as Rubén Darío in Spanish, and Walt Whitman in English.
26. Jousse, *The Oral Style*, 114.
27. Jousse, *The Oral Style*, 127.
28. Jousse, *The Oral Style*, 130.
29. Jousse, *The Oral Style*, 130.
30. Compare the biblical reference to "eating the scroll" in Ezek 2:9—3:11.
31. Wolters, *The Song*, 61.
32. Wolters, *The Song*, 67.
33. Wolters, *The Song*, 73.
34. Wolters, *The Song*, 99.

were "no more poets than were the Prophets and the Rabbis of Israel, Jesus, Saint John, Saint Paul etc."[35] For this reason, Jousse prefers the term "recitations" rather than "poetry."

Chapter 14, "Oral Composers," presents the thesis that Jesus used the traditional oral formulae of the Jewish people to engage his audiences as he taught them the secrets of the kingdom of heaven. From Matt. 13:52, for example, Jousse interprets the saying about treasures being brought from a "storeroom" as a reference to memory and its storing capacity.

Therefore, understanding the recitations of Jesus and other oral composers of the New Testament is greatly aided by the internalization of the propositional gestures that existed in their Aramaic oral milieu.[36] Jousse's example of Jesus's short parable of the pearl of great value immediately brings the first line of Prov 31:10 into focus—"A valiant woman who can find, her worth is beyond pearls" (my translation). The issue of orality in regard to Prov 31:10–31 is not one of whether the poem was composed orally or in writing. Rather, it is one of how such poetry was composed by the adaptation of oral formulae, or in Jousse's words, "propositional gestures." According to Jousse, Jesus adapted these to make his teaching memorable and understandable. Proverbs 31:10–31 comes from an earlier but similar oral milieu.

Chapter 15, "Mnemonic Faculties in Oral Style Milieux," uses various ethnic case studies that support Jousse's theory of oral composition to argue for the accurate memorization of Jesus' parables in his oral milieu. However, allowance is also made for gradual change in grammar and vocabulary over time so that ancient recitations may appear to be contemporary with traditional ones. This endorsement of memorization while allowing for linguistic change undermined historical-critical methods, which were in favor in Jousse's time. A focus on memory also allows a much older dating of the original proverbs on which Prov 31:10–31 is based, despite historical-critical arguments for more recent dating on the basis of vocabulary.

The final three chapters of *The Oral Style* examine other mnemonic tools in recitations, expanding the focus from one line to greater units. Chapter 16, "Mnemotechnical Devices within the Rhythmic Schema," introduces examples of other linguistic devices such as alliteration, assonance, and rhyme, which occur within the rhythmic schema of a

---

35. Jousse, *The Oral Style*, 137.
36. Jousse, *The Oral Style*, 148.

parallel line. Jousse notes that such mnemonic devices often naturally occur within the phonology and grammar of a language, and modern written poetry is actually a late rediscovery of "age-old performance tools."[37] Chapter 17, "Mnemotechnical Devices within the Recitative," examines oral techniques of memorizing blocks of gestures which include rhyme patterns and framing segments bounded by key words. In addition, Jousse includes the method of counting; and Prov 31:10–31 with its twenty-two line alphabetic acrostic is a specifically Hebrew method for this. Chapter 18, "Mnemotechnical Devices within a Recitation," looks at the mnemonic devices (refrains, keys words, and the acrostic) that bind several recitatives into a recitation. For example, Jousse describes 1 Cor 13 as three recitatives made up of untranslatable formulae from Hebrew and Aramaic strung together like pearls "combined in a new and striking fashion by the incomparable mastery" of Paul.[38]

In summary, Jousse points out what may seem obvious but is seldom commented on. Firstly, that what are called "poetic devices" in modern literary analysis were originally mnemonic, not aesthetic (or artificial). His analysis reveals the same features that contemporary literary analysis highlights in Hebrew poetry and in Prov 31:10–31. However, he goes beyond form to state that the purpose of these devices is to aid memorization. Secondly, he is able to show that the same Hebraic oral style (both rhythmic schema and specific phrases) continued to be used by Jesus and his disciples.

The influence of Jousse (primarily his assertion of mnemonic function) can be seen most recently in Dobbs-Allsopp's literary analysis of Hebrew poetry.[39] Like Jousse, Dobbs-Allsop begins his analysis with Lowth and includes comparative cultures and historicity in his literary analysis. There are frequent references to Jousse throughout Dobbs-Allsopp's essays as he uses "an informing orality" to "temper or reframe" the governing assumptions of "'high' literature (and highly literate) criticism practiced by Lowth (and most critics since)."[40] Dobbs-Allsopp does not make the mistake that some of Jousse's immediate followers made of creating a strong division between orality and literacy. Instead, he uses

---

37. Jousse, *The Oral Style*, 191.
38. Jousse, *The Oral Style*, 218.
39. Dobbs-Allsopp, *On Biblical Poetry*.
40. Dobbs-Allsopp, *On Biblical Poetry*, 5.

Jousse's ideas to illuminate the understanding of selections of Hebrew poetry.

The next section will demonstrate a similar orally informed understanding of Prov 31:10–31.

The Acrostic Recitation

Prov 31:10–31 is an acrostic text of twenty-two lines with each line beginning with a consecutive letter of the Hebrew alphabet.[41] Superficially, it could be argued that the poem is formed around the written alphabet and Jousse's oral style has little relevance. However, letters are simply approximations of spoken phonemes. Shaping a poem so that the first letter of each line matches consecutive phonemes shows awareness of sound as much as awareness of writing. Moreover, the alphabet is a mnemonic device and important for the memorization and performance of the text. It may also be used as a means of indexing orally composed lines for memorization and recitation. Jousse gives the nonbiblical example of an Arab "Raoui" who could recite one hundred pre-Islamic rhythmic verses for each letter of the alphabet (2,700 recitations).[42] It is quite possible that the individual lines (or parts thereof) of the valiant-woman poem existed in isolation before they were grouped into alphabetic order. Indeed, many modern collections of proverbs are arranged in exactly this alphabetical order.[43]

Unfortunately, this acrostic format has tended to distract scholars from the oral features of the poem. Bruce Waltke observes that the alphabetic acrostic nature of the poem has prevented analysis of other "embroidered" poetic features.[44] The acrostic form is generally accepted as an overriding artistic device, leaving little room for further poetic analysis.[45]

The Enclosed Recitatives

A threefold Joussian approach to an oral text can be deduced from the titles of the last three chapters of Jousse's *Oral Style*. Firstly, an oral text is

---

41. There are eleven other clearly alphabetic acrostic poems (Pss 25; 34; 37; 111; 112; 119; 145; Lam 1, 2, 3, 4).

42. Jousse, *The Oral Style*, 170.

43. E.g., Brougham and Reed, *The Reed Book of Maori Proverbs*.

44. Waltke, *The Book of Proverbs*, 514.

45. E.g., Lucas, *Proverbs*, 195.

An Oral Perspective of Proverbs 31:10–31 113

a recitation that can be broken into smaller recitatives made up of rhythmic schemas. Secondly, the acrostic structure makes the boundaries of the recitation clear. Thirdly, the rhythmic schema in Prov 31:10–31 is manifest in the individual lines that make up the twenty-two verses.

While the external boundaries of the whole poem (recitation) are marked by the beginning and end of the alphabetic structure, it is more difficult to find smaller sections (recitatives) enclosed within the poem. At first, there seems to be little connection between the lines. As a result, different authors divided it into various sections. The analysis below is based on Jousse's observation that recitatives are often bounded by repeated key words. In other words, the recitative begins with a line containing the key word and ends with a line which repeats the same word.

TABLE 4.2: RECITATIVES IN PROVERBS 31:10–31

Recitative 1: vv. 10–14 Value	אשת־חיל מי ימצא ורחק מפנינים מכרה	10
	בטח בה לב בעלה ושלל לא יחסר	11
	גמלתהו טוב ולא־רע כל ימי חייה	12
	דרשה צמר ופשתים ותעש בחפץ כפיה	13
	היתה כאניות סוחר ממרחק תביא לחמה	14
Recitative 2 vv. 15–18 Work, food, strength	ותקם בעוד לילה ותתן טרף לביתה וחק לנערתיה	15
	זממה שדה ותקחהו מפרי כפיה [ק= נטעה] כרם	16
	חגרה בעוז מתניה ותאמץ זרעותיה	17
	טעמה כי־טוב סחרה לא־יכבה [ק= בלילה] נרה	18
Recitative 3 Chiasm vv. 19–20	ידיה שלחה בכישור וכפיה תמכו פלך	19
	כפה פרשה לעני וידיה שלחה לאביון	20
Recitative 4 vv. 21–25 Clothing	לא־תירא לביתה משלג כי כל־ביתה לבש שנים	21
	מרבדים עשתה־לה שש וארגמן לבושה	22
	נודע בשערים בעלה בשבתו עם־זקני־ארץ	23
	סדין עשתה ותמכר וחגור נתנה לכנעני	24
	עז־והדר לבושה ותשחק ליום אחרון	25
Recitative 5 vv. 26–27 Wisdom	פיה פתחה בחכמה ותורת־חסד על־לשונה	26
	צופיה הליכות ביתה ולחם עצלות לא תאכל	27
Recitative 6 vv. 28–31 Praise	קמו בניה ויאשרוה בעלה ויהללה	28
	רבות בנות עשו חיל ואת עלית על־כלנה	29
	שקר החן והבל היפי אשה יראת־יהוה היא תתהלל	30
	תנו־לה מפרי ידיה ויהללוה בשערים מעשיה	31

The recitation can be split into six recitatives with three occurring in each half of the recitation. Key words are highlighted in the table above. The first recitative is bounded by repetition of the word רחק, meaning "remote" or "far off." The word is used as an implicit (31:10) and explicit (31:14) metaphor for rarity or value. The second recitative (31:15–18) is bounded by לילה "night" and describes diligent working. A tightly structured chiasm around repetition of synonyms for "hand" (יד and כף) follows as a two-line recitative (31:19–20). These key words are also the initial acrostic words of their respective lines, and they finish the first half of the recitation.

The second half of the recitation (31:21–25) begins with a new recitative focusing on the new theme introduced by the chiasm's reference to weaving "clothing" (לבש). This is followed by a two-line recitative, which Wolters interprets as containing a unique bilingual pun.[46] The first line (31:26) is a beautiful (but ambiguous) definition of חכמה ("wisdom"): ותורת־חסד "teaching of kindness" / "law of grace." The second line begins with the unique spelling of the Hebrew participle צופיה "looking well to," which according to Wolters is probably a Hebrew transliteration of the Greek σοφία ("wisdom"). Jousse's marking of recitatives through key words supports this assertion, as it links these two verses together. The final recitative (31:28–31) revolves around the word for "praise," הלל.

While the identification of six recitatives is useful for the purposes of memorization and performance, there is also a cohesive whole, and there are even two balanced halves. Yoder's analogy of a literary mosaic is apt, but more in line with Prov 31:10–31 would be the analogy of a quilt, each panel stitched together by the acrostic and the repetition of key words and themes.

Rhythmic Schema

The six recitatives fit into two equal halves of eleven lines containing three recitatives each. This two-part structure of the poem reflects Jousse's law of bilateralism. He taught that human communication is intimately connected to the symmetrical nature of our bodies. This structure results in the parallelism that is not only observable in Hebrew poetry but, according to Jousse, primary to all human thought and communication. The chiasm in vv.19–20 is another example of this bilateralism with יד

---

46. Wolters, *The Song*, 30–41.

("hand"), שלח ("extend"), and כף ("palm") repeated symmetrically across the two verses.

Bilateralism is also reflected in what Jousse calls a "rhythmic schema." "Each balancing of each rhythmic laryngo-buccal schema is naturally composed of a certain number of syllables ... A rhythmic schema, so to speak, elaborates itself by the balanced recitation of two, and sometimes three, approximately propositional parallel gestures."[47] It is important to note the word "approximately" because Jousse is speaking of a natural, not mechanical, system of rhythm or meter. He would agree with Watson's statement, "No single poem is consistently written in one metrical pattern."[48]

Proverbs 31:10–31 is a clear example of Jousse's rhythmic schema. James Kugel reveals that Saint Jerome believed that the metrical structure of Prov 31:10–31, the later acrostic psalms (119 and 145), and Deut 32 all had the same iambic tetrameter.[49] However, Kugel also points out that Jerome never made explicit his basis for counting meter and was in all probability "proceeding by trial scansions."[50] Kugel's own explanation of meter seems to be the most consistent. Meter is simply a product of both parallelism and terseness creating balanced lines of only four or five major words. Hence meter is not the driving force of Hebrew poetry but only "part of a complex of equivalences."[51] A stylistically faithful translation may appear rhythmic at times, but that rhythm should be a result of the binary structure and terseness of most lines rather than structure and terseness being caused by a metrical rule of rhythm.

A superficial analysis of rhythm based on these concepts is displayed below. The definition of a major word is somewhat subjective as adverbs and pronouns are generally not included.

---

47. Jousse, *The Oral Style*, 114.
48. Watson, *Classical Hebrew Poetry*, 98.
49. Kugel, *The Idea of Biblical Poetry*, 155.
50. Kugel, *The Idea of Biblical Poetry*, 156. Scansion here refers to an imposed meter on a line of text.
51. Kugel, *The Idea of Biblical Poetry*, 71.

TABLE 4.3: RHYTHMIC SCHEMA IN PROVERBS 31:10–31

Structure	Verses
Three words in A followed by three in B	10, 11, 12, 13, 14, 18, 19, 20, 21, 22, 23, 24, 25, 26, 27, 31
Three words in A followed by four in B	16
Three words in A followed by two in B	17, 28
Triplet 3:3:2	15, 30
Four words in A followed by three in B	29

The table above shows that disruption to rhythm occurs at the end of the first half of the poem (vv. 15–17), leading up to the chiastic structure (v. 19), and from v. 28, which is the beginning of a chorus of praise, to end the poem. Rhythmic schemas may also therefore contribute to the bilateral structure of the whole poem.

Rhythmic Schemas and Mnemotechnical Devices

Jousse's third level of analysis of the individual line goes beyond parallelism to include "Mnemotechnical Devices within the Rhythmic Schema." He believed that the oral style promotes rhyme for mnemonic as much as aesthetic reasons.[52] In Prov 31:10–31 the feminine ending of most verbs and many nouns emphasizes the femininity of the subject, creates a thematic uniformity through the poem, and often signals the end of a verse in the way that the acrostic consonant signals the beginning. Verses 10, 12, 13, 14, 15, 17, 18, 22, 26, 28, 29, and 31 all end in the third person singular feminine particle, and there are other instances at the end of the beginning half of each verse (11a, 17a, 18a, 22a, 23a, 25a, 26a, 27a, 28a, 31a). The stress pattern on these particles should also contribute to rhythm, which while difficult to analyze in biblical Hebrew feels natural during recitation. Moreover, when a clause does not have a feminine ending, there is often a semirhyming verb ending with an /a/ or /ar/ sound (e.g., 10a, 11b, 12a . . .).

Alliteration, while not as prevalent, is also present. A few verses appear to have deliberate repetition of the initial acrostic.[53] Jousse's

---

52. Kugel, *The Idea of Biblical Poetry*, 139.

53. V. 11a (בטח בה לב בעלה), v. 18a (טעמה כי טוב סחרה) and v. 26a (פיה פתחה).

observation that such features aid memory is relevant to alliteration as well as rhyme. However, the memory aid here is more concerned with lexical choice than structure. Table 4.4 suggests underlined incidents of alliteration (repetition of initial-syllable consonants in a verse) and bold occurrences of assonance (repetition of vowel sounds).

TABLE 4.4: ASSONANCE AND CONSONANCE

10: אשת־חיל <u>מִ</u>י י<u>מְ</u>צא ורחק <u>מִ</u>פנינים <u>מִ</u>כרה
11: <u>בָּ</u>טח <u>בָּ</u>ה <u>לֵ</u>ב <u>בַּ</u>עלה ושל<u>לָ</u> <u>לֹ</u>א יחסר
12: גמלתהו טוב ולא־<u>רָ</u>ע כל י<u>מֵ</u>י חי<u>יהָ</u>
13: דרשה צמר ו<u>פִ</u>שתים ותעש בחפץ כפ<u>יהָ</u>
14: היתה כאניות סו<u>חֵ</u>ר ממר<u>חָ</u>ק תביא לל<u>חמָהּ</u>
15: ותקם בעוד <u>לַיְלָ</u>ה ותן טרף <u>לַ</u>ביתה וחק <u>לַ</u>נערתיה
16: <u>זָמְמָ</u>ה שדה ותקחהו <u>מִ</u>פרי כפיה [ק= נטעה] כרם
17: חגרה בעוז מת<u>נֵ</u>יה ות<u>אַ</u>מץ זרעו<u>תֶיהָ</u>
18: <u>טָ</u>עמה כי־<u>טָ</u>וב סחרה <u>לֹ</u>א־יכבה [ק= <u>בַּלַיְלָ</u>ה] נרה
19: ידיה שלחה בכישור וכפיה תמכו פלך
20: כפה פרשה לעני וידיה שלחה לאביון
21: <u>לֹ</u>א־תירא <u>לַ</u>ביתה משלג כי כל־ביתה <u>לָ</u>ב<u>שׁ</u> <u>שָׁ</u>נים
22: מרבדים ע<u>שָׂ</u>תה־לה <u>שֵׁשׁ</u> וארגמן ל<u>בוּשָׁהּ</u>
23: נודע <u>בַּשְּׁ</u>ערים <u>בַּ</u>עלה <u>בְּשִׁ</u>בתו עם־זקני־ארץ
24: סדין ע<u>שְׂתָה</u> ותמכר וחגור נתנה לכנעני
25: עז־והדר לבו<u>שָׁהּ</u> ות<u>שְׂ</u>חק ליום אחרון
26: <u>פִּ</u>יהָ <u>פָּתְ</u>חה בחכמה ותורת־חסד על־לשונה
27: <u>צוֹ</u>פיה ה<u>לִי</u>כות ביתה ו<u>לֶ</u>חם עצלות לא תאכל
28: קמו בניה ויאשרוה בעלה ויה<u>לְלָהּ</u>
29: רבות <u>בָּנות</u> עשו חיל ו<u>אַתְּ</u> עלית על־כלנה
30: שקר <u>הַ</u>חן ו<u>הֶ</u>בל <u>הַ</u>יפי אשה יראת־יהוה <u>הִ</u>יא תת<u>הַלָּ</u>ל
31: תנו־לה מפרי ידיה ויהללוה בשערים מעשיה

The ends of clauses (cola) are often in bold, which emphasizes the assonance (often rhyme) of the strong /a/ endings, which become noticeable in recitation. This pattern is observable through the whole recitation and clearly demarcates many parallel clauses. Consonance and often alliteration are noted by underlined letters. This analysis on the first recitative shows מ occurring four times in or near word-initial position in 31:10.

בּ starts three of the first four words in 31:11, while יּ is prominent four times in the last two words of 31:12. מ occurs twice, while ח occurs three times in 31:13. Similar patterns are found through the following recitatives except for the chiasm in 19–20, which relies on its own internal structure for memorization.

While the exact rhythm stress of ancient Hebrew is unknown, it can be assumed that the features of assonance and consonance would have influenced the rhythm. Robert Alter cites Hrushovski to state that Hebrew poetry has a "free rhythm" based on a cluster of principles (semantic, syntactic, prosodic, morphological, and phonetic).[54] Experimentally, the process of memorization through oral performance highlights repetition of key words, assonance, and consonance. Listening to these features gives an automatic rhythm to a performance.

Jousse advocates a very corporeally rooted analysis of oral text. He claims that for Semites the center of life is "in the throat, in the nefesh, and not in the head."[55] Jousse writes of understanding Homer's Greek poetry only through memorization and recitation where he could "feel" the formulations in his own mouth.[56] Ultimately, the lexical roots of words are "vocal gestures of a sort."[57] This is the central point of Jousse's thesis. Humans react to the universe through gestures, which are expressed physically and orally in order to be conveyed from generation to generation through structured, memorable verbal propositions.

The frequency of rhyme and alliteration noted in tables 4.2 and 4.4 is not noted in academic commentaries. Even the acrostic structure is usually considered a superficial artifice, unrelated to performance or memorization. Giffone argues that the acrostic is purely for viewing pleasure and there is no memory-aid function. His argument is based on the claim that "There is no peculiar 'acrostic vocabulary' or 'acrostic grammar.'"[58] This argument ignores both the simplicity of the alphabetic acrostic as a memory prompt and the variety of forms employed in all Hebrew poetry. There is no particular vocabulary or grammar needed for memorization. All memorable forms of sound play and rhythm are

---

54. Alter, *The Art of Biblical Poetry*, 7.
55. Jousse, *The Oral Style*, xxvi.
56. Jousse, *The Oral Style*, xxvi.
57. Jousse, *The Oral Style*, xxvi.
58. Giffone, "A 'Perfect' Poem," 50.

strung together in what Jousse calls a "necklace of pearls," which can be recalled and performed at will.

Translating from an Oral Perspective

Translation of Prov 31:10–31 tends to focus on individual words or on the dynamic equivalence of a clause. Little attention is given to the connected aspects of performance and memorization. Those translators who deal with performance or memorization tend to focus on only one feature. For example, *The Knox English Old Testament* (1950) shows an acrostic but fails to show the parallelism of the Hebrew. André Chouraqui's French translation (1985) highlights the parallelism but ignores the sound play and the acrostic (except for the Hebrew letter being printed at the start of each line). Perhaps the most comprehensive is Alter's English translation (2010).[59] Although Alter comes from a literary perspective, he focuses on the same issues raised by Jousse, complaining that most translators who "ride roughshod over the Hebrew syntax and are obtuse about the word choices of the Hebrew writers and would scarcely think that the play of sound of the Hebrew words or the way they inscribe double meanings was part of the translator's task."[60] While Prov 31:10–31 in Alter's translation captures a sense of rhythm, there is no acrostic format or careful attention paid to alliteration or rhyme that could facilitate memory. Alter's focus is on literary style, not oral performance.

The translation below tries, in Dobbs-Allsopp's words, to be "informed by orality"[61]—that is, to be informed by the oral style in the way Jousse has described it. It has already been demonstrated that this style, in the original Hebrew, facilitates memorization, which allows for repeated performances and transferal from one generation to another. Thus, the acrostic form is essential to the structure of the poem. This form is aided by what James Kugel describes as "a complex of equivalences" found throughout Hebrew poetry.[62] The equivalent features (in addition to the initial acrostic) that have been highlighted in this translation include parallelism (with clauses containing similar but idiosyncratic rhythm),

---

59. Alter, *The Wisdom Books*, 332–34.
60. Alter, *The Art of Bible Translation*, 77.
61. Dobbs-Allsopp, *On Biblical Poetry*.
62. Kugel, *The Idea of Biblical Poetry*, 71.

syntactic order to highlight rhyme, lexical choice influenced by alliteration, and lexical repetition when a word is repeated in Hebrew.

Recitative 1

> 10. A warrior woman who will win, far away her worth from jewels
> 11. Believed by her bridegroom she, no spoil lacking he
> 12. Causing him good not bad, all her lifelong days
> 13. Desiring wool and weave, willingly she worked her hands
> 14. Even as the ships of trade, far away she brought her bread.

Aside from the acrostic form, alliteration is the most obvious feature that has been translated into Recitative 1. For example, in v. 10 the /m/ sound of the Hebrew has been replaced by a /w/ sound in English, while in v. 11 both languages repeat the sound of the initial consonant three times. This effect is simulated at a clause level rather than for individual words; although in v. 12, "lifelong days" is a happy alliterative equivalence of ימי חייה. The key word רחק, which begins the second part of the first (v.10) and last (v.14) lines, is intentionally translated the same: "far away." There is also an attempt to replicate some of the grammatical rhyme through the poem by the word order of v.11, even though this line does not rhyme in the Hebrew.

Alter describes translation as an art form of trying to convey important effects seen in the original. Sometimes the result is not perfect, but it is "nevertheless preferable to not communicating the effect of the original at all."[63] Thus, while it would be preferable to translate features such as rhyme and wordplay onto the same words where they occur in Hebrew, at least the use of such features, albeit on different words, is imitated in parts of the poem.

Recitative 2

> 15. From the night she rose, fed her family, for her servants portions too

---

63. Alter, *The Art of Bible Translation*, 92.

16. Gained title to the field she selected, palmed the profit to plant a vineyard
17. Girded in strength, strong in her arms
18. Insuring the good of her trade, her lamp at night does not fade.

Alliteration is not as strong in recitative 2, although this is used in v. 15 to imitate the rhythm of each section beginning with the prefix for "and" in Hebrew. Key words repeated through the poem, such as לילה ("night"), סחר ("trade"), and כף ("palm") are translated consistently although a small pun is played on the word "palm" in v. 16 to both represent the phrase "fruit of her hands" in the Hebrew and to keep the consistent translation. Rhyme is also reflected in v. 18. The translation in v. 17 may appear to have regressed into what Alter would call the error of dynamic equivalence.[64] Novick makes the case for both concrete and abstract interpretations of the idioms contained in the Hebrew.[65] In this case, brevity and acrostic form took precedence in translation over concrete explanation.

Recitative 3

19. Joined her hands to the distaff, her palms held the spindle
20. Kept her palm to reach the poor, her hands to join the oppressed.

There is no attempt to interpret v. 19 with more contemporary or technically specific language. The chiastic structure is clearly important at the center of this poem; however, it is usually lost in translation. The juxtaposition of daily work with justice and mercy is best conveyed by structure. These lines became powerful for me when I had the privilege of observing an Akha commune committee reviewing a woman's literacy and numeracy project in rural Laos. The ornately clothed Akha women of the village had a powerful presence in the meeting, while their hands worked weaving homegrown cotton garments on the portable apparatus they carried with them nearly everywhere.

It will be noticed that the translation tends to indicate the past tense. Siegismund argues that the *qatal* verb form is mistranslated into present

---

64. Alter, *The Art of Bible Translation*, 29.
65. Novick, "She Binds Her Arms."

tense in nearly all translations.[66] This is an example of translation bias, which turns a past-tense description (ideal or imaginary) into an explicit behavioral lesson. To translate in the present tense may reveal a hermeneutic bias of interpreting this scripture as didactic instruction rather than metaphorical poetry. Such a bias reduces this text into some kind of poetic code for the correct behavior of a married woman.[67]

Recitative 4

21. Lacked her family fear of snow, clothed in scarlet her family go
22. Making herself tapestry, clothed in purple linen finery
23. Noted her bridegroom at the gates, where with the rulers he deliberates
24. Offering her linen garments for sale, cloth to gird a Canaanite male
25. Putting on clothes of strong dignity, she laughs at the days to come.

While only one of these five verses (v. 22) contains rhyming clauses in the Hebrew, the translation rhymes four of them to facilitate memorization and to reflect the rhyme that occurs throughout the poem because of the feminine ending. Verse 24 has an unusual translation to reflect the repeated word חגור ("gird") from v. 17.

Recitative 5

26. Quick wisdom from her mouth sprung: the law of grace on her tongue
27. Reason wisely watched her family's ways; no idle bread she ate.

Verse 26 has been made to rhyme to reflect the Hebrew and aid memorization. Wolters's assertion that a bilingual pun is being made in v. 27 with the Greek σοφία ("wisdom") and the Hebrew participle צופיה ("keep watch") cannot be shown, but both words are included in the translation.[68]

---

66. Siegismund, "Death of a Virtuous Woman?"

67. For an interpretation as moral teaching see for example: Branch, "Proverbs 31:10–31."

68. Wolters, *The Song*, 30–41.

Recitative 6

28 Sons of hers rise—bless her, Bridegroom—praise her

29 Too many daughters act as warriors, but you excel them all

30 Untrue is favor, beauty is vain, but a woman fearing The Name, they shall praise her

31 Value her with the profit of her hands; her works in the gates praise her.

Three of the four verses in the final recitative end with the phrase "praise her," which is an attempt to imitate the rhyme of the third person feminine in Hebrew and to allow a rhythmic emphasis in performance.

The Hebrew word for "fruit" is translated as "profit" in the final verse to be consistent with the translation and pun in v. 16. Similarly, the key word חיל from the first line continues to be translated as "(act as a) warrior" in v. 29.

Evaluation and Conclusion

If nothing more, the attempt to translate in a more oral style has highlighted some of the complexity of Hebrew poetry, which reinforces Kugel's description of "a complex of equivalences."[69] Although lexical equivalence has been removed from its common position of primary importance in translation, there is a new emphasis on consistent translation of repeated words to reflect the poetic techniques of repetition and structure found within the poem. Balanced with this is the acrostic structure and the desire for alliteration. Rhyme has also been added.

One criticism that could be made of this English translation is that there is little consistency, but this reflects the Hebrew. One line will contain alliteration, another will have rhyming clauses, and another suddenly switches to a three-part parallelism. Lines are not enjambed, and there is no evidence of conjunctions linking one verse to another.[70] The poetic features aid memorization and performance of one or two lines rather than providing unity.

---

69. Kugel, *The Idea of Biblical Poetry*, 71.

70. The Hebrew for v. 15 does begin with the conjunction "and," but this is forced by the acrostic pattern demanding a word beginning with ו.

This diversity supports the claim that single or double verses were originally independent oral sayings. These are the pearls described by Jousse, which have been strung together in the acrostic. An additional binding is the repeated key words, which are especially clear at the beginning and end of each of the six recitatives.

Jousse's oral perspective has analytical, pedagogical, and practical benefits. From an analytical perspective, it provides an explanatory framework for word choice, word repetition and sentence structure. On a surface level, the results differ little from the literary perspective articulated by Alter and others. More profound is the sense of ongoing composition from an oral milieu. This echoes the idea of dialogic truth articulated by Bakhtin.[71] The implications of this will begin to be addressed in the final paragraphs of this section.

Pedagogical advantages refer to deeper engagement with biblical Hebrew for students of language and Scripture. My experience of memorizing the Hebrew text with an emphasis on alliteration, rhyme, and the acrostic has reinforced an understanding of vocabulary, syntax, and grammar. The additional exercise of trying to translate style as well as words has forced me to grapple with possibilities of meaning within the confines of meaningful performance. Regardless of the quality of the result, performance has given life to the text and conscious connection with the original Hebrew.

Finally, practical value refers to the ability of readers to carry text within them. The text is no longer bound to the printed or electronic page. Instead, it can be meditated on in daily life. Verses can be linked to breathing and recited during exercise. When one is reading other texts, the poem can be mentally referred to, facilitating intertextual dialogue. Proverbs have always been applied, adapted, and mixed within diverse situations. This cannot take place until those proverbs are memorized. Jousse describes this process in the following way:

> We must add an in-depth study of the living, expressive, and rhythmic geste. Bookish man has said: "To know by heart is not to know," not realizing that this means wiping out ninety percent of the knowledge of all human beings.[72]

One future direction for further study of Prov 31:10–31 has already been mapped out by Jousse's methodology. Adaptations and references to

---

71. Bakhtin, *Problems*.
72. Jousse, *The Anthropology of Geste and Rhythm*, 25–26.

lines in the text of the poem can be found in the teachings of Jesus and other New Testament "writers." (Jousse would call them speakers.) For example, Luke 12 contains several familiar-sounding phrases and themes which are arguably sourced from Prov 31:10–31. The two formulae found in Luke 12:35, "Keep your loins girded and your lamps burning," are almost direct quotations from 31:17–18. Moreover, Jesus makes frequent references to trade, clothing, farming, giving portions to servants, marriage, mothers, and daughters. These are the settings in which each pearl of Prov 31:10–31 is set.

Such a study would deepen our understanding of Christ as human and Israelite operating through an oral medium and in an oral milieu. It would also bring the challenge of approaching scripture in a similar grounded and embodied way. Truth is something to be lived out in dialogue with others, past and present, not something to be individually analyzed or objectified.

Bibliography

Alter, Robert. *The Art of Bible Translation*. Princeton: Princeton University Press, 2019.
———. *The Art of Biblical Poetry*. New York: Basic Books, 1985.
———. *The Wisdom Books: Job, Proverbs, and Ecclesiastes: A Translation with Commentary*. New York: Norton, 2010.
Bakhtin, Mikhail. *Problems of Dostoevsky's Poetics*. Translated by R. W. Rotsel. Minneapolis: University of Minnesota Press, 1984.
Branch, Robin Gallaher. "Proverbs 31:10–31: A Passage Containing Wisdom Principles for a Successful Marriage." *Koers: Bulletin for Christian Scholarship* 77.2 (2012) art. #49. 9pp.
Brougham, A. E., and A. W. Reed. *The Reed Book of Maori Proverbs*. Revised by Tīmoti Kāretu. Auckland: Reed, 1999.
Camp, Claudia V. *Wisdom and the Feminine in the Book of Proverbs*. Bible and Literature Series 11. Sheffield: Almond, 1985.
Chouraqui, André, trans. *La Bible*. Paris: Desclée de Brouwer, 1986.
Dobbs-Allsopp, F. W. *On Biblical Poetry*. New York: Oxford University Press, 2015.
Giffone, Benjamin D. "A 'Perfect' Poem: The Use of the Qatal Verbal Form in the Biblical Acrostics." *Hebrew Studies* (2010) 49–72.
Hurowitz, Victor Avigdor. "The Seventh Pillar—Reconsidering the Literary Structure and Unity of Proverbs 31." *ZAW* 113 (2001) 209–18.
Jousse, Marcel. *The Anthropology of Geste and Rhythm*. Edited and translated by Edgard Sienaert and Joan Conolly. 2nd ed. Durban, South Africa: Mantis, 2000.
———. *The Oral Style*. Translated by Edgard Sienaert and Richard Whitaker. Albert Bates Lord Studies in Oral Tradition 6. New York: Garland, 1990.
———. *In Search of Coherence: Introducing Marcel Jousse's Anthropology of Mimism*. Edited and translated by Edgard Sienaert. Eugene, OR: Pickwick Publications, 2016.

———. *Memory, Memorization, and Memorizers: The Galilean Oral-Style Tradition and Its Traditionists*. Edited and translated by Edgard Sienaert. Biblical Performance Criticism Series 15. Eugene, OR: Cascade Books, 2018.

———. *The Parallel Rhythmic Recitatives of the Rabbis of Israel*. Translated with notes by Edgard Sienaert. Paris: Association Marcel Jousse, 2021.

———. *Le style oral rythmique et mnémotechnique chez les verbo-moteurs*. Paris: Beauchesne, 1925.

Knox, Ronald, trans. *The Holy Bible: A Translation from the Latin Vulgate in the Light of the Hebrew and Greek Originals*. London: Burns & Oates, 1956.

Kugel, James L. *The Idea of Biblical Poetry: Parallelism and Its History*. Baltimore: Johns Hopkins University Press, 1998.

Lord, Albert B. *The Singer of Tales*. Harvard Studies in Comparative Literature 24. Cambridge: Harvard University Press, 1960. Reprint, New York: Atheneum, 1968.

———. *The Singer of Tales*. 2nd ed. Edited by Stephen A. Mitchell and Gregory Nagy. Cambridge: Harvard University Press, 2000.

Lucas, Ernest C. *Proverbs*. Two Horizons Old Testament Commentary. Grand Rapids: Eerdmans, 2015.

Novick, Tzvi. "'She Binds Her Arms': Rereading Proverbs 31:17." *Journal of Biblical Literature* 128 (2009) 107–13.

Parry, Milman. "Studies in the Epic Technique of Oral Verse-Making I: Homer and Homeric Style." *Harvard Studies in Classical Philology* 41 (1930) 73–147.

Rad, Gerhard von. *Wisdom in Israel*. Translated by James D. Martin. London: SCM, 1972.

Siegismund, Kasper. "The Death of a Virtuous Woman? Proverbs 31.10–31: Gnomic Qatal, and the Role of Translation in the Analysis of the Hebrew Verbal System." *Journal for the Study of the Old Testament* 43 (2019) 284–300.

Waltke, Bruce K. *The Book of Proverbs, Chapters 15–31*. New International Commentary on the Old Testament. Grand Rapids: Eerdmans, 2005.

Watson, Wilfred G. E. *Classical Hebrew Poetry: A Guide to Its Techniques*. Journal for the Study of the Old Testament Supplement Series 26. Sheffield: Sheffield Academic Press, 2009.

Wolters, Al. *The Song of the Valiant Woman: Studies in the Interpretation of Proverbs 31:10–31*. Carlisle, UK: Paternoster, 2001.

Yoder, Christine Roy. *Proverbs*. Abingdon Old Testament Commentaries. Nashville: Abingdon, 2009.

5

What Use Is Jousse?
Oral Form as a Mnemonic Device in the Hodayot

SHEM MILLER

Although Marcel Jousse passed away before the publication of the bulk of the Dead Sea Scrolls, he had certainly heard of them. In his final lecture at Sorbonne University in the late 1950s, Jousse compares the dead, written, Hebrew scrolls of the Judean desert with the living, oral, Aramaic targumim of rural Galilee:

> The Dead Sea Scrolls, however amazing and intriguing a discovery, belong outside a truly real and living oral milieu: they would compare to a monastic and scholastic *Grande Chartreuse*, a monastery that would have written in dead Latin, amid living French people speaking a living French language. From the desert of Judea and its neo-Hebrew manuscripts, I see an almost stillborn Essenism petrified within its monastery, and, from rural Galilee and its living oral targum, I see a Yeshuan *Besoreta* blossoming forth and carried by the peasant memory to all corners of the world.[1]

As Jousse recognized, his view of the Qumran community and the Dead Sea Scrolls was affected by his (self-described) experience as both "traditionist peasant" and a Jesuit anthropologist.[2] I suspect his point of view

---

1. Jousse, *Memory*, 37.
2. Jousse, *Memory*, 37.

was also influenced by some trends in early Dead Sea Scrolls scholarship, which compared Qumran to a monastery and Essenes to celibate monks.[3] That being said, I suspect Jousse would have eventually placed the Dead Sea Scrolls inside—not outside—the "truly real and living oral milieu" of ancient Judea. The eventual publication of commentaries, versions, and targumim in the Dead Sea Scrolls, as well as Jousse's theoretical understanding of orality and memory, would have demanded it. Indeed, as I explore in this essay, Jousse's largely overlooked, innovative theory of a Palestinian "oral style" can be used to illuminate the mnemonic techniques and oral setting of the Scrolls.

Central to Jousse's theory of an oral style is its fundamentally formulaic nature. The oral style, in the cryptic words of Jousse, "lives solely by formulism."[4] With this in mind, this essay considers the use of three formulaic techniques of the oral style, which Jousse dubbed "formula-facets," "formulaic equivalencies," and "clamp-words."[5] As a case example, I will explore the use of these techniques in an anthology of poetic thanksgiving hymns called the Hodayot (or the Thanksgiving Hymns). Using Jousse's theory, I contend that the prominence of incipits, word pairs, key words, and lists in the Thanksgiving Hymns suggests they were stylized for memorization and transmitted through oral performance. In a nutshell, these literary devices helped ancient readers memorize and perform texts.

As you may have recognized, the title of this essay refers to an article by Jan Assmann called "Form as a Mnemonic Device: Cultural Texts and Cultural Memory." In this article, Assmann argues—similar to Jousse—that certain forms of speech have a mnemonic function.[6] "Only by acquiring certain additional distinctive features of form and genre," according to Assmann, "is an utterance capable of staying in memory and remaining accessible to later recourse, repetition, elaboration, and commentary."[7] Some literary devices explicitly functioned as mnemonic devices that enabled ancient readers to more efficiently perform, memorize, and navigate texts. For example, alphabetic acrostics segment poetic

---

3. Concerning the view that Qumran was a monastery, see Broshi, "Was Qumran, Indeed, a Monastery?" Concerning celibacy and women at Qumran, see Schuller, "Women in the Dead Sea Scrolls."

4. Jousse, *Memory*, 46.

5. Jousse, *Memory*, 46–56.

6. Assmann, "Form as a Mnemonic Device," 72–73.

7. Assmann, "Form as a Mnemonic Device," 72.

lines in a manner that assists oral performance and memorization.⁸ Borrowing Assmann's ideas, we could think of these types of literary devices as memory-making forms.

Initial Formula-Facets or Incipits

The first memory-making form that I will consider is a formula-facet. As with many of Jousse's neologisms, we need to unpack his dense terminology. Most broadly, formula-facets are a type of formulaic speech. But this definition is not very helpful because Jousse's conception of formulism includes a wide gamut of ideas, such as formulas, repetition, variants, doublets, key words, and abbreviations. More specifically, an initial formula-facet may be defined as an introductory formula, such as "And it happened in those days . . ." or "Once upon a time . . ."⁹ But Jousse's understanding of a formula extends beyond a standard, dictionary definition—that is, a stock term, phrase, or line repeated in a literary composition. Most basically, as Kelber points out, a formula (for Jousse) denotes a sound bite, "a recitational unit of *speech* that was always composed of more than a single word."¹⁰ In addition, according to Jousse's theory, this sound bite should serve a mnemonic and performative function. The purpose of formulas was to render oral discourse memorable, operational, and stable.¹¹ Finally, and most importantly, initial formula-facets are "adaptable" and "susceptible to constant change."¹² Hence, Jousse chose the term, "facet," as it "expresses the possible variability of the formulas and their equivalences."¹³ Overall, an initial formula-facet is like a fluid, adaptable introductory formula.

Nor should one equate Jousse's formula with the definition employed in oral-formulaic theory—namely, a stock phrase that (1) expresses an essential idea, (2) exhibits a fixed metrical value, and (3) enables composition in performance.¹⁴ To be sure, Jousse shared many

---

8. Concerning the functions of an acrostic, see Watson, *Classical Hebrew Poetry*, 197–200; Concerning the use of acrostics as a pedagogical device, see van der Toorn, *Scribal Culture*, 98–100, 116.

9. Jousse, *Memory*, 53–54.

10. Kelber, Foreword to Jousse, *Memory*, xxi (italics added).

11. Kelber, Foreword to Jousse, *Memory*, xxi.

12. Jousse, *Memory*, 53.

13. Jousse, *Memory*, 53.

14. For a definition of formulas in oral-formulaic theory, see Rodríguez, *Oral*

views with his contemporary and collaborator Milman Parry, the father or oral-formulaic theory.[15] For example, both viewed formulaic language as an essential building block of traditional texts and oral discourse. Unlike Parry, however, Jousse was not primarily interested in using formulas to identify oral tradition or oral composition in written texts. Rather, Jousse—as an anthropologist—sought to uncover *universal* laws that operate in oral discourse and oral performance. As summarized by Kelber, "the purpose of the book [i.e., *Le Style Oral*] was to identify anthropological laws of formulism, mimism, memory, bilateralism, rhythm and gestures that regulate and energize oral discourse and performance."[16] In this sense, Jousse's concept of formulas was more a harbinger of Ong than a reflection of Parry. In Ong's discussion of formulas, for example, he also seeks to identify universal characteristics of orally based thought and expression.[17]

Turning to the Dead Sea Scrolls, one can find ample examples of initial formula-facets throughout a variety of genres. The incipits in the Hodayot, however, provide a salient example. As is well-known among Dead Sea Scrolls scholars, the Hodayot's anthology has been divided into two classes of hymns with divergent literary styles and social contexts.[18] Even more importantly for our interests, the bifurcation of the Hodayot is partly based on form-critical criteria such as divergent formulas that introduce each hymn. According to this theory, the so-called Teacher Hymns compose the middle of the Cave 1 Hodayot manuscript (1QH^a 9:1—19:5) and begin with "I thank you, O Lord, that" (אודכה אדוני כי). The founder of the Community, the Teacher of Righteousness, authored these hymns, and they describe the Teacher's experiences of suffering and redemption. These hymns employ "I" language and fit best in a private, devotional context. The so-called Community Hymns make up the beginning and end of the Cave 1 Hodayot manuscript (1QH^a 1:1—8:41, 19:6—28:1ff.) and begin with the incipit "Blessed are you, O Lord"

Tradition, 20; Tate, "Formulas."

15. Concerning Jousse's collaboration with Parry, see Kelber's foreword to Jousse, *Memory*.

16. Kelber, Foreword to Jousse, *Memory*, xiii.

17. Ong, *Orality and Literacy*, 36–57.

18. For helpful overviews of early scholarship on the division of Teacher and Community Hymns, see Hasselbalch, *Meaning and Context*, 2–12; Schuller, "Recent Scholarship on the Hodayot," 119–20, 133–46.

(ברוך אתה אדוני), amongst others.[19] They employ "we" language, are less personal, and deal with more general concerns such as "divine salvific action and the human condition."[20] They best suit a context of public worship.

As I have briefly discussed elsewhere, however, inconsistency complicates this form-critical basis of division.[21] The incipits are a good case in point. The most compelling evidence for a form-critical division occurs in the Teacher Hymns. As one would expect, almost all of the extant incipits between 1QH^a 9:1—19:5 begin with "I thank you, O Lord, that" (אודכה אדוני כי).[22] In addition, this incipit can be partially reconstructed in two additional psalms (cf. 1QH^a 15:29; 16:5). Interspersed through this overarching consistency, however, we do encounter some outliers. For example, one hymn begins with the incipit of a Community Hymn (not the Teacher Hymn). Although not entirely extant, the incipit in 1QH^a 17:38 is usually reconstructed as "B[less]ed are yo[u, O Lord]" (ב]רו[ך את]ה אדוני]). Moreover, another incipit includes both formulas (Community Hymn and Teacher Hymn). In 1QH^a 13:22, the initial scribe wrote אודכה אדוני. Subsequently, another scribe erased and replaced this incipit with ברוך אתה—the incipit of the Community Hymns. Finally, in 1QH^a 18:16 one finds "Blessed are you, O Lord, God of Compassion" (ברוך אתה אדוני אל הרחמים). This formula either subdivides this hymn into two parts (1QH^a 17:38—18:14; 18:16—19:5) or indicates the beginning of a new hymn (18:16—19:5).[23] If the latter is correct, then we have a third Teacher Hymn beginning with the incorrect incipit.

Turning to the incipits of the Community Hymns (1QH^a 1:1—8:41, 19:6—28:1ff.), the evidence is more problematic for several reasons. First, the correct formula occurs only twice, and both instances are reconstructed.[24] The first instance is entirely reconstructed and therefore conjectural (1QH^a 7:12). The editors of the *editio princeps* have restored

---

19. For a description of the incipits, see Stegemann, "The Number of Psalms in 1QHodayot^a," 220–22.

20. Schuller, "Prayer, Hymnic, and Liturgical Texts," 154.

21. Miller, "Role of Performance," 362–64.

22. Cf. 1QH^a 10:22; 10:33; 11:20; 11:38; 12:6; 13:7; 13:22; 15:9; 15:37.

23. Concerning the subdivision of this hymn, see Stegemann, "The Number of Psalms in 1QHodayot^a," 215–16; Stegemann and Schuller, DJD 40: 236.

24. A third occurrence may be partially extant in 1QH^a 6:19. According to Stegemann and Schuller, however, this formula introduces a subdivision rather than a new hymn. See Stegemann, "The Number of Psalms in 1QHodayot^a," 213–15; Stegemann and Schuller, DJD 40: 89–90.

the beginning of this line as, "[Blessed are you, God Most High]" ([ברוך אתה אל עליון]).[25] And the second instance is partially reconstructed (1QH[a] 7:21). Only three letters of this incipit are extant: "Bless[ed are you, God of compassion]" ([ברו]ך אתה אל הרחמים). Overall, we do not have one fully extant instance of the correct incipit beginning a Community Hymn.

Second, a form-critical bifurcation of the hymns is problematic because the incipit of the Teacher Hymns, as well as a slight variation, occurs twice in the Community Hymns (cf. "[I thank] you, O Lord," [אוד]ך אדוני] in 1QH[a] 6:34 and "I thank you, O my God, that," אודכה אלי כי in 1QH[a] 19:6). Third, at least four of these hymns are prescribed "for the Maskil"—an authoritative teacher and liturgical master in the sectarian movement (1QH[a] 5:12 [*hodayah* 5:12—6:33]; 7:21 [*hodayah* 7:21—8:41]; 20:7 [*hodayah* 20:7—22:42]; 25:34 [*hodayah* 25:34—27:3]).[26] Last, and most important for the topic of this article, the incipits of the Community Hymns are inconsistent and exhibit subtle variations. Consider, for example, the multiformity of the following four incipits prescribed for the Maskil: (1) 1QH[a] 5:12 contains "[A psalm for the In]structor," [מזמור למ]שכיל; (2) 1QH[a] 7:21 contains "Bless[ed are you, God of compassion, with a] song, a psalm for the Inst[ructor]," [ברו]ך אתה אל הרחמים ב[שיר מזמור למש]כיל; (3) 1QH[a] 20:7 contains "[For the Instruc]tor, [th]anksgiving and prayer," [למשכי]ל [ה]ודות ותפלה; (4) 1QH[a] 25:34 contains "For the Instructor, a psa[lm, a song]," למשכיל מזמ[ור שיר].

This sort of multiformity is not limited to incipits prescribed for the Maskil. In fact, as the chart below displays, no two incipits of a Community Hymn are identical.

INCIPITS IN THE COMMUNITY HYMNS

1QH[a]	Hebrew	Translation
5:12	[מזמור למ]שכיל	[A psalm for the In]structor
6:19	[ברוך אתה] אדוני	[Blessed are you], O Lord
6:34	[אוד]ך אדוני	[I thank] you, O Lord

---

25. Stegemann and Schuller, DJD 40: 99–100.

26. My division of the individual hymns follows Stegemann ("The Number of Psalms in 1QHodayot[a]," 228–29).

7:12	[ברו]ך אתה אל עליון]	[Blessed are you, God Most High]
7:21	ברו]ך אתה אל הרחמים ב[שיר מזמור למש[כיל]	Bless[ed are you, God of compassion, with a] song, a psalm for the Inst[ructor]
19:6	אודכה אלי כי	I thank you, O my God, that
19:18	[וא]נ]י אודכה אלי	[And, as for me,] I thank you, O my God
20:7	[למשכי]ל [ה]ודות ותפלה	[For the Instruc]tor, [th]anksgiving and prayer
25:34	למשכיל מזמ[ור שיר]	For the Instructor, a psa[lm, a song]

Overall, the picture that emerges from examining the formulaic introductions of the hymns is far hazier than one might imagine according to prevailing form-critical theory. There is no consistent incipit used for the Community Hymns, incipits of both classes sometimes introduce the wrong class of hymn, and the incipits of the Community Hymns exhibit a variety of subtle variations.

What are we to make of this? On the one hand, these data undermine a form-critical bifurcation of the Hodayot into two classes of hymns with different uses, private and communal. More interesting for our concerns, however, the emerging picture fits neatly with Jousse's theory of the Palestinian oral style. In fact, I suspect Jousse would have expected this sort of multiformity in the Hodayot's introductory formulas. To be sure, as Jousse argues, the formulas function to stabilize oral texts. But, as Kelber notes, "stability was not to be confused with immobility."[27] In other words, Jousse is also keenly aware that formulaic language is also adaptable language.[28] Just as memory is never verbatim recollection, so formulaic speech is never mechanical repetition.[29] Perhaps this is why Jousse chose to emphasize that the Palestinian oral style lived by *propositional* formulism rather than *stereotypical* formulism.[30] In Jousse's

---

27. Kelber, Foreword to Jousse, *Memory*, xxi.
28. Kelber, Foreword to Jousse, *Memory*, xxi; Jousse, *Memory*, 47.
29. Jousse, *Memory*, 47.
30. Jousse, *Memory*, 46, 49, 61.

words, "formulism and individualism" only "seem incompatible," as each traditionist makes formulas work for himself or herself.[31]

The multiformity of Jousse's "formulism" is particularly evident in the incipits of the Community Hymns, where word substitutions, additions or omissions, and reordering occur frequently. Although I prefer the term, "multiforms," we could also think of these variations as "memory variants" or "oral variants." A few brief examples from table 5.1, above, will demonstrate my point. Concerning word substitutions, one can quickly observe a variety of synonyms that occur after the phrase "Blessed are you." For instance, 1QH[a] 6:19 has "Lord" (אדוני), 1QH[a] 7:12 has "God Most High" (אל עליון), and 1QH[a] 7:21 (cf. also 1QH[a] 18:16) has "God of compassion" (אל הרחמים). Concerning additions or omissions, consider the end of the rather long incipit in 1QH[a] 7:21: "Bless[ed are you, God of compassion, with a] song, a psalm for the Inst[ructor]." Interestingly, the word, "psalm" (מזמור), has been added above the column line thus: ברו]ך אתה אל הרחמים ב[שיר מזמור למש]כיל]. This superscription provides a clear example of an addition containing a synonym for the word, "song" (שיר). Moreover, by comparing this incipit (i.e., 1QH[a] 7:21) with another incipit in 1QH[a] 7:12, we also find an example of reordering. Whereas the end of 1QH[a] 7:21 reads, "[a] song, a psalm for the Inst[ructor]," 1QH[a] 7:12 begins with "For the Instructor, a psa[lm, a song]." The word order is inverse. Overall, the multiformity of the Hodayot's incipits is consistent with the types of variations found in texts that are held in the mind and reproduced through speech.

Formulaic Equivalences or Variants

The second memory-making form that I will consider is what Jousse calls formulaic equivalences. Although Jousse's understanding of formulaic equivalencies covers a wide variety of ideas, my discussion below will focus on two specific connotations—namely, variant readings and word pairs.[32] The complex textual tradition of the Thanksgiving Hymns poses a plethora of thorny problems for assessing variant readings. There are a total of eight manuscripts of the Hodayot, two from Cave 1 and six from Cave 4. In addition, the textual evidence suggests that some Cave 4 manuscripts represent earlier collections, which were eventually combined

---

31. Jousse, *Memory*, 46.
32. Jousse, *Memory*, 47, 49.

into the anthology of hymns represented by 1QH^a and 4QH^b (4Q428). In fact, out of all six Cave 4 manuscripts, only 4QH^b (4Q428) is similar in both order and length to our most complete copy from Cave 1 (1QH^a).[33] 4QH^e (4Q31) contains a different order of hymns than in 1QH^a, and 4QH^a (4Q427), and 4QH^a (4Q427) contains a different order of hymns than in 1QH^a, 4QH^b (4Q428), and 4QH^c (4Q429).[34] In addition, 4QH^a (4Q427) may have originally contained only Community Hymns.[35]

Given this complex textual history, it is not surprising that a variety of variant readings exist among the Hodayot manuscripts. On the one hand, some variants reflect the different orthographic conventions of scribes. Compared with the usual pronominal suffix of ך- in 1QH^a, for instance, parallel passages in 4QH^a (4Q427) typically contain the extended form כה-.[36] As pointed out by Schuller, "the suffixes of the second and third person are generally the extended forms" in 4QH^a (4Q427).[37] Alternatively, the extended form of the second person suffix consistently occurs in 1QH^a 7:12–20, which leads Stegemann and Schuller to conclude that these lines "may have been copied from a different *Vorlage* [than the rest of 1QH^a cols. 4–8 which predominately contain the short form]."[38]

On the other hand, some variants represent scribal errors, corrections, and editing. For instance, in 1QH^a 20:5 the *vav* of ש{ו}קט has been secondarily erased to correct a spelling mistake (i.e., שקט instead of שוקט). As an example of scribal editing, ומ[וכיחי אמת] was changed to ומ[וכיחי] צדק in 1QH^a 10:6. Note that אמת is expunctuated (which indicates a correction), and צדק is superscripted above אמת. Since ומוכיחי צדק also occurs in one parallel passage in a Cave 4 copy of the Hodayot (cf. 4QpapH^f [4Q432] 3 2), it has been suggested that this variant is based upon another textual tradition for this phrase. In Schuller's words, "it is likely that Scribe C was correcting to another manuscript, whether 4QpapH^f or yet another copy with the same reading."[39] And this conclusion is reasonable, because in some places 1QH^a appears to have

---

33. Schuller, "Some Contributions," 278–87; Schuller, "The Cave 4 Hodayot Manuscripts," 137–50.

34. Schuller, DJD 29: 86, 203.

35. Schuller, DJD 29: 86.

36. E.g., compare רחמיכה in 4QH^a (4Q427) 1 2 with רחמיך in 1QH^a 19:21. Schuller, DJD 29: 85–86; *Qumran Cave 4*, 85–86; Stegemann and Schuller, DJD 40: 100.

37. Schuller, DJD 29: 85, *Cave 4*, 85.

38. Stegemann and Schuller, DJD 40:100.

39. Stegemann and Schuller, DJD 40: 135.

been corrected to agree with other Cave 4 copies of the Hodayot, such as 4QHᵃ (4Q427) and 4QHᶜ (4Q429).⁴⁰

That being said, some variant readings could also have originated in oral performance and scribal memory. The explanation of variant readings, according to the editors of the *editio princeps*, is primarily based upon the presupposition that variants are textual. In other words, variants in one copy derive from other copies of the same passage. But some variants cannot be definitively explained as scribal errors or textual corrections. For example, we find a perfect verb versus an imperfect verb⁴¹ or a pronominal suffix on a noun in one instance and the lack thereof in another.⁴² In addition, parallel portions of different copies sometimes contain different nouns, verbs, or prepositions.⁴³ For example, we find להודיע in 1QHᵃ 26:31 versus להופיע in 4QHᵃ (4Q427) 7 ii 12, both of which were expunctuated (marked for deletion) at some stage. Or we find לערמת in 4QHᵃ 10:1 versus לעומת in 1QHᵃ 21:11. As Schuller has noted concerning the last two examples, it is ultimately impossible to determine which of the two variants for each is original.⁴⁴

These examples illustrate what Parry and Carr call "good variants," as they make perfect sense within the sentence.⁴⁵ Both readings are semantically, grammatically, and morphologically correct. The problematic

---

40. Schuller, DJD 29: 88, 182.

41. E.g., see (1) דבקה in 4QHᶜ (4Q429) 3 4 // תדבק in 1QHᵃ 13:33; (2) והיו in 4QHᵇ (4Q428) 8 1 // ויהיו in 1QHᵃ 14:17. For other differences in the morphology of verbs, see (1) יעודני in 4QHᵃ (4Q427) 7 i 9 // יו[ע]ד[ני] in 1QHᵃ 26:6 (concerning these bi-spellings, see Schuller, DJD 29: 102); (2) שמע 4QHᵃ (4Q427) 7 ii 20a // לשמוע in 4QHᵇ (4Q428) 21 1 (perfect verb vs. infinitive); (3) יחשבו in 4QHᶜ (4Q429) 2 8 // יחשובו in 1QHᵃ 13:28 (*piel* vs. *qal*); and (4) לה[מ]ס in 4QpapHᶠ (4Q432) 3 5 // למוס in 1QHᵃ 10:8 (*hiphil* vs. *qal*).

42. E.g., see (1) באשמתם וית[גול]ל[ו] in 4QHᶜ (4Q429) 4 i 12 // יתגוללו באשמה in 1QHᵃ 14:25; (2) גבורתכה in 4QHᵃ (4Q427) 7 ii 15 // גבורה in 1QHᵃ 26:34; (3) סודי in 4QHᶜ (4Q429) 4 ii 7 // סוד in 1QHᵃ 14:29; (4) אנחתי in 1QHᵃ 13:35 (cf. also 4QpapHᶠ [4Q432] 11 1) // אנחה in 4QHᶜ (4Q429) 3 7.

43. For examples noun substitutions, see (1) לערמת in 4QHᵃ (4Q427) 10 1 // לעומת in 1QHᵃ 21:11; (2) רוח in 4QHᵃ (4Q427) 7 ii 8 // רום in 1QHᵃ 26:27 (cf. also 4QHᵉ [4Q431] 2 7); (3) וקו in 4QpapHᶠ (4Q432) 6 3 // וקץ in 1QHᵃ 11:29. For an example of different verb, see יגבירהו in 4QHᵃ (4Q427) 7 ii 9 // יגביה in 1QHᵃ 26:28. For examples of a preposition substitutions, see (1) ועם in 4QHᵃ (4Q427) 8 i 10 // ועד in 1QHᵃ 7:18; (2) עד תום in 4QHᶜ (4Q429) 4 ii 12 // עם תום in 1QHᵃ 14:31.

44. Stegemann and Schuller, DJD 40: 135; Schuller, DJD 29:117.

45. Carr, *The Formation*, 17–21; Carr, "Orality, Textuality, and Memory," 166–67; Parry, *The Making of Homeric Verse*, 268. For more on the topic of "good variants," see Miller, *Dead Sea Media*, 252–54.

nature of an exclusively text-centered approach to variants is precisely why Jousse preferred the terminology "formulaic equivalencies," as he argued that variants should not be conceived in terms of textual discrepancies or synoptic problems.[46] According to Jousse, the presence of formulaic equivalencies provide evidence that ancient Jewish texts were stored in the mind and produced from memory. The Palestinian oral style, according to Jousse, "lives for the memory and in the memory."[47] And the "fluid" character of oral texts naturally reflects the "liquid" nature of human memory.[48] Seen from this perspective, variants do not derive from other texts but rather from the mind of the scribe. This is an important distinction because scribal memory includes not only the memory of written copies but also oral performance. Variant readings can thus express "different reflections" or "variable facets" of the same thing that are generated by the mind and produced during performance.[49]

A paradigmatic example of these "good variants" occurs in 1QH[a] 20:5 and its parallel passages in two Cave 4 copies. At first blush, the sentence in 1QH[a] reads, "[And I will dwe]ll securely in a ho[ly] dwelling [in] quiet and ease" (ואשב[ה לבטח במעון קו[דש ב]ש{ו}קט ושלוה]). After close examination, however, the editors of the *editio princeps* noted the trace of a letter superscripted above (the *qoph* of) קו[דש] by a different scribe.[50] According to the editors, "the trace is almost certainly the arm of a *shin* and probably the first letter of presence [ש]לום"; moreover, there is a scribal mark (a dot) before the *qoph*, indicating that "there is an alternative reading (not a deletion)."[51] Thus, if the editors are correct, we have the traces of what Person and Talmon call a "double reading," a textual variation that preserves two equally valid and alternative readings within the same manuscript.[52] And the second possible reading with "peaceful" instead of "holy" would read as follows: "[And I will dwe]ll securely in a peac[eful] dwelling [in] quiet and ease."

Even more striking, overlapping portions of two Cave 4 copies of the Hodayot contain two additional readings of this passage bringing the

46. Jousse, *Memory*, 47.

47. Jousse, *Memory*, 46.

48. Kelber, foreword, in Jousse, *Memory*, xxi.

49. Jousse, *Memory*, 49, 53.

50. Stegemann and Schuller, DJD 50: 254.

51. Stegemann and Schuller, DJD 40: 254–55.

52. Talmon, "Synonymous Readings," 343–45; Person, "Formulas and Scribal Memory."

total to four formulaic equivalencies. 4QH[a] (4Q427) 3 2 preserves a third reading with neither "holy" nor "peaceful": "[And I will dwell se]curely in a dwelling of quie[t and ease]" ([ואשבה לב]טח במעון שק]ט ושלוה]).[53] Finally, according to the editors' hypothetical reconstruction, 4QH[b] (4Q428) 12 ii 1 may preserve a fourth reading lacking "quiet and ease": [And I will dwell] securely in a dw[elling of peace and blessing] ([ואשבה] לבטח במ]עון שלום וברכה]). Stegemann and Schuller's highly complex explanation of these variants rests on a text-centered hermeneutic, which focuses on uncovering an original text and identifying variants resulting from scribal errors.[54] But these variants are not errors. Essentially, these variations add, omit, or exchange words, but the gist of the sentence remains relatively similar. As a result, it is impossible to identify a so-called "original text" behind these types of variants. These types of "good variants" offer evidence that the Hodayot were stored in the mind and transmitted through oral performance.[55]

Formulaic Equivalencies or Word Pairs

Jousse's concept of formulaic equivalencies also bears a striking resemblance to the concept of word pairs in Hebrew poetry. According to Jousse's example, the phrase, "shepherd's *warning*, in the morning," is formulaically equivalent to, "shepherds *delight*, in the night."[56] This couplet contains pairs of antonyms that alternate between words in parallel lines. Morning is a near antonym with night, just as warning is to delight. This type of semantic and lexical parallelism between lines and words in Hebrew poetry is reminiscent of word pairs in Hebrew poetry. In biblical studies, a theory of word pairs emerged in early twentieth-century scholarship that attempted to explain why certain words in Hebrew poetry frequently go together, like morning and evening or night and day. And the

---

53. I should note that both 1QH[a] and 4QH[a] (4Q427) conclude this sentence with the same appositional clause. According to 1QH[a], the complete sentence is "[And I will dwe]ll securely in a ho[ly] {peac[eful]} dwelling [in] quiet and ease, [in peac]e and blessing in the tents of glory and salvation" (בשלו]ם וברכה באהלי כבוד וישועה]). According to 4QH[a] (4Q427), the complete sentence is "[And I will dwell securely in a dwelling of quie[t and ease], [in] peace and blessing [in the tents of glory and sal]vation" ([ב]שלום וברכה [באהלי כבוד ויש]ועה]).

54. Stegemann and Schuller, DJD 40: 254–55.

55. For a full discussion of memory variants, see Miller, *Dead Sea Media*, 226–66.

56. Jousse, *Memory*, 50–51.

answer, it seemed, was unearthed in Ras Shamra. Although scholars of the Hebrew Bible long ago noted that certain words are frequently paired together in parallel clauses, it was not until the discovery of the Ugaritic texts that a theory of a stock body of fixed word pairs became prominent in the field of biblical studies. According to this theory, word pairs are analogous to oral formulae, which comprise a literary tradition common to both Israel and Canaan.[57] Consequently, extensive lists—veritable lexicons—were compiled, which eventually grew to such an extent that some started to question the practical viability of stock word pairs.[58]

Drawing on psycholinguistic theory, Adele Berlin proposed an elegant redefinition of "word pairs" in terms of lexical parallelism. Word pairs, according to Berlin, are "nothing more or less than the products of normal word associations that are made by all competent speakers"—that is, word pairs "derive from commonly held associations between words."[59] Likewise, Kugel defined word pairs as "conventionally associated terms of synonyms and near-synonyms, and of antonyms and near-antonyms."[60] Thus, although recent studies of word pairs (in biblical poetry) and word associations (in psycholinguistics) undermine the theory of word pairs as a sort of oral lexicon, it also underscores their function in oral-traditional texts.

As pointed out by Stanley Gevirtz's study of word pairs in oral poetry, word pairs served a mnemonic function.[61] Similar to catchphrases, these formulaic equivalencies function as mnemonic hooks to assist memorization and recitation. Word pairs, as Jousse pointed out, also function to demonstrate an oral poet's mastery over a traditional text. In the words of Jousse, formulaic equivalency displays "mastery in traditional oral-style performance."[62] The more mastery an oral poet has with a given text, the more formulaic equivalencies one should expect

---

57. Culley, *Oral Formulaic Language*, 12–39; Watters, *Formula Criticism*, 39–91.

58. Berlin, *Biblical Parallelism*, 66. For a critique of word-pairs, see Craigie, "Parallel Word Pairs in Ugaritic Poetry," 136–37. For an extensive lists of word pairs, see Dahood, "Ugaritic-Hebrew Parallel Pairs," 71–382.

59. Berlin, *Biblical Parallelism*, 68. Berlin extends this idea to parallelism when she suggests that "the whole process of parallelism is related in some way to the process of association. Just as any competent speaker can generate a word pair, so any competent speaker can generate a parallel line. Presumably, this is done through an associative process similar to that of word association" (*Biblical Parallelism*, 89).

60. Kugel, *The Idea of Biblical Poetry*, 33.

61. Gevirtz, *Patterns*, 10.

62. Jousse, *Memory*, 47.

in his or her performance. Rather than an extensive list of stock associations memorized by oral tradents, word pairs are simply the normal associations *generated* and *recalled* by competent speakers. And as such, they function to aid poets in the composition, memorization, and performance of traditional texts.

Let us take a brief look at a few examples of word pairs in action. The authors of the Hodayot often employed word pairs to describe anatomical parts, such as "tongue" (לשון) and "lips" (שפה) in 1QH[a] 10:9, 12:17, 15:14–15, 16:37, and 26:12. The following example is typical of anatomical word pairs:

Word Pairs in 1QH[a] 17:29–31

For you knew me from (the time of) my *father* (מאבי),
    and from the <u>womb</u> (ומרחם) [you sanctified me],
    [and from the <u>belly</u> (ומבטן)] of my *mother* (אמי) you have nurtured me.
And from the <u>breasts</u> (ומשדי) of my pregnant mother I received your compassion,
    and in the <u>bosom</u> (ובחיק) of my wet nurse your [kindness] was great.

Drawing on psycholinguistic laws of associations, Berlin posits that a word will elicit very particular associations based on paradigmatic and syntagmatic rules.[63] These associations include "clang responses" (or rhyming), the word itself, and a number of near synonyms and near antonyms.[64] As the above examples illustrate, two of the most common are synonyms (e.g., womb and belly, breasts and bosom, man and person) and antonyms (e.g., father and mother, bitter and sweet). In the Hodayot, word pairs in the form of near synonyms frequently involve path terminology (cf. 1QH[a] 12:5, 14:27, 15:17–18, 21:22–23) and sin terminology (cf. 1QH[a] 4:24, 9:27–29, 12:30–31, 14:9–11, 22:33). Sometimes word pairs also describe physical objects, such as "bar" (בריח) and "door" (דלת) in 1QH[a] 11:19, 13:39, 14:30–33, or abstract ideas, such as "heart" (לב) and "soul" (נפש) in 1QH[a] 7:23, 8:28, 10:30, 16:33, 18:32–33.

---

63. Concerning word associations in psycholinguistics, see Deese, *The Structure*, 160–70; Clark, "Word Associations," 271–75.

64. Berlin, *The Dynamics*, 69. Clang responses are words that sound like or rhyme with the stimulus. The word *dog*, for example, would elicit *hog, fog, log, cog*, etc. There is no semantic connection between the words (Clark, "Word Associations," 272–73).

Clamping or Parallelism

The final memory-making form that I will consider is what Jousse calls "clamp-words." According to Jousse, clamping is a mnemonic aid and structuring device common in the Palestinian oral style. Jousse defines clamping as the balancing or overlapping of propositional phrases with similar meanings or sounds.[65] In other words, clamping is the repetition of words, phrases, or sounds between lines or larger units within a text (oral or written). Jousse identifies three systems of clamping. He dubs the first system "annomination," which essentially denotes lexical parallelism or semantic parallelism—that is, the repetition of the words (lexical) or lines (semantic) with similar meanings.[66] Jousse calls these types of parallel words or phrases clamp-words. The second and third systems Jousse calls "avocalization" and "acconsonantization," which essentially denote two different kinds of phonological parallelism.[67] The former is assonance or the repetition of vowels, whereas the latter is alliteration or the repetition of consonants.[68] These types of parallel words are called clamp-rhymes and clamp-alliterations. In my discussion below, I will focus on two different examples of annomination or clamp-words: key words and lists.

Clamp-words or Key Words

As I noted above, Jousse's concept of clamp-words essentially denotes lexical and semantic parallelism. But we could also describe this phenomenon as "key words," because the purpose of clamping is to facilitate the memorization and recitation of an oral text. In a nutshell, clamp-words enable the performer to move through the macro structure of a text, from one proposition to the next, by linking lines and strophes through the repetition of sounds and meanings. Likewise, key words do not simply reiterate identical content; rather, they are a mnemonic

---

65. Jousse, *Memory*, 54. Or, as he describes elsewhere, clamping occurs when the oral performer "strives to begin the first proposition of each following recitative by a word or sound identical to the proposition at the end of the preceding recitative" (*Memory*, 55).

66. Jousse, *Memory*, 54–55. For a definition of lexical and semantic parallelism, see Berlin, *The Dynamics*, 64–69, 88–94.

67. For a definition of phonological parallelism, see Berlin, *The Dynamics*, 103–6.

68. Jousse, *Memory*, 55.

"seconding" device, which aids in retention and comprehension.[69] The balanced echo between key words aids fluency and memory. Most importantly, keywords (like clamp-words) are performance cues, because they provide structural organization and thematic coherence. Essentially, key words function to unite a series of propositions into a single movement that is memorable through its repetitive form.

As an example of clamp-words in the Dead Sea Scrolls, let us return to the Hodayot. In past scholarship, the prevalent use of key words in the Hodayot has contributed to negative assessments of its style. According to Jacob Licht, for example, the Hodayot "does not seem to possess any high degree of literary merit"; moreover, its poetry is repetitive "to the point of monotony."[70] In my view, however, keywords are a product of the oral-written textuality of the Hodayot's hymns, which were designed to be memorized and performed. Repetition of key words is therefore not the result of hackneyed, uncreative style. It is a sophisticated poetic device aimed at creating structural organization and thematic coherence.

Both Bonnie Kittel's and Barbara Thiering's work on the Hodayot emphasize how grouping key words creates thematic coherence within individual hymns. Oftentimes, as Kittel notes, key words are grouped in the first strophe and are "carried from the opening unit all the way to the close of the poem."[71] In *hodayah* 10:22–32, for example, נפש occurs six times and חסד, שוא, and בבריתכה twice. These are the most repeated nouns in this *hodayah*; moreover, these key words are introduced in the first strophe.[72] The authors of the Hodayot also cluster key words in places other than introductions. This observation led Thiering to

---

69. This "seconding" aspect of parallelism was emphasized by Kugel, who defined parallelism as "A, and what's more, B" (*The Idea of Biblical Poetry*, 8, 51–54).

70. Licht, "Thanksgiving Scroll," 1–2. For other early studies that describe the Hodayot's poetry as chaotic, uncreative or repetitive compared to biblical poetry, see Kraft, "Poetic Structure," 16–17; Gaster, *The Scriptures*, 120.

71. Kittel describes these kinds of keywords as "link words." See Kittel, *The Hymns*, 171. The repetition of keywords introduced in the opening unit is also found in biblical poetry. See van der Lugt, *Rhetorical Criticism*, 469.

72. For another notable example, see the repetition (1) of כבוד, סוד and פלא (3x) and אמת (5x) in *hodayah* 19:6–17; (2) לבב, אמת and פשע in *hodayah* 10:5–21; and (3) לב and עם (9x), the verbal root of פנה (8x), and ברית (6x) in *hodayah* 12:6—13:6. Last, see *hodayah* 16:5—17:36, which is organized around the theme of "water in the world": מים (12x) and עולם (9x). In every example, these key words occur in the first strophe of *hodayah*.

hypothesize the existence of so-called "gather-lines."⁷³ For example, in *hodayah* 11:20–37, 1QHª 11:24 gathers words from the previous lines (1QHª 11:21–23).⁷⁴

Key words also often provide structural organization in the Hodayot. Key words can signal a decisive turning point and establish poetic macrostructure (stanzas and strophes). In *hodayah* 11:20–37, for example, key words organize the poem into two distinctive parts. As several commentators note, beginning at 1QHª 11:30 "it is as if a new poem has begun" and a "completely different vocabulary is introduced."⁷⁵ This turning point is achieved, in part, by the repetition of new key words in the last half of the poem. Key words also thematically organize strophes and demarcate strophic boundaries. For example, consider the use of the term "truth" (אמת) in *hodayah* 15:29–36. In this particular hymn, אמת begins the first line, and is repeated at the beginning of the next three strophes. In this way, keywords can unify the strophe and delimit strophic boundaries.

Annomination or Lists

A list is three or more parallel words or cola in consecutive or sequential order. Although lists also occur in biblical poetry, they are more integral to the verbose poetic style of the Hodayot.⁷⁶ As Kittel described, "quite often" within a strophe "parallel structures and terms are employed over more than a bicolon or tricolon."⁷⁷ In these cases, she continues, "lines do not break down easily into sets of bicola or tricola, but instead the parallel features are arranged in elaborate patterns over the entire unit."⁷⁸ Sometimes elaborate patterns form a simple series of descriptive words.

---

73. Thiering, "Poetic Forms," 190–91. Kittel calls this form of repetition a "double line" (*The Hymns*, 172).

74. For more examples, see 1QHª 11:14 (gathers words from lines 15–18), 1QHª 11:27 (gathers words from lines 18–20), and 1QHª 11:12 (gathers words from lines 8–11).

75. Hughes, *Scriptural Allusions*, 218–19. See also Newsom, *Symbolic Space*, 260; Kittel, *Hymns*, 71–72.

76. E.g., Prov 6:12–15, 17; Song 4:1–5; 6:4–7; Ezek 1:26–28; Isa 30:27–28; 32:3–6; Pss 115:5–7; 135:16–17. For a discussion of lists in Hebrew and Ugaritic poetry, see Watson, *Classical Hebrew Poetry*, 351–56.

77. Kittel, *The Hymns*, 159.

78. Kittel, *The Hymns*, 159. Kittel also considers listing a stylistic feature of the Hodayot (*The Hymns*, 161–63).

For example, a list of pools cataloging springs of streams, springs of water, a watered garden, and a pool is found in 1QH^a 16:5–6 of *hodayah* 26:5—27:36.[79] Oftentimes, these simple series also exhibit forms of grammatical parallelism. In 1QH^a 17:28 of *hodayah* 16:5–17:36, for example, a list describes aspects of God's protective care over his servant in five morphologically and syntactically parallel epithets: [מפלטי] ("my place of refuge"), מנוסי ("my shelter"), משגבי ("my stronghold"), סלע עוזי ("my strong rock"), and ומצודתי ("my fortress").

The majority of lists in the Hodayot, however, are more complex than a simple series. A list of God's attributes together with the associative location in *hodayah* 19:6–17 offers an illustrative example. Truth, righteousness, knowledge and might are listed together with God's mouth, hand, thought, and strength. In addition to the syntactic and morphologic parallelism between these four lines, the correspondence between attributes and their associative location forms a distinctive internal-line parallelism.[80] Another list describing God's attributes is located in 1QH^a 19:8–10 of *hodayah* 19:6–17. This list of nine cola describes the mercy, strength, glory and greatness of God. Similar to 1QH^a 19:10–11, corresponding syntactic and morphologic parallelisms tie the cola together as a list.[81]

Lists in the Hodayot often contain a series of the narrator's anatomical parts. These anatomical lists, which vary widely in length from three to eleven cola, describe a variety of themes ranging from the providence of God to the affliction of the author. For example, in 1QH^a 19:7–8 of *hodayah* 19:6–17, a short list describes the parts of the speaker's body that give praise to God. 1QH^a 16:33–37 of *hodayah* 16:5—17:36 contains a longer anatomical list. In this list, twelve body parts (heart, flesh, loins, arm, joint, hand, leg, knees, foot, arm, tongue, and mouth) compare the author's affliction to someone trapped in Sheol. Each colon progressively

---

79. For more examples of lists with a simple series, see 1QH^a 15:18; 16:6; 18:10.

80. The four cola are syntactically parallel, and even the ordering of their constituents is parallel for all four lines. Each of the attributes of God constitutes the subject, while each of the associative locations is an object. Morphologically each of the attributes of God ends with a second person singular possessive pronominal suffix, each colon begins with a *vav* conjunction and ends with a ה, and the second through the fourth colon also have a ב preposition.

81. A partial list also extends into lines 1QH^a 19:11–12, describing various attributes of God.

describes the condition of his broken body, detailing how the entire body is powerless to extricate the speaker from his predicament.[82]

Similar to key words, lists do not simply reiterate identical content; rather, they provide a "balanced echo of something already said."[83] As Alter has noted, even in cases where multiple forms of the "same" concept are listed, parallelism between these associated terms does not denote identical meaning but rather "dramatization."[84] Consider, for example, the dramatization and intensification created by the anatomical list in 1QH^a 17:30–33, which describes God's providential care over the author. This list not only catalogues the various body parts associated with the speaker's birth and infancy, but it also describes a chronological progression of events from conception to early childhood.[85] It begins with God knowing the speaker before his conception. The list proceeds with a progression from his conception in the mother's uterus, growth in her womb, nursing during infancy, growth to a toddler (with his wet nurse), and finally his maturation into a child. The chronological progression extends into adulthood and old age in this same strophe after the conclusion of this list. Images of parental nurturing pervade this last section of *hodayah* 16:5—17:36, where a parental metaphor is applied to God. The author has not known his father and has been forsaken by his mother, but God has become his surrogate mother and father.[86]

As I previously discussed, listing is a memory-making form in poetic compositions that facilitates oral performance and memory. This memory function of listing is illuminated by Pasternack's study of Old English poetry. Old English poetry—similar to poetry in the

---

82. Each colon typically contains one body part, although in two instances each colon contains two parts. For other examples of anatomical lists, see 1QH^a 15:5–8 of *hodayah* 13:22—15:8, which lists eleven body parts of the narrator in a similar fashion as 1QH^a 16:33–37. Finally, 1QH^a 15:5–8 consists of a detailed description of the speaker's body both internally and externally. The author of this hymn describes the arms, joints, legs, eyes, ears, heart, skeleton, and bowels, as they react to the sin and destruction of the wicked.

83. Havelock, *The Muse Learns to Write*, 73.

84. The movement of meaning between parallel terms, according to Alter, "is one of heightening or intensification, of focusing, specification, concretization, and even what could be called dramatization" (Alter, *The Art of Biblical Poetry*, 19).

85. Syntactic parallelism also punctuates each colon of the list with a prepositional phrase (usually מן) that introduces each body part.

86. Hughes, *Scriptural Allusions*, 166–67. 1QH^a 15:23–25 of *hodayah* 15:29–36 contains a similar list, which draws upon the imagery of an infant.

Scrolls—contains patterns, in which words, syntax, and rhythm regularly repeat. Pasternack's study shows how these parallelisms often "unite a series of verses into a single movement and create a list that is memorable through its repetitive form."[87] In the Hodayot, infinitive lists provide a paradigmatic example of the mnemonic function of listing.[88] Infinitive lists are memorable because each line is syntactically, morphologically, and semantically parallel. Infinitive lists are essentially a form of morphologic and syntactic parallelism, in which each colon begins with an infinitive construct (typically with a *lamed* prefix) and sometimes a *vav* conjunction. Moreover, this morphologic parallelism directs the reader back to the first clause. Thus, to use Jousse's terminology, the initial infinitive functions as an initial formula-facet for every line in the list. For example, in 1QH^a 6:20–21 of *hodayah* 5:12—6:33 the poet describes how God places understanding in the heart of his servant *so that he can do* each of the described actions in the list. Other examples of infinitive lists can be found in 1QH^a 14:13–15 of *hodayah* 13:22—15:8 and 1QH^a 19:13–17 of *hodayah* 19:6–17.

Similar to most of the world's oral poetry, poetry in the Hodayot often gravitates toward repetitive expression, such as parallelism, key words, and listing.[89] This repetition—similar to Jousse's notion of clamping—adds structure and facilitates both memorization and performance. According to Jousse's terminology, the "sequencing," "successivisation," and "imbrication" presented by clamping helps to create internal cohesion within an oral text.[90] Or, as Bauman notes, "the persistence of invariant elements and the structural principles underlying parallel constructions serve as mnemonic aids to the performer of a fixed traditional text or enhance the fluency of the improvisational or spontaneous performance."[91] In short, "internal cohesion" is created through "external connection."[92]

---

87. Pasternack, *The Textuality*, 71–72.

88. Kittel also points out the existence of infinitive lists in her analysis of the poetic techniques of the Hodayot (*The Hymns*, 59, 159).

89. Concerning the use of repetition in oral poetry from around the world, see Finnegan, *Oral Poetry*, 129.

90. Jousse, *Memory*, 54–55, 58–60.

91. Bauman, *Verbal Art*, 19.

92. Jousse, *Memory*, 58.

Conclusion

Although the contributions of Marcel Jousse have been largely overlooked in past scholarship, his work offers many insights into the oral-written textuality of ancient Jewish literature. When thinking specifically about how Dead Sea Scrolls scholarship could benefit from using Jousse's theory of a Palestinian oral style, one word comes to mind: *memory*. For Jousse, memory is integral to the Palestinian oral style. And in Dead Sea Scrolls scholarship, not nearly enough attention has been paid to the intersection of memory and textuality. In this essay, I examined three specific memory-making forms discussed by Jousse: formula-facets, formulaic equivalencies, and clamp-words. We discovered that these techniques share many commonalities with the use of incipits, multiformity, word pairs, key words, and lists in the Hodayot. This, in my opinion, is not mere coincidence. Similar to the Aramaic proverbs and the sayings of Jesus explored by Jousse, the Hodayot and other poetic texts in the Dead Sea Scrolls emerged from a milieu in which texts were primarily experienced through the spoken word and stored in the human mind. The prominence of these techniques suggests that the Hodayot's style—like Jousse's Palestinian oral style—cannot be understood apart from orality and memory.

Bibliography

Alter, Robert. *The Art of Biblical Poetry*. New York: Basic Books, 1985.
Assmann, Jan. "Form as a Mnemonic Device: Cultural Texts and Cultural Memory." In *Performing the Gospel: Orality, Memory, and Mark*, edited by Richard A. Horsley et al., 67–83. Minneapolis: Fortress, 2006.
Bauman, Richard. *Verbal Art as Performance*. Prospect Heights, IL: Waveland, 1984.
Berlin, Adele. *The Dynamics of Biblical Parallelism*. 1985. Reprint, The Biblical Resource Series. Grand Rapids: Eerdmans, 2008.
Broshi, Magen. "Was Qumran, Indeed, a Monastery? The Consensus and Its Challengers, an Archaeologist's View." In *Caves of Enlightenment: Proceedings of the American Schools of Oriental Research Dead Sea Scrolls Jubilee Symposium (1947–1997)*, edited by James H. Charlesworth, 19–37. North Richland Hills, TX: Bibal, 1998.
Carr, David M. *The Formation of the Hebrew Bible: A New Reconstruction*. Oxford: Oxford University Press, 2011.
———. "Orality, Textuality, and Memory: The State of Biblical Studies." In *Contextualizing Israel's Sacred Writings: Ancient Literacy, Orality, and Literary Production*, edited by Brian B. Schmidt, 161–73. Society of Biblical Literature Early Judaism and Its Literature 22. Atlanta: Society of Biblical Literature, 2015.
Clark, Herbert H. "Word Associations and Linguistic Theory." In *New Horizons in Linguistics*, edited by John Lyons, 271–86. Harmondsworth, UK: Penguin, 1975.

Craigie, Peter C. "Parallel Word Pairs in Ugaritic Poetry: A Critical Evaluation of Their Relevance for Psalm 29." *Ugarit-Forschungen* 11 (1979) 135–40.

Culley, Robert C. *Oral Formulaic Language in the Biblical Psalms*. Near and Middle East Series 4. Toronto: University of Toronto Press, 1967.

Dahood, Mitchell. "Ugaritic-Hebrew Parallel Pairs." In *Ras Shamra Parallels: The Texts from Ugarit and the Hebrew Bible*, vol. 1, edited by Loren R. Fisher, 71–382. Analecta Orientalia 49. Rome: Pontifical Biblical Institute, 1972.

Deese, James Earle. *The Structure of Associations in Language and Thought*. Baltimore: Johns Hopkins University Press, 1966.

Finnegan, Ruth. *Oral Poetry: Its Nature, Significance and Social Context*. 1977. Reprint, Eugene, OR: Wipf & Stock, 2018.

Gaster, Theodor H. *The Scriptures of the Dead Sea Sect*. London: Secker & Warburg, 1957.

Gevirtz, Stanley. *Patterns in the Early Poetry of Israel*. Studies in Ancient Oriental Civilizations 32. Chicago: University of Chicago Press, 1963.

Hasselbalch, Trine Bjørnung. *Meaning and Context in the Thanksgiving Hymns: Linguistic and Rhetorical Perspectives on a Collection of Prayers from Qumran*. Society of Biblical Literature Early Judaism and Its Literature 42. Atlanta: Society of Biblical Literature, 2015.

Havelock, Eric A. *The Muse Learns to Write: Reflections on Orality and Literacy from Antiquity to the Present*. New Haven: Yale University Press, 1988.

Hughes, Julie A. *Scriptural Allusions and Exegesis in the Hodayot*. Studies on the Texts of the Desert of Judah 59. Leiden: Brill, 2006.

Jousse, Marcel. *Memory, Memorization, and Memorizers: The Galilean Oral-Style Tradition and Its Traditionists*. Edited and translated by Edgard Sienaert. Biblical Performance Criticism Series 15. Eugene, OR: Cascade Books, 2018.

Kelber, Werner H. Foreword to *Memory, Memorization, and Memorizers: The Galilean Oral-Style Tradition and Its Traditionists*, by Marcel Jousse, xiii–xxiii. Edited and translated by Edgard Sienaert. Biblical Performance Criticism Series 15. Eugene, OR: Cascade Books, 2018.

Kittel, Bonnie Pedrotti. *The Hymns of Qumran: Translation and Commentary*. Society of Biblical Literature Dissertation Series 50. Atlanta: Society of Biblical Literature, 1981.

Kraft, Charles F. "Poetic Structure in the Qumran Thanksgiving Psalms." *Biblical Research* 2 (1957) 1–18.

Kugel, James L. *The Idea of Biblical Poetry: Parallelism and Its History*. Baltimore: Johns Hopkins University Press, 1981.

Licht, Jacob. "The Doctrine of the Thanksgiving Scroll." *Israel Exploration Journal* 6 (1956) 1–13, 89–101.

Lugt, Pieter van der. *Rhetorical Criticism and the Poetry of the Book of Job*. Oudtestamentische Studiën 32. Leiden: Brill, 1995.

Miller, Shem. *Dead Sea Media: Orality, Textuality, and Memory in the Scrolls from the Judean Desert*. Studies on the Texts of the Desert of Judah 129. Leiden: Brill, 2019.

———. "Role of Performance and Performance of Role: Cultural Memory in the Hodayot." *Journal of Biblical Literature* 137 (2018) 359–82.

Newsom, Carol. *The Self as Symbolic Space: Constructing Identity and Community at Qumran*. Studies on the Texts of the Desert of Judah 52. Leiden: Brill, 2004.

Ong, Walter J. *Orality and Literacy: The Technologizing of the Word.* New Accents. London: Routledge, 2002.
Parry, Milman. *The Making of Homeric Verse: The Collected Papers of Milman Parry.* Edited by Adam Parry. Oxford: Clarendon, 1971.
Pasternack, Carol Braun. *The Textuality of Old English Poetry.* Cambridge Studies in Anglo-Saxon England 13. Cambridge: Cambridge University Press, 1995.
Person, Raymond F., Jr. "Formulas and Scribal Memory: A Case Study of Text-Critical Variants as Examples of Category-Triggering." In *Weathered Words: Formulaic Language and Verbal Art,* edited by M. Frog and William Lamb, 147–72. Washington, DC: Center for Hellenic Studies, 2021.
Rodríguez, Rafael. *Oral Tradition and the New Testament: A Guide for the Perplexed.* Guides for the Perplexed. London: Bloomsbury, 2014.
Schuller, Eileen M. "The Cave 4 Hodayot Manuscripts: A Preliminary Description." *Jewish Quarterly Review* 85 (1994) 137–50.
———. "Prayer, Hymnic, and Liturgical Texts from Qumran." In *The Community of the Renewed Covenant: The Notre Dame Symposium on the Dead Sea Scrolls,* edited by Eugene Ulrich and James C. VanderKam, 153–71. Christianity and Judaism in Antiquity 10. Notre Dame: University of Notre Dame Press, 1994.
———. "Recent Scholarship on the Hodayot 1993–2010." *Currents in Biblical Research* 10 (2011) 119–62.
———. "Some Contributions of the Cave Four Manuscripts (4Q427–432) to the Study of the Hodayot." *Dead Sea Discoveries* 8 (2001) 278–87.
———. "Women in the Dead Sea Scrolls." In *Methods of Investigation of the Dead Sea Scrolls and the Khirbet Qumran Site,* edited by Michael O. Wise et al., 115–31. New York: New York Academy of Sciences, 1994.
Schuller, Eileen M. et al. *Qumran Cave 4:20: Liturgical Texts, Part 2.* Discoveries in the Judean Desert 40. Oxford: Clarendon, 2009.
Stegemann, Hartmut. "The Number of Psalms in 1QHodayot^a and Some of Their Sections." In *Liturgical Perspectives: Prayer and Poetry in Light of the Dead Sea Scrolls,* edited by Esther G. Chazon et al., 191–234. Studies on the Texts of the Desert of Judah 48. Leiden: Brill, 2003.
Stegemann, Hartmut, and Eileen M. Schuller. *1QHodayot^a with Incorporation of 1QHodayot^b and 4QHodayot^{a-f}.* Discoveries in the Judean Desert 40. Oxford: Clarendon, 2009.
Talmon, Shemaryahu. "Synonymous Readings in the Textual Traditions of the Old Testament." *Scripta Hierosolymitana* 8 (1961) 335–83.
Tate, Aaron P. "Formulas." In *The Dictionary of the Bible and Ancient Media,* edited by Tom Thatcher et al., 146–48. London: Bloomsbury, 2017.
Thiering, Barbara. "The Poetic Forms of the Hodayot." *Journal of Semitic Studies* 8 (1963) 189–209.
Toorn, Karel van der. *Scribal Culture and the Making of the Hebrew Bible.* Cambridge: Harvard University Press, 2007.
Watson, Wilfred G. E. *Classical Hebrew Poetry: A Guide to Its Techniques.* Journal for the Study of the Old Testament Supplement Series 26. Sheffield: JSOT Press, 1984.
Watters, William R. *Formula Criticism and the Poetry of the Old Testament.* Beiheft zur Zeitschrift für die alttestamentliche Wissenschaft 138. Berlin: de Gruyter, 1976.

6

Sound, Memory, and the Oral Style

MARGARET E. LEE

Marcel Jousse and the Oral Style

The recent translation into English by Edgard Sienaert of the works of Marcel Jousse presents an important opportunity to broaden our understanding of the New Testament and especially the Gospels as narratives of works and deeds attributed to Jesus. Jousse lectured in Paris from 1931 to 1957,[1] between the ending of the old quest for the historical Jesus and the beginning of the new quest. Although he did not engage with the quest, Jousse's aims align in some ways with old questers, who sought a foundation for biblical study in methods that would connect the person of Jesus with theological claims about him in the councils and subsequent tradition, enabling the biblical tradition to serve then as a warrant or, alternatively, a critique of those theological traditions. As a Jesuit priest, Jousse revered the teachings of Jesus as unique and sacred. As an anthropologist, he espoused a scientific approach to interpretation, based on empirical data and articulated with precision.

    Jousse's concern with precision revealed itself in the profusion of neologisms in his work. While these complicate the task of coming to terms with his insights, they signal Jousse's drive to escape conventional

---

1. Kelber, foreword in Jousse, *Memory*, xiii.

methodological restraints and to think about communication in new ways. His cross-cultural study of preliterate societies and the oral transmission of traditions in ancient and modern cultures sensitized Jousse to the physiological basis of communication and the crucial role of memory in verbal art, especially before the invention of print. His insights can therefore enlighten those today who seek to better understand the composition and transmission of the Jesus traditions.

Jousse's theory of "mimism" maintains that human expression imitates physical processes in the phenomenal world. He asserted that speech replicates physical movements outside themselves that humans apprehend or "intussuscept."[2] Because humans fundamentally experience themselves as bilateral beings, they store their recollections of these natural movements in memory in balanced forms, which they communicate orally in rhythmic patterns or schemas.[3] According to Jousse, the physiological basis of human learning implies that speech fundamentally conveys physical movement, or *geste*. Jousse argued that the "propositional *geste*," not the word, composed the fundamental language unit.[4] He defined the propositional *geste* as an expression that predicates an action by an actor, directed toward someone or something that is acted upon.[5] Concrete, rhythmic, propositional *gestes* remain stable in memory and are accurately recalled.[6] Moreover, culturally determined propositional patterns emerge in the process of oral transmission, exhibiting distinctive characteristics, such as those discernible in the Palestinian ethnic milieu and in a Galilean oral style.[7] These persist over time and reflect a shared, traditional history. The use of writing, according to Jousse, interferes with this natural process by interposing a graphic code between one's perception of external rhythmic movements and the propositional *gestes* imitating them that are stored in memory.[8] Jousse claimed that the use of static signs to represent concrete physical movements burdens human expression with abstractions and replaces the rhythmic balance of

---

2. Jousse, *In Search*, 13.
3. Jousse, *In Search*, 260–91; Jousse, *The Oral Style*, 125, 229.
4. Jousse, *The Oral Style*, xxvi, 53; Jousse, *Memory*, 102, 155, 330.
5. Jousse, *In Search*, 15–17.
6. Jousse, *Memory*, 307; Jousse, *The Oral Style*, 127, 146.
7. Jousse, *Memory*, 152–53, 391–93.
8. Jousse, *In Search*, 105–7.

oral style with a linear logic.[9] He labeled as "algebrosis" the tendency to reduce concrete experience to arbitrary signs. He explains:

> I created the word "algebrosis" from existing terminology. We can perform no scientific function at present without *algebra*, in which a voluntary process of simplification takes place and signs are assigned meaning by consensus. In *algebrosis* the signs or words, which are *gestes*, can mean 'anything' because we no longer see their connection with the real [sic] they originally referred to. We live by a system in which all *gestes* are diminished and degraded, be they corporeal, manual, laryngo-buccal or graphic, because they are emptied of their original concretism.[10]

As applied to the New Testament Gospels, Jousse's approach viewed Jesus of Nazareth as fully embedded in the oral style of balanced, mnemonic, "propositional *gestes*" that are communicated through speech. Jousse maintained that Jesus, a Jewish, Aramaic-speaking Palestinian peasant, would necessarily have employed in his speech the rhythmic patterns of his local milieu, which derived not directly from the Hebrew Bible but from the Aramaic targumim as they existed in the oral stage of their compilation and transmission, before they were written down.[11] Jesus' teachings, Jousse insisted, were recorded by bilingual "apprehenders" who heard them repeated by Peter, Matthew, John, or persons with direct connections to these privileged original auditors.[12] The oral style of these original witnesses ensured accurate, verbatim transmission in Aramaic.[13]

Jousse asserted that neither "transcription" nor "translation" properly characterizes the recording process that the apostles' apprehenders employed. Rather, these unknown persons with direct lines to eyewitness testimony "transferred" the "recitatives" of Jesus's teachings from the balanced, propositional rhythms of the Aramaic targumim to correlative patterns of "Hellenistic Greek."[14] Jousse attributed variations among the

---

9. *The Oral Style*, 84, 102.

10. Quoted from an audio recording of one of Jousse's lectures at the Sorbonne by Edgard Sienaert in his "Introduction" to Jousse, *Memory*, 8. Jousse's statement should not be construed as erecting a Great Divide between speaking and writing, since he clearly states elsewhere that print, not writing, dissolves the oral style (*Oral Style*, 132, 195).

11. Jousse, *Memory*, 26.

12. Jousse, *The Oral Style*, 176–80.

13. Jousse, *Memory*, 71, 307.

14. Jousse, *Memory*, 26–34, 94–97, 244.

gospel narratives to the different personalities and styles of the gospel transfer-transcribers.[15] Thus Jousse dismissed the Synoptic problem as a "pseudo-problem" that can be explained in terms of the individual personalities of the Jesus tradition's transmitters.[16] The resulting canonical Gospels therefore present Jesus' sayings and deeds in written forms that preserve their substructure in the Aramaic targumim while also distorting them with Greek constructions that align only imperfectly with the Aramaic *ipsissima verba Jesu*.

A more accurate presentation of Jesus's teachings can be reconstituted, Jousse maintained, from the patterns that characterize the oral style, aligned with their Aramaic precursors. Since Jousse's understanding of the oral style affirms that its fundamental linguistic unit is not the word but the formula or propositional *geste*,[17] word-for-word translations further distort Jesus's message. Jousse rejected the sort of "scorched-earth criticism" in which "nothing authentic must be left standing,"[18] as espoused by critics such as Alfred Loisy, whom Jousse labeled a "pulverisor of texts."[19] Jousse claimed that, because its philological methods focus on words and not propositions, they failed to recognize the balanced rhythms of the oral style and the propositional structures integral to Jesus's oral teaching.[20]

Subsequent scholarship necessitated the updating of some of Jousse's premises regarding his reconstruction of Christian origins and the oral and written transmission of Jesus traditions. Jousse's outdated premises include the presumption that the evangelists enjoyed personal access to apostolic eyewitness testimony, the early dating of the gospels, the privileged status of the canon, and tacit acceptance of the narrative of Christian origins presented in the Acts of the Apostles. But Jousse cannot be held accountable for developments in New Testament interpretation that postdate him. Any appraisal of the value of Jousse's insights for contemporary New Testament study must assess the utility of his notion of the oral style. This rubric can organize salient discussion points. In so

15. Jousse, *Memory*, 105, 299.
16. Jousse, *Memory*, 66, 96–105.
17. Jousse, *Memory*, 102, 155.
18. Jousse, *Memory*, 316.
19. Jousse, *Memory*, 312.
20. Jousse, *Memory*, 315–16.

doing, we stop at the phrase's first word, *the*, which implies a singular and universal phenomenon.

The implication that oral style functions in a single way across time and space invites questions concerning the extent to which we may generalize about its characteristics. Jousse argued for distinctive features of first-century Aramaic traditions, features that were eventually encoded in the Aramaic targumim. He spoke of "Palestinian," "Greek," and "Hebraic" modes of communication as if they were uniformly expressed across their respective cultures and without specifying whether his categories of classification derived from linguistic, geographic, or religious criteria. Jousse illustrated his theories about the Jesus traditions only by reference to canonical works, without accounting for the composition and transmission of noncanonical evidence for these traditions. It therefore becomes difficult to determine which traits might best characterize the oral style generally, and which are distinctive of specific cultural manifestations of oral style.

More fundamentally, Jousse applies his theory of mimism to other traditions outside the ancient Mediterranean world where a mimetic understanding of language does not necessarily obtain. For example, Jousse occasionally points to ancient Chinese Taoist literature to support his notion of the propositional *geste* in oral style.[21] But David Hinton, perhaps the premiere contemporary translator of classical Chinese literature into English, points to fundamental differences between the mimetic understanding of language in the West and the language found, for example, in the *Tao Te Ching*, which, like the New Testament Gospels, preserves spoken teachings (of Lao Tzu) and the oral traditions associated with them. Hinton explains that Taoist cosmology does not view human beings as ontologically separate from the natural world in which they live, as does Western philosophy. Taoist cosmology eliminates the distinction between subject and object, inside and outside.[22] In Taoist thought and in the Ch'an Buddhist forms into which it evolves, an individual identity center does not exist. Rather, Hinton explains, humans are seen to arise from the unitary existence-tissue that continually generates and regenerates all things. Language is not understood as imitating reality, as in Western linguistic theory. An entity is said to exist only as and when language names it, thereby conferring the entity's temporary phenomenological

---

21. Jousse, *The Oral Style*, 55–56, 163.
22. Hinton, *Awakened Cosmos*, 6–7; Hinton, *China Root*, 3–4.

status. Thus, language mediates and participates in Tao, the "Way" that generates and transforms all things in the ongoing journey from Absence to Presence and back to empty Absence. Accordingly, Chinese grammar fails to specify the precise relationship between juxtaposed ideograms in classical Chinese poetry. The blank space between its complex written signs plays an active role in communication by mediating empty Absence, the primal, wild state of the phenomenal world, and inviting mystical meditation on various possibilities of signification.[23]

By contrast, Western philosophy posits human actors who understand themselves to possess discrete identities, distinct from the external entities in the phenomenal world. Their separate identity centers imitate in their oral and written expressions the movements of extrinsic objects and forces.[24] Jousse challenged any hard distinction between the perceiver and objects perceived. His theory of mimism posited an organic connection between a human perception and the object perceived, and he insisted that "interaction is the all-important element" in mimism.[25] Still, in the end Jousse's theory of language necessarily retained the Western ontological separation of the perceiver and the perceived; it understands language as mimesis. Thus, written Chinese might not express propositional *gestes* in precisely the way Jousse specifies. These considerations raise questions regarding the absolute universality of an oral style.

The crucial component of the oral style is certainly *oral*, an insufficiently precise term for the study of verbal art that exhibits features of both spoken and written transmission. By *oral* Jousse seems to mean not just spoken but unwritten, indicating that his methodology pursues unwritten speech, a phenomenon ultimately unavailable by reading written works, including the New Testament. Jousse maintained that written compositions preserve aspects of the structures that organize spoken recitations. While he acknowledged that the Gospels were not orally composed in the manner of the Homeric epics, he asserted that the Gospels preserve recitations that were orally composed, such as the Sermon on the Mount,[26] which Jousse classified as Jesus's "rhythmo-catechism,"[27] and the Magnificat, which, Jousse maintains, was orally composed by

23. Hinton, *Awakened Cosmos*, 18–19, 60–65.
24. Jousse, *In Search*, 112–13, 245.
25. Jousse, *In Search*, 17.
26. Jousse, *The Oral Style*, 65, 146–53.
27. Jousse, *Memory*, 44–57, 129.

Mary the mother of Jesus.[28] Jousse seemed to identify such oral structures intuitively, based primarily on his perception of the balance that derives from human bilateralism. Reliable analysis of oral style as preserved in written compositions requires clearer criteria than Jousse provided for discerning in written materials the precise boundaries of orally composed components.

Subsequent studies, such as Catherine Hezser's examination of Jewish literature in Roman Palestine, reveal a vast variety of written modes, even among Palestinians with little or no literacy. Hezser's analysis uncovers written works in a multiplicity of languages that employ various materials, and whose variations in form and content frequently correlate with particular social roles and educational experiences.[29] Jousse did not acknowledge this level of complexity. Hezser's more comprehensive analysis indicates both a low literacy level in Roman Palestine and the primacy of speech and memory in that milieu, as suggested by its widely diverse written artifacts. Her work indicates that there remains room to expand our models of oral and written traditions to account for ways in which oral and written sources interpenetrate in ancient compositional processes, especially since written compositions were "published" primarily through speech.

Finally, the oral style hypothesizes an important function for *style*. For Jousse, style—not words or even Jesus's Aramaic language—is what persists in New Testament writings that is traceable to Jesus. Jousse imagined illiterate Palestinian peasants such as Mary, Peter, and Jesus himself as speakers in the oral style, whose actual recitations were "transfer-transcribed" out of Aramaic and into Greek in a kind of Christian diaspora from Palestine to Rome wherein the teachings of a Jewish Jesus became Greek Christianity.[30] A gap remains between Jousse's abstraction of a particular style and the diverse materials that exhibit it. Even in the presence of a unique Palestinian oral style, we need to account more precisely for the compositional processes that might preserve its stylistic features.

Jousse argued that oral style, preserved in writing, reflects "without contamination"[31] the original, orally composed recitations that are traceable to Jesus and his ear-witnesses. These considerations become

---

28. Jousse, *Memory*, 32, 57.
29. Hezser, *Jewish Literacy*.
30. Jousse, *Memory*, 87–105, 176.
31. Jousse, *Memory*, 71.

problematic in view of the many intervening decades between Jesus's teachings and the composition of the Gospels. But even if Jousse correctly maintained that "the eyes of a silent modern reader" can "recognize on the printed page the rhythmo-pedagogic structures of the oral performance,"[32] he did not specify precisely what such a discovery of oral style can tell us about the Jesus traditions. Oral-style communication may have originated with other speakers than those Jousse supposes, and methods of recording such communication were likely diverse. As we explore the new dimensions revealed in an Aramaic, Palestinian oral style we need to account more precisely for the compositional processes at work in materials that reveal oral style. Further investigation could explore such issues as the engagement of conventional materials in literature outside the Jesus traditions, the style(s) evident in extracanonical literature of the Jesus traditions, and the possibility that written compositions can imitate oral styles in the interest of verisimilitude.

This brief summary of the oral style suggests problematic aspects of Jousse's theory but also, and more importantly, some of his crucial contributions to our understanding of the New Testament. While Jousse's claims regarding the singularity and universality of the oral style remain questionable, his observations about nonwritten communication in cultures with minimal literacy highlight the important role of memory in spoken communication. Jousse reminds us that in the ancient Roman world, memory served as the archive for oral tradition. Jousse's appreciation of memory's central role in verbal art before the invention of print furnishes a necessary corrective for imprecise categories such "orality," "literacy," and even "performance." But subsequent scholarship regarding communication media in the ancient world illustrates a deeper integration of speech and writing in antiquity than Jousse has imagined. We now know that memory plays the crucial role not just for spoken communication but also for literary composition in memorial cultures.

Jousse's theory of the oral style may not be able to lead us back to a tradition's original, spoken event, but his insistence on the physicality of communication and its concrete, empirical basis focuses our attention on speech, supported by memory, as the primary mode of transmission for Jesus traditions, written and unwritten. Even though stylistic features cannot necessarily identify sources of oral or written traditions, they

---

32. Jousse, *Memory*, 140.

enable us to discern structural features that organize literary works and provide clues to their composition and reception.

In the spoken communication of both oral and written traditions, these structural features are implemented by sound. Sound mediates the storage and retrieval of oral and written traditions in memorial space and organizes ancient written compositions for their spoken performance and auditory reception. Jousse called for a "rhythmo-typography" of the biblical material to enable the discernment of its spoken rhythms and balance,[33] while acknowledging the inherent challenges of graphically depicting auditory phenomena.[34] I have argued for the use of sound mapping, the visual display of audible evidence, to illustrate audible patterns in written compositions and to better situate the interpretive task in the context of ancient media culture.

What Is a Sound Map?

A sound map is a visual display of audible evidence. Sound mapping analyzes ancient written works as spoken sound. Sound maps admit a variety of graphic formats and facilitate various analytical techniques, but in their simplest form, sound maps graphically display audible patterns in ancient Greek compositions. The theoretics for sound mapping are set forth in *Sound Mapping the New Testament*.[35]

Sound mapping entails an analytical process, not a full-scale interpretive method. It serves as an essential prelude to interpretation because it discerns the structures that organize written compositions and facilitate their storage in and retrieval from memory. As does Jousse, sound mapping affirms that the fundamental language unit is not the word but the sound group in which it is embedded. Jousse discerned "propositions" that compose these units while sound mapping employs the ancient designation for a grammatically coherent unit of speech, the colon.

The procedures for sound mapping derive from ancient reflections on Greek composition. *Sound Mapping the New Testament* explores the Greek notion of συμπλοκή, the primary metaphor for written composition in Greek antiquity. Συμπλοκή denotes "combination," but the term designates a particular kind of combination and not ordinary mixing.

---

33. Jousse, *Memory*, 237.
34. Jousse, *The Oral Style*, 102; Jousse, *Memory*, 149.
35. Lee and Scott, *Sound Mapping*.

Συμπλοκή refers to situations in which elements are combined under tension and become indistinguishable from each other after having been combined. The word can refer to a wrestling hold and even to sexual intercourse but most often συμπλοκή refers to weaving, where warp and weft threads combine to form an integral fabric.

Although the metaphor of woven fabric for written composition may seem opaque to modern readers, its aptness appealed to ancient writers for whom the processes of textile production connected more intimately with daily experience. The metaphor analogizes a written manuscript to the organized warp threads on a loom, while the weft symbolizes the human voice, a composition's sound when spoken aloud. The warp establishes a woven fabric's structure but without the weft, no fabric exists; its warp threads hang loose and possess no integrity. Similarly, according to the ancient metaphor of written composition as συμπλοκή, a composition comes into existence only when actualized by vocal sound. Without the human voice, a written composition lacks integrity. Just as a woven fabric requires both warp and weft, the interlacement of speech and writing constitute an ancient written composition.[36]

Συμπλοκή as a metaphor for written composition highlights the creative tension between speech and writing and their interlacement in ancient Greek composition, just as warp and weft threads must be held under tension to be interlaced to form a woven fabric. The ancient media environment cannot properly be described as *orality*, in the sense of that term as it applies to the epic tradition, nor should it be characterized as *performance*, as that term relates to the rhetorical tradition. Neither are modern notions of reading and writing as silent and private endeavors appropriate to the ancient media environment. Instead, written composition in antiquity used both written and oral materials in a manner that reflects a deep interpenetration of writing and speech in memorial space, even in communities with little or no literacy. Sound mapping serves as a valuable analytical tool precisely because it explores this interlacement of speech and writing in compositional συμπλοκή.

Ancient Scribal Practice

Recent scholarship exploring ancient scribal practice facilitates a more comprehensive understanding of the ways that speech and writing

---

36. Lee and Scott, *Sound Mapping*, 72–77.

interpenetrate in ancient literary composition than we find in Jousse's work. Alan Kirk's *Q in Matthew: Ancient Media, Memory, and Early Scribal Transmission of the Jesus Tradition* richly describes ancient scribal practice, especially as it pertains to the Synoptic tradition. Kirk explores scribal techniques with particular attention to source utilization and asks how these techniques inform our understanding of the compositional process active in the Jesus tradition. Kirk observes that the two-document hypothesis has so far failed to explain adequately how Luke and Matthew used their sources, Mark and Q, in composing their Gospels.[37] He set out to test the provisions of the two-document hypothesis against analogous examples of source utilization in ancient scribal practice. As test cases, Kirk examined the primary passages in Matthew's Gospel that have given scholars reason to challenge the two-document hypothesis: Matthew's rearrangement of Q sayings in the Sermon on the Mount and his transpositions of Mark's narrative in Matt 8–12. Kirk hypothesizes that Matthew would have employed a single set of scribal practices to incorporate both sources into his Gospel, so Kirk set out to discover what these compositional practices may have entailed. In Kirk's and my analysis, "Matthew" refers to the unknown evangelist of the First Gospel, not an apostle of Jesus or one of his "transfer-transcribers."

Kirk's exploration of ancient scribal practice emphasizes two important concepts for our purposes. The first is the notion of the scribe, not as "transfer-transcriber," as Jousse maintains, but as tradent.[38] Like Kim Haines-Eitzen, who argues that Christian scribes were active users of the traditions they copied,[39] Kirk insists that ancient scribes of the Synoptic tradition occupied the role of tradent as preservers of tradition for the communities they served. Scribes served neither as mere copyists who simply transcribed material from one physical surface to another, nor as authors in the modern sense, with our emphasis on individual creativity. Instead, scribal tradents strove to preserve faithfully those traditions deemed worthy of and useful to their communities. Such a task, Kirk argues, necessarily implies an ethical responsibility to reshape the traditions they transmit so as to address their community's unique circumstances.[40] Thus we find a saying such as Matt 13:52, "a scribe trained for

---

37. Kirk, *Q in Matthew*, 151–83, 306–9.
38. Kirk, *Q in Matthew*, 40–42, 110–23.
39. Haines-Eitzen, *Guardians*, 16, 130.
40. Kirk, *Q in Matthew*, 97.

the kingdom of heaven . . . brings from his treasure (θησαυρός) the new and the old,"⁴¹ an aphorism that also figures prominently in Jousse's work as a figure for the composition of the Gospels.⁴² The treasure to which Matt 13:52 refers is memory; in fact, θησαυρός typically functions as a powerful metaphor for memorial space in the ancient world.⁴³

The second important concept for the present argument that Kirk employs is the memorial function of *topoi*. Kirk explains in detail how ancient memorial arts trained the memory to store both written and oral traditions for reliable retrieval. He emphasizes that materials stored in memory were arranged in structured sequences by conventional *topoi*, and that both the storage and retrieval of such materials was heavily influenced by the physical characteristics of their sources.⁴⁴ In the written Q source, for example, component sayings were organized on papyrus rolls by *topoi*, which were committed to memory in an ordered sequence.⁴⁵ When accessed in memory, those *topoi* were mentally scanned forward in sequence. Individual sayings became available in memorial space only when their governing *topos* was activated in memory.⁴⁶

Kirk's reconstruction of this method of source utilization improves upon Jousse's notion of "pearl-lessons," individual sayings or oral teachings, and "counter-necklaces," the linear sequences in which they were supposedly arranged.⁴⁷ Jousse envisioned elements of oral tradition organized in groups like beads on a string and connected by "clamp-words,"⁴⁸ which Jousse extended to "clamp-*sounds*" (italics in the original), repeated sounds and rhyming sounds that associate materials stored in memory. Sound mapping, too, shows the fundamental role played by the repetition of sounds in phonemes, syllables, and cola, in building a composition's structure.⁴⁹ Still, Jousse's schema failed to account for the different arrangements of sayings in Q and Matthew's Sermon on the Mount, whereas Kirk's reconstruction of Matthew's use of Q materials arranged by *topoi* more successfully accounts for the Sermon's final form. Sound

41. Kirk, *Q in Matthew*, 183.
42. Jousse, *Memory*, 152; Jousse, *The Oral Style*, 147.
43. Kirk, *Q in Matthew*, 143; Lee and Scott, *Sound Mapping*, 66.
44. Kirk, *Q in Matthew*, 131–42.
45. Kirk, *Q in Matthew*, 181–82.
46. Kirk, *Q in Matthew*, 136–37.
47. Jousse, *Memory*, 56–68.
48. Jousse, *Memory*, 55–56, 386.
49. Lee and Scott, *Sound Mapping*, 135–58.

mapping takes the next step by illustrating how audible signals mediate the compositional processes Kirk describes.

Kirk concludes that Matthew's scribal project consisted of using Mark's Gospel as his narrative frame, connecting Q sayings to narrative pegs in Mark and diverging from his sources when incorporating them into his own new deliberative framework. Matthew's variations from Q, Kirk explains, often stem from the fact that he accesses Q sayings in forward order by *topos*, not by individual saying.[50] Consistent with typical scribal practice, Kirk observed, sometimes Matthew also scans a source in forward order multiple times to retrieve appropriate sayings.[51]

Kirk's masterful study accounts in meticulous detail for Matthew's rearrangements of his source material and for the deep interpenetration of speech and writing in memorial culture. His analysis also fills critical gaps in the two-document hypothesis and affirms its value in accounting for the literary relationships among the Synoptic Gospels. Although Kirk does not finally resolve, or claim to resolve, all the challenges that the two-document hypothesis presents, important implications of his work abound. Significant for our purpose is Kirk's finding that variation from a source derives from a scribe's persuasive goal and not from the type of source, written or oral.[52] Although it has become common to associate variation from a source with oral transmission and alignment with a source with written transmission, Kirk points out that ancient scribal practice and Matthew's compositional project demonstrate otherwise. Kirk writes, "The media vectors moved in both directions: the material, spatial, and visual properties of the written artifact affected and reacted upon the oral enactment and oral utilization of the work."[53] Thus oral traditions can be retrieved reliably from the memorial θησαυρός without variation, just as compositions can diverge significantly from written sources depending upon a scribe's purpose. Finally, Kirk's study demonstrates the importance of structure in written compositions, and especially the extent to which the physical structure of a written tradition influences its storage in memory, its subsequent retrieval, and its

---

50. Kirk, *Q in Matthew*, 215.
51. Kirk, *Q in Matthew*, 86.
52. Kirk, *Q in Matthew*, 218.
53. Kirk, *Q in Matthew*, 107.

incorporation into a new composition.⁵⁴ The following analysis will illustrate these dynamics.

Once Again, Sound

Kirk's work on ancient scribal practice as it pertains to Matthew's Gospel analyzes the gospel's final form in terms of written-source utilization. His focus on written materials should not be understood to diminish the importance of speech and memory. Kirk affirms that conventional *topoi* were available primarily from memory, even when written sources were used. Moreover, Kirk paved the way for sound analysis in his acknowledgment that the access to materials stored in memory was "assisted by the acoustic channel."⁵⁵ Sound is the key for storing a composition in memory, for accessing traditional materials in memorial space, and for unifying elements in a new configuration. Thus, Matthew's συμπλοκή preserves traditional materials in a manner that is heavily influenced by Q's physical characteristics as Matthew establishes a *new* mnemonic structure for his own composition. The structures that organize source material in memory and account for its retrieval in memorial space are built and implemented by sound.

Since both Jousse and Kirk prominently illustrate their proposals about gospel composition with reference to the Sermon on the Mount, three examples from the Sermon will illustrate how sound mediates both memorial composition and auditory reception.⁵⁶

Example #1: The Beatitudes

The Beatitudes exhibit primary strategies of Matthew's συμπλοκή throughout the Sermon on the Mount. Sound mediates these strategies. A sound map reveals how audible cues activate Q *topoi* in memorial space, trigger connections to Matthew's programmatic concerns, and establish a new structural framework for the Sermon and for the gospel.

---

54. Kirk, *Q in Matthew*, 107.
55. Kirk, *Q in Matthew*, 144.
56. For sound maps and fuller treatments of the audible patterns in the Sermon on the Mount see Lee, "A Method for Sound Analysis"; Lee, "Matthew: The Musical"; Lee, "Melody in Manuscript"; Lee, "Sound and Structure"; Lee and Scott, *Sound Mapping*; and Scott and Dean, "Sound Map of the Sermon."

The Beatitudes in Matthew and Q

Matthew 5:3–11	Q 6:20b–23
Μακάριοι οἱ πτωχοὶ τῷ πνεύματι ὅτι . . . μακάριοι οἱ πενθοῦντε ὅτι . . . μακάριοι οἱ πραεῖς ὅτι . . .	Μακάριοι οἱ πτωχοὶ ὅτι . . . [μακάριοι οἱ κλαίοντες νῦν ὅτι . . .]
μακάριοι οἱ πεινῶντες καὶ διψῶντες τὴν δικαιοσύνην ὅτι . . . μακάριοι οἱ ἐλεήμονες ὅτι . . . μακάριοι οἱ καθαροὶ τῇ καρδίᾳ ὅτι . . . μακάριοι οἱ εἰρηνοποιοί ὅτι . . . μακάριοι οἱ δεδιωγμένοι δικαιοσύνης ὅτι . . .	μακάριοι οἱ πεινῶντες νῦν ὅτι . . .
μακάριοί ἐστε ὅταν ὀνειδίσωσιν ὑμᾶς . . . χαίρετε καὶ ἀγαλλιᾶσθε . . .	μακάριοί ἐστε ὅταν μισήσωσιν ὑμᾶς . . . χάρητε ἐν ἐκείνῃ τῇ ἡμέρᾳ . . . καὶ σκιρτήσατε . . .

Matthew preserves the Q beatitudes (6:20b–23) and their familiar and distinctive sound signature: repeated initial sounds (μακάριοι οἱ)[57] and a repeating internal format for component units in the Beatitudes sequence (μακάριοι οἱ . . . ὅτι . . .). His first four beatitudes (5:3–6) intensify the effect of repeated initial sounds by naming the blessed groups using an initial π sound (οἱ πτωχοί, οἱ πενθοῦντες, οἱ πραεῖς, οἱ πεινῶντες). Matthew achieves this effect by means of two modifications of the Q beatitudes. First, he moves the third Q beatitude (μακάριοι οἱ κλαίοντες) into second position and changes the name of the blessed group from οἱ κλαίοντες to οἱ πενθοῦντε. He also changes their fate from γελάσετε to παρακληθήσονται, reiterating the initial π sound in both modifications. With only a slight shift in meaning, Matthew thereby intensifies Q's repetition of opening sounds by repeating an initial π sound. Matthew's second strategy to intensify Q's repeated initial sounds is to insert a third beatitude (μακάριοι οἱ πραεῖς) before Q's third beatitude, again reiterating the initial π sound in the name of the blessed group. Then, Q's third (Matthew's fourth) beatitude (μακάριοι οἱ πεινῶντες) sustains the pattern, repeating an initial π sound. Thus Matthew's first four beatitudes transmit Q's first three beatitudes while reinforcing their distinctive sound shape.

After Matthew's first four beatitudes and between Q's third and fourth beatitudes, Matthew inserts four beatitudes of unknown provenance (5:7–10) that reflect his programmatic concerns. He fashions

---

57. Jousse, too, notes the significance of repeated initial sounds in the Beatitudes, see Jousse, *Memory*, 239.

this new material in the Q beatitude format (μακάριοι οἱ ... ὅτι ...) and frames them in his fourth (5:6) and eighth beatitudes (5:10) with a repetition of ἡ δικαιοσύνη, one of Matthew's primary narrative themes. Audible links connect all of Matthew's added beatitudes to subsequent Sermon *topoi*. Most of these audible links derive from Q, suggesting that sound triggers these connections in memorial space and contributes to the coherence of Matthew's emerging set of Sermon *topoi*.

Matthew's Innovations on Q Beatitude Sounds

μακάριοι οἱ <u>πτωχοί</u> τῷ πνεύματι ...
μακάριοι οἱ <u>π</u>ενθοῦντε ...
μακάριοι οἱ <u>π</u>ραεῖς ...
μακάριοι οἱ <u>π</u>εινῶντες καὶ διψῶντες <u>τὴν δικαιοσύνην</u> ...
μακάριοι <u>οἱ ἐλεήμονες</u> ...
μακάριοι <u>οἱ καθαροὶ τῇ καρδίᾳ</u> ...
μακάριοι <u>οἱ εἰρηνοποιοί</u> ...
μακάριοι <u>οἱ δεδιωγμένοι</u> ἕνεκεν <u>δικαιοσύνης</u> ...
μακάριοί ἐστε ὅταν ὀνειδίσωσιν ὑμᾶς ...
χαίρετε καὶ ἀγαλλιᾶσθε ...

Kirk points out that the added beatitudes also thematically link with subsequent and distinctive Matthean *topoi* that function programmatically for the Sermon and the gospel.[58] A sound map of the M beatitudes reveals that audible cues, many of which come from Q, trigger subsequent Matthean *topoi*.

---

58. Kirk, *Q in Matthew*, 190-93.

Audible Cues from Q in Matthew's Beatitudes

Matthew's beatitude	Later echoes in Matthew's Sermon	Q parallels
5:5 μακάριοι οἱ πραεῖς, ὅτι αὐτοὶ κληρονομήσουσιν **τὴν γῆν**.	5:13 ὑμεῖς ἐστε τὸ ἅλας **τῆς γῆς**...	//Q 14:34
	5:18 ... ἕως ἂν παρέλθῃ ὁ οὐρανὸς καὶ **ἡ γῆ** ...	//Q 16:17
	5:35 ... μήτε ἐν **τῇ γῇ** ...	No Q parallel
	6:10 ... ὡς ἐν οὐρανῷ καὶ ἐπὶ **γῆς**	//Q 11:2-4 (does not include ἡ γῆ)
	6:19 μὴ θησαυρίζετε ὑμῖν θησαυροὺς ἐπὶ **τῆς γῆς**	//Q 12:43 (does not include ἡ γῆ)
5:7 μακάριοι οἱ **εἰρηνοποιοί**, ὅτι αὐτοὶ υἱοὶ θεοῦ κληθήσονται.	6:2-4"Ὅταν οὖν ποιῇς **ἐλεημοσύνην μὴ** ... σοῦ δὲ ποιοῦντος **ἐλεημοσύνην** ... ὅπως ᾖ σου ἡ **ἐλεημοσύνη**	No Q parallel
5:8 μακάριοι οἱ καθαροὶ **τῇ καρδίᾳ**, ὅτι αὐτοὶ τὸν θεὸν ὄψονται.	5:28 πᾶς ὁ βλέπων γυναῖκα πρὸς τὸ ἐπιθυμῆσαι αὐτὴν ἤδη ἐμοίχευσεν αὐτὴν ἐν **τῇ καρδίᾳ** αὐτοῦ.	No Q parallel
	6:21 ... ὅπου γάρ ἐστιν ὁ θησαυρός σου, ἐκεῖ ἔσται καὶ **ἡ καρδία** σου.	//Q 12:34
5:9 μακάριοι οἱ εἰρηνοποιοί, ὅτι αὐτοὶ **υἱοὶ** θεοῦ κληθήσονται.	5:45 ... ὅπως γένησθε **υἱοὶ** τοῦ πατρὸς ὑμῶν τοῦ ἐν οὐρανοῖς.	//Q 6:35
5:10 μακάριοι οἱ **δεδιωγμένοι** ἕνεκεν δικαιοσύνης, ὅτι αὐτῶν ἐστιν ἡ βασιλεία τῶν οὐρανῶν.	5:11 μακάριοί ἐστε ὅταν ὀνειδίσωσιν ὑμᾶς καὶ **διώξωσιν**	//Q 6:22
	5:44 ... προσεύχεσθε ὑπὲρ τῶν **διωκόντων** ὑμᾶς	No Q parallel

As Kirk has argued,[59] Matthew's memorial competence in his sources enables him to navigate Q *topoi* nimbly as he structures his own programmatic concerns.

Having amplified distinctive audible features of the Q beatitudes (repeated initial sounds and a repeating format for each beatitude), Matthew sustains the use of repeated initial sounds throughout the Sermon and uses audible cues to link new sections of the Sermon to previous sections. For example, the final Q beatitude shifts from the third grammatical person (μακάριοι οἱ πτωχοί) to the second person (μακάριοί ἐστε). Matthew preserves both this shift to the second person and the full, fourth Q beatitude in his ninth beatitude. In the subsequent Sermon section (5:13-16), Matthew maintains the second grammatical person and introduces the salt-and-light sayings with the same initial sounds (ὑμεῖς ἐστε τὸ ἅλας τῆς γῆς [5:13]; ὑμεῖς ἐστε τὸ φῶς τοῦ κόσμου [5:14]), deviating from the format of his source, Q14:34-35 (salt) and Q11:33 (light).

---

59. Kirk, *Q in Matthew*, 115, 192, 194.

In the following and highly redactional section (5:17-20), Matthew sets up an antithetical structure that opens with a negative imperative (μὴ νομίσητε), followed by an οὐκ/ἀλλὰ construction, a format absent from the Q parallel (Q 16:16-17). Again, Matthew here builds on a Q *topos* but alters its format to comport with his unique, emerging structure. He elaborates the antithetical format created in 5:17-20 in his next Sermon section, the antitheses (5:21-48). While exhibiting a clear antithetical structure, the antitheses all begin with repeated initial sounds (ἠκούσατε ὅτι ἐρρέθη [τοῖς ἀρχαίοις]) and employ the same internal format in each component unit. That format draws a sharp antithesis between the opening formula for each component section (ἠκούσατε ὅτι ἐρρέθη) and Jesus's subsequent teaching, introduced in all five component units by ἐγὼ δὲ λέγω ὑμῖν. In this way the audible organization of the antitheses aligns both with the antithesis format established in 5:17-20 and with the sound structure employed in the Beatitudes and the salt-and-light section. Implementation of these techniques requires a more sophisticated compositional strategy than the use of repeated "clamp-words," as Jousse proposes, since they do not depend solely on simple, sequential repetition but also on the artful arrangement of key sounds to build a complex structure.

Structure of Matt 5:3-48

(5:3-12)
Μακάριοι οἱ ... **ὅτι** αὐτῶν (αὐτοί)... (8x)
μακάριοί ἐστε ...

(5:13-16)
Ὑμεῖς ἐστε τὸ ἅλας τῆς γῆς ...
Ὑμεῖς ἐστε τὸ φῶς τοῦ κόσμου ...

(5:17-20)
Μὴ νομίσητε ὅτι ἦλθον καταλῦσαι τὸν νόμον ἢ τοὺς προφήτας
    οὐκ ἦλθον καταλῦσαι
    ἀλλὰ πληρῶσαι

(5:21-48)
Ἠκούσατε ὅτι ἐρρέθη τοῖς ἀρχαίοις Οὐ φονεύσεις ...   ἐγὼ δὲ λέγω ὑμῖν ...
Ἠκούσατε ὅτι ἐρρέθη Οὐ μοιχεύσεις ...   ἐγὼ δὲ λέγω ὑμῖν ...
Πάλιν ἠκούσατε ὅτι ἐρρέθη τοῖς ἀρχαίοις Οὐκ ἐπιορκήσεις ...   ἐγὼ δὲ λέγω ὑμῖν ...
Ἠκούσατε ὅτι ἐρρέθη Ὀφθαλμὸν ἀντὶ ὀφθαλμοῦ ...   ἐγὼ δὲ λέγω ὑμῖν ...
Ἠκούσατε ὅτι ἐρρέθη Ἀγαπήσεις τὸν πλησίον σου ...   ἐγὼ δὲ λέγω ὑμῖν ...

Example #2: The Lord's Prayer

Matthew situates the Q Lord's Prayer in a section of the Sermon typically referred to as the cult didache (6:1–18). Kirk observes, "'Cult Didache,' the label often given to this sequence, smuggles in the notion that this is a distinct source,"[60] explicitly critiquing the notion that style indicates source and calling out a faulty reconstruction of ancient media culture. Matthew organizes this section around a set of *topoi* from his native tradition (and not from Q *topoi*) that enumerates conventional elements of cult piety: almsgiving, prayer, and fasting. Logically, Matthew associates the Q Lord's Prayer with the central *topos* on prayer in this triad, but in so doing he elaborates the three strategies employed earlier in the Sermon: preservation of audible cues in Q, repeated initial sounds, and a repeating internal format for component units within a section. To organize his repeating internal-unit structure, Matthew creates an antithetical format for the cult didache *topoi* similar to the format established in 5:17–20.

Repeating Format of Matthew's Cult Didache

Almsgiving	Ὅταν οὖν ποιῇς ἐλεημοσύνη μὴ ... ἀμὴν λέγω ὑμῖν ... σοῦ δὲ ...
Prayer	Καὶ ὅταν προσεύχησθε (//Q 11:2) μὴ ... ἀμὴν λέγω ὑμῖν ... σοῦ δὲ ...
Fasting	Ὅταν δὲ νηστεύητε μὴ ... ἀμὴν λέγω ὑμῖν ... σοῦ δὲ ...

Matthew amplifies this template with a "leftover" from the Q saying on light, οὐδεὶς λύχνον ἅψας εἰς κρύπτην τίθησιν (Q11:33). Although Matthew preserves this Q saying in 5:15, he does not include there Q's reference to hiding (εἰς κρύπτην). Matthew incorporates this "leftover" fragment in the antithetical structure he invents for his cult didache. Kirk shows how "using up" unused elements from previously activated *topoi*

---

60. Kirk, *Q in Matthew*, 202 n. 49.

aligns with normal scribal practice.[61] Matthew's cult didache iterates the phrase twice at the end of each component unit. (Matthew's third unit on fasting modifies the phrase to ἐν τῷ κρυφαίῳ.) Thus Matthew transforms a "leftover" from Q into a significant structural element that articulates a distinctive Matthean theme.

"Leftover" Fragment in Cult Didache Structure

Almsgiving	Ὅταν οὖν ποιῇς ἐλεημοσύνη
	μὴ ...
	ἀμὴν λέγω ὑμῖν ...
	σοῦ δὲ ...
	    ὅπως ᾖ σου ἡ ἐλεημοσύνη **ἐν τῷ κρυπτῷ**
	    καὶ ὁ πατήρ σου ὁ βλέπων **ἐν τῷ κρυπτῷ** ἀποδώσει σοι

Prayer	Καὶ ὅταν προσεύχησθε
	μὴ ...
	ἀμὴν λέγω ὑμῖν ...
	σοῦ δὲ ...
	    κλείσας τὴν θύραν σου πρόσευξαι τῷ πατρί σου τῷ **ἐν τῷ κρυπτῷ**
	    καὶ ὁ πατήρ σου ὁ βλέπων **ἐν τῷ κρυπτῷ** ἀποδώσει σοι

Fasting	Ὅταν δὲ νηστεύητε
	μὴ ...
	ἀμὴν λέγω ὑμῖν ...
	σοῦ δὲ ...
	    μὴ φανῇς τοῖς ἀνθρώποις νηστεύων ἀλλὰ τῷ πατρί σου **τῷ ἐν τῷ κρυφαίῳ**
	    καὶ ὁ πατήρ σου ὁ βλέπων **ἐν τῷ κρυφαίῳ** ἀποδώσει σοι

Additional audible signals from Q organize and reinforce the antithetical structure Matthew devises for the cult didache. The initial sounds of Matthew's internal-unit format (Ὅταν, ὅταν προσεύχησθε) repeat the opening sounds of the Q 11:2 *topos* on prayer (ὅταν προσεύχησθε), which Matthew preserves in the middle unit of his cult didache, the unit on prayer.

---

61. Kirk, *Q in Matthew*, 86, 215.

Q Elements in the Structure of Matthew's Cult Didache: ὅταν προσεύχησθε
Ὅταν οὖν ποιῇς ἐλεημοσύνη
    μὴ ...
    ἀμὴν λέγω ὑμῖν ...
    σοῦ δὲ ... ἐν τῷ κρυπτῷ ... ἐν τῷ κρυπτῷ

Καὶ **ὅταν προσεύχησθε**
    μὴ ...
    ἀμὴν λέγω ὑμῖν ...
    σοῦ δὲ ... ἐν τῷ κρυπτῷ ... ἐν τῷ κρυπτῷ

Ὅταν δὲ νηστεύητε
    μὴ ...
    ἀμὴν λέγω ὑμῖν ...
    σοῦ δὲ ... ἐν τῷ κρυφαίῳ ... ἐν τῷ κρυφαίῳ

In addition, the recurring statement, ἀμὴν λέγω ὑμῖν, that separates the prohibition (μὴ . . .) from the positive command (σοῦ δὲ . . .) in each component unit derives from the opening of Q 11:9: κἀγὼ ὑμῖν λέγω.

Q Elements in the Structure of Matthew's Cult Didache: ἀμὴν λέγω ὑμῖν
Ὅταν οὖν ποιῇς ἐλεημοσύνη
    μὴ ...
    ἀμὴν λέγω ὑμῖν ...
    σοῦ δὲ ... ἐν τῷ κρυπτῷ ... ἐν τῷ κρυπτῷ

Καὶ ὅταν προσεύχησθε
    μὴ ...
    ἀμὴν λέγω ὑμῖν ...
    σοῦ δὲ ... ἐν τῷ κρυπτῷ ... ἐν τῷ κρυπτῷ

Ὅταν δὲ νηστεύητε
    μὴ ...
    ἀμὴν λέγω ὑμῖν ...
    σοῦ δὲ ... ἐν τῷ κρυφαίῳ ... ἐν τῷ κρυφαίῳ

Matthew inserts the Q prayer into his antithetical format in his unit on prayer, appending the Lord's Prayer to the second iteration of his established pattern. In so doing, Matthew reiterates the opening syllable of προσεύχησθε (προς) in the two introductory statements he creates, one appended at the beginning of the cult didache before the first unit on almsgiving, and another as a preface to the prayer itself at the end of the cult didache's second unit on prayer.

Audible Structure of Matthew's Cult Didache

Προσέχετε [δὲ] τὴν δικαιοσύνην ὑμῶν …
μὴ ποιεῖν ἔ**μπροσ**θεν τῶν ἀνθρώπων πρὸς τὸ θεαθῆναι αὐτοῖς …

    Ὅταν οὖν ποιῇς ἐλεημοσύνη
        μὴ …
        ἀμὴν λέγω ὑμῖν …
        σοῦ δὲ … ἐν τῷ κρυπτῷ … ἐν τῷ κρυπτῷ

    Καὶ ὅταν **προσ**εύχησθε
        μὴ …
        ἀμὴν λέγω ὑμῖν …
        σοῦ δὲ … ἐν τῷ κρυπτῷ … ἐν τῷ κρυπτῷ

Προσευχόμενοι δὲ μὴ βατταλογήσητε ὥσπερ οἱ ἐθνικοί …
Οὕτως οὖν **προσ**εύχεσθε ὑμεῖς …

    Ὅταν δὲ νηστεύητε
        μὴ …
        ἀμὴν λέγω ὑμῖν …
        σοῦ δὲ … ἐν τῷ κρυφαίῳ … ἐν τῷ κρυφαίῳ

In these ways, Matthew's cult didache coheres audibly in sound and structure with previous Sermon sections. Matthew builds on audible cues from Q, then organizes Sermon sections using repeated opening sounds, a repeating internal format for component units in each section, and the antithetical structure Matthew devises in 5:17–20. Matthew's articulation of his established structural signals becomes more elaborate and innovative as the Sermon progresses, consistent with the demands of auditory delivery. Considering the complexity of Matthew's συμπλοκή in the cult didache, it should come as no surprise that the cult didache functions programmatically for both the Sermon and the Gospel, articulated through Matthew's distinctive concerns (such as hidden righteousness, right relationship with the Father, and the contrast between his audience and the scribes and Pharisees) and audibly keyed by repeating sound patterns.

Example #3: The Golden Rule

The so-called Golden Rule occurs in 7:12, near the end of Matthew's Sermon, and is generally thought to conclude the Sermon's penultimate section before the Sermon ends with Matthew's rendition of Q's warnings (Q

13:24, Q 6:43–45) and judgments (Q 46–49). Although no consensus has yet been reached in the history of interpretation regarding the Sermon's structure,[62] most commentators would accept the following list as a fair representation of the Sermon's macro-organization.

Structure of the Sermon on the Mount (Matt 5:3–7:27)
Beatitudes (5:3–12)
Salt and Light (5:13–16)
Validity of the Law (5:17–20)
Antitheses (5:21–48)
Cult didache (6:1–18)
Social issues (6:19–7:12)
Warnings and judgment (7:13–27)

Three problems attend this scheme. First, the scheme fails to account for the Sermon's unity. Why this list of sections? How are the sections related, and why do they occur in this order? Kirk's explanation derives from his understanding of ancient scribal practice. He argues that Matthew incorporates the Q sermon into his own deliberative framework by beginning with the Q sermon's opening *topos* (the Beatitudes), ending with the Q sermon's closing *topos* (two builders), and developing two "courses" of *topoi* in between. Matthew's first course of *topoi* (5:13–48), Kirk argues, concerns relationships with others while the second course of *topoi* (6:1—7:12) pertains to the human relationship with God. The two courses of *topoi* intersect in Matthew's cult didache, wherein Matthew implicitly argues that right relationships with God and others are inextricably linked: one must relate properly with others to be seen as righteous before God, and must relate properly with God to interact righteously with others.[63] Kirk's explanation is logical as far as it goes, but it does not fully account for the Sermon's unity or macrostructure, since these aims lie beyond his already ambitious project.

The second problem with the Sermon's macro-organization as depicted above pertains to the coherence of the Sermon section thought to end with the Golden Rule (6:19—7:12). Commentators have labeled this section variously as they strain to find some organizing principle or common thread unifying this collection of sayings.

---

62. For a summary of this lack of consensus, see Lee and Scott, *Sound Mapping*, 309–14.

63. Kirk, *Q in Matthew*, 205.

Third, an apparent disjuncture separates Matt 5:3—6:18 from the rest of the Sermon (6:19—7:27). Matthew 5:3—6:18, which includes the Beatitudes, the salt-and-light sayings, the section upholding the endurance of the law, the antitheses, and the cult didache, exhibits a coherence of sound and sense that often survives even in English translation. Shifts in topic and tone seem to align in these sections, so that structural boundaries appear natural and aligned with the series of topics articulated. In 6:19—7:27, however, the alignment of sound and sense seems to break down, so its structural skeleton remains elusive. Moreover, Matt 6:19—7:27 exhibits the highest level in the Sermon of variation from Matthew's sources. Kirk has shown that variation from a source occurs as Matthew aligns his source material with his own deliberative framework.[64] Kirk goes so far as to state that adjusting Q units to Matthew's deliberative framework and orienting them to "the cardinal points of Matthew's gospel itself . . . is the *raison d'être* of the Sermon M units."[65] But if intensive redactional activity tends to mark passages that reflect Matthew's persuasive purpose, why has the structure of this part of the Sermon, and thus its purpose, so far eluded the Sermon's commentators?

The traditional solution to these problems is to posit a structuring effect exerted by an *inclusio* formed by the phrase, ὁ νόμος καὶ οἱ προφῆται (the law and the prophets), which occurs in 5:27 and 7:12. But again, multiple problems trouble this proposal. First, the *inclusio* theory implicitly trivializes the portions of the Sermon that lie outside the *inclusio*. Yet we have seen how the Beatitudes function programmatically for the Sermon, both in terms of sound and sense. Their crucial thematic and structural role is difficult to explain for a section that lies outside the *inclusio* with its supposed structural significance. Second, the use of *inclusio* to unify an extensive run of material (5:17—7:12) has no apparent analog in normal ancient scribal practice. In other words, the dynamics of auditory reception do not support the *inclusio* theory. A single repetition of a phrase cannot effectively unify so many highly organized, intervening sounds, because the repeated phrase simply cannot persist in memory under such conditions. Ultimately, the *inclusio* theory fails to account for the Sermon's integrity as a product of Matthew's συμπλοκή.

The structural proposals described above share a common flaw: they defy the dynamics of auditory reception. Sound mapping resolves this conundrum that has bedeviled the history of the Sermon's interpretation.

64. Kirk, *Q in Matthew*, 204, 215–18, 221, 223.
65. Kirk, *Q in Matthew*, 217.

A sound map shows that the coherence of 6:19—7:12 seems problematic precisely because it incorrectly discerns the section's boundaries. As a matter of fact, the Sermon's final sections exhibit the same structural features that characterize the Sermon up to this point. When analyzed by sound, Matt 6:19—7:27 is shown to consist of three sections that employ repeated opening sounds and repeating internal formats that organize each section's component units.

Audible structure of Matt 6:19—7:27
(6:19-7:6)
       Μὴ θησαυρίζετε (repeated 5x) (6:19-34) (//Q12:33-34)
           μὴ μεριμνᾶτε (repeated 5x)
       Μὴ κρίνετε (7:1-5)
       Μὴ δῶτε τὸ ἅγιον τοῖς (7:6)
(7:7-20)
       Αἰτεῖτε καὶ δοθήσεται ὑμῖν (7:7-12)(//Q11:9-13)
          ζητεῖτε καὶ εὑρήσετε
          κρούετε καὶ ἀνοιγήσεται ὑμῖν
       Εἰσέλθατε διὰ τῆς στενῆς πύλης (7:13-14)
       Προσέχετε ἀπὸ τῶν ψευδοπροφητῶν (7:15-20)

(7:21-27)
       Οὐ πᾶς ὁ λέγων μοι Κύριε κύριε (7:21-23)(//Q6:46-47)
       Πᾶς οὖν ὅστις ἀκούει μου τοὺς λόγους τούτους (7:24-27)

As if to reinforce his established organizing strategies, Matthew multiplies repeating opening sounds in the first unit of section 6:19—7:6 (θησαυρ- [five times]; μὴ μεριμνᾶτε [five times]) and in the first unit of 7:7-20 where three imperative verbs ending in -εῖτε or -ετε occur in quick succession in 7:7 (αἰτεῖτε, ζητεῖτε, κρούετε). Imperative verbs with similar endings occur at the beginning of 7:13 (εἰσέλθατε) and 7:15 (προσέχετε), completing the established scheme of repeated sounds at the beginning of each component unit in a section. Moreover, the three final Sermon sections themselves represent a sustained antithesis, with one section organized by negative imperatives (μὴ θησαυρίζετε [6:16]; μὴ κρίνετε [7:1]; μὴ δῶτε [7:6]), followed by a section whose component units begin with positive imperatives (αἰτεῖτε [7:7]; εἰσέλθατε [7:23]; προσέχετε [7:15]). The Sermon ends with a section of warnings and judgments whose two component units begin with similar sounds (οὐ πᾶς

[7:21]; πᾶς οὖν [7:24]). Crucially, no structural division occurs at 7:12, the Golden Rule. Rather, 7:12 concludes the middle unit of the penultimate Sermon section 7:7–20.

Sound mapping reveals the Sermon's structural skeleton and thereby provides access to its distinctive persuasive purpose. The functions of Matthew's final Sermon sections cohere with organizational strategies employed throughout the Sermon and mediated by sound. Matthew's antithetical arrangement of 6:16—7:27 reshapes Q's parenesis, transforming its future-oriented apocalyptic framework into a present-oriented, sapiential outlook that focuses Matthew's audience on their present task: making disciples of the nations. Thus Matthew, as a scribe trained for the kingdom, transmits traditional materials reshaped by his συμπλοκή to deliver a radical message, urging his audience to look beyond the boundaries of their own community.

As Kirk has persuasively argued, Q's physical form influences the structure of Matthew's Sermon as he accesses Q memorially in forward order by *topos*. Matthew's συμπλοκή results in a Sermon that is formulaic for his Gospel, naming Matthew's thematic concerns and keying them with audible cues that associate formulaic elements with their subsequent elaboration outside the Sermon. Thus, Matthew's transmission of traditional materials ultimately articulates a radical message. Sound mediates this complex communicative task. Sound emerges as the primary means for navigating memorial space, the mechanism that implements Matthew's persuasive purpose, and the fundamental key to the Gospel's structure and meaning.

Conclusions

The foregoing examples from the Sermon on the Mount affirm that Jousse's basic insight holds: the New Testament Gospels exhibit formulaic characteristics, and these features present for analysis crucial clues to the Gospels' composition and reception. Jousse's notion of the oral style cannot fully account for the significance of these features since he attributes their formulaic quality to a stage of unwritten transmission. We now know that oral traditioning of this type can occur at various points and in multiple ways in a written work, and not just at a single, early stage of transmission. We also know that unwritten elements discernible in the Gospels, such as sequences of conventional *topoi* in the Sermon on the Mount (almsgiving, prayer, fasting), also feature prominently in the compositional process, in addition to a saying's balanced, rhythmic format.

Jousse's effort to align patterns discernible in the gospel narratives with precursors in the Aramaic targumim opens important avenues of understanding that can influence and sometimes correct our interpretation of their semantic meaning and cultural significance. It remains doubtful, however, that these Aramaic patterns can ultimately take us back to Jesus himself. A full assessment of Jousse's contributions to historical Jesus study and to translation informed by Aramaic targumic material ranges beyond this chapter's scope and my expertise. But significant for our purpose in evaluating Jousse's notion of the oral style is the notion of fidelity that they imply. For Jousse, the replication of Aramaic patterns in the Greek New Testament Gospels provides a pathway to original testimony about Jesus because, Jousse claims, balanced, formulaic patterns are designed to be recalled verbatim. Kirk's study substantially problematized this contention, showing that accuracy of transmission does not necessarily correlate to the type of source, oral or written. Kirk's examination of ancient scribal practice informs his reconstruction of the scribal tradent's work, which is also fundamentally concerned with fidelity. The tradent, Kirk argues, experiences an ethical imperative to faithfully transmit traditions held to be crucial to a community's identity. This means that a tradent necessarily reshapes those traditions to address a community's current concerns and is not restricted to verbatim repetition. Paradoxically, Jousse's model explains variations among the Gospels in terms of the individuality of the evangelists, who nevertheless transmit Jesus's teaching accurately, whereas Kirk's model insists that individuality held little value for scribal tradents, who necessarily reshaped conventional traditions they passed down in the service of remaining faithful to these valued traditions by rendering them accessible to and useful by their audiences.

Jousse nevertheless upholds a more fundamental insight: that communication in societies before the use of print relied primarily on speech and, therefore, on memory, to hand down their traditions, even when those societies used manuscripts. Kirk has reconstructed some of the memorial processes at work in the composition of a gospel that employs literary sources. His reconstruction affirms the value of the two-document hypothesis as a useful response to the Synoptic problem, while acknowledging that further refinement of this hypothesis may still be necessary. Kirk's reconstruction sharpens our understanding of the evangelist as a scribal tradent, reshaping and thereby faithfully transmitting valued traditions to a vital community. Kirk and Jousse both demonstrate that memory, not documents, serves as communication's archive and storehouse, and that memorial processes remain fundamental to oral and written composition.

Jousse's insistence on communication's physical, empirical basis provide an important corrective to interpretive methods embedded in a silent print culture. To be remembered and transmitted in memorial societies, traditions must first be spoken, heard, and remembered. Audible patterns facilitate the storage and retrieval from memory of a society's valued materials. The New Testament Gospels exhibit an oral style to the extent that they rely on sound patterns to organize traditional materials and thereby abet a tradent's reshaping of those materials as they are transmitted.

The three approaches to New Testament material discussed here—those of Jousse, Kirk, and sound mapping—all depend on close reading of written documents for evidence of auditory and memorial processes. All three recognize the inherent irony of searching for speech sounds in silent literature, but they also recognize that manuscripts are all we have of the ancient recitations that compose the New Testament. These approaches differ in their ultimate aims. Jousse identified a Palestinian oral style based on his observation in the Gospels of the kind of bilateral balance and parallelism found in the Aramaic targumim. This distinctive style, Jousse claimed, provides access to the oral composers of its underlying recitations. Kirk's project seeks to understand just one aspect of ancient composition, the use of written sources, without speculating about how those sources were first recorded. His detailed exploration of ancient scribal practice recognizes and fully appreciates the crucial roles that speech, memory, and the multimedia transmission of conventional *topoi* play in the ancient processes of handing down valued traditions. Where Jousse's methodology sought to uncover Jesus's own teachings as he spoke them, Kirk's analysis sheds light on the tradent's persuasive purpose in reshaping traditional materials for a new audience.

Sound mapping discerns a composition's audible structure, providing important clues to its composition and interpretation. With Jousse and Kirk, sound mapping seeks an empirical basis for analysis. Sound furnishes this empirical foundation. By plotting sound patterns in written works, sound mapping illustrates sound's fundamental role across the whole range of communication, encompassing spoken recitations, storage and retrieval of recited material from memory, and the persuasive power of written documents in their final forms, including documents composed using material from other written compositions. These different approaches share a focus on speech and memory in composition and contribute complimentary insights to New Testament interpretation.

Bibliography

Haines-Eitzen, Kim. *Guardians of Letters: Literacy, Power, and the Transmitters of Early Christian Literature*. Oxford: Oxford University Press, 2000.

Hezser, Catherine. *Jewish Literacy in Roman Palestine*. Texts and Studies in Ancient Judaism 81. Tübingen: Mohr Siebeck, 2001.

Hinton, David. *Awakened Cosmos: The Mind of Classical Chinese Poetry*. Illus. ed. Boulder, CO: Shambhala, 2019.

———. *China Root: Taoism, Ch'an, and Original Zen*. Boulder, CO: Shambhala, 2020.

Jousse, Marcel. *In Search of Coherence: Introducing Marcel Jousse's Anthropology of Mimism*. Edited and translated by Edgard Sienaert. Eugene, OR: Pickwick Publications, 2016.

———. *Memory, Memorization, and Memorizers: The Galilean Oral-Style Tradition and Its Traditionists*. Edited and translated by Edgard Sienaert. Biblical Performance Criticism Series 15. Eugene, OR: Cascade Books, 2018.

———. *The Oral Style*. Translated by Edgard Sienaert and Richard Whitaker. Albert Bates Studies in Oral Tradition 6. New York: Garland, 1990.

———. *Le style oral rythmique et mnémotechnique chez les verbo-moteurs*. 1925. Reprint, Paris: Fondation Marcel Jousse, 1981.

Kirk, Alan. *Q in Matthew: Ancient Media, Memory, and Early Scribal Transmission of the Jesus Tradition*. Library of New Testament Studies 564. New York: Bloomsbury T. & T. Clark, 2016.

Lee, Margaret E. "A Method for Sound Analysis in Hellenistic Greek: The Sermon on the Mount as a Test Case." DTheol diss., Melbourne College of Divinity, 2005.

———. "Matthew: The Musical." *Currents in Theology and Mission* 37 (2010) 479–87.

———. "Melody in Manuscript: The Birth Narrative in the Gospel of Matthew." In *Testimony, Witness, Authority: The Politics and Poetics of Experience*, edited by Tom Clark et al., 86–107. Newcastle upon Tyne: Cambridge Scholars, 2013.

———. "Sound and Structure in the Gospel of Matthew." In *From Text to Performance: Narrative and Performance Criticisms in Dialogue and Debate*, 97–130, edited by Kelly R. Iverson, 97–130. Biblical Performance Criticism Series 10. Eugene, OR: Cascade Books, 2014.

Lee, Margaret Ellen, and Bernard Brandon Scott. *Sound Mapping the New Testament*. 2nd ed. Biblical Performance Criticism Series 18. Eugene, OR: Cascade Books, 2022.

Scott, Bernard Brandon, and Margaret E. Dean. "A Sound Map of the Sermon on the Mount." In *Treasures New and Old: Recent Contributions to Matthean Studies*, edited by David R. Bauer and Mark Allan Powell, 313–80. Society of Biblical Literature Symposium Series 1. Atlanta: Scholars, 1996.

7

Jousse, Oral Composition, and the Gospel of Mark

JOANNA DEWEY

For this collection of articles exploring the importance of the work of Marcel Jousse for biblical studies, I shall focus on the formation of the Gospels, particularly the Gospel of Mark. I shall contrast Jousse's understanding of gospel formation with that of the form critics and finally with my own understanding of the Gospel of Mark as an oral composition. Then I shall address a few issues raised by Jousse's understanding of gospel development.

Before turning to my specific topic, I need to address some general issues in regard to Marcel Jousse. Jousse, the twentieth-century French anthropologist and Jesuit priest, was a "verbomotor"; that is, he was an oral communicator who used his voice and body to communicate, and who did scholarship demonstrating that many oral cultures functioned this way. Indeed, he would say that there are laws governing all oral cultures. He was strongly of the opinion that writing basically saps the life out of everything. He was antagonistic toward bookish culture, for he saw it as crippling oral memorial values. Rather, life is in the oral world; memory was/is central. Speech was fashioned to enable and reinforce memory.

Jousse describes oral compositions as follows: "The age-old structures of oral style bring into existence things far from ordinary, closely-strung 'pearls' with a hundred facets, shaped with infinite care by human mouths over centuries . . . They are pearls, jewels with many highlights, from which strings of beauty and truth have been made."[1] For Jousse, the Gospels are pearls. Although the time between Jesus and the composition of the Gospels is quite short, Jousse considers them pearls honed over centuries since Jesus and the Gospels were carriers of Aramaic targumic traditions that had been in the making for a long time. Jousse uses the term "pearl" both to refer to whole gospels and to refer to portions of a gospel. He uses the term "necklace" to refer to a whole gospel. Since there are seven clear divisions in the Gospel of Matthew, he also uses the term "seven-strand necklace" for a gospel. Small or larger portions are often referred to as facets of a jewel. For Jousse, the Gospels are oral jewels. "Necklace" always refers to a larger unit, usually a gospel. He also uses the term "counter-necklace" to refer to a whole gospel: "counter" in the sense of rhythmic counting—perhaps of the seven strands.[2] "Pearls," "jewels," and "facets" are used more or less interchangeably for smaller units within the Gospels.

Jousse was fascinated with Jesus (whom he called Yeshua, the Aramaic form of the name). He viewed him as a Galilean, Aramaic-speaking, peasant, an oral communicator in Israel's Aramaic targumic tradition. In first-century Palestine, people were speaking Aramaic and no longer understood Hebrew. The targumim are Aramaic renderings of the Hebrew texts. A literate scribe would read the Hebrew text aloud, and then a person whom Jousse calls a transferor would speak the passage in Aramaic, transferring it orally from Hebrew to Aramaic.[3]

A portion of Jousse's work is available in English in three volumes. The first is a book originally published by Jousse in 1924, *The Oral Style*. The other two are essays and dictations by Jousse and transcriptions of his lectures that were selected, translated, and introduced by Edgard Sienaert—*In Search of Coherence: Introducing Marcel Jousse's Anthropology of Mimism* (2016) and *Memory, Memorization, and Memorizers: The Galilean Oral Style Tradition and Its Traditionists* (2018). It is this last book that provides my understanding of Jousse's view of gospel formation. Jousse, however, never set forth his view in a comprehensive, systematic fashion. Rather he makes scattered references to Jesus, the Gospels, and tradition throughout many of the lectures and essays. I have done my best to be faithful to his ideas *and* to systematize his thought.

---

1. Jousse, *The Oral Style*, 240 n32.
2. Jousse, *Memory*, 126.
3. In due course the Targumic traditions were written down.

Jousse's work was taken up by some students of oral literature. Jousse and Milman Parry, the Homeric scholar, influenced each other. And Jousse may have influenced Albert Lord and Walter Ong. Lord and Ong have greatly influenced me in my understanding of oral composition and the formation of Mark. However, among biblical critics in the twentieth century, Jousse's work was used primarily by Birger Gerhardsson and a few others arguing for more verbal accuracy in the Jesus traditions.[4] Jousse's work was not taken up by the source critics, who tried to solve the interrelationships of the Synoptic Gospels on the basis of written texts and who were (and sometimes still are) obsessed over the minor agreements of Matthew and Luke against Mark. Nor was his work taken up by the form critics, who were attempting to investigate what they understood as the short oral phase of transmission. On the one hand, I learned a great deal about the Synoptic tradition in my 1970s graduate training from working through the Gospel parallels in Greek and working through Bultmann's form-critical *History of the Synoptic Tradition*. On the other hand, if Jousse's contemporary biblical critics and my own teachers had had some grasp of oral-style and oral-memory traditioning processes, biblical research would have advanced more quickly and, in my opinion, would have reflected the development of the gospel traditions more in alignment with ancient communication dynamics.

Given the failure of mainstream gospel scholarship to connect with Jousse's work, it is important to grasp his understanding of memorization. While Jousse speaks often of memorizing or memorization, he does *not* mean word-for-word, exact memorization the way we were taught to memorize in school—a concept of memorization based on the fixed print medium. Jousse does speak of Jesus explicitly teaching his disciples, and he certainly does see stability in tradition and memory. Yet he is fully aware of constant variations. He talks of fluid texts. He writes: "'Texts' are structural 'tissues,' 'webs' of formulas . . . They are 'fluid' in the sense that any one formula . . . can either be replaced by another formula of approximate equivalence, or omitted, or emphasized."[5] Jousse cites the following example:

---

4. A recent study of Gerhardsson suggests that he was offering a serious challenge to form criticism. In his own time, the form critics rejected his work primarily on a dating issue and did not deal with his challenge. See Kelber and Byrskog, eds., *Jesus in Memory*.

5. Jousse, *Memory*, 337–38.

And he saw him	and he fell to his face	
And he saw him	and he fell at his feet	
And he saw him	and he fell to his knees	
And he saw him	and he fell to the ground	
And he saw him	and he ran towards him	and he fell at his face[6]

The same variability applies not only to narrative as shown in the example above. It also occurs in sayings of Jesus found in the Gospels. Jousse shows the "recitational variants" in the Lord's Prayer:

Our Father who art in Heaven	Our *Abba* of Heaven
Our daily bread	Our bread to come
Remit us our debts	Remit us our sins
Do not lead us	Do not lead us
In temptation	To the test[7]

Jousse attributes the left-hand column to Jesus (found in Matt 6:9–13) and the right-hand column to Paul (found in Luke 11:2–4). Variations are to be expected.

Finally, the same flexibility applies to larger elements of composition as well. Episodes can be added in or omitted; the order of episodes can vary. Jousse writes:

> The users of the traditional memory know what to expect from substitutions, omissions, and transpositions of the structural elements regardless of whether these structural elements operated at the level of a strand, a half-strand, a pearl-lesson or a pearl-facet. Memorization is utilization and therefore adaptation.[8]

> The oral style is *intercalary*: interpolation allows insertion or removal of any facet-formula from the whole pearl-lesson to meet immediate rhythmo-catechistic needs. What we are confronted with today is the static form of what was essentially and primarily alive in the intercalary formation. Our fixed version of today was once one form *among many others* . . . Our inert, fixed text does not reflect what was once a moving and living mimodrama.[9]

Jousse notes that there are only twenty verses in the whole gospel material that are rigorously identical.[10] There is always variation and adapta-

---

6. Jousse, *Memory*, 338.
7. Jousse, *Memory*, 51.
8. Jousse, *Memory*, 134.
9. Jousse, *Memory*, 56 (italics original).
10. Jousse, *Memory*, 97.

tion. That is to be expected. So, while Jousse speaks often of memory and memorization, he does not mean word-for-word memory as those of us accustomed to print media expect.

Jousse's Understanding of Gospel Development

As noted above, Jousse was fascinated with Jesus. Jousse asserts that Jesus' followers, the twelve whom he calls "apprehenders," memorized Jesus' sayings in Aramaic, always with variations. They could do this quite easily not only because Jesus used repetition in his teaching but also because they themselves were immersed in the Aramaic targumic tradition. They were already familiar with the various formulas. The apprehenders not only learned Jesus' teachings but they also experienced his deeds. Peter, as the chief apprehender, strung the sayings and the deeds together on a "counter-necklace."[11] Jousse writes:

> No one who studied the necklace and the pearls in any depth, either in single units or as a global whole, could ever see them again as a higgledy-piggledy patchwork of odd bits and pieces composed haphazardly and separately. The sense of unity and direction they convey is such that only a single creative genius could have conceived such a brilliant and uniquely pedagogical tool.[12]

For Jousse, the creative genius is unquestionably Jesus. Peter comes next as the composer of the original counter-necklace.[13] Jousse pictures Peter in Jerusalem teaching the other eleven. Thus, for Jousse, a full gospel narrative of Jesus' sayings, deeds, and passion narrative takes shape in Aramaic very quickly and entirely orally.

Jousse posits a similar process of "transferring" the gospel narrative from Aramaic to Greek as that of the transferring of a biblical passage from Hebrew to Aramaic. Just as there were transferors who orally transferred (translated) the Israelite tradition from Hebrew into Aramaic, so there were *sunergoi* (the Greek word Paul uses for his coworkers) who transferred the oral Aramaic gospel into Greek orally, and who at some point put it in writing. We have the three written Synoptic Gospels, which Jousse views as simply oral variants. Similarly, I might add, Albert Lord,

---

11. Jousse, *Memory*, 107.
12. Jousse, *Memory*, 111.
13. Jousse, *Memory*, 107.

the scholar of oral literature, noted that the Synoptic Gospels seemed to him to "have the appearance of three oral traditional variants of the same narrative and non-narrative materials."[14] Scholars such as Jousse and Lord, who were familiar with oral literature with all of its oral variations introduced by different tellers and by the same teller on different telling occasions, perceive the Gospels as different oral versions.[15]

Jousse views the Gospel of Matthew as the fullest and the closest to Peter's Aramaic form of the gospel. He observes that we could not discern the seven "pearls" (portions) in Mark if we did not have Matthew's seven clearer divisions.[16] He posits that each of our Synoptic Gospels had its own *sunergos*, the coworker/transferrer who transferred the material from Aramaic to Greek. He notes that we do not know who the *sunergos* was for Mattai (that is, who transferred his Aramaic gospel into the Greek of our Gospel of Matthew). Jousse views Mark as the *sunergos* for Peter (transferring the Aramaic gospel into the Greek Gospel of Mark), and Luke as the *sunergos* for Paul (transferring the Aramaic gospel into the Greek Gospel of Luke).

If a biblical scholar trained in text-oriented source, form, and redaction criticism pursued Jousse's thought analytically, this scholar might conclude that there were three Aramaic gospels, each transferred into Greek once, resulting in our three canonical Synoptic Gospels. I do not think this is Jousse's view. I suggest, rather, that he imagines one Aramaic gospel first composed orally by Peter, the chief apprehender, which was then told and retold with many different variations, and then got transferred into Greek in various ways—again being told and retold. These transferors would have been bilingual in Aramaic and Greek. By associating Mark with Peter and Paul with Luke, Jousse is following the traditional associations and solidly grounding the authority of the New Testament writings. All three of the Gospels are transfers of the prior Aramaic narrative of sayings and deeds that was told in various ways. Jousse insists that the style of the Gospels is not fundamentally Greek, but a transfer of an original Aramaic retaining Aramaic patterns and formulas.

---

14. Lord, "The Gospels," 90.

15. If the Synoptic Gospels are oral variants, there is no need to posit a written source 'Q' to explain the agreements between Matthew and Luke that cannot be explained by their use of the Gospel of Mark. Is it perhaps that Q is just a figment of scholarly imagination?

16. Jousse, *Memory*, 107.

According to Jousse, writing comes in as a useful aide-mémoire, but the writing process is deeply informed by oral sensibilities and oral dynamics. Writing basically serves the oral memory process. A similar view is held today by the British text critic D. C. Parker, whose interest is in manuscript transmission, not oral dynamics. He works with individual ancient manuscripts not with our reconstructed standard Greek texts. Parker concludes, "The gospels were written rather to support than to replace the oral tradition."[17] He continues, "The written texts are only a part of the process by which the traditions about Jesus were passed on. The traditions were told and retold, written and rewritten, in oral tradition and in successive versions of texts."[18] Thus, Parker would agree with Jousse's supposition that each of our extant Greek Synoptic Gospels is simply a singular instance of multifold oral traditional renderings fixed in writing. Jousse writes, "Our fixed version of today was once one form *among many others* that remained living, acting and teaching."[19] One should not speak of the particular version of the writing we have today as the original. It is merely the particular example that happened to survive in writing.

Jousse trusts the historical accuracy of much that we would question today. We no longer share his faith in the accuracy of the transmission of Jesus' sayings. Most of us affirm Markan priority and consider Matthew and Luke as expansions of Mark, whether we consider the process to be totally dependent on manuscripts, or whether oral memory played the more significant role. Many of us doubt that Paul was fully familiar with an Aramaic gospel that Luke then transferred into Greek.[20] It should be observed that while Jousse assumes the historicity, his primary interest is in the oral style and memory and not in questions of historical fact.

In summary—one, Jousse insists on the formation of the Gospels as a largely oral process; two, Jousse sees the development of the tradition as highly dependent on specific individuals, known or unknown; three, he sees the basic gospel narrative taking form first in Aramaic by Peter; and, four, he sees the transfer from Aramaic into Greek as fundamentally retaining Aramaic structures and formulations. Above all, he

---

17. Parker, *The Living Text*, 19.
18. Parker, *The Living Text*, 179.
19. Jousse, *Memory*, 56.
20. Jousse, *Memory*, 110.

understands the process as fundamentally oral, even the composition of entire gospels. I will return to these issues below.

Form-Critical Understanding of the Development of the Gospels

Today, Jousse strikes us as historically naïve. On that point, he probably does not differ much from his contemporary New Testament source and form critics, although the form critics began increasingly chipping away at historicity. Where he differed strikingly from them was in his insistence that the creation and transmission of Jesus' and the gospel's message was a live, oral process based on memory. Here, Jousse understands the first-century oral/memorial media culture far better than the form critics.

Early twentieth-century scholars were studying the Gospels on media assumptions derived from the print culture they knew. It was the only media culture they knew since television and the internet were still in the future. The first serious challenge to the ubiquity of print norms for all cultures really did not come until 1962 when Marshall McLuhan—the man who coined "the medium is the message"—published *The Gutenberg Galaxy*. Print media are fixed as neither the oral nor the manuscript media are.

Once some consensus emerged on Markan priority, biblical scholars turned their attention to the question of how the gospel material developed from the time of Jesus around 30 CE to the existence of the first Gospel, Mark, dated around 70 CE. Since for them, writing was obviously primary, they considered the oral stage to be a phase that ended when the written Gospels were composed. German scholars were at the forefront of form criticism: Martin Dibelius published his first edition of *From Tradition to Gospel* in 1919, and Rudolf Bultmann published his first edition of *The History of the Synoptic Tradition* in 1921. Marcel Jousse initially published his work, *The Oral Style*, in 1924. Unfortunately, there was no fruitful dialogue between the two approaches.

The form critics turned their attention to studying individual pericopes (miracle stories, pronouncement stories, and so forth) and to looking for their *Sitz im Leben* (situation in life) where such stories would have been useful in preaching, teaching, or community formation. They did much fruitful work analyzing individual passages. However, they understood the process of development mostly as an anonymous community process—a process of adapting, expanding, and at times creating passages to meet the needs of particular situations. Since they assumed that writing was necessary to create longer sections of material consisting of multiple passages, they argued that the passages developed and traveled as single units in the oral phase. They considered longer sections of connected narrative, such as the passion narrative or the controversy stories of Mark 2:1–28, as early written texts. The transmission occurred in Greek. Then around the time of the Roman-Jewish War (in about 70 CE) someone who came to be called Mark put the scattered individual oral pericopes and a few written longer sections together in writing that was considered to lack literary order and coherence, however. In Bultmann's view, Mark was not master of his material.[21]

There was not much oral about this process. Given the approximately forty-year time gap between Jesus' time and a written gospel, composition had to have been an oral phase. For the form critics, the oral stage was merely a phase: the episodes had to survive and develop from the days of Jesus until they were incorporated in a written document. In contrast to Jousse's understanding, (1) there was no Aramaic narrative of Jesus' sayings and deeds; (2) indeed there was no narrative combining Jesus' sayings *and* deeds of any sort until around 70 CE when Mark compiled one in writing; (3) the development of the pericopes in the brief oral phase was largely a community process, not the work of gifted individuals, known or unknown; and (4) there was no consideration of a transfer from an Aramaic tradition to the Greek gospel. The visions of Jousse and the form-critics could hardly be more different.

My Understanding of the Development of the Gospel of Mark

From form criticism biblical scholars moved on first to redaction criticism. Assuming that the various pericopes were known as separate items and were only combined in writing, redaction critics sought to identify the editorial links in the Synoptic Gospels by which the gospel writers combined the individual units into a connected narrative. Both form critics (interested in the oral stage) and redaction critics (interested in the editorial work to combine the passages) were fundamentally asking historical questions of how and when the material emerged. Scholars, myself included, then moved on to narrative criticism, viewing each gospel

21. Bultmann, *The History*, 350.

in its entirety as an intentional written composition with a message to convey. As scholars looked at the Gospel of Mark as a narrative in its own right, we increasingly saw Mark as master of his material—indeed as the composer of a creative masterpiece.

Beginning in the early 1980s with the publication of Werner Kelber's *The Oral and the Written Gospel* and Thomas E. Boomershine's founding of *The Bible in Ancient and Modern Media* group as a program unit within the Society of Biblical Literature, Kelber and Boomershine have pressed biblical scholars to recognize the radically different and much more oral media world of antiquity. Literacy rates in antiquity were low, with perhaps as little as 5 percent of the population literate.[22] Even elite males, who were fully literate, functioned largely orally. They would compose by dictating to literate slaves, and slaves would frequently read a written text aloud to them. Reading was communal and aloud, and much storytelling and information was communicated orally with no or extremely little recourse to writing. Kelber's and Boomershine's work was (and in some ways still is) groundbreaking.

Learning from the work of Kelber and Boomershine and reading scholars in media and orality studies such as Walter Ong, Albert Lord, and John Miles Foley, I became convinced that *Mark was orally composed in Greek*. The gospel is of an appropriate length for oral performance and is composed in ways that facilitate remembering for both performer and audience. That the Gospel works well as an oral performance is evidenced by Alec McCowen's successful performance of it on London and Broadway stages beginning in the late 1970s. Further, I suggest that as an oral narrative it became widely known throughout the empire and therefore survived to become part of the New Testament canon, in spite of the fact that most of its content is contained in Matthew and Luke.[23] I am not the first or the only one to argue for oral composition of the Gospel of Mark. Antoinette Wire[24] and Pieter J. J. Botha[25] have presented sustained arguments for oral composition. Today it remains a minority position in academic scholarship although more scholars are looking at oral composition as playing an important role in the formation of Mark.[26]

---

22. Harris, *Ancient Literacy*; Hezser, *Jewish Literacy*.
23. Dewey, *The Oral Ethos*, 157–169.
24. Wire, *The Case for Mark*.
25. Botha, *Orality*, 163–90.
26. E.g., Elder, "The Media Matrix."

In the first place, the Gospel's style is thoroughly oral. Viewing Mark on the basis of Walter Ong's description of oral style demonstrates that Mark is throughout oral in style. Ong summarizes oral characteristics as follows: content is combined in additive rather than subordinating relationships; the structure is aggregative rather than analytic or linear; the content is also repetitious or 'copious,' close to the human world, agonistically toned, and empathetic and participatory rather than objectively distanced.[27] These characteristics describe Mark well.[28]

Furthermore, Mark composes material into a whole in ways typical of oral composition. In *Preface to Plato*, Eric A. Havelock argues that Plato's attack on poetry or mimesis in book 10 of the *Republic* is an attack on the oral mindset.[29] Plato considers the content of mimesis to be merely opinion or *doxa*, which has three limitations. One, it is made up of happenings (*gignomena*), not abstract thought; two, the happenings are concrete and can be easily visualized (*horata*); and, three, they are many (*polla*)—that is, pluralized, not organized according to cause and effect.[30] Mark has many miracles, two feeding stories, three passion predictions, and so forth. This oral mindset, as Havelock describes it, seems an excellent description of Mark's Gospel. Teaching is embedded in narrative; even the so-called Markan summaries can be easily visualized as distant film shots. Visualizing the story helps both the performer and the audience to remember and follow the story.

Havelock's essay on oral composition in *Oedipus Rex* is very helpful for understanding the seemingly unorderly composition of Mark.[31] He describes the oral method of composition as the *echo principle*:

> What is to be said and remembered later is cast in the form of an echo of something said already; the future is encoded in the present. All oral narrative is in structure continually both prophetic and retrospective ... Though the narrative syntax is paratactic—the basic conjunction being 'and then,' 'and next'— the narrative is not linear but turns back on itself in order to assist the memory to reach the end by having it anticipated somehow in the beginning.[32]

27. Ong, *Orality and Literacy*, 37–49.
28. Dewey, *The Oral Ethos*, 97–101.
29. Havelock, *Preface to Plato*.
30. Havelock, *Preface to Plato*, 181.
31. Havelock, "Oral Composition."
32. Havelock, "Oral Composition," 183.

Jousse, Oral Composition, and the Gospel of Mark   191

There could hardly be a better description of Mark's narrative.[33] In conclusion, Mark is throughout composed in an oral style. Composition in an oral style does not exclude the existence of written versions. I will come back to issues of oral/written interface.

In contrast to the form critics, and also distinct from Jousse, I argue further that Mark is not composing the narrative from scattered individual episodes but rather is building on a growing narrative tradition. As noted above, form criticism has customarily assumed that Mark composed the Gospel from the bits and pieces of oral tradition and perhaps from a short written source or two. All that we now know about how oral tradition operates suggests that this assumption of form criticism is wrong, deriving more from the critics' own immersion in print culture than from how tradition operates. Typically, tradition is remembered by gathering stories around a hero (fictional or real), not by remembering disparate individual episodes. The larger story consists of episodes connected by "and next," "and then," which the storyteller can combine in various ways in telling a larger narrative.

Studies from the three fields of folklore, oral tradition, and oral history all suggest that traditions are likely to coalesce into a continuous narrative or narrative framework fairly quickly. During the middle of the last century, Thorleif Boman, on the basis of his study of folklore, introduced to New Testament studies the thesis that traditions typically gathered into larger continuous narratives.[34] He concluded that no narrative based on history ever emerged out of individual items that circulated for decades independently. Rather such a narrative grew gradually into a more comprehensive narrative about a person.[35] Jan Vansina, the student of African oral traditions and oral history, asserted that traditions "adhere to the 'great man,'" coalescing into larger blocks of connected narratives about that person.[36] Walter Ong wrote, "Most, if not all, oral cultures generate quite substantial narratives or series of narratives."[37] All agree against the form-critical assumption of transmission of disparate, small episodes. It seems much more probable that Mark was building on, refining, and developing an oral tradition that had already created a

---

33. Dewey, *The Oral Ethos*, 63–78, 86–90.
34. Boman, *Jesus Überlieferung*.
35. Boman, *Jesus Überlieferung*, 31.
36. Vansina. *Oral Tradition*, 108.
37. Ong, *Orality and Literacy*, 140.

continuous, more-or-less coherent narrative. It should be noted that the development of an early continuous narrative does not mean that the early narrative is more historically accurate—or for that matter, less accurate. It just means a connected story is likely to begin early and gradually grow. Writing is not required to produce a longer narrative.

Of course, in the media world of antiquity, writing and orality constantly interacted. I would hazard that the Gospel of Mark was first put into writing around 70 CE shortly after it began to circulate orally. But the existence of a manuscript in writing does not stop oral performance. As Albert Lord noted, oral literature is a genre not a phase.[38] The Gospel continued to be told even after it existed in manuscript. As Jousse suggests, writing was used to support oral renderings. I think Mark was composed and transmitted primarily orally, but that does not exclude earlier and later written versions. We really cannot speak of an original Gospel of Mark, since beginning at the time when the person we call Mark put his individual stamp on the gospel story, followed by the repeated recirculation of the story between oral telling and written versions, we do not know how close our reconstructed Markan text is to what Mark told around 70 CE.[39] Jousse was surely correct when he observed, "Our fixed version of today was once one form *among many others* that remained living, acting and teaching."[40]

To summarize the similarities and differences between Marcel Jousse's picture of the composition of Mark and my own view: We both reject the position of the form critics that the episodes traveled individually until they were put together in writing. We both agree that the Gospel was composed orally. We both agree that manuscripts interacted with oral performances, and that our fixed version was not the original but rather one particular version that survived in manuscript form. We disagree about when and how the Gospel was composed. Jousse views Peter as the primary creator of the Gospel shortly after Easter. For Jousse, Mark is the transferor (*sunergos*) who heard Peter preach in Rome and who put down in Greek writing Peter's preaching. In contrast, I have argued that narratives grow and begin to take shape early but develop more slowly. I see the primary creative act as Mark's, who put his stamp on the growing oral narrative. Overall, Jousse was certainly correct to stress the central

---

38. Quoted in Keck, "Oral Traditional Literature," 114.

39. Our first manuscripts of more than very small fragments of Mark are fourth century. See Dewey, *The Oral Ethos*, 170–82; and Wire, *Performance*, 21–70.

40. Jousse, *Memory*, 56.

role of memory. Oral development and oral transmission of the Gospel of Mark was far more important than we biblical scholars have generally realized.

A Few Concluding Observations

First, was there a full Aramaic gospel connecting Jesus' life and death? Was Jousse correct in supposing Peter told and taught a fully connected narrative of Jesus' life and death? These are actually two questions. One, did Peter compose a full gospel narrative? As noted above, Jousse pictures Peter sitting in the Jesus community in Jerusalem teaching the disciples. I doubt it. No, it takes some time for a longer narrative to take shape, and for theological interpretation to evolve—from several years to a few decades. Stories do gather around a hero but not instantly.

Then, were there Aramaic connected narratives that were developing? Probably. Also probably Aramaic oral narratives interacted with Greek oral narratives. Scholars do not agree on how widely Greek was spoken in Galilee and Judea in the first century. We know the elite used Greek, and we generally assume the lower classes, who were overwhelmingly not literate, spoke Aramaic. It is possible that many spoke Greek as well. So it is likely that Aramaic narratives were developing, and that they interacted with the developing Greek narratives. Narratives or narrative? I would suggest most likely a basic narrative with many variations. My position of a basic oral narrative with multiple variations is similar to both Jousse's and Lord's positions. In regard to the existence of Aramaic narratives we cannot say anything more; we simply lack sufficient data.

Second, how much of the development of the gospel traditions was anonymous community evolution (as the form critics thought), and how much was the work of particular individuals whose names we often know (as Jousse posits)? I suspect it was the work of many, many individuals. One individual tells an account that he or she learned from someone else, and then another, and so on. Most of these individuals are anonymous—*we* do not know their names or geographic locations. (Storytellers probably were known in their local communities, and farther afield if they were traveling storytellers. Part of an audience's evaluation of a story was its evaluation of the performer.) Jousse and other scholars of oral literature stress that the individual storyteller stamps his or her own individuality on their storytelling. I think that the Gospel grew as various storytellers told and retold the narrative, adapting and expanding it. I think the Gospel of Mark has the imprint of a really gifted storyteller, and there may have been other gifted ones both before and after him. Are these individuals whose names we know? We undoubtedly know some of their names, but most of them we probably do not. In this sense, the form critics were right to posit anonymous development. If you posit, as I do, that the Gospel of Mark was composed in the East, not in Rome,[41] all we really know about Mark is that the name Mark, a common name, became associated with the Gospel of Mark. We know little if anything about the historical composer of the Gospel of Mark.[42]

Third, is the Gospel of Mark transferred from Aramaic, retaining Aramaic structures? I have already rejected the idea that Mark simply transferred Peter's original narrative into Greek and wrote it down. But a more fundamental question remains: Does the Gospel reflect Aramaic in its structures and rhythms, or is it simply in an oral Greek style? Jousse insists that the basic pattern of the Gospels is Aramaic not Greek. He states flatly, "The New Testament is not in Greek: It is a transfer in Greek of an original Aramaic text."[43] Furthermore, Jousse writes:

> The traditional system of transfer from Aramaic into Greek is such that, beneath the Greek translation, the Aramaic structures are easily perceived . . . [A] Greek writer, writing in Greek written style, could never have executed the astounding 'stylistic miracle' of unconsciously composing phrases that, once transferred into Aramaic, would be so very *characteristic* of the structures of Aramaic oral style, complete with its double bilateralism and its traditional formulaic parallelisms.[44]

The Gospel of Mark is certainly not composed in formal Greek written style. Bultmann's conclusion that Mark was not master of his material reflects the Gospel's lack of proper Greek written style. A comparison of Mark's style to that of Hebrews or Ephesians or even to the Gospel of Luke shows how much simpler and less sophisticated Mark's syntax is. Furthermore, Mark does contain structures similar to "Aramaic oral style, complete with its double bilateralism and its traditional formulaic parallelisms." Rather than a transfer from Aramaic, I would posit that Mark is composing in Greek using typical Greek oral style and patterning. Jousse

41. Dewey, "A Galilean Provenance."
42. For a different view, see Black, *Images*.
43. Jousse, *Memory*, 328.
44. Jousse, *Memory*, 265 (italics original).

argues for universal laws of oral composition, comparing Homeric, Vedic, Chinese, and Hebrew sources.[45] Oral patterns and formulations in Greek likely resemble oral patterns and formulations in Aramaic. What Jousse sees as underlying Aramaic is probably just Mark's *oral* Greek style. So I suggest that it is likely that the similarities to Aramaic are due to what Jousse would call the universal characteristics or laws of oral narrative, rather than to a specific transfer from Aramaic. The similarity of Mark's structures to those that Jousse sees as peculiarly Aramaic may just be similarities of typical oral discourse.[46] After all, we do not have much Koine Greek *oral* literature to compare with the Gospel of Mark.

While the style of Mark may be simply Greek oral style, the content of the Gospel clearly reflects the Aramaic targumic tradition. Jousse suggests that the transferors into Greek were likely Greek speakers and Palestinian thinkers.[47] Although I do not consider Mark a transferor of the tradition from Aramaic to Greek, Mark is certainly quite familiar with much of the Hebrew tradition and continually alludes to it. The composer of the Gospel of Mark might accurately be described as a Greek speaker and a Palestinian (or diasporic Jewish) thinker. I do not believe the Gospel of Mark was transferred from Aramaic, but the Gospel reflects great familiarity with the Jewish tradition.

In conclusion, then, Jousse has presented a substantial argument for the central role of oral memory in the composition of the Gospels. He is certainly correct that narratives the length of Mark can be composed orally. His rejection of the form-critical view that individual passages remained independent until they were combined in writing has stood the test of time and is becoming more widely shared by biblical scholars. Jousse shared his understanding of the historical reliability of the traditions with many early twentieth-century critics—an understanding we largely no longer share today. Thus some of his views seem naïve today. Finally, whatever the particulars, the process of gospel formation and transmission owes far more to oral memory and oral performance than is generally acknowledged. Scholarship would have advanced more speedily and more accurately if we had taken Jousse's challenges seriously in the last century.

---

45. Jousse, *The Oral Style*.

46. For a different view, see Chilton et al., eds., *A Comparative Handbook to the Gospel of Mark*.

47. Jousse, *Memory*, 99.

Bibliography

Black, C. Clifton. *Mark: Images of an Apostolic Interpreter.* Studies on Personalities of the New Testament. 1994. Reprint, Minneapolis: Fortress, 2001.

Botha, Pieter J. J. *Orality and Literacy in Early Christianity.* Biblical Performance Criticism Series 5. Eugene, OR: Cascade Books, 2012.

Boman, Thorleif. *Die Jesus-Überlieferung im Lichte der neueren Volkskunde.* Göttingen: Vandenhoeck & Ruprecht, 1967.

Bultmann, Rudolf. *Die Geschichte der synoptischen Tradition.* Forschungen zur Religion und Literatur des Alten und Neuen Testaments 29. Göttingen: Vandenhoeck & Ruprecht, 1921.

———. *The History of the Synoptic Tradition.* Translated by John Marsh. New York: Harper & Row, 1963.

Chilton, Bruce D. *A Galilean Rabbi and His Bible: Jesus' Use of the Interpreted Scriptures of His Time.* Good News Studies 8. 1984. Reprint, Eugene, OR: Wipf & Stock, 2013.

Chilton, Bruce et al., eds. *A Comparative Handbook to the Gospel of Mark: Comparisons with Pseudepigrapha, the Qumran Scrolls, and Rabbinic Literature.* New Testament Gospels in Their Judaic Contexts 1. Leiden: Brill, 2010.

Dewey, Joanna. "A Galilean Provenance for the Gospel of Mark?" *Forum,* 3rd ser., 2 (2013) 101–20.

———. *The Oral Ethos of the Early Church: Speaking, Writing, and the Gospel of Mark.* Biblical Performance Criticism Series 8. Eugene, OR: Cascade Books, 2013.

Dibelius, Martin. *Die Formgeschichte des Evangeliums.* Tübingen: Mohr Siebeck, 1919.

———. *From Tradition to Gospel.* Translated by Bertram Lee Woolf. The Scribner Library. New York: Scribner, 1965.

Elder, Nicholas A. "The Media Matrix of Early Jewish and Christian Literature: Reading Joseph and Aseneth and Mark as Textualized Oral Narratives." PhD diss., Marquette University, 2018.

Foley, John Miles. *How to Read an Oral Poem.* Urbana: University of Illinois Press, 2002.

———. *Immanent Art: From Structure to Meaning in Traditional Oral Epic.* Bloomington: Indiana University Press, 1991.

———. *The Singer of Tales in Performance.* Voices in Performance and Text. Bloomington: Indiana University Press, 1995.

Gerhardsson, Birger. *Memory and Manuscript: Oral Tradition and Written Transmission in Rabbinic Judaism and Early Christianity.* Translated by Eric J. Sharpe. Acta Seminarii Neotestamentici Upsaliensis 22. Lund: Gleerup, 1961.

———. *Memory and Manuscript: Oral Tradition and Written Transmission in Rabbinic Judaism and Early Christianity.* Translated by Eric J. Sharpe. Rev. ed. Biblical Resource Series. Grand Rapids: Eerdmans, 1998.

Harris, William V. *Ancient Literacy.* Cambridge: Harvard University Press, 1989.

Havelock, Eric A. "Oral Composition in the *Oedipus Tyrannus* of Sophocles." *New Literary History* (1984) 175–97.

———. *Preface to Plato.* Cambridge: Belknap, 1963.

Hezser, Catherine. *Jewish Literacy in Roman Palestine.* Texts and Studies in Ancient Judaism 81. Tübingen: Mohr Siebeck, 2001.

Jousse, Marcel. *Memory, Memorization, and Memorizers: The Galilean Oral-Style Tradition and Its Traditionalists.* Edited and translated by Edgard Sienaert. Biblical Performance Criticism Series 15. Eugene, OR: Cascade Books, 2018.

———. *The Oral Style.* Translated by Edgard Sienaert and Richard Whitaker. Albert Bates Lord Studies in Oral Tradition 6. New York: Garland, 1990.

———. *Le style oral rythmique et mnémotechnique chez les verbo-moteurs.* Paris: Beauchesne, 1925.

Keck, Leander E. "Oral Traditional Literature and the Gospels: The Seminar." In *The Relationships among the Gospels: An Interdisciplinary Dialogue,* edited by William O. Walker, Jr., 103–22. Trinity University Monograph Series in Religion 5. San Antonio: Trinity University Press, 1978.

Kelber, Werner. *The Oral and the Written Gospel: The Hermeneutics of Speaking and Writing in the Synoptic Tradition, Mark, Paul, and Q.* Philadelphia: Fortress, 1983. Reprint, Voices in Performance and Text. Bloomington: Indiana University Press, 1997.

Kelber, Werner, and Samuel Byrskog, eds. *Jesus in Memory: Traditions in Oral and Scribal Perspectives.* Waco: Baylor University Press, 2009.

Lord, Albert B. "The Gospels as Oral Traditional Literature." In *The Relationships among the Gospels: An Interdisciplinary Dialogue,* edited by William O. Walker, Jr., 33–91. Trinity University Monograph Series in Religion 5. San Antonio: Trinity University Press, 1978.

———. *The Singer of Tales.* Harvard Studies in Comparative Literature 24. Cambridge: Harvard University Press, 1960.

McLuhan, Marshall. *The Gutenberg Galaxy: The Making of Typographic Man.* Toronto: University of Toronto Press: 1962.

Ong, Walter J. *Interfaces of the Word: Studies in the Evolution of Consciousness and Culture.* Ithaca: Cornell University Press, 1977.

———. *Orality and Literacy: The Technologizing of the Word.* New Accents. London: Methuen, 1982.

———. *The Presence of the Word: Some Prolegomena for Cultural and Religious History.* New Haven: Yale University Press, 1967.

Parker, D. C. *The Living Text of the Gospels.* Cambridge: Cambridge University Press, 1997.

Vansina, Jan. *Oral Tradition as History.* Madison: University of Wisconsin Press, 1985.

Wire, Antoinette Clark. *The Case for Mark Composed in Performance.* Biblical Performance Criticism Series 3. Eugene, OR: Cascade Books, 2011.

8

Origin and Techniques of the Biblical Recitations[1]

MARCEL JOUSSE

Introduction: Man, Maker of Material and Intellectual Tools

When Man sought to create a physical tool, he invented those metals that, by fusion, make bronze, a fluid matter that hardens in the shape of the mold into which it has been poured.

When Man sought to create an intellectual tool, it was his gesture, in all its fluidity, that allowed him to capture the multitude of gestures in his surroundings.

This very fluidity, however, renders gesture fragile and transitory, and Man came soon to understand that the liquid bronze of his gesture could crystallize and solidify with the insertion of an element he had within him: rhythm. This is how we, humans, arrive at this most curious anthropological feature of the gesture—that is simultaneously fluid and solid.

Rhythm, a Tool of Solidification

Whenever any question about gesture in the tradition is brought up, these two elements must be taken into account: the gesture as fluid and the gesture as *rhythmically* solidified.

---

[1]. School of Anthropology, 19 March 1934. Original title: "Les récitations de style oral" [The Oral-Style Recitations].

It is pure genius to come to understand that rhythmizing the gesture is solidifying the gesture. And the brilliant invention of rhythm is realized from the beginning of all civilizations. The perception that "People always dance. They are perpetual dancers," was fundamentally wrong. People do not *dance*; they make "rhythmic gestures." How fortunate, because it is these rhythmic gestures that allow the solid transmission of their traditions! Likewise we are told, "All people started with poetry," creating the impression that people made rhythmed speech as a form of art. This is totally wrong. What they did was purely pedagogical and therefore utilitarian.

When at some stage the bronze axe replaced the flint ax, it was not because bronze was more artistic, but because bronze was easy to smelt and of unmatched solidity. Equally, when we come across rhythmic speech, it is not because it is more beautiful, but because rhythmic speech is more stable.

Do you see the need to understand the various stages the invention and use of human tools went through? I take the opportunity here to thank Mr. Chesneau,[2] whose diligent presence is always encouraging, but who also kindly offered me a small volume he wrote. It was when reading this that I made the connection between the bronze tool and rhythmed speech. There is this most curious thing indeed: that the making of the bronze axe and the making of the corporeal-manual gesture both happened as a result of the discovery of the *solidifiable fluid*. It is most interesting to see how physical and intellectual human tools follow each other.

It is this that makes the anthropological laws so valuable. Man has very few laws. Anthropologists will work for centuries, for millennia perhaps, and still, they will discover but very few anthropological laws.

At present, whenever we want to study the human being, we cut him up. Look at the poster advertising our courses: sociology, ethnography, ethnology, anthropology, linguistics, zoology... they all look like small pieces of Man seemingly impossible to put together again, chunks of a human serpent unable to locate its wounds and so to become whole again. This School's green poster, with its diverse titles, creates the impression of a science in search of itself.

What I attempt to do in linguistic anthropology is to show just how wide this field truly is.

---

2. Gabriel Chesneau (1859–1937), director of the School of Mines in Paris, a regular presence at Jousse's lectures.

The Unexplored Richness of the Anthropology of Gesture

A few minutes ago I was asked by a colleague, "But how will you manage to speak for years to come on a subject as narrow as language?" Alas! I would like to have at least another twenty years before me to do just the alphabet of this daunting matter.

In fact, language has never been studied. And there you have this remarkable man, one of the luminaries of this School, who wonders how one can speak of language for so long, when I, on the other hand, am terrified by the prospect of no more than some twenty-odd years to treat this subject!

Why such a question? Because no one has bothered about language. At the School of anthropology, I was met with great sympathy, but I am absolutely certain that no one knows anything about the subject, with one or two exceptions perhaps, such as Dr. Papillault,[3] who is, regrettably, gravely ill.

A few years ago, I was invited to give a lecture on gesture at a Belgian university. Before the lecture, Father Sertillanges,[4] a truly nice and remarkable man—you must have read his books and have heard him speak so eloquently—mused, "The psychology of gesture! How will he be able to speak for an hour on gesture? When a public speaker has made a gesture upwards, another downwards, another to the left, another to the right, that's more or less all one can say about gesture . . ." An intelligent man, he came to listen and told me afterwards, "I wondered what one could say about gesture. I see now that it is an immense subject that demands hundreds of years of research by a thousand scholars."

Invariably, when someone brings something new, the social milieu proves to be unprepared to receive it. And I am quite sure that if all those professors who figure on the poster were asked to teach my subject for twenty years, they would need at least twenty years prior to prepare. One does not waltz into a science, in mine no more easily than in any other. Richness and depth come with time.

If Mr. Chesneau were told, "Ten minutes suffice for one to understand algebra," I am quite sure he would answer, "I spent part of my life in algebra and I am far from having exhausted all the possible combinations of those little algebraic signs." My colleague's question about how I would

---

3. Georges Papillault (1863–1934), director of the École d'Anthropologie at the time of his death.

4. Antonin Sertillanges (1863–1948), professor of moral philosophy at the Catholic University of Paris.

fill my teaching hours when talking about gesture just proves how new the matter is and how little developed still and understood. Until now, no one has dealt with gesture as significative and logic expression: "What could you possibly say?" Let this dear professor rest assured: I have programs ready for the next twenty years.

What I bring might be new, but things did progress, and the problem of language is no longer viewed today as it was two years ago. When you open Dr. Dumas's treatise on psychology,[5] which is authoritative, worldwide, you find language defined as a *mimic and significative gesticulation*. That was not the case at all before, and these words about language—"gesticulation," "mimism"—were not in use.

We need to clear people's minds and show them that there is, in this desert, many blooms not yet seen and even unsuspected. Language, that *most common* of all things, is also the least studied and therefore the least known. And here is my logic: I must lead you to get a feel for the subject, as my study moves ahead, logically, *progressively*, in the way of geometric theorems. All thought that is its own master and in control of itself has to proceed in successive and interlocking waves.

In my first year of lecturing, I showed you how the mimic gesture blossoms as corporeal and manual language. I traced before you this most formidable development that no one, until then, suspected, because nobody had ever bothered with gesture as a tool of expression and intercommunication. Human gesture was left to die, just as, for long years, all those flint axes—Manmade tools—were trampled on, because no one knew what lay beneath. In our soil, people, for centuries if not millennia, pushed away with the tip of their shoes, all those small pieces of flint that they mistook for just stones, just rounded pebbles. This happened when an entire specialized science would come into being, one that would pick up those pebbles and say: "This is the work of Man's crafting hand."

Similarly, there lay, in the human gesture that looked like something haphazardly flailing around, a science in waiting, a science altogether much richer than the axes made of flint. It was a science not dealing with objects in ten, fifteen or twenty different shapes, but a science engaging the uncountable richness of human thought.

Never before had it been said that gesture is capable of expressing even the richest human thinking *without* recourse to *oral language*. This

---

5. Georges Dumas, *Nouveau traité de psychologie*, 6 vols. (Paris: Alcan 1930–1949) (New treatise on psychology). The article is by André Ombredane (1871–1956), "Le langage, gesticulation significative, mimique et conventionnelle" (1933) (Language as significant, mimic and conventional gesticulation).

expressive capacity of gesture remains to this day so little recognized that anyone unfamiliar with my work is totally ignorant of the question. It is too new for them, and it is indeed so new that only a few specialists who are by trade obliged to study language know about it. I can confidently say that even my colleagues in this School—with at best two or three exceptions—are totally unaware of what it is that I am bringing. It seems to frighten them, and it is a fear that I put as a jewel on my lapel—if I had the good fortune of having such. It is a young researcher's pure joy!

The Crystallization of the Pearl-Lessons

Having firmed up his recitation by the introduction of rhythm, what did Man do with the resulting small blocks that I have called recitatives?

To "crystallize," as I showed you in an earlier lecture, has always been one of Man's main preoccupations, and Man crystallized his recitations in the form of *parallel recitatives*. We saw how the rules of resonance applied and how what was expressed in recitative 1 would reflect or echo in recitative 2. In the milieu of the rabbis of Israel, such small blocks were most judiciously called: *pearls*.

"Pearls" is a most expressive term. What one does is similar to counting the beads of a necklace. Such was this sense of crystallization that a series of those small crystallizations of pearls was indeed called a *necklace*. We come across this technique everywhere.

There never is an undefined string of pearls, and when one has to recite, not two, but ten, fifteen, or thirty recitatives, these pearls are put in an ordered sequence. What we have is this *[Jousse draws a figure on the blackboard]*: an imaginary recitative 1, here, is parallel to a recitative 2. What happens when there is a recitative 3? How will these three relate; how can they be linked up? All oral peoples have tried to create such linkages, not just a linking of ideas, which is meaningless, but a linking of gestures.[6] This then is the shape of a "didactic necklace": recitative 0 is followed by 1 and 2, set next to each other,

R 0

Rec 1   Rec 2

---

6. Jousse replaces the terminology of metaphysics with a gestural terminology: *ideas*, *images* do not exist, "They are *mimemes*, things done with the body." School of anthropology, 01/03/37. See n. 15.

They are symmetrically linked by words. When in this oral necklace the word *dove* occurs in Recitative 1, you will invariably find here, in recitative II, the word *dove*. If there is *bow*, there will be a corresponding *bow* here. When you find *to die*, further on, there will be *to die*, in this spot; or the word *warrior*, and, in parallel, *warrior*. And so on. This is all-important in recitation because, if the recitation is well established, no one pearl can be left out: the recitation is encased, enchained, in this mnemotechnical necklace.

At the École des Hautes Études,[7] I will apply this anthropological law to the *Lamentations* of Jeremiah. I will show—it has been noticed before, but never explained—why the first verseline of *Lamentations* contains a word that will come up again in the last line; the second verse of the *Lamentations* is repeated in the last verse but one. This process is well-known in Israel (there are a number of Israelites here who follow me very assiduously), it is called: clamping.

The Clamp-Words

In the clamping method, one takes the first letter and positions it in relation to the last letter; the second letter is set in relation to the last letter but one in the Hebraic alphabet. This looks like a curious method of recitation, but it is what we ourselves do with a sheaf of loose pages: we number them: 1, 2, 3, 4, etc. . . . and the dispersed notes find their place in an ordered whole. Dispersion happens very easily too in purely oral recitation of the "pearl-lessons." In the Gospel recitatives, for example, those "pearl-lessons" that were transposed when put in writing, how can they be put in the right order again? Through our knowledge of the laws of oral composition.

The Palestinians, like many oral-style peoples, had no numbering comparable to our Arab numbering: 1, 2, 3, and so on. Many of these peoples numbered things by the letters of the alphabet: Aleph, Bet, Gimel, Dalet . . . *the letters of the alphabet were used as numbers*. This explains why, Catholic or not, if you follow the rites of the holy week, you will hear those most beautiful lamentations begin with: aleph, bet, etc., because what you are hearing are oral-style recitations improvised by the Nabis of Israel. To retain their pearl necklaces correctly, they ordered

---

7. The École des Hautes Études is a prestigious institution for public research and higher education in Paris where Jousse taught from 1933 until 1945 at the invitation of Maurice Goguel, the dean of the Protestant Faculty of Theology.

them, beginning with the letters of the alphabet: the recitation begins with aleph, which gives you the letter *A*, which is also the number *one*, and one continues the numbering by the letters of the alphabet: *aleph, bet, gimel* = 1, 2, 3 . . . And so, the beginnings of the recitatives link up, with the initial letter-number articulation serving as a clamp.

We simply have no idea of the care oral peoples took to keep their traditions intact. We busied ourselves until now quasi-exclusively with dead tools. Writing froze us, and dynamic anthropology[8] questions this stranglehold writing has on us. Remember that the role of writing as we know it among us is only a few centuries old. All that went before was altogether more interesting, more human! When I was young, by far the largest part of the peasants of the Sarthe were illiterate. Were they clearly inferior or superior to us? I believe that they were in many aspects our superiors. I was often ashamed because my memory compared badly with theirs. They were marvelous people. In the evening hours, when one or another grandmother began to recite the old Sarthois traditions, it was a pure wonder of simplicity and finesse. What guided them? The melody and the rhymes, both very much what we have here, at the beginning of the lamentations in the Hebraic milieu. The inborn sense of *the laws of memory* in many peoples of oral style is quite astounding.

This explains why my best laboratory is not the experimental laboratory, but the ethnic laboratory. Those peoples had a fine-tuned perception of their feelings and for thousands upon thousands of years—it is impossible to give a precise number—they used empirically all the laws of memory for the portage and transmission of their traditions. True anthropology of gesture must get a maximum grasp of manual and oral expression wherever it is still alive. And, with the help of these manual and oral gestures, anthropologists must research, for example in the Palestinian literature, which laws played a part and how.

The work to be done on the oral literature of the rabbis is enormous and has hardly been touched upon. These were men who put in writing only their Bible, their Torah, which their people carried orally. There were among them remarkable men, such as Rabbi Hillel, Rabbi Aqiba, and Rabbi Gamaliel, whom we totally ignore! For centuries, they did not

---

8. Marcel Jousse's *anthropology of gesture* is the dynamic science of the living human, an *anthropos* who is an indivisible psychophysiological compound, and who manifests himself solely through gestures, visible or invisible. It is this human as a complexus of gestures that the *science* anthropology has as its sole object to see and observe, and not to invent and construct.

put anything in writing, as happened with the Gallic Druids, who knew writing but did not use it for their pedagogy—they always wanted to keep their teaching oral.

The rabbis of Israel, on the contrary, felt the need, at some given moment, to "put in writing" what they had carried and transmitted orally for a hundred, two hundred, four hundred, six hundred years. This formidable encyclopedia is the Aramaic transfer-targum of the Hebraic Torah. It is our task to look into these texts "put in writing" and to find out about the laws governing these oral transmissions. This research is important, even for our ordinary reading of the Bible. Whenever we, Catholics or Protestants, pick up our gospel, or our Bible, if we are Israelites, we see these stylistic processes in operation, and we wonder: "Why, for what reason, is this structured in this way?"

Until now, the Talmud had been looked upon as a pile of texts and rather a mess. In fact, it is an accumulation of oral recitations linked by a verbal logic, which is not necessarily an internal logic. The rabbis linked their recitations by words. Obviously, translated words do not always have the same resonance in the foreign language. That is how the impression is created of a heap of little pieces haphazardly thrown together. But there is a very powerful linkage present. It is not unlike a necklace of pearls strung on an invisible silk thread.

If I have brought anything to the mechanics of the recitatives, it is surely this law of *clamping* by what I have called *clamp-words*.

At the École des Hautes Étude, I will show that this system of clamping proves with anthropological certainty (apologetical certainty is not my concern) that there are in our Greek Gospels Aramaic linkages that are no longer operational in the Greek transfer-translations. Clamping only works in Aramaic, and it is proof that the original texts were Aramaic compositions in oral style. It is absolutely impossible to deny that an entire series of clamp-words was composed in Aramaic, when, by translating the Greek back into Aramaic, the linkages reemerge in all their original logic.

This was never before pointed out because the research remained forever focused on writing and not on the laws of memory in oral-style milieus. When, later, I will deal with the processes at work in the *ethnic* Palestinian oral-style milieu, I will refer you back to what I have explained to you here, today, from an *anthropological* point of view. What I am sharing with you here is the discovery of the laws that operate in Man, as *anthropos*. At the École des hautes-études, I show how these anthropological laws are adapted in a particular ethnic milieu, a particular alphabet and a particular mechanism of expression—and especially in the Palestinian milieu.

There are still oral-style civilizations to be studied closely, such as the civilization of the Tuaregs, which Father de Foucauld[9] has understood so admirably. The French government sponsored the publication of two volumes of this admirable savant: *The Recitations of the Tuaregs* and a third collection of recitatives is to appear soon. Theirs is a most fascinating literature and among them, as in other oral-style peoples, there are men and women capable of improvising oral compositions that resemble like sisters the recitations of the Palestinian milieu. Why? Simply because the laws of memory are, everywhere, not identical, but analogous. Man is always Man. As anthropologists, our task is to verify these laws ethnically, once we have understood their anthropological mechanism.

I have shown you, in large strokes, the mechanism of the recitation in the milieus of oral style. In the next three lectures I will deal with the rhythmopedagogical use of this oral style. What will become obvious is that once we know what has been developed in this immense laboratory of oral style, we would be foolish to try to create a pedagogy, when we can make use of a pedagogy that has worked so well and survived so admirably.

Applying the Laws of Recitation to Pedagogy

I have lately been reading the pedagogical writings of Mr. Marion.[10] His pedagogy has not aged, because it is rooted in the fundamental laws, which are the anthropological laws. It struck me how this truly prodigious man intuited these laws, and how he felt anthropology was the direction to take. Which it is, of course!

Look the world over and see how these fundamental laws have been known for thousands of years. Here in France, for example, the sense that verse was easier to learn than prose—which is why La Fontaine[11]

---

9. Charles de Foucauld (1858–1916), explorer and hermit, *Poésies Touarègues: Dialecte de l'Ahaggar*, 2 vols. (Paris: Leroux, 1925–1930).

10. Henri Marion (1846–1896), philosopher and educator. His lectures were published as *Leçons de psychologie appliquée à l'éducation* in 1882 and reprinted in 2000 (Lectures in Psychology Applied to Education) in Brookline, Massachusetts, by Adamant Media Corporation.

11. Jean de La Fontaine (1621–1695), his collections of fables are standard texts in

rhymed and rhythmed his fables—originated from a concern, not with poetry, but with memory. Our commandments of God and of the Catholic Church are in that form, balanced and rhythmed—again, not for the sake of poetry. And if poetry had been the aim, it surely was not achieved. What was achieved, however, was the recovery of the 8 + 8 balancing of syllables. How curious that all these men, who had not the slightest notion of the anthropological laws we bring into play now, would have sensed that the 8 + 8 balancing was the way to teach small children, and with rhymes as a system of clamping. Children recite these commandments spontaneously, balancing admirably their text from 8 to 8 or from 6 to 6, as in:

> Oui je viens dans son temple adorer l'Éternel...[12]
> Yes, I come to his temple to worship the Lord...

This balancing by the children may well have escaped the attention of the people who composed the text in octosyllables.

Pedagogy does not have to invent itself; it needs to rediscover itself in us, which is a very different matter. Pedagogy must be built on knowledge of human mechanics. And that is why our task as anthropologists is so daunting, and why it will remain so, increasingly. We need to study the laws of memory among all those peoples who still practice them, in order to find out how to apply them in our present pedagogical milieu. We hear all around us, "We must return to a pedagogy that is more alive." Pedagogy, however, is not created on paper, but in the living being. Go to the peoples who do not care about paper at all because they do not know paper, or who, if they know writing, use writing as a testimonial and not as our books meant for everyday reading.

I will show you next year how writing was known in a many ethnic milieus but was kept under the guard of scribes and priests. Texts were "control texts" that served as a rectifier of the recitation. You wouldn't have seen people walking about with an obelisk in their pockets or steles of Hammurabi. The enormous blocks you find in the Louvre Museum were not our small deluxe pocket handkerchiefs. Our present-day handbooks are an altogether recent invention.

I remember reading as a child about a chatelaine who had to sell quite a number of sheep to buy a missal. A missal was an extraordinary

---

the French high school curriculum.

12. Jean Racine (1639–1699), from the play *Athalie* (Athaliah), act 1, scene 1, line 1, a classic of the French school curriculum.

thing to possess! I also remember those formidable medieval knights who, we were told, had one great failing: they could not write! To sign a document, those lords who-could-not-write dipped their finger in the ink and put their mark on the paper. Which is not extraordinary at all and quite normal: these are our present-day fingerprints and the true scientific, unfalsifiable signatures. What seems strange to us from afar is simple common sense. These people did not have our great need for writing. When they had finished waging war, they sat in an armchair, as you will do this evening, and they had before them a "loudspeaker." It was not our radio presenter; it was a troubadour or *trouvère* who came to tell them, in rhythmomelodic form, in units of eight and eight or of four and six syllables, their exploits or those of their ancestors. It was the *Song of Roland*[13] and other stories. It was their story.

We no longer have such compositions truly made for listening. Our present-day speakers on the radio feel more like gentlemen reading aloud from the written page. I found myself a couple of hours ago at a lecture where the lecturer read a paper, with that small gesture of someone who "drinks like a hen," looking as he did at his paper, then lifting his head to look at his audience, and then on to his paper again . . . There is no way that this man, who wrote his text at his desk, could in any way observe the laws of proper breathing that make speech pleasant to listen to. He could have gone on reading his paper forever, whereas a lecturer who teaches verbally has to submit himself to the laws of human expression: if his sentence is too long, it will get stuck in his throat; if it is well breathed, well respired, it will go down perfectly and the audience will listen to it without tiring.

Our pedagogy has for far too long ignored the laws of memorization *by audition*. We are told from all sides: "Let us return to life." "Let us return to things that are adapted to children." It is this that I have shown you. It is not difficult, but it is extremely complicated, because it is life and it will take some twenty years to be understood and applied in pedagogy.

There is a relentless dismantling of the mechanisms of memory in our children. Children as young as eight and nine all of a sudden become estranged, as if they are no longer what they used to be. What is happening? After my outline of the anthropological laws of gesture, our psychiatrists came to understand disorders such as aphasia and apraxia as a *breaking down* of gestures. Not enough attention has been paid to

---

13. The *Chanson de Roland* is a French epic poem from the late eleventh century.

the *building up* of gestures in children. The anthropological laws *are not created* by anyone. To be respected and made use of, they must first be known and investigated.

Conclusion: The Science of Mimism

It is good, I think, at the end of a series of lectures such as these, to look back and to say, like the small child who finishes his page of writing and sticks out his tongue, "That's it." We too have this year done a fine page of writing, and if not I, then at least my collaborator-stenographer here who makes digital gestures while I make laryngobuccal gestures.

What has my teaching brought this year? *Mimism*: the unknown law of Man.[14] It is mimism that allows us to grasp the human mechanisms in their primordial genesis and to prove that, unfortunately for him, *Man has no ideas*; that Man has no images either, those terrible images that have always troubled the psychiatrists; that *Man* has no need at all to *know writing in order to know something*. There have been formidable civilizations that lived from oral style, like the ancient Gauls. I recently argued, against an authority in the field, the value and superiority of the Gallic pedagogy over a number of other contemporaneous pedagogies. To the retort "If the Gauls were that masterful, something of that mastery would have been left," I said: "Something was left, and it was this: it is precisely because the Gauls were such remarkably determined men that they felt compelled by their tradition to preserve their teaching in oral form."

---

14. *The law of human mimism.* There is no *ex*pression without prior *im*pression, and human expression is, in content and in form, the expression of prior impression by the universe. In form: ours is an interactional universe in which everything is acting on everything else and is likewise acted upon; human expression mimes this universal formula as in the linguistic proposition of the subject (actor), verb (acting), complement (acted upon), and manifests in gestures that are corporeally global, engaging the whole body, or specialized as manual, ocular, auricular, and oral, when through the organs of speech. In content: what sets Man apart in the universe, is a capacity to mime the unconscious actions of the universe, to store them as units of things mimed or *mimemes*, and to bring them into consciousness as propositions: "People greater than I am will see further than I see, but I do know that I brought an all-important law when I said: 'The Anthropos is a propositionally miming animal' because, alone among all the animals of the creation, Man is capable of replaying the interaction of the real: an acting one—acting on—an acted upon . . . He may well not understand the interaction objectively, in the detached form of what are called words, but he can understand it *within himself*, as a triphasic proposition." École des hautes études, 23d October 1940.

We have unfortunately very recently lost Camille Jullian.[15] I recommend that you read his work. Carefully researched and beautifully written, it will show you just how much the Gallic civilization was able to carry in a purely oral form. Overconfident as we are in our writing system, we have neglected and disdained those civilizations of the memory, and we failed to research them properly.

With the anthropology of gesture an immense laboratory opens up before us. And it is not, as some thought at first, the narrowness of the discipline that should frighten us, but rather its breadth and depth. There is no shortage of work to be done, as a daunting amount of labor awaits us. However, after thirty years of study, I master the subject. Every year from now, logically, calmly, knowingly, I will divide the subject for you, *artificially*. As I cannot give you everything at once, I will separate it out in the most logical form possible.

We started, two years ago, with congenital human mimism. In this academic year, we looked at the transition from global gesture to oral gesture, and next year we will arrive logically at the appearance of writing in the form of shadow play and at the necessary passage of this mimography to phonography, with the language of gesture evolving slowly into oral language. In the process, those same "ideograms" or rather mimograms, as I am calling them now, will serve to articulate sounds. And when the sound will little by little detach itself from the object and become "algebraized," the need will no longer be felt to have, in the writing, a mimic reproduction of the object, because this mimic reproduction will no longer recall the object, but the vocal sound.

Whatever the algebrizations that occurred in the course of millennia, we cannot, at present, explain the shape of the letters we write with, without having recourse to the primordial *mimism* that I have brought here as essential law of the dynamic anthropology.

In the presence of savants, I have established a science.

---

15. Camille Jullian (1859–1933), *Histoire de la Gaule*, 8 vols. (Paris: Hachette 1908–1926).

9

The Au/Orality of the Aramaic Gospel

BRUCE CHILTON

La Sarthe and Au/Orality

La Sarthe is a *département* in France, with a land mass roughly that of Delaware, defined by a meandering river from which it takes its name. Except for Le Mans, which is la Sarthe's principal city, small towns and villages predominate. In one of these, Beaumont-sur-Sarthe, Marcel Jousse was born in 1886. In another, Fresnay-sur-Sarthe, he died in 1961.[1] Apart from that background in la Sarthe, he could not have crafted the definition of anthropology that he pioneered, he could not have emerged as the kind of anthropologist that met that definition, and he could not have made his formidable contribution to understanding the development of the Gospels and to assessing how the Gospels continue to shape human action.

This chapter assesses how Jousse's background influenced him, by his own account. It then takes up two interrelated subjects: his pioneering investigation of Aramaic substrata within the Gospels and his particular emphasis upon *mimêsis* as the anthropological key to both how the substrata were produced and how they can be understood. This leads to a final consideration of the prospect of continued investigation along the trajectory that he set out.

---

1. See Baron, *Mémoire vivante*.

The culture of Jousse's village, and the formative influence of his mother in particular, was received by the ear and practiced by the mouth. Although he mastered several languages and disciplines of study from an early age, public education had not yet raised the level of general literacy in the region to its modern standard. Even to this day, there are villages in la Sarthe where life is conducted for the most part without reference to the literate culture of Paris, which is frequently regarded as being as foreign and linguistically distorted as it is hegemonic. Because he excelled in his studies, Marcel Jousse might easily have left this world behind. Instead, he chose to learn from it, making la Sarthe a touchstone by which he assessed new forms of learning as he acquired them.

The natal village of Marcel Jousse lies north of Le Mans; south of that city, I have stayed in the village of Chenu every year for nearly forty years. There, too, la Sarthe proves to provide a thriving river of language by ear and by mouth—hence, "au/orality" in the title of this essay and this section. Much as Jousse describes in his recollections, one can still hear and learn the songs and stories that accompany every family celebration, and there is a disproportionately high number of these as compared to in urban and suburban settings I have encountered. In recent years Claude Ribouillaut has collected the music of celebration, as well as that of the two World Wars that marked la Sarthe in many ways.[2] Of course, the very act of collection objectifies music, and makes it a possible preserve of professionals. In la Sarthe, songs and stories do not belong to such a group; they circulate and can be claimed for performance by individuals only for a short period of time. Then the compositions continue their lives with other performers, selected usually for reasons of either status or talent. Au/orality is more a communal and collaborative enterprise than an authorial activity.

The purpose of such offerings is not entertainment in itself, although their value as such can be very high. The purpose of a story or song might, quite to the contrary, be vengeance: to keep at bay some segment of the village community by means of remembered wrongs and enduring resentments. An allusive reference to possible collaboration when la Sarthe was occupied under the Third Reich, or alleged association with the Communist Party during the same time, is sufficient to bracket some people out of au/orally defined circles of association. Sometimes the oral performance is more like a list than a narrative, and enables

---

2. Ribouillaut, *La Musique au Fusil*.

the organization of village hunts for deer or boar, which are rigorously (and legally) communal, rather than an individual's sport. Commercial transactions also live in au/oral memory, establishing serial patterns of exchange of commodities outside the detection of tax collectors that can be highly complex and might involve transactions far outside the area. Local politics, of course, is at base an au/oral enterprise in the village, although written publicity and the occasional poison-pen letter shoved under doors might also feature; what appears in writing, however, only makes sense in terms of what has been heard already and then explained subsequently by word of mouth. The culture of language by ear and mouth does not exclude the eye, but the written word remains subservient to the meanings that au/orality establishes. What is heard and said means more than what is written and read.

One marker of au/orality in la Sarthe is that the language spoken is not simply standard French. Those from outside the village often take this as a sign of a lack of education or of a lower-class "dialect," but at times wording serves to signal the preserve of the ear and the mouth. The people of Chenu, for example, call themselves *Catunuciens* (or *Catoniciens*), a term that historically links them to the ancient name of the village in Latin, *Catunucius*.³ As commonly pronounced, however, the term sounds more like *Châteaunuciens*, so encapsulating a relationship to *le Château*, by which is meant both the building and the families that have inhabited it over several centuries. Yet that derivation of the term is categorically denied by many in Chenu, who see *le Château* as an alien feature of village life. Derivation from Latin *Catunucius* seems far preferable to these objectors and is probably more accurate in critical terms. In any case, even as the language of Chenu is used, signification is a matter of dispute.

Across the street from where I stay with family, the pork butcher—a person of high accomplishment—speaks in a way that only villagers can understand fully, but he conducts his business flawlessly. If you ask him for directions, for example, he will tell you to proceed to one set of crossroads or another, but instead of the standard French *carrefour*, he will call that a *courouail*, an evident derivative from the rarely found Latin term.⁴ Of course he doesn't think of derivations when he speaks of a *courouail* to his fellow *Catunuciens*, but his language performs who he

---

3. See Carrè de Busserolle, *Dictionnaire Géographique*, 232.
4. See Sarzana, *De romanorum imperatorum*, 37.

is. As Marcel Jousse would explain, he is a true *verbo-moteur*, an engine of language.

Aramaic Au/Orality and Retroversion

Marcel Jousse applied his firsthand knowledge of au/orality to the Gospels, and he did so globally, not piecemeal. Had he attempted a catalog of connections, he would have never arrived at the point of understanding patterns of usage, which was his goal, rather than the atomistic analysis of individual sayings. In any case, the works of Aramaists such as Gustaf Dalman were well-known when he engaged in his research,[5] and he actively collaborated with scholars of the New Testament such as Maurice Goguel.[6] The work of cataloging was already well underway during his period; his task was synthesis and insight, on the assumption that catalogs were ready to hand. But those unfamiliar with the literature and evidence that he assumes might wrongly gather the impression that Jousse merely projected the model of his childhood onto the texts. In fact, however, he was accounting for express features of the texts, features that mark their au/oral origins.

Language carries signs of its provenience. The Gospels include not only Aramaic words in transliteration but also full phrases. A partial list would include prominent examples, some of them so well-known that they have arrived as possible expressions in English, despite having passed through several languages during the course of transmission. These instances are widely acknowledged; less adequately appreciated is that today it is possible to collate transliterations in the Gospels with historical examples of Aramaic, so that a retroversion into first-century forms of the language is possible.[7] Here the Greek transliteration is compared to retroverted Aramaic of the period, with a translation:

---

5. See, for example, Dalman, *Die Worte Jesu*.
6. An influence documented in Jousse, *In Search of Coherence*, 68.
7. See Flesher and Chilton, *The Targums*, 409–21.

Transliteration	Retroversion	Translation
Taleitha qoum	Taliyta' qumiy	Girl, arise (Mark 5:41)
Korban	Qorbana'	Qorban (Mark 7:11)
Rabbei/rabbounei	Rabiy/Rabouniy	Rabbi (Mark 9:5; 10:51)
Mamônas	Mamôna'	Mammon (Luke 16:9, 11, 13)
Geennas	Geyhinam	Gehenna (Mark 9:43, 45, 47)
Abba	'Abba'	Abba (Mark 14:36)
Golgotha	Golgata'	Golgotha (Mark 15:22)
Elôi, elôi, lama sabakhthanei?	'Eliy, 'Eliy, lamah sabaqtaniy?	Eloi, Eloi, lama sabachthani? (Mark 15:34)

Linguistic shifts involved in these variations are fascinating, and have been explored in literature cited here. The present investigation only needs to attend to the fact of the connections and variations together; the mutations that appear among Greek, Aramaic, and English variants are commensurate with the assimilation of expressions from la Sarthe into standard French. Jousse built these indications into his systematic description of how au/orality can link materials together in a way that influenced Millman Parry,[8] Thorleif Boman,[9] and Birger Gerhardsson.[10] But beyond these suggestions of structuring principles derived from the Aramaic language, he also proposed engaged attention to the targumim in particular.

To some extent, his reasoning reflects awareness that even after targumim were written, the work of the translator or *meturgeman* within a synagogue remained oral, a matter of recitation from memory rather than from a written source. This practice distinguished the reading of Hebrew from the performance of Aramaic. The *meturgeman* epitomized the challenge of permitting au/orality to survive and even prosper in an increasingly literate environment. In addition, Jousse recognized that some of the interpretations of the targumim correlate with those offered by Jesus in the Gospels.

Before we turn to targumic correlations with the Gospels, we need to confront a factor that has seriously disrupted the reception of Jousse's

---

8. As discussed by Werner Kelber in his foreword to Jousse, *Memory*, xiv–xv.
9. Boman, *Die Jesus-Überlieferung*.
10. Gerhardsson, *Memory and Manuscript*.

work. As he was writing, one consensus regarding the dating of the targumim was breaking up in favor of another, and well after his withdrawal from activity for reasons of health in 1957 the consensus changed again. At the end of that process, however, Jousse's findings hold up remarkably well.[11]

The standard dating endorsed by Gustaf Dalman posited that a targum to the Pentateuch preferred within rabbinic Judaism, called Targum Onqelos, was the base targum. In addition, Pinkhos Churgin by Jousse's time had already identified elements in Targum Jonathan to the Prophets that also went back to the first century of the Common Era.[12] These targumim, developed and used by rabbis of the Babylonian Talmud, came to be thought of as written in Babylonian Aramaic. Then, in 1930, Paul Kahle published his highly influential essays on the manuscripts discovered in the Cairo Geniza.[13] He claimed that they represented Palestinian Aramaic, and that—although the manuscripts dated from between the seventh and the fourteenth centuries—they reflected a much earlier "Palestinian targum." His dating and account of the development of Aramaic was accepted by Alejandro Díez Macho, Matthew Black, and Martin McNamara.[14]

From that perspective, the claim became current that the targumim used by Marcel Jousse were too late for comparison with the New Testament. "Late" and "early," of course, are always relative terms in targumic scholarship. Without question, the targumim are later than the origin suggested in rabbinic literature, which would put them in the time of Ezra. But at times Jesus is associated with usages reflected in the targumim. As Jousse worked, he and T. W. Manson could point to the interpretation of Isa 6:10 in Mark 4:12, where parables are told in order to avoid understanding by those who do not repent, so that they are not forgiven (rather than healed, as in the Masoretic Text and the Septuagint).[15] The Targum takes the passage in the same way, just as it also associates Gehenna with the phrase "where their worm does not die and their fire is not quenched"

---

11. For the discussion of linguistics that follows Flesher and Chilton, *The Targums*, 151–66 and 267–83.

12. Churgin, *Targum Jonathan*.

13. Kahle, *The Cairo Geniza*.

14. See Díez Macho, *Neophyti 1*; Black, *An Aramaic Approach*; McNamara, *Targum and Testament*.

15. For the cases discussed in this paragraph, see Manson, *The Teaching of Jesus*, 74–81; Evans, *To See and Not Perceive*; Flesher and Chilton, *The Targums*, 385–408.

(Targum Isa 66:24 and Mark 9:48), and takes up the proverbial expression that those who wield the sword die by it (Targum Isaiah 50:11), which Matt 26:52 reflects. Even if Kahle's hypothesis had been confirmed, much of the evidence that Jousse builds upon would have remained viable in exegetical terms, because the date of a given tradition is not determined by the dating of the document in which it appears.

As it happens, however, Kahle's hypothesis has not been confirmed in any case. The work of compiling *The Comprehensive Aramaic Lexicon* has resulted in a complete typology of the development of Aramaic, the world's oldest continuously spoken language.[16] That massive project—based on earlier studies by Preben Wernberg-Møller, Anthony D. York, and Steven A. Kaufman[17]—which is easily accessible with links to many of the primary sources (including targumim), makes it clear that the so-called Palestinian targumim linguistically arrived after the period of the Dead Sea Scrolls, and that the targumim to which Jousse had recourse, Onqelos and Jonathan, better represent first-century usage when considered in association with the Scrolls. The dating of their manuscripts is medieval, while the finds in the Cairo Geniza bridge the Byzantine and medieval periods, but the language of Onqelos and Jonathan more closely correlates with provable examples of Aramaic from the first century.

In a sense, however, the controversy over the dating of dialects of Aramaic is a side issue, since the Gospels were in any case composed in Greek. Stepping behind the texts into Aramaic tradition will always require retroversion. New Testament scholarship carries a natural Hellenistic preference, which is exacerbated by appeals to claims that the original teaching of Jesus required no recourse to Aramaic, since he spoke Greek. That linguistic model of first-century Galilee, which also encouraged the portrait of Jesus as a Cynic,[18] has fared no better than the hypothesis of a primitive Palestinian targum.

Yet it would be a parody of Jousse's insight simply to translate Gospels into Aramaic of the appropriate period and to claim that is the precedent of the texts as they stand. Rather, what is necessary is a clear indication that material in the written Gospels conveys what was substantially related first with the au/oral tradition. Two examples of that follow.

16. See Kaufman, *The Comprehensive Aramaic Lexicon*.
17. See Wernberg-Møller, "An Inquiry"; York, "The Dating"; Kaufman, "Dating the Language."
18. See, for example, Eddy, "Jesus as Diogenes?"

Marcel Jousse himself retroverted the Lord's Prayer into Aramaic, although the secondary literature since his time has privileged other retroversions, by Joachim Jeremias and Joseph A. Fitzmyer.[19] Unlike Jeremias and Fitzmyer, however, Jousse understood that the au/oral Lord's Prayer would not include the additions of Matthew and Luke, so that it is a rhythmic, efficient model. Of the two versions of the Lord's Prayer in the New Testament (Matt 6:9–15; Luke 11:2–4), Luke's is widely considered the earlier in form. Matthew presents what is, in effect, a commentary woven together with the prayer. The relative sparseness of Luke has won it virtually unanimous recognition among scholars as the nearest to the form of an outline which Jesus would have recommended. Even so, Luke includes an explanation of the responsibility implied in being forgiven, as a schematic presentation of the Matthean and Lukan renderings makes clear:

Matthew	Luke
Our father,	Father,
who is in the heavens,	
your name will be sanctified,	your name will be sanctified,
your kingdom will come,	your kingdom will come.
your will happen	
as in heaven, even on earth.	
Our bread that is coming,	Our bread that is coming,
give us today,	be giving us each day,
and forgive us our debts,	and release us our sins
as we also have forgiven our debtors,	because we also ourselves release everyone who is indebted to us,
And do not bring us to the test,	And do not bring us to the test.
but deliver us from the evil one.	

The model unfolds under two major headings:

I) an address of God (1) as father, (2) with sanctification of God's name, and (3) with vigorous assent to the coming of God's kingdom;

II) a petition for (1) bread, (2) forgiveness, and (3) constancy.

The two major headings are clearly distinguished in grammatical terms. The address of God in the Greek text is as a third person, a father, and is followed by imperatives in the third person ("your name be

---

19. For further discussion and bibliographical references, see Chilton, *Jesus' Prayer and Jesus' Eucharist*.

sanctified," "your kingdom come"), while the plea for bread—which as Jousse correctly saw is "coming," not merely "daily"—is in the imperative of the second person ("give"), as is the appeal for forgiveness ("forgive"), and constancy ("do not bring").

Assessed by its individual elements, the Lord's Prayer may be characterized as a fairly typical instance of the Judaic piety of its period. To call God "father" was—as such—nothing radical, and the association of his fatherly care with his actual provision for prayerful Israel is attested in Ps 68:5. The same passage shows that the connection of God's holiness to his fatherhood was seen as natural, and the importance of sanctifying God's name within the earliest of rabbinic texts of prayer—such as the Kaddish—is well-known. That his holiness is consistent with people being forgiven and accepted by him is also unexceptionable. Finally, the idea that God's being king amounts to a "kingdom" which was about to be revealed is amply precedented within the targumim, and they insist upon the loyal response of God's people to that revelation:

'abba'/	father/source
yitqadash/ shemakh/	your name will be sanctified
te/tah malkhutakh/	your kingdom will come
hav/ li yo/ma' lakh/ma' d'a/teh	give me today the bread that is coming
ushebaq/ li yat choba/ti	and release me my debts
ve'al/ ta'aley/ni lenisyon/a'.	not bring me to the test

Comparable elements of rhythm and succinct expression are also present within a teaching that supposes the continued functioning and local practice of the temple in the Gospels (Mark 7:15):[20]

la'/ demibar/a' debar 'enash/a'
d'a/tah beyh demta/mey
bar/a' min d'a/ten min/
bar 'enash/a' 'iyleyn/ demta/men.

There is not from outside the person
That goes in him, pollutes
Except what goes out from
The person, these things pollute.

---

20. For further discussion, see Chilton, "A Generative Exegesis." This retroversion, and other retroversions of Mark are available in Chilton et al., eds, *A Comparative Handbook*.

The stroke (/) is used to help describe the poetics of the assertion, which divides into two statements, each of three beats followed by two or three beats. Using *bar* for "outside"[21] (in the phrase *demin bar*), produces a repetition of sound with "person" (*bar 'enasha'*). "Person" itself is repeated in the last line, so as to emphasize closure. The use of *bar* is echoed in "except that" (*bera' min*),[22] linking the two lines by the same sound which opens the first line strikingly. The participle of "pollute" (from *tema'*)[23] dominates the sense of the entire *mashal*.

Conventional wisdom has it that the statement attributed to Jesus in Mark 7:14–15 lies at the heart of the chapter. The Jesus Seminar is representative both of that conventional wisdom, and of what is usually done with the consensus. The saying is accepted as "a categorical challenge to the laws governing pollution and purity," and is attributed to Jesus.[24]

From the present point of view, the saying might be attributed to Jesus or not: the issue of substance is that an argument by assertion is being made about defilement. The assertion is easily construed in Aramaic attested from Jesus' period and place,[25] and is more attractive when it is so rendered. Rendering the aphorism into Aramaic obviously makes it no more and no less a saying of Jesus. That it can be so rendered, and is memorable in Aramaic, simply helps to confirm the suggestion that the circle of Jesus confronted the issue of defilement. The circle was characterized by fellowship at meals involving various people with different practices of purity. That description applies to the period of Jesus' own activity, and to the period after his death when others appeared to lead the movement. In either phase, the circle of Jesus needed to cope with the social issue of possible defilement as one member of Israel (with one set of practices) met another member of Israel (with a different set of practices). The Jesus Seminar uncritically accepts the present context of the saying, limited to a dispute about foods, as the generative concern of

---

21. See Fitzmyer and Harrington, *A Manual*, 52 (= no. 7.8.4).

22. Cf. Fitzmyer and Harrington, *A Manual*, 124 (= no. 29B.22.23). The result is that *min bar* appears in the first line, and *bera' min* in the second.

23. I have used a form of the *pael*, of which the infinitive appears in Fitzmyer and Harrington, *A Manual*, 114 (= no. 29B.20.15).

24. See Funk and Hoover, *Five Gospels*, 69.

25. See both Kaufman, *The Comprehensive Aramaic Lexicon*; and Fitzmyer and Harrington, *A Manual*, where the forms used here are attested. The pointing, of course, is a largely a matter of supposition on the basis of later texts, and a simplified scheme is employed here for that reason.

the saying.²⁶ If it is a *mashal* from the circle of Jesus, its setting cannot be determined from the literary context with which later circles associated the aphorism.

For the circle of Jesus, a common meaning attributed to the aphorism appears to be a distortion: that Jesus was concerned only with moral, as distinct from cultic matters (cf. the interpretation of the saying in Matt 15:15-20; Mark 7:17-23). That portrayal suited the packaging of the Gospels for a Greco-Roman audience, and it continues to serve the interests of ethical religionists today, but it is far from the historical matrix of Jesus' saying at its generative moment, as an instrument to bridge diverse practices of purity.

Both the Lord's Prayer and the Mark 7:15, then, when retroverted into the Aramaic au/orality that produced them, emerge as carefully honed, rhythmic paradigms, linguistic gestures (joined, according to Jousse's observation, with physical gestures) that deal with the two poles that defined Jesus' movement: the approach of God and the issue of defilement. Both those concerns were ambient and beyond the capacity of any one person or group within the movement to deal with them. Yet they needed to be addressed by any and all members of the community, because they arose by the very act of community, and for that need to be addressed, an au/oral culture that had given birth to the movement continued to give it life.

Anthropology

In both cases, the prayer of Jesus and the aphorism in regard to defilement, Jousse's approach involves more than narrowly linguistic analysis. He insisted in a lecture given in 1941, "What I bring here is a new science: the anthropology of *geste*."²⁷ *Geste* is difficult to render, and it is wise not to make it synonymous with "gesture" in current English. The sense of a deliberate action is clearly involved for Jousse, and he stressed how articulated action, whether with wording or without, expressed "the anthropology of thought elaborated by the whole body."²⁸ This whole-body

---

26. For that reason, the version of the saying in Thomas 1:14, which specifies what goes into "your mouth," is taken to be as original as what is in Mark. It seems much more likely that the setting in Thomas (eating what is given you during missionary journeys; cf. Luke 10:8-9) has influenced the wording.

27. Quoted from a 1941 lecture: Jousse, *In Search*, 6.

28. Quoted from a 1951 lecture: Jousse, *In Search*, 7.

dedication to the idea, involving analysis of all kinds of gestes—"manual, ocular, auricular, laryngo-buccal, olfactive, gustatative"—makes the science of Jousse seem daunting in its scope, but for him precisely in that scope lies the "true anthropologist's bewilderment and anguish: in the fact that we think *with all the fibres of our body*."[29] Jousse's enthusiasm conveys itself in what he says, and because his work was itself an oral performance, its rhetoric is of lush proportions from time to time. For the sake of this discussion, I leave aside as much as possible his many neologisms, but these have been brilliantly expounded on the basis of Jousse's own explanations by Edgard Sienaert.

These bodily "fibres," in Jousse's analysis, convey the key for their own decipherment. That key is what Aristotle called *mimêsis* and Jousse calls "mimisme," in which there is a "law of universal mimology, namely, that *we are*, through all the fibres of our body, through all the fibres of our organs, *congenital mimers*."[30] This *mimêsis* is not merely from person to person in Jousse's analysis; rather, borrowing from the image of Pierre Janet, he asserts, "Between the action of the universe and the reaction of the human stands the switch of the human conscientizing mechanism, the gestuation that turns a phenomenon into a mimeme."[31] *Mimêsis*, because it is the means by which human beings grasp the universe, is also the means by which they may grasp themselves.

Contemporary Discussion of Mimêsis

At the time that Jousse developed his anthropology, Roger Caillois, associated with Georges Bataille in the Collège de Sociologie,[32] also focused on the issue of *mimêsis*, portraying its operation as inherent within the animal world.[33] His essays, "La mante religieuse" and "Mimétisme et psychasthénie légendaire," exercised considerable influence within surrealist circles,[34] most enduringly in a classic monograph that remains

---

29. Quoted from a 1934 lecture: Jousse, *In Search*, 7. All italics are as in Sienaert's rendering.

30. Quoted from the same 1934 lecture: Jousse, *In Search*, 7 (italics original).

31. Quoted from a 1935 lecture: Jousse, *In Search*, 35.

32. See Falasca-Zamponi, "A Left Sacred or a Sacred Left?"

33. See the influential articles Caillois, "La mante religieuse"; and Caillois, "Mimétisme et psychasthénie légendaire."

34. See Cheng, "Mask, Mimicry, Metamorphosis."

in print since its publication in 1938.[35] Jousse's overlap with a theme associated with a famous and influential surrealist may help to explain some of his many problems with his Catholic hierarchy. In any case, both Jousse and Caillois, the first a dedicated practitioner of au/oral *mimêsis*, the second a famously literate investigator of mimetic links, emphasized the unifying capacity of *mimêsis*, whether among human beings or between people and their environment. By means of the contribution of Caillois, the surrealist appeal to the affinity between humans and animals found its theoretical apology, while in the case of Jousse, the mimetic capacities of people mirror the mimetic influence of God. That is the basis of Jousse's statement that "in the mimodrama of the creation, divine mimism humanized Man. In the mimodrama of the Communion, human mimism divinized Man."[36]

As they pursued their differing approaches, Caillois and Jousse opened the prospect of an analytic resort to *mimêsis* in the assessment of how and why human beings communicate. Without their influence, it seems improbable that Erich Auerbach's famous book, *Mimesis*, could have been produced. Yet as the subtitle of Auerbach's work indicates, he applies the term, not on the basis of Aristotle's usage, but Plato's, and is concerned with the concept in terms of the literary representation of reality. To be sure, Plato is only a point of departure, since Auerbach does not assume that "reality" is a given; rather, it is always constructed. Language for him involves a figural process of representation, which literature discloses by means of its *mimêsis*.[37] Such has been the influence of this book in modern discussion that representation has tended to supersede the more dynamic appraisal of *mimêsis*, as the basis of action, in Aristotle. In recent years, this has been the case most prominently in the work of René Girard.

Girard's intervention began with his study *Deceit, Desire, and the Novel* by focusing on the nineteenth century, just the period in which Auerbach saw an overturning of classical styles of presentation.[38] Girard

---

35. See Caillois, *Le mythe et l'homme*.

36. Jousse, *In Search*, 53, quoting from a lecture given in 1943.

37. Although he is frequently said to be rather inchoate in his approach, it seems to me that Auerbach's "Epilogue" is cogent in this regard; see Auerbach, *Mimesis*, 554–58; and Hovind, "Figural Interpretation."

38. See Girard, *Deceit, Desire, and the Novel*, noting that its title in the original French edition, *Mensonge romantique et verité Romanesque*, makes the debt to Auerbach more explicit. A fuller assessment of Girard's contribution, especially in respect

developed an approach to *mimêsis* in competitive terms, and characteristically emphasized the mimetic potential for violence—and the inevitability of its sporadic outbreak—throughout his oeuvre. He describes the mimetic process in a way that is at odds with Jousse's analysis. The desire featured in Girard's title is not for the object that is desired, but an impulse to assume the desire of a competitor. Nothing promotes desire but someone else's desire. This is a mimetic analysis in both Platonic and Aristotelian terms, since a faulty representation (the mistake of thinking one wants what another wants), and a dynamic action (the attempt to supplant the desiring other) are together at the root of the response.

Having developed his approach in a reading of Proust, Stendhal, and Dostoevsky in particular, Girard became convinced that he had uncovered a fundamental human reflex and problem. Defined in these terms, *mimêsis* must inevitably lead to conflict, and under conditions of stress even to violence. On this understanding, mimetic jealousy is not merely a novelistic conceit, but an underlying problem of humanity in civilization. Girard pursued that lead into the development of religions in their origins, operating in an anthropological mode reminiscent of Jousse's. Repeatedly in his many works he asserts that all societies, precisely because they are societies of mimetic human beings (in Girard's distinctive sense), enter into jealous conflict with one another, each person attempting to eliminate a rival.

The relief of this rivalry comes about by means of sacrifice in Girard's model. In order to deal with mimetic jealousy across a society, a scapegoat for the tension that has been generated by *mimêsis* is found. The scapegoat is charged with the social dysfunction of the community and for any conditions that may afflict it, such as famine or plague. The release of violence against these scapegoats is the origin of sacrifice, according to Girard, in every culture that has ever existed. The elimination of the scapegoat in fact relieves tension within the community, at least until its next crisis, and for that reason the scapegoat is mythologized into a willing victim, and eventually can be conceived of as a god.

In recent discussion Girard's influence has been considerable, to the point that a scholarly organization, the Colloquium on Violence and Religion, has been formed to forward his model. Notably, the colloquium describes itself as an "International Association of Scholars

---

to sacrifice, is available in Chilton, *The Temple of Jesus*, 15–25; and Chilton, "The Eucharist."

of Mimetic Theory,"[39] in which the *mimêsis* is as described by Girard, rather than by Plato, Aristotle, Caillois, or Jousse. Much as Jousse's influence suffered because targumic studies took a different direction from his, so *mimêsis* in his sense (and Aristotle's as well as Caillois's) has been eclipsed by Girard's model in much contemporary discussion. In the case of the targumim, as we have seen, a consensus that parted company with Jousse has been reoriented so as to encourage his approach, with critical adjustments. Similarly, Girard's model of *mimêsis* has been subjected to correction.

The most prominent of the correctors was, until his death in 2015, René Girard himself. In response to criticism, he came to emphasize that not all *mimêsis* needs to result in a sacrificial crisis. He acknowledged that "the good *mimesis*" offered a way out, by offering patterns of response that could avoid, reduce, and even eliminate violence.[40] The New Testament, he thought, was the paragon of this alternative mimetic path. Girard's expression of this aspect of his theory attracted criticism, because he portrayed Christianity as the one religion that offered a break with the mimetic past of humanity, in that Jesus was portrayed as blameless when he was victimized. But that evident exceptionalism aside, he did come to analyze *mimêsis* in more properly Aristotelian terms, in that the trajectory of a mimetic act depended on the character of what was imitated.

That also was Jousse's point of departure. For him, "the Galilean Pastor is indeed becoming incarnate in both the old and the new Aramaically targumizing formulas."[41] Wording, in other words, is an encapsulation of mimetic action, and that wording is deliberately sown (to use a metaphor dear to Jousse) in order to engender, extend, and intensify that action. This to him was the true *Kêpha'*, the rock of tradition. Transcribing this last dictation to his assistant, Jousse exclaimed, "It is too beautiful! It is too beautiful! If it were stronger, it would kill me." He then suffered from an attack from which he never fully recovered.[42]

---

39. See COV&R. https://violenceandreligion.com/.

40. See Girard's own account of his evolution in Astell and Goodhart, eds, *Sacrifice, Scripture, and Substitution*, 36–69.

41. Jousse, *Memory*, 144.

42. Jousse, *Memory*, 147.

Mimetic Retroversion

The beauty that entranced Jousse, and to which he gave frequent expression in his works, was the capacity of *mimêsis*, not to represent or distort reality (the point of departure for Auerbach and Girard alike in their reliance on Plato), but to frame the activities by which human beings in turn frame their reality. For this reason, he was concerned not only with the recovery of wording, but also with the discovery of rhythm, repetition, and structure within the Aramaic language. For him this was as crucial a feature of retroversion as the choice of the correct language and vocabulary. Although he referred to the "oral style," it was on the clear understanding that style inheres in the substance of what is said.

Within the retroversions developed here, the poetics are rhythmically driven, and for that reason the natural stresses of Aramaic have already been indicated as embedded in the wording. On that basis, we now attend to those stresses as an aspect of the mimetic arc of the compositions.

Within the Lord's Prayer, the rhythm is simple, but rises to a double climax in two waves. In the first wave, a single stress is followed by two lines of two stresses, and then a final line of four stresses:

> 'abba'/
> yitqadash/ shemakh/
> te/tah malkhutakh/
> hav/ li yo/ma' lakh/ma' d'a/theh.

In this way, the sparse humility in the request for bread is provided with a fitting emphasis after the mounting emphasis on eschatology in the first three lines. Then, in the second wave, a line of two stresses is followed by a line of three stresses:

> ushebaq/ li yat choba/ti
> ve'al/ ta'aley/ni lenisyon/a'.

The addition of 'ameyn/ at the close would result in a symmetry with the opening of the prayer as a whole, but in substance the Lord's Prayer ends with a rising number of stresses again, to convey the transition of the prayer into the activities that it implies within itself.

In contrast, the aphorism in regard to uncleanness is expressed by means of a self-contained rhythm:

> la'/ demibar/a' debar 'enash/a'
> d'a/tah beyh demta/mey
> bar/a' min d'a/ten min/
> bar 'enash/a' 'iyleyn/ demta/men.

In this case, the three stresses in the first, third, and fourth lines establish a rhythm that secures the sense of a foundational whole. Within that whole, the second line stands out for its *missing* beat, relatively speaking, and that is just the point of the aphorism: the issue of what truly pollutes.

In each case, the Lord's Prayer and the aphorism on defilement, rhythm conveys meaning along with the wording concerned. The Prayer is an impetus to action, the *mimêsis* of the one who taught and teaches the Prayer and at the same time an engagement of the one to whom prayer is offered, while the aphorism is an act of concentration on how to avoid the uncleanness that is highlighted: by means of greater caution—in acting rather than in consuming.

Prospect

Recourse to the contribution of Marcel Jousse evidently requires critical adjustment. Since his time, the discipline of targumic and Aramaic studies has undergone a sea change. Fortuitously, the revolution involved has to an extent involved coming full circle, in the sense that targumim on which he relied, subsequent to his death considered to be well after the period of the New Testament, have now been shown to represent a form of Aramaic that was spoken during the first century. Still, the availability of many more kinds of targumim and a much richer understanding of the Aramaic language mean that retroversion as practiced by Jousse needs revision.

Comparison of Jousse's "Aramaic Targumic Formulas of the Our Father," with the version offered here is instructive.[43] The diction is comparable in most instances, although he did not have the benefit of resources only developed after his work was completed, so that some of the vocabulary must be adjusted. Perhaps more importantly, although Jousse's version is shorter, more compact, and rhythmically better defined than the Greek of Matthew, Luke, or the Didachê, Jousse retroverted into Aramaic some elements that scholars have widely agreed to be interpretative elements added in the Matthean version (here underlined); "our father that

---

43. Jousse, *Memory*, 346–90, 394–95.

is in heaven," "your will be done as in heaven so on earth," "as we remitted to our debtors," "but free us from evil." Jousse wrote during a time when the liturgical dominance of Matthew's version accorded it greater prominence in scholarly reconstruction than it merited. Because he accorded with that fashion, the rhythmic structure of two waves described here is missed, and the prayer becomes a formulaic and contained composition, more a series of aphorism than an impulse articulated in order to elicit action.

Discussion of *mimêsis*, like that of the targumim, might also at one time have seemed to leave Jousse behind in the advance of the field in another direction altogether. But René Girard's attention to the workings of his own mimetic model and his willingness to engage in criticism has shown, to his critics and supporters as well as to himself, that mimetic action need not only consist in concealment. Jousse's properly Aristotelian conception of *mimêsis* obviates the emphasis on distortion in Erich Auerbach's and Girard's innovative applications of a Platonic conception. Nonetheless, in this regard Jousse did not specify how he saw mimetic activity in relation to what people encounter in their environment, although he was eager to emphasize his insight that "mimism *is* metaphor—transfer from cosmic movement as unconscious action-interaction to anthropological movement conscious as geste-proposition."[44]

In the absence of a definable way in which the natural environment might be described as mimetic, Jousse's insistence upon "cosmic movement as unconscious action-interaction" might be seen as more a theological assertion than a genuine extension of his anthropology. Yet in the recent past a view of physical matter itself has arisen and has been applied to the question of human consciousness so as to offer a surprising new prospect for Jousse's approach globally.

Quantum Mimêsis

During the course of the twentieth century, matter appeared to be both less and more than it seemed to be. The electron that once was supposed to be a subatomic unit that orbited around a nucleus was no longer conceived as such. Rather, the electron might sometimes be measurable as a value of energy, and sometimes as a particle, but not as both at the same time. Expressed at the level of the atom, that may seem an abstract

---

44. Jousse, *In Search*, 35, from a lecture given in 1935.

observation, but it proves to pose a fundamental challenge to a mechanical model of physical nature.

Erwin Schrödinger developed an equation that showed that particles could best be described as waves of energy. But if that is the case, could a particle really be in more than one place at the same time, like a wave of light? Schödinger denied that idea, and worked out a thought experiment, known as "Schrödinger's Cat,"[45] to express his objection. Quantum physics would have it that an electron's actual location in space and time only holds for the moment of observation; uncertainty shrouds where it is at another time or for another observer. To illustrate why that issue is troublesome, Schrödinger imagined a cat put at risk of poisoning inside a sealed box. The release of the poison was conditional on a Geiger counter detecting radiation at a marginal level that was also sealed in the box. Such a value that might or might not be picked up, since the precise position of all the subatomic particles involved (in the source of radiation and the Geiger counter) could not be determined in advance. Quantum uncertainty suggested that the cat would only be dead, or alive, when an observer opened the box. Schrödinger demurred, insisting that the cat was either dead or alive, independently of what someone might see after the fact of this strange experiment.

Schrödinger's illustration backfired after he set it out. Some physicists took his thought experiment, as well as his fundamental equation that represents quanta in terms of waves, to show that every quantum might occupy several positions at once. Only an observation can say what occurs in any given case. This means that it is true for that observation, and only that observation.[46] That implies that *each* position of particles such as electrons corresponds to different universes; at all times, people also might inhabit many worlds. Popularly called the "multiverse," this interpretation has proven extremely popular,[47] and profoundly controversial. It was just the corollary that Schrödinger disputed.

Recently, Roger Penrose, a Nobel laureate (2020) as a result of his work on black holes, has offered a resolution of this problem. At the same time, he has related his model of physical relations to an understanding of consciousness. If it is the case that all objects are subject to "superposition," such that they might be in one place or in other places, and if the

---

45. Bhaumik, "Is Schrödinger's Cat Alive?"
46. See Everett, "The Theory," 98.
47. See Kaku, *Parallel Worlds*.

multiverse is an unconvincing conclusion to draw from that, then there must be a better model. In Penrose's robust—but still controversial—theory, the superposition resolves itself as a result of the gravitational attraction *between* the quanta. They snap into place in what is conceived of as a resolution of time and space by "orchestrated objective reduction."[48] That resolution is the origin of consciousness, in that the brain is capable of detecting these moments when multiple potentials are resolved into single realities.

Both at the level of the relationships between quanta, and at the level of the claim that the brain can actually detect the emergence of such relationships, Penrose's contribution remains hypothetical. But the hypothesis involves positing a mimetic relationship between quanta, such that one quantum structures another in their mutual influence, and the perception of that relationship by a neurological process that is itself mimetic. In Jousse's language, it is a case of relating "cosmic movement as unconscious action-interaction to anthropological movement conscious as geste-proposition."[49]

The linkage between *mimêsis* in human beings, such that it structures their social relations, and *mimêsis* in the natural world, such that it makes conscious process possible, is expressed emphatically in Jousse's oeuvre, but its status has been more aspirational than demonstrable. It is possible, however, that an approach by means of the continued research suggested by Roger Penrose will offer Jousse's claims a fresh foundation. In his conversation with his assistant, Gabrielle Baron, after his crisis of health, Jousse reflected on his outburst, "It is too beautiful . . ." He asked her if she had seen "the two large shadows on the mountain who were walking away."[50] She did not, perhaps because what Jousse was perceiving was *mimêsis* itself, a force binding people together, expressed in the Aramaic teaching of Jesus, and finally embedded in the universe. If so, it is doubtless recoverable.

---

48. See Hameroff and Penrose, "Consciousness in the Universe"; Chilton, *Resurrection Logic*, 197–201.

49. Jousse, *In Search*, 35.

50. Baron, *Mémoire vivante*, 147; see also Jousse, *Memory*, 147.

Bibliography

Astell, Ann W., and Sandor Goodhart, eds. *Sacrifice, Scripture, and Substitution: Readings in Ancient Judaism and Christianity*. Christianity and Judaism in Antiquity Series 18. Notre Dame: University of Notre Dame Press, 2011.

Auerbach, Erich. *Mimesis: The Representation of Reality in Western Literature*. Translated by William Trask. 1953. Reprint, Princeton: Princeton University Press, 2003.

Baron, Gabrielle. *Mémoire vivante. Vie et oeuvre de Marcel Jousse*. Paris: Le Centurion, 1981.

Bhaumik, Mani. "Is Schrödinger's Cat Alive?" *Quanta* 6.1 (2017) 70–80.

Black, Matthew. *An Aramaic Approach to the Gospels and Acts*. 3rd ed. Oxford: Clarendon, 1967.

Boman, Thorleif. *Die Jesus-Überlieferung im Lichte der neueren Volkskunde*. Göttingen: Vandenhoeck & Ruprecht, 1967.

Caillois, Roger. "La mante religieuse: De la Biologie à la Psychanalyse." *Minotaure* 5 (1934) 23–16.

———. "Mimétisme et psychasthénie légendaire." *Minotaure* 7 (1935) 5–10.

———. *Le mythe et l'homme*. Paris: Gallimard, 1938.

Carré de Busserolle, J.-X. *Dictionnaire géographique, historique et biographique de l'Inde et Loire et de l'ancienne province de Touraine*, Volume II. Mémoire de la Societé Archéologique de la Touraine XXVIII. Tours: Rouillé-Ladevèze, 1879.

Cheng, Joyce. "Mask, Mimicry, Metamorphosis: Roger Caillois, Walter Benjamin and Surrealism in the 1930s." *Modernism/modernity* 16.1 (2009) 61–86.

Chilton, Bruce. "The Eucharist and the Mimesis of Sacrifice." In *Sacrifice, Scripture, and Substitution: Readings in Ancient Judaism and Christianity*, edited by Ann W. Astell and Sandor Goodhart, 140–54. Christianity and Judaism in Antiquity Series 18. Notre Dame: University of Notre Dame Press, 2011.

———. "A Generative Exegesis of Mark 7:1–23." *Journal of Higher Criticism* 3.1 (1996) 18–37.

———. *Jesus' Prayer and Jesus' Eucharist: His Personal Practice of Spirituality*. Valley Forge, PA: Trinity, 1997.

———. *Resurrection Logic: How Jesus' First Followers Believed God Raised Him from the Dead*. Waco: Baylor University Press, 2019.

———. *The Temple of Jesus: His Sacrificial Program within a Cultural History of Sacrifice*. University Park: Pennsylvania State University Press, 1992.

Chilton, Bruce et al., eds. *A Comparative Handbook to the Gospel of Mark: Comparisons with Pseudepigrapha, the Qumran Scrolls, and Rabbinic Literature*. The New Testament Gospels in Their Judaic Contexts 1. Leiden: Brill, 2010.

Churgin, Pinkhos. *Targum Jonathan to the Prophets*. Yale Oriental Series—Researches XIV. New Haven: Yale University Press, 1927.

Dalman, G. *The Words of Jesus: Considered in the Light of Post-Biblical Jewish Writings and the Aramaic Language*. Translated by D. M. Kay. 1902. Reprint, Eugene, OR: Wipf & Stock, 1997.

———. *Die Worte Jesu: Mit Berücksichtigung des nachkanonischen jüdischen Schrifttums und der aramäischen Sprache*. Leipzig: Hinrichs, 1898.

Díez Macho, Alejandro. *Neophyti 1. Targum Palestinense Ms de la Biblioteca Vaticana*. 6 vols. Madrid-Barcelona: Consejo Superior de Investigaciones Científicas, 1968–1979.

Eddy, Paul Rhodes. "Jesus as Diogenes? Reflections on the Cynic Jesus Thesis." *Journal of Biblical Literature* 115 (1996) 449–69.

Evans, Craig A. *To See and Not Perceive. Isaiah 6:9–10.* In *Early Jewish and Christian Interpretation*. Journal for the Study of the Old Testament Supplement Series 64. Sheffield: Sheffield Academic, 1989.

Everett, Hugh, III. "The Theory of the Universal Wave Function." In *The Many-Worlds Interpretation of Quantum Mechanics*, edited by Bryce S. DeWitt and R. Neil Graham, 3–32. Princeton Series in Physics. Princeton: Princeton University Press, 1973.

Falasca-Zamponi, Simonetta. "A Left Sacred or a Sacred Left? The 'Collège De Sociologie', Fascism, and Political Culture in Interwar France." *South Central Review* 23 (2006) 40–54.

Fitzmyer, Joseph A., and Daniel J. Harrington. *A Manual of Palestinian Aramaic Texts*. Biblica et Orientalia 34. Rome: Pontifical Biblical Institute Press, 1978.

Flesher, Paul V. M., and Bruce Chilton. *The Targums: A Critical Introduction*. Studies in Aramaic Interpretation of Scripture 12. Leiden: Brill, 2011.

Funk, Robert W., and Roy W. Hoover, eds. *The Five Gospels: The Search for the Authentic Words of Jesus*. New York: Macmillan, 1993.

Gerhardsson, Birger. *Memory and Manuscript: Oral Tradition and Written Transmission in Rabbinic Judaism and Early Christianity*. Translated by Eric J. Sharpe. Acta Seminarii Neotestamentici Upsaliensis 22. Lund: Glerup, 1961.

———. *Memory and Manuscript: Oral Tradition and Written Transmission in Rabbinic Judaism and Early Christianity*. Translated by Eric J. Sharpe. Rev. ed. Biblical Resource Series. Grand Rapids: Eerdmans, 1998.

Girard, René, *Deceit, Desire, and the Novel: Self and Other in Literary Structure*. Translated by Yvonne Freccero. Baltimore: Johns Hopkins University Press, 1965.

———. *Violence and the Sacred*. Translated by Patrick Gregory. Baltimore: Johns Hopkins University Press, 1977.

Hameroff, Stuart, and Roger Penrose. "Consciousness in the Universe: A Review of the 'Orch OR' Theory." *Physics of Life Reviews* 11 (2014) 39–78.

Hovind, Jacob. "Figural Interpretation as Modernist Hermeneutics: The Rhetoric of Erich Auerbach's *Mimesis*." *Comparative Literature* 64 (2012) 257–69.

Jousse, Marcel. *Memory, Memorization, and Memorizers: The Galilean Oral-Style Tradition and Its Traditionalists*. Edited and translated by Edgard Sienaert. Biblical Performance Criticism Series 15. Eugene, OR: Cascade Books, 2018.

———. *In Search of Coherence: Introducing Marcel Jousse's Anthropology of Mimism*. Edited and translated by Edgard Sienaert. Eugene, OR: Pickwick Publications, 2016.

Kahle, Paul. *The Cairo Geniza*. 2nd ed. Oxford: Blackwell, 1959.

Kaku, Michio. *Parallel Worlds: A Journey through Creation, Higher Dimensions, and the Future of the Cosmos*. New York: Doubleday, 2004.

Kaufman, Stephen A, ed. *The Comprehensive Aramaic Lexicon*. http://cal.huc.edu/.

———. "Dating the Language of the Palestinian Targums and Their Use in the Study of First-Century CE Tests." In *The Aramaic Bible: Targums in Their Historical Context*, edited by D. R. G. Beattie and M. J. McNamara, 118–141. Journal for the Study of the Old Testament Supplement Series 166. Sheffield, England: JSOT Press, 1994.

McNamara, Martin. *Targum and Testament Revisited: Aramaic Paraphrases of the Hebrew Bible*. Rev. ed. Grand Rapids: Eerdmans, 2010.

Manson, T. W. *The Teaching of Jesus*. 2nd ed. Cambridge: Cambridge University Press, 1955.

Ribouillaut, Claude. *La Musique au Fusil: Avec les Poilus de la Grande Guerre.* Arles: Rouergue, 1996.
Sarzana, Guiseppi. *De romanorum imperatorum ac summorum pontificum sollicitudine et provvidentia in conservandis veteribus monumentis.* Florence: Excudebat, 1828.
Wernberg-Møller, P. "An Inquiry into the Validity of the Text Critical Argument for an Early Dating of the Recently Discovered Palestinian Targum." *Vetus Testamentum* 12 (1962) 312–30.
York, Anthony D. "The Dating of Targumic Literature." *Journal for the Study of Judaism* 10 (1979) 49–62.

10

Marcel Jousse, the Synoptic Problem, and the Past and Future of Gospel Studies

MATTHEW D. C. LARSEN

This chapter is an exploratory and conceptual exercise, and perhaps a bit of a provocation, using the work of Marcel Jousse to think with my own field of ancient Christianity, and particularly the history of scholarship about the production of early gospel tradition. Rather than presenting data from antiquity and seeking to prove a *what*, *how*, or *when* type of question, this essay deals with concepts and considers a what-if type of question: namely, what might have happened if gospel scholars had paid attention to the work of Jousse nearly a century ago. I take up the work of Jousse on orality in first-century Palestine, the Synoptic problem, and the past, present, and possible future(s) of gospel studies.

Unlike other contributors in this volume, I am not an expert on Marcel Jousse. I am a cultural historian of ancient Christianity, and I have published on the emergence of gospel tradition in written form. Although I am not qualified to account for the full range of Jousse's thought or writings over the course of his career, I focus in this chapter on how Jousse felt his work related to the emergence of gospel tradition, and how Jousse's work may be able to help gospel scholars reimagine elemental questions in our field. I must apologize up front that I will rely here on some of my previous publications on early gospel tradition.

I focus particularly on what scholars have called the Synoptic problem. This has traditionally been understood as follows: how to solve the literary relationship between the early gospel traditions now known as the Gospel according to Mark, the Gospel according to Matthew, and the Gospel according to Luke. But, of course, from a methodological point of view, the problematic terms here are "problem" and "literary relationship." Yet, these are the terms of engagement for the Synoptic problem. Consequently, any adjudication of the problem is confined to the rubric of *Literaturkritik*.

There is another way, however. To think outside the traditional gospel studies box, I will engage with Jousse's work, published in French nearly a century ago, in the recent translation *Memory, Memorization, and Memorizers: The Galilean Oral-Style and Its Traditionists*. This will give us the chance to move away from a literary or "bookish" (to use Jousse's term) paradigm to think about an orality paradigm, on the one hand, and a fluid-textual paradigm, on the other. I put Jousse's *Memory, Memorization, and Memorizers* in conversation with my own work on textual fluidity and gospel tradition, especially my 2018 monograph, *Gospels before the Book*, as well as some of my other articles and chapters.[1] Jousse's work and my own work, from very different angles, both point out and call into question the validity of some of the more modern bookish assumptions of gospel studies.

In this chapter, I will think critically and constructively about the past and future of gospel studies and entertain the question: what would have happened if scholars of early gospel tradition had taken the insights of Jousse more seriously. How might the field of gospel studies have looked different? What different paths might the form critics have taken? How might the practices of redaction critics and textual critics have been different, had the field been less shot through with what Marcel Jousse called "algebrosis"?[2] Would the Synoptic problem still have been regarded

---

1. Larsen, "Accidental Publication"; Larson, *Gospels before the Book*; Larson, "Correcting the Gospel"; "The Real-and-Imagined Biography of a Gospel Manuscript"; Larson, "According to Mark as Hypomnemata"; Larson, "The Publication of the Synoptics"; "Listening with the Body"; Larsen and Letteney, "Christians and the Codex."

2. Jousse's term "algebrosis" should probably be explained to the readers. Jousse states, "I created the word 'algebrosis' from existing terminology. We can perform no scientific function at present without *algebra*, in which a voluntary process of simplification takes place and signs are assigned meaning by consensus. In *algebrosis* the signs or words, which are *gestes*, can mean 'anything' because we no longer see their connection with the real they originally referred to. We live by a system in which all *gestes* are diminished and degraded, be they corporeal, manual, laryngo-buccal or graphic, because they are emptied of their original concretism" (Jousse, *Memory*, 8). Jousse, then, associates the algebraic mind with Greek and Latin modes of thinking

as a problem at all? Or would the complex constellation of overlapping and interlocking gospel traditions instead have been imagined as an inevitable and living process? What new possibilities would or could have emerged?[3]

Along the way, I will gesture to the similarities and differences between Jousse's approach and my own work on the emergence of early written gospel tradition. I believe my work, almost all of it done without knowledge of Jousse's work, is augmented by Jousse's framework and insights, although I come at matters from different corners than Jousse does; in turn, Jousse's framework is improved and strengthened by my work, and mine by his.

Reconsidering the Past and Present

Our current media situation allows us new perspectives on the issue of textual change and multiplicity. This is perhaps because we are living in an increasingly digital or even post-printing-press era, with the result that we are in a better position to see what intellectual blind spots had previously been caused by "bookish" assumptions created by the rise and death of the author in the mid-twentieth century. Put otherwise, our different media situations allow us to see things differently. So, in turning to Jousse, we turn again to questions of textual fluidity, on the one hand, and speech, on the other. On both we can learn from Jousse and in turn update his thinking. Yet we can never go back to or re-create the past. To try to do so would be both counterproductive and is in fact impossible. Each day we can make a new future, and as we do so, it is essential to reconsider the past from our new present situation.

But we do not return to a previous century of scholars simply by going backwards in time, which would be both impossible and undesirable. We reconsider the past with new questions and insights about how reading and writing practices work, both in our own moment and in antiquity. One of the arenas where we have made progress is in the field of

---

and communication (Jousse, *Memory*, 190), as opposed to Jewish ones.

3. Of the items mentioned above—that is, form criticism, redaction criticism, textual criticism, the Synoptic problem—I will mainly focus on the latter. Yet, I mention the others because I believe they are all related, both in terms of the history of the discipline, and in how the discipline of gospel studies is methodologically partitioned. At the pediment of each of the issues mentioned stands the Synoptic problem. Without it, the architecture of the discipline needs to be rethought.

book history, which focuses on questions related to how the technology and the idea of the book was constructed and developed across history.[4] Developments in a variety of fields have made it easier for us to see how gospel scholars of a previous century were operating within a printing-press framework as unknowingly as fish swim in water. The work of scholars in the field of book history has made it impossible to assume that books have always existed, or to continue to regard them as normal and inherently more valuable and more reliable than oral tradition—and to question the assumption that when we say "book," we all know what a book really is. In this regard, we are positioned to return to a previous century of scholars critically and constructively.

For Bultmann and the form critics, what was important were the strategies for transmitting and changing stories from the moment they were first spoken up through the period of their retelling until the time they were captured in the form of "the book."[5] That is, how do we account for the time from the initial utterance, whether by Jesus or someone else, followed by the vicissitudes of oral transmission, and the creation of discrete, stable, and self-contained books that we call gospels? By looking at how people transmitted oral tradition, they developed theories that allowed them to peel back the layers of the onion, so to speak. Put bluntly, they cared about what happened from circa 30 CE to circa 70 CE and what happened before the gospels were frozen in a written medium as books. They "failed" to recover what was uttered in 30 CE, but they believed they made some progress in determining how the stories changed over this critical period between their "original" utterance and its "solidification" in "books." Subsequent "fluidity" of the tradition "after the book" was beyond the purview of the form critics, as they saw it, because they were working under the mistaken assumption that the textualized medium provided a safeguard of stability.

---

4. Here are a few key works on book history. McKenzie, *Bibliography and the Sociology of Texts*; Chartier, *The Order of Books*; McGann, *The Textual Condition*; Eisenstein, *The Printing Press as an Agent of Change*.

5. I am thinking here of the key works on form criticism: Bultmann, *Die Geschichte der synoptischen Tradition*; Dibelius, *Die Formgeschichte des Evangeliums*. In some ways, this was a movement that led to a series of important culs-de-sac, and some may regard it as failure. As I shall argue here, we return today to the question of form, and how stories and texts change over time. While the form critics failed in their effort to get back to some original moment of creation, we now have better tools to track the forward-moving change to living tradition, in both its oral and textual components.

Redaction critics emerged in the 1950s and 1960s and shifted the question to the genius of the author, which in this case meant the producers of gospel tradition as author-figures. What was critical for them was tracing the creativity of the author as he used previous sources to craft his own book.[6] From this moment, the genius lay not in the initial utterance or in the community of oral transmitters of tradition, but in the author-figure of the so-called evangelist. Again, put bluntly, they cared about what happened between the creation of the first gospel book and the last gospel book, circa 70 to 100 CE. When it came to sources from the second century, redaction critics handed the baton to noncanonical scholars or textual critics, depending on the nature of the source. Oral tradition before the period of the book was a mist of the bard now gone; changes to the tradition after they were immortalized in the book format was the weakness of faulty scribes.

The Book as Controlling Metaphor

In all of this, there is an overlooked problem. There is the assumption of "the book" at the heart of scholarly history. That is, not just a book but a framing idea of bookishness, or, put differently, the controlling metaphor of *the book*.[7] As God spoke in Genesis 1 on the first day, "Let there be light!" and all else flowed thereafter, so the biblical scholar in the beginning uttered, "Let there be books!" and all subsequent questions emerged from a bookish foundation. What differentiates form criticism from redaction criticism, as well as source criticism and text criticism, too, is the assumption of a singular moment (or series of singular moments) wherein a gospel emerges as a book, complete and frozen in time. All these modes of critique essentially track how gospel traditions change. But "we philologists" have placed one type of change in one category and

---

6. The key works of redaction criticism are Marxsen, *Der Evangelist Markus*; Perrin, *What is Redaction Criticism?* Anthony Hanson in a review of Perrin's book succinctly defined redaction criticism, then the "latest method of Gospel criticism," as "an analysis of the Gospels with the aim of discovering what was in the mind of the evangelist as he wrote." See Hanson, Review of Norman Perrin, *What Is Redaction Criticism?* Note the optimism and positivity of approach in the relation to the mind and intent of the author-figure. The practice of redaction criticism remains active in gospel scholarship, at least more so than form criticism.

7. On the book as metaphor, see Mroczek, *The Literary Imagination*, 50.

another type of change in another category based on the metaphor of the book and our aesthetic judgments.[8]

For instance, the person who produced the textual tradition that we now call the Gospel according to Luke used other prior sources in the creation of his own instantiation of gospel tradition. Is that change a part of the transmission history of those sources? No, or at least not in the traditional framing of gospel scholars, because the Gospel according to Luke has been thought of as a book, and is part of Scripture—the Bible, the Book par excellence. Both the producer(s) of the Gospel according to Luke and the scribes of the so-called Western text both changed the previous versions of sources before them. Yet when the scribes of the so-called Western text did to Luke-Acts what the compiler of the Gospel according to Luke did to his sources, is this treated in the same way?[9] No, of course not; but why not? Twentieth-century gospel scholars treated the Gospel according to Luke and the Western text differently because many assumed that the author Luke wrote finished books, completed and complete at a specific moment in time, whereas later Western scribes were not authors and lacked agency.[10] But what if we introduce another metaphor besides "the book," with its concomitant figures of the author and the scribe? What if we don't assume finality but vibrant fluidity as the controlling metaphor? If we do not begin a priori with the assumption of the book as the organizing principle, what is left of the infrastructure of biblical studies, and what remains of what Marcel Jousse called "the Synoptic pseudo-problem"?

---

8. With the language of "we philologists," I am referencing the title of Nietzsche's 1875 unpublished essay (though published posthumously) "We Philologists," not self-identifying as a philologist.

9. The Western text of Acts is roughly 10 percent longer than the Alexandrian version. See Metzger, *A Textual Commentary*, 259–60: "The Western text is nearly one-tenth longer than the Alexandrian text, and is generally more picturesque and circumstantial, whereas the shorter text is generally more colorless and in places more obscure." A similar assessment could be made of how the Gospel according to Luke reworked the Gospel according to Mark, although the latter is occasionally more colorful.

10. Strange, *The Problem of the Text of Acts*.

The Problem of the Book and Marcel Jousse on the Synoptic (Pseudo-)Problem

Jousse intuited much of this almost a century ago. Jousse was lecturing in Paris from 1931 to 1957.[11] The first edition of his book, *The Oral Style* was published in 1925. Importantly, his work temporally coincided with the rise of form criticism, with Martin Dibelius publishing *Die Formgeschichte des Evangeliums* in 1919 and Rudolf Bultmann publishing *Die Geschichte der synoptischen Tradition* in 1921. While broadly coinciding chronologically with the rise of form criticism, Jousse was siloed off from the form critics and was very much on his own constructing a very different path.

Part of the reason why Jousse could clearly see the problem with the Synoptic problem was because of his work on orality, memory, and performance. He knew that to switch metaphors away from the book would have profound and fundamental implications. I have argued that at the nexus of so many of the fundamental questions about the gospel tradition (text, source, and redaction criticism) is the issue of the Synoptic problem, and I believe Jousse would agree with me in this regard.[12]

By my count, in *Memory, Memorization, and Memorizers* alone, he refers to the Synoptic problem (or closely related issues) sixteen times, and his conclusion is that the assumption of the book and bookish philology (he links this not only with Greco-Roman literary techniques but also Greco-Roman ways of thinking) is the sole impetus behind what has come to be called the Synoptic problem.[13] He refers to the "bothersome so-called Synoptic Problem." He wrote that the Gospels were "not merely books for reading" but for reciting. That is, they are not pieces of literature to be read by an individual in silence, but scripts to be memorized and performed with improvisation. Jousse held that

> For memory-aids [the Gospels] are, and not merely books for reading. Being themselves without memory, our critics forget to study the evidence and operation of memory in these texts. That is why the Synoptic Problem is an amnesic problem. Were the problem properly identified, a great many questions would be clarified, and some would simply disappear.[14]

---

11. See Kelber's introductory chapter in this volume, "The Work of Marcel Jousse in Context."

12. See Larsen, "The Publication of the Synoptics."

13. It is telling that many of Jousse's critical remarks are qualified as "bookish."

14. Jousse, *Memory*, 44 (see also p. 305).

Amnesia caused the Synoptic problem, for Jousse, and the amnesia was in the minds of gospel scholars who had forgotten (or never learned) how memory worked in first-century Palestine. To identify the problem would not solve but rather dissolve the Synoptic problem as such. Jousse also stated that "It is this diversiform seder with its seven strands that caused the improperly, and so bookishly called Synoptic Problem. There is no Synoptic Problem. There is only the fact of the Palestinian seder with all its accompanying rhythmo-catechistic implications."[15]

For Jousse, if gospel scholars were to switch the controlling metaphor from author-scribe to apprehender-reciter, the Synoptic problem would disappear. But the person who approaches the complexities from the perspective of the "Greco-Latinizing bookish critic . . . will invent for himself the most insoluble pseudo-problems imaginable. Such a pseudo-problem does not exist; it is the synoptic pseudo-problem, a problem that does not exist."[16] The Synoptic problem was not solvable, for Jousse, because it is not a problem of antiquity but a problem of modern book culture, and outside of the paradigm and controlling metaphor of the book it is only a pseudo-problem.[17] Jousse himself saw the matter from another perspective:

> My position is, *the solution to our evangelical literature lies in the targums,* for the simple reason that the targums are a *popular literature,* essentially popular, . . . Thus, Yeshua and his apprehenders . . . did what seemed to them the appropriate thing to do: to reconstruct a new story with the old formulas. That then is, in sum, my solution to the neo-testament problem of the Synoptics, one for anyone well-disposed to use.[18]

15. Jousse, *Memory,* 66.

16. Jousse, *Memory,* 96.

17. As a side note, Jousse did not comment on the history of the Synoptic problem qua problem, although it would have arguably strengthened his argument. While the first person to articulate an explanation for the obvious literary relationship between the canonical Gospels is usually understood to be Augustine, and his view held sway until the modern Western period, the relationship between the Synoptic Gospels was not regarded as a problem until the emergence of modern critical scholarship. For more on this history, see, for example, Watson's chapters "Augustine's Ambiguous Legacy" and "Dismantling the Canon: Lessing/Reimarus" in *Gospel Writing,* 13–113.

18. Jousse, *Memory,* 166 (italics original). I would distance myself from the term "popular" literature, especially of the kind that looks to romanticize the divinely inspired poetry of "common folk." See the critique here of Walsh, *The Origins,* 50–104. Jousse may perhaps be viewed by some as somewhat guilty of such. Yet I see his intervention not in the "popular" but in studying how people told and retold stories in ancient Jewish contexts.

"To reconstruct a new story with the old formulas" is a consequential statement, one that is quite different from the identity of Jesus developed by the mainstream of twentieth-century gospel scholarship. Not only did Jousse claim to resolve the Synoptic problem as a problem of modernity, but he also, commendably, attempted to resettle Jesus more fully in his ancient Jewish historical context, which many scholars after him missed during the second quest for the historical Jesus. Jousse, then, like Birger Gerhardsson, relied on later rabbinic tradition and comparative orality studies.[19] Jousse, however, unlike Gerhardsson, principally relied on the targumic traditions, which began orally in rabbinic Judaism and eventually were written down. There are targumic scrolls in Qumran, which suggests some of the targumic traditions may in fact have existed even in the first century BCE, such as 11Q Targum Job.[20] Jousse's case for a living (= oral) Aramaic, targumic tradition in first-century Galilee is therefore rendered more plausible than attempts like Gerhardsson's.[21] To wit, the contribution of Bruce Chilton to this volume is important.

Jousse argued that the gospel tradition consists of "fluid texts." By this he seemed to mean a text that is fixed in its written form but fluid in its improvised performance. He did not seem to question the solidity of "books" or of textual traditions, treating them as fixed, stable things. Once written down, texts assume a form of stability, however brief and temporary it may seem.

Symbiotic Fluidity in Text, Tradition, and Performance

To my mind, Jousse (at least in *Memory, Memorization, and Memorizers*) connected his concept of fluidity with recitation, performance, and improvisation, not with textuality and writtenness.[22] He still worked with the controlling metaphor of books as fundamentally stable and performance as the key component of fluidity. Texts change over, for Jousse, but they can be most basically categorized as stable.[23] For him, these fixed

---

19. Gerhardsson, *Memory and Manuscript*; *The Reliability*.

20. See Kaufman, "The Job Targum from Qumran."

21. See Kelber's introductory chapter in this volume, "The Work of Marcel Jousse in Context."

22. See esp. Jousse, *Memory*, 30–31, where the term "fluid texts" is used. Yet even there, when read in context, the fluidity is a product of performance. Jousse does not there consider the fluidity of textualization itself.

23. Here I may disagree with other contributors to the volume. In my defense, I am

texts required performance, and it was the act of performance that was inevitably fluid. Improvisation does not change the written text. Jousse still links writtenness with stability. In Jousse's view, books were not fluid; their performance was. In this way, for him, this means that the so-called Synoptic problem is in fact a pseudo-problem based on misguided, bookish assumptions and solved strictly by understanding oral recitation. So, a return to Jousse would, at a minimum, raise the question: is the Synoptic problem still a problem?

But we cannot simply return to Jousse completely on his own terms and in his own time. Nor should we desire to do so. We can, however, make use of Jousse's forgotten insights and cautions and then put them in conversation with current scholarly exchanges. We have made advances in the intervening years. To begin, his claims of the uniqueness and historical exemplarity of Jesus's mimetic teaching needs to be tamped down and historically situated both in the ancient Mediterranean contexts as well as the contexts of Jousse's own biography as a Jesuit academician working in early twentieth-century France. Additionally, Jousse could be charged with creating too sharp a binary between Judaism, on the one hand, and Hellenization, on the other; further, he could be accused of conflating Hellenistic and Roman culture in the term *Greco-Roman*.[24] Lastly, he might be accused of idealizing a simple, pure, and popular origin to the Gospels. At his best, though, Jousse offers a meaningful alternative framework for thinking about how gospel tradition emerged, one in which there are not multiple discrete books but a constellation of oral traditions.

More directly related, however, to my chapter here on the Synoptic problem and the past and future and gospel studies is another matter. One of the recent areas of active research has been around how ancient people read and how they wrote, or ancient reading and writing practices.[25] We now have a more nuanced approach to ancient textualities, reading practices, and writing practices. These advances, in my view, expand several of Jousse's claims about ancient writing practices by offering small challenges that in fact strengthen his overall conclusions about the

---

working with Jousse's view as expressed in *Memory*, and I am not aware that Jousse changed his mind or expressed himself differently elsewhere.

24. See, e.g., Hengel, *Judaism and Hellenism*; Petersen, "Paul the Jew."

25. Carr, *Holy Resilience*; Hezser, *Jewish Literacy*; Person, *From Conversation to Oral Tradition*; Kirk, *Memory and the Jesus Tradition*; Mroczek, *The Literary Imagination*; Gurd, *Work in Progress*; Johnson, *Readers and Reading*.

Synoptic problem as a pseudoproblem. While Jousse saw the fluidity of performance as exposing the Synoptic problem as a pseudoproblem, my own work on the fluidity of written texts in gospel tradition, and the work of others on fluidity in ancient Jewish texts and Greek and Roman text, further underscores Jousse's position. I read Jousse as viewing the performance of script as pushing the fluidity of texts; I argue for a symbiotic fluidity between text and performance. To Jousse's constellation of oral traditions I add the reality of a constellation of textual traditions. These work in tandem to undermine the modern bookish assumptions necessary to formulate such a thing as a Synoptic problem.

Jousse refers several times to "fluid texts," which he calls by "an apparently contradictory but perfectly adequate name."[26] But Jousse is thinking of a particular kind of fluidity: the texts "vary 'fluidly,' not only from one reciter to another, but also, for the same reciter, from one day to another."[27] Put in other words, the written texts themselves are considered as fixed products, but the recitation or performance is inherently fluid. In this way, Jousse is both ahead of his time as well as a product of his time.[28] He is decades ahead of other form critics in terms of thinking about how fluidity works, but in the company of the form critics by thinking of a text as a stable product rather than an ongoing process.

Recently, however, a variety of scholars working in the fields of classics, ancient Judaism, New Testament, ancient Christianity, late antiquity, and medieval studies have noted that texts themselves, and not just their performances, are fluid.[29] John Bryant in his book *The Fluid Text* refers to texts as having an energy.[30] Perhaps because we are accustomed to

---

26. Jousse, *Memory*, 30.

27. Jousse, *Memory*, 31.

28. I suppose an imaginary interlocutor might interject, "Yes, but once it is written down, a text is fixed until or unless it is—in whatever form—changed, rewritten or re-oralized." Of course, but this still offers a perspective trapped within a controlling metaphor of text as stable, when it is not, and certainly was not in antiquity. To untangle the Synoptic pseudoproblem, we must go to the root of the matter, which is the controlling metaphor of textual stability. Jousse viewed the apprehension and recitation of the tradition as the source of the Synoptic pseudoproblem. I would agree but add that the inherent instability of textuality in antiquity is a further contributing factor, not a safeguard against change.

29. Breed, *Nomadic Text*; Najman, "The Vitality of Scripture"; Gurd, *Work in Progress*; Peirano, *The Rhetoric*; Mroczek, *The Literary Imagination;* Larsen, *Gospels before the Book*; Parker, *The Living Text*; Rebeillard, *The Early Martyr Narratives*; Dahlmann, "Textual Fluidity."

30. Bryant, *The Fluid Text*. For the purposes of comparing my own work with that

technologies like Google Docs or Wikipedia, we can see clearly now how both before and after the book (and truthfully the book and the printing press never really did away with this), written works can be productively viewed not as stable products but as processes. My own work has shown how many different ancient cultures shared the idea of a utilitarian form of writing that was explicitly designed to be rewritten, to become something else, to change, to be augmented, co-opted, fixed, or undermined. In this way, fluidity relates to both the oral recitation and the ongoing process of writing.[31] There is an interwoven relationship between writing and performance, and both contribute to a textual tradition's fluidity. In fact, Jousse's framework, while not escaping entirely from the controlling metaphor of textual stability, provides a useful position for describing the symbiotic relationship between oral and textual fluidity.[32]

My book *Gospels before the Book* shows how, without the assumption of author-figures and self-contained, stable books, the emergence of the textual traditions that we call the Gospels according to Matthew, Mark, Luke, and John, along with the Gospel according to Thomas, the Gospel according to Peter, and dozens of others, are concrete evidence that the gospel tradition did not become stabilized once written. Gospel writing was an ongoing act that moved well into the second and third centuries and beyond. The textualization of the gospel did not serve as a stabilizing feature. By the existence of the different written iterations of the gospel, and the various forms of individual iterations (such as the endings of Mark), we have clear evidence that the textualization of the gospel tradition was part and parcel of its vitality and fluidity. Rather than viewing gospel tradition as a set of separate and distinct books published by unique "authors," I show that it is more historically credible to view the emergence of textualized gospel tradition through the lens of open, unfinished, and revisable ancient writing practices. That is, the textual traditions we now call the Gospel according to Matthew and the Gospel according to Mark would likely not have been viewed by a late

---

of Jousse, it is interesting that I use Bryant's theory in my own approach, and Bryant's theory is based on both book and screenplay (i.e., performance).

31. See here, for example, the work of Ulrich, *The Dead Sea Scrolls*, 11–12: "the scribes were also updating the tradition and making it relevant to the current situation" (11). For Ulrich, the history of the Hebrew Scriptures is one of "revised editions of traditional material." He offers numerous examples. See also Siker, *Liquid Scripture*.

32. One might counter that with writing comes a degree of scribal stability that remains in place unless or until it gives way to recitational performance or rewriting. Yet I maintain that the act of textualization itself creates fluidity in big and small ways.

first- or early second-century reader as two similar but different books by different authors, but as two different instantiations of the same living and changing textualized tradition. This claim about textual fluidity does not exclude performance and improvisation of tradition as an additional site of variance. The two phenomena both symbiotically support fluidity.

Jousse was right to see how performance and memory created variance, and "variants are not fertile ground for synoptic problems, but are as many proofs of mastery in traditional oral-style performance."[33] That is, the existence of textual variants does not constitute the basis for a Synoptic problem, but textual variants themselves are proof of the performance, improvisation, and reperformance of gospel tradition in the oral style. The more one performs a text, the more variance of the tradition one is likely to find.

But the issue goes further than Jousse realized. The variance of tradition was as native to oral performance as it was to textual production. Jousse was mistaken to view text as inherently stable and moribund. "The text," for Jousse, "was as secure as our catechisms," and "the laws of oral style did not much apply in this text [i.e., of the Gospels]."[34] The processes of reading and writing practices in antiquity created fluidity, and the assumptions of textuality in antiquity worked rather more like a Google doc than a printed volume. The insights that Jousse had about fluidity in oral performance have a parallel, *mutatis mutandis*, in ancient textuality and writing practices, and the emergence of gospel tradition itself is proof of this, as my own work has shown. In fact, the matter goes one step further: the fluidity of the oral performance and the fluidity of the textual production are mutually beneficial and connected in a process that is not unilateral.

---

33. Jousse, *Memory*, 47.

34. Jousse, *Memory*, 393. This may be a place where Jousse's too clean bifurcation of Jewish and Greco-Roman culture presents a problem for his theory. The gospels, for him, were still heavily oral, formulaic texts, situated thoroughly in a first century Palestinian context. Jousse sees "algebrosis" was setting in with their Greek and Latin translations, and with the scholars' bookish approaches. In this, he is both working with categories of Jewish vs. Hellenistic vs. Roman that are too distinct as well as viewing the Greco-Roman context as the bookish (i.e., stable) one.

A Comparison: Homeric and Gospel Tradition on Pluriformity, Performance, and Titles

Let me illustrate this with the well-known examples from antiquity—the works of Homer—and how this example sheds light on gospel tradition. Homer's works were initially orally performed and memorized.[35] The tradition was preserved through re-presentation of the stories over centuries, if not millennia. During this period, the performance of Homer was a debated issue. Plato did not approve of a certain type of Homeric performing specialist.[36] He described this performer as follows:

> "Then the narrative that he will employ will be the kind that we just now illustrated by the verses of Homer, and his diction will be one that partakes of both, of imitation and simple narration, but there will be a small portion of imitation in a long discourse—or is there nothing in what I say?" "Yes, indeed," he said, "that is the type and pattern of such a speaker." "Then," said I, "the other kind of speaker, the more debased he is the less will he shrink from imitating anything and everything. He will think nothing unworthy of himself, so that he will attempt, seriously and in the presence of many, to imitate all things, including those we just now mentioned—claps of thunder, and the noise of wind and hail and axles and pulleys, and the notes of trumpets and flutes and pan-pipes, and the sounds of all instruments, and the cries of dogs, sheep, and birds; and so his style will depend wholly on imitation in voice and gesture, or will contain but a little of pure narration."[37]

The performance of Homer that Plato disdained so much, but that perhaps was not uncommon during the time, involved improvising the "text" of Homer with all manner of animal and nature sounds.[38] It was more like a staged performance each time, and less like the Victorian image of someone reading a book to children as they sit around the reader. The text was primarily oral, and this orality allowed the textual tradition to live and breathe and move in a thousand different directions to meet the needs of the performer and the audience. This undoubtedly created a growing and even mushrooming textual component to the Homeric

---

35. See, e.g., Nagy, *Homer the Preclassic*.
36. See Kivy, *The Performance of Reading*, 7–10.
37. Plato, *Republic* 3.396e–397c, trans. Shorey.
38. See, e.g., Havelock, *Preface to Plato*.

stories, produced by the oral performance, which would then further influence the textual version, and so on and so forth goes the cycle. But, again, the symbiotic relationship between fluidity in the oral and the textual realms goes deeper still.

Later, in the third and second centuries BCE, the Alexandrian grammarians (such as Aristarchus) began to establish revised and corrected versions of Homer's works in authoritative written forms.[39] Yet, this process of textualizing Homer did not entirely or even necessarily eliminate diverse forms of Homer's works. With each new corrected edition, the text of Homer changed a bit more, with one more option on the table.

The parallel between the versions of Homeric tradition and the emergent textual variance of gospel tradition becomes tighter when titular particularity attached to the Gospels (in the second half of the second century CE) is put in its historical context. Important for the purposes of this chapter, the titles that came to be attached to these different versions were "Homer's *Iliad*, according to [name/city]," with [name/city] referring to the name of the corrector or the edition used in a city.[40] Similar things happened with Virgil's *The Aeneid*, with late antique Latin grammarians, and there the growth and vibrancy of the textual tradition was not a "problem" but something to be embraced.[41]

The growth of gospel tradition in the first couple centuries is like (though, of course, not identical to) the growth of Homeric tradition. I do not mean this in terms of content but in terms of textuality and orality, stability and fluidity, multiplicity and vitality. Both were initially uttered, then later recited, then written down, then recited again, then written down again, then recited again, and so forth. Some people cared to establish something like a corrected version of the tradition in writing. Some of these editions came to be called Gospel, according to [name]. Others seemed more concerned with the performance and vibrancy of the tradition. The form of the titles given to the corrected edition of a certain text of Homer and the various iterations of the written gospel are obviously parallel phenomena. Homer's *Iliad* (or *Odyssey*) according to [name of the corrector] comes in the form κατά plus the name of the person in the accusative. This is explicitly *not* the formula used to denote authorship. For

---

39. See Larsen, "Correcting the Gospel," 80–84. I am setting aside here the question about the Alexandrian library, and focusing on the work of grammarians who edited the textual strands of Homer.

40. West, *Studies in the Text*, 46–67.

41. Peirano, *The Rhetoric*, 242–63.

that, one would use the genitive: Homer's *Iliad*. The formula "according to [name]" in antiquity uniformly and exclusively denotes not the author but the name of the corrector of a fluid and pluriform textual tradition.[42] I suggest that similar and unique titles were attached to both traditions, because they were similar phenomena: both involve a complex blend of textualization, editorial work, oral performance, and improvisation.

As I have shown elsewhere, during the course of the second century CE the formula of "according to [name]" is applied to different editions of the gospel, with Irenaeus as the earliest literary evidence.[43] Prior to that, a gospel was an oral proclamation, and once it began to be textualized, the gospel was the Lord's gospel or the gospel of Jesus (Mark 1:1), who is not the author but is the authorizing and originating figure of the proclamation and textualization. Different iterations of the pluriform and fluid gospel come to be assigned to different people, none using the genitive of authorship but rather the "according to [name]" formula. This labels the so-called evangelists not as the authors but as the revisers, correctors, or reworkers of the fluid and pluriform textual tradition known as the gospel.

In both Homer and the gospel, we have then similar examples of traditions that look less like single books and more like vibrant constellations of textual traditions. In both, we have an authorizing/originating figure who never wrote a book, but whose text took on its own energy and changed in various ways. In both, we have a tradition that exists in many separate yet related and authorized forms. In both, we can reimagine the interwoven relationship of fluidity between oral recitation and writing practices.

Rereading the Shape of Gospel Tradition— Again—with the Insights of Jousse

The shape of gospel tradition is an area in which orality and ancient writing practices influence one another. Much of Jousse's work shows how the intercalation of gospel tradition relates to oral style of performance, improvisation, and storytelling in first-century Palestine.

> What we are confronted with today [i.e., in the text of the Gospels] is the static form of what was essentially and primarily alive

---

42. Larsen, "Correcting the Gospel," 80–84.
43. On the manuscript evidence, see Larsen, "Correcting the Gospel," 86–89.

> in the intercalary formation. Our fixed version of today was once one form *among many others* that remained living, acting and teaching. And today, with three versions of a living and fluid pearl before us, we will never know with certainty if, in practice, and before a certain apprehender, there was somewhere an ephemeral insertion or omission. Our inert, fixed text does not reflect what was once a moving and living mimodrama.[44]

The language here is dense and full of jargon, but the contrasting ideas are clear. Jousse meant that we will never know how the gospel was recited and performed in specific ancient contexts, and the written version may trick us into thinking of the gospel tradition as primarily static in its written form. True, but when he produces the binary of now-written-fixed versus then-performed-fluid, he invites the mistaken idea that the written text *back then* was also fixed and inert. It was not even in the "Greco-Latinizing" contexts, as I show in *Gospels before the Book*, and this is where I view my own work as correcting and strengthening Jousse's claim about the Synoptic pseudoproblem.[45] The key part is this: Textual revision was an integral part of ancient writing practices and functioned in a similar way that recitation functioned for Jousse—as necessarily creating fluidity of tradition. The more texts were used, the more they tended to be reworked. On the other hand, a similar sort of intercalation (sandwiching of stories, or placing stories side by side for later use and reuse) can be seen in a particular form of ancient writing, too: in ὑπομνήματα and *commentarii*, or ancient note collection.[46] Ancient note-taking is similar in that notes were organized by key words and topics. This is exemplified well in the anecdote by Aulus Gellius in his *Attic Nights*. In the following quotation from his preface, he reflected on the organization of his writing:

> But in the arrangement of my material, I have adopted the same haphazard order that I had previously followed in collecting it. For whenever I had taken in hand any Greek or Latin book, or had heard anything worth remembering, I used to jot down whatever took my fancy, of any and every kind, without any definite plan or order; and such notes I would lay away as an aid to my memory, like a kind of literary storehouse, so that when the need arose of a subject or a word (*aut rei aut verbi*) which I

---

44. Jousse, *Memory*, 56.
45. Larsen, *Gospels before the Book*, 11–78.
46. Larsen, *Gospels before the Book*, 11–78, 121–26.

chanced for the moment to have forgotten, and the books from which I had taken it were not at hand, I could readily find and produce it.[47]

We see this same sort of organization in the earliest strands of gospel tradition. As I showed in *Gospels before the Book*, this sort of intercalation and organization appears in the Gospel according to Mark. The Gospel according to Mark also adds an element of bracketing stories in order to hold various collections of notes together, such as beginning a collection by grouping stories about healing a blind man or feeding a multitude.[48] This seems to be another way that the orality and textuality work in similar ways. Contrary to Jousse, we do not need to bifurcate the oral and the written to make sense of the issue of intercalation in gospel tradition. Orality and textuality both serve to promote such intercalary style; in fact, in terms of emergence of gospel tradition, they both do.

The processes of orality and performance have, *mutatis mutandis*, counterparts in the textual revision and fluidity. The collation and organization described by Aulus Gellius, in addition to the textual revision and alteration described in *Gospels before the Book*, do not work in exactly the same way as Jousse's orality, but—and this is the important part—both Jousse's orality and my textual fluidity work against the modern bookish assumptions necessary to formulate something like the Synoptic problem.

All of this, of course, does not undercut Jousse's insight that the Synoptic problem is a pseudoproblem. In fact, it strengthens it. It is not that the Synoptic problem has been "solved" but that, in this new light, it comes to be seen as simply a badly formulated question. Jousse viewed the so-called Synoptic problem as simply a misunderstanding of how memory and orality worked in Palestine and thus the three so-called Synoptic Gospels were not "little books composed half and half of Deeds and Sayings, in which three authors scratch[ed] about haphazardly." For him, this "is a vain plumitive fantasy that, explaining nothing, muddles everything."[49] Thus, "there is no Synoptic Problem. There is only the fact of the Palestinian seder with all its accompanying rhythmo-catechistic implications . . . Include memory in the equation, and everything falls

---

47. Aulus Gellius, *Noct. att. praef.* 1–2; translation from Larsen, *Gospels before the Book*, 126.

48. Larsen, *Gospels before the Book*, 127–35.

49. Jousse, *Memory*, 66.

... in[to] place; exclude memory and include writing, and you have a recipe for the most inextricable of pseudo-problems textual criticism ever encountered."[50] To this I would add the complementary idea: there is only ever the concrete evidence of textual revision and fluidity going farther and farther back, and never a pristine "original" moment of book-published-by-author. It is not that it is "turtles [of revision] all the way down," but for all practical purposes, from where we now sit, this may be a distinction without difference. In Jousse's model and my own, we cannot get back to the original, but we are left with ample data to track its evolution in subsequent iterations. Jousse's insight on orality and performance in conjunction with my work on textual fluidity suggest we move from a backward-looking model searching for bookish origins; that we instead look for a forward-moving model that incorporates the vitality of both the oral and textual dimensions.[51]

Conclusion

So then, we stand to learn from Jousse's insights about how orality and memory show how the Synoptic problem, and consequently much of gospel scholarship, is asking the wrong question. The Synoptic problem, as traditionally conceived, has presupposed that the problem of the significant overlap of the three Synoptic Gospels is a bookish problem, produced by three ancient authors who published three ancient books, and the solution to this bookish problem is to be solved by bookish means.[52] Jousse, then, pulls the rug out from under the Synoptic problem by showing the problem to be a modern one concocted by modern Western scholars with bookish assumptions.

But we must also now teach Jousse that writing itself, far from always serving to stabilize, is also a source of vitality that produces fluidity and multiplicity. Inverting the language of Paul in 2 Cor 3:4–6, then, it is not just that the oral spirit and memory that gives life; so does the letter. The studies by Jousse nearly a century ago on orality push against the idea of the so-called Synoptic problem; my more recent studies on textual

---

50. Jousse, *Memory*, 66.

51. In Larsen, *Gospels before the Book*, 152, I suggest Robert Darnton's cultural-historical storytelling model as potentially generative.

52. It is curious, then, in this scenario that no one in antiquity accused the Synoptic authors of plagiarism. On plagiarism, see McGill, *Plagiarism in Latin Literature*. See also Richards, "Was Matthew a Plagiarist?"

fluidity and gospel tradition offer an additional blow the idea from a different direction. One can hope that this one-two punch could be enough to stun the so-called Synoptic problem, and perhaps invite future scholars to consider a different paradigm.

Using a historically disciplined imagination, I craft a story and an analogy for purposes of illustration of how orality and textuality both symbiotically create a context of vitality and multiplicity in relation to the emergence of gospel tradition. First, the story. If I were able to go back in time and ask first- or second-century Christians which theoretical solution to the Synoptic problem is correct, it is not that they would think one is right and others are wrong; it is that they would probably find all the popularized scholarly theories far too linear. More likely, they would not appreciate the question at all. Second, I return to an analogy mentioned above. It only makes sense to think of standing on the surface of Jupiter or Uranus if one's frame of reference is a two-dimensional map of the solar system rather than the material reality of giant gas planets. On the contrary, one cannot touch the surface of a giant gas planet in the same way one can touch the surface of Earth or Mars. On a giant gas planet, rather, there is a "there there," but not a terra firma on which to stand. Textualized gospel tradition in the first couple of centuries is less terra firma and more gas giant, less stable books and more complex, moving constellation of various strands of textualized gospel tradition. There is a symbiotic relationship between the various strands of tradition as well as between the oral and the written, and without the binary of oral as fluid and written as fixed.

In conclusion, I turn to a question that Werner Kelber asks in his foreword to Jousse's *Memory, Memorization, and Memorizers*:

> In New Testament studies, form criticism dominated the work of the Quest, the study of the synoptic tradition, and the interpretation of the gospels. But what, one asks again, would our understandings of Jesus, the synoptic tradition, and the gospel be today, had the form critics allowed their own categories to be challenged, or at least modified, by Jousse's model of oral style?[53]

From where I sit, to ask this question is to ask about the past and future of gospel studies. To incorporate Jousse's insights into the current landscape of the field would involve both taking seriously his work on oral style as well as updating his views on textual fluidity. One fundamental

---

53. Kelber, foreword in Jousse, *Memory*, xxiii.

implication for the future of gospel studies, according to Jousse himself, would be to ask: Is the Synoptic problem actually a pseudoproblem produced by our own intellectual blind spots? If we can take that elemental question seriously, then we have already come a long way towards taking Jousse seriously.

Bibliography

Breed, Brennan W. *Nomadic Text: A Theory of Biblical Reception History*. Indiana Series in Biblical Literature. Bloomington: Indiana University Press, 2014.

Bryant, John. *The Fluid Text: A Theory of Revision and Editing for Book and Screen*. Editorial Theory and Literary Criticism. Ann Arbor: University of Michigan Press, 2002.

Bultmann, Rudolf. *Die Geschichte der synoptischen Tradition*. 3rd ed. Forschungen zur Religion und Literatur des Alten und Neuen Testaments 29. Göttingen: Vandenhoeck & Ruprecht, 1957.

———. *The History of the Synoptic Tradition*. Translated by John Marsh. New York: Harper & Row, 1963.

Chartier, Roger. *The Order of Books: Readers, Authors, and Libraries in Europe between the Fourteenth and Eighteenth Centuries*. Translated by Lydia G. Cochrane. Stanford: Stanford University Press, 1994.

Carr, David M. *Holy Resilience: The Bible's Traumatic Origins*. New Haven: Yale University Press, 2014.

Dahlmann, Britt. "Textual Fluidity and Authorial Revision: The Case of Cassian and Palladius." In *Monastic Education in Late Antiquity: The Transformation of Classical Paideia*, edited by Lilian I. Larsen and Samuel Rubenson, 281–305. Cambridge: Cambridge University Press, 2018.

Dibelius, Martin. *Die Formgeschichte des Evangeliums*. 3rd ed. Tübingen: Mohr Siebeck, 1959.

———. *From Tradition to Gospel*. Translated by Bertram Lee Woolf. The Scribner Library. New York: Scribner, 1965.

Eisenstein, Elizabeth L. *The Printing Press as an Agent of Change: Communication and Cultural Transformation in Early-Modern Europe*. 2 vols. Cambridge: Cambridge University Press, 1980.

Gerhardsson, Birger. *Memory and Manuscript: Oral Tradition and Written Transmission in Rabbinic Judaism and Early Christianity*. Translated by Eric J. Sharpe. Acta Seminarii Neotestamentici Upsaliensis 22. Lund: Gleerup, 1961. Rev. Ed. Biblical Resource Series. Grand Rapids: Eerdmans, 1998.

———. *The Reliability of the Gospel Tradition*. Peabody, MA: Hendrickson, 2001.

Gurd, Sean Alexander. *Work in Progress: Literary Revision as Social Performance in Ancient Rome*. American Classical Studies 57. Oxford: Oxford University Press, 2012.

Hanson, Anthony. Review of Norman Perrin, *What Is Redaction Criticism? Scottish Journal of Theology* 23 (1970) 494–95.

Havelock, Eric. *Preface to Plato*. Cambridge: Belknap, 1982.

Hengel, Martin. *Judaism and Hellenism: Studies in Their Encounter in Palestine during the Early Hellenistic Period*. Translated by John Bowden. 1974. Reprint, Eugene, OR: Wipf & Stock, 2003.

Hezser, Catherine. *Jewish Literacy in Roman Palestine*. Texts and Studies in Ancient Judaism 81. Tübingen: Mohr Siebeck, 2001.

Johnson, William A. *Readers and Reading Culture in the High Roman Empire*. Classical Culture and Society. New York: Oxford University Press, 2010.

Jousse, Marcel. *Memory, Memorization, and Memorizers: The Galilean Oral-Style and Its Traditionists*. Translated and edited by Edgard Sienaert. Biblical Performance Criticism Series 15. Eugene, OR: Cascade Books, 2018.

Kaufman, Stephen A. "The Job Targum from Qumran." *Journal of the American Oriental Society* 93 (1973) 317–27.

Kelber, Werner H. Foreword to *Memory, Memorization, and Memorizers: The Galilean Oral-Style and Its Traditionists*, by Marcel Jousse, xiii–xxiii. Translated and edited by Edgard Sienaert. Biblical Performance Criticism Series 15. Eugene, OR: Cascade Books, 2018.

Kirk, Alan. *Memory and the Jesus Tradition*. The Reception of Jesus in the First Three Centuries 2. London: T. & T. Clark, 2018.

Kivy, Peter. *The Performance of Reading: An Essay in the Philosophy of Literature*. New Directions in Aesthetics 3. Malden, MA: Blackwell, 2009.

Larsen, Matthew D. C. "Accidental Publication, Unfinished Texts and the Traditional Goals of New Testament Textual Criticism." *Journal for the Study of the New Testament* 39.4 (2017) 362–87.

———. "According to Mark as Hypomnemata: From Working Document to Pre-Literary Draft." In *Mark and Genre: Micro and Macro*, edited by Jacob Mortensen. Studia Aarhusiana Neotestamentica, forthcoming.

———. "Correcting the Gospel: Putting the titles of the gospels in historical context." In *Rethinking "Authority" in Late Antiquity*, edited by A. J. Berkovitz and Mark Letteney, 78–103. Routledge Monographs in Classical Studies. New York: Routledge, 2018.

———. *Gospels before the Book*. New York: Oxford University Press, 2018.

———. "Listening with the Body, Seeing through the Ears: Contextualizing Philo's Lecture Event in *On the Contemplative Life*." *Journal for the Study of Judaism* 47 (2016) 447–74.

———. "The Publication of the Synoptics and the Problem of Dating." In *The Oxford Handbook of the Synoptic Gospels*, edited by Stephen Ahearne-Kroll. Oxford Handbooks. New York: Oxford University Press, forthcoming.

———. "The Real-and-Imagined Biography of a Gospel Manuscript." *Early Christianity* 12 (2021) 103–31.

Larsen, Matthew D. C., and Mark Letteney. "Christians and the Codex: Generic Materiality and Early Gospel Traditions." *Journal of Early Christian Studies* 27 (2019) 383–415.

Marxsen, Willi. *Der Evangelist Markus: Studien zur Redaktionsgeschichte des Evangeliums*. 2nd ed. Forschungen zur Religion und Literatur des Alten und Neuen Testaments. Göttingen: Vandenhoeck & Ruprecht, 1959.

———. *Mark the Evangelist: Studies on the Redaction History of the Gospel*. Translated by James Boyce et al. Nashville: Abingdon, 1969.

McGann, Jerome J. *The Textual Condition*. Princeton Studies in Culture/Power/History. Princeton: Princeton University Press, 1991.

McGill, Scott. *Plagiarism in Latin Literature*. Cambridge: Cambridge University Press, 2012.

McKenzie, D. F. *Bibliography and the Sociology of Texts*. Cambridge: Cambridge University Press, 1999.

Metzger, Bruce M. *A Textual Commentary on the Greek New Testament*. Stuttgart: United Bible Societies, 1975.

Mroczek, Eva. *The Literary Imagination in Jewish Antiquity*. New York: Oxford University Press, 2016.

Nagy, Gregory. *Homer the Preclassic*. Berkeley: University of California Press, 2012.

Najman, Hindy. "The Vitality of Scripture within and beyond the 'Canon.'" *Journal for the Study of Judaism* 43 (2012) 497–518.

Nietzsche, Friedrich. "Wir Philologen." *Kritische Studienausgabe* 8:1–96 (1875) 121–27.

Parker, David. *The Living Text of the Gospels*. Cambridge: Cambridge University Press, 1997.

Peirano, Irene. *The Rhetoric of the Roman Fake: Latin Pseudepigrapha in Context*. Cambridge: Cambridge University Press, 2012.

Perrin, Norman. *What Is Redaction Criticism?* Guides to Biblical Scholarship: New Testament. 1969. Reprint, Eugene, OR: Wipf & Stock, 2002.

Person, Raymond F. *From Conversation to Oral Tradition: A Simplest Systematics for Oral Traditions*. Routledge Studies in Rhetoric and Stylistics 10. London: Routledge, 2016.

Petersen, Anders Klostergaard. "Paul the Jew Was also Paul the Hellenist." In *Paul the Jew: Rereading the Apostle as a Figure of Second Temple Judaism*, edited by Gabriele Boccaccini and Carlos A. Segovia, 273–99. Minneapolis: Fortress, 2016.

Plato. *The Republic*. English and Greek. English translation by Paul Shorey. 2 vols. Loeb Classical Library. Cambridge: Harvard University Press, 1942.

Richards, E. Randolph. "Was Matthew a Plagiarist? Plagiarism in Greco-Roman Antiquity." In *Christian Origins and the Establishment of the Early Jesus Movement*, edited by Stanley E. Porter and Andrew W. Pitts, 108–33. Texts and Editions for New Testament Study 12. Early Christianity in Its Hellenistic Context 4. Leiden: Brill, 2018.

Rebeillard, Éric. *The Early Martyr Narratives: Neither Authentic Accounts nor Forgeries*. Divinations: Rereading Late Ancient Religion. Philadelphia: University of Pennsylvania Press, 2020.

Siker, Jeffrey. *Liquid Scripture: The Bible in the Digital World*. Minneapolis: Fortress, 2017.

Strange, William A. *The Problem of the Text of Acts*. Society for New Testament Studies Monograph Series 71. Cambridge: Cambridge University Press, 1992.

Ulrich, Eugene. *The Dead Sea Scrolls and the Origins of the Bible*. Studies in the Dead Sea Scrolls and Related Literature. Grand Rapids: Eerdmans, 1999.

Walsh, Robyn Faith. *The Origins of Early Christian Literature: Contextualizing the New Testament within Greco-Roman Literary Culture*. Cambridge: Cambridge University Press, 2021.

Watson. Francis. *Gospel Writing: A Canonical Perspective*. Grand Rapids: Eerdmans, 2013.

West, Martin L. *Studies in the Text and Transmission of the Iliad.* 2001. Reprint, Berlin: de Gruyter, 2015.

11

Conclusion

Implications of the Work of Marcel Jousse

WERNER H. KELBER

> Orality-literacy theorems challenge biblical study perhaps more than any other field of learning.
> —Walter J. Ong, SJ
> *Orality and Literacy: The Technologizing of the Word*, 173

The Relevance of Jousse

To assert that some of Jousse's views on the Bible and biblical scholarship are dated by current scholarly standards is stating the obvious. Among the contributors to this volume, Dewey questions Jousse's assent to the idea of an initial Petrine Aramaic Gospel of Matthew and casts doubt on the premise that the Greek of Mark's Gospel reflects Aramaic patterns and diction. Lee observes that Jousse has underrated the level of complexity that typifies the oral-scribal-memorial communications world, and she criticizes his inclination to link oral style directly with known individual personalities of the early Jesus movement. The readers of this volume will not only encounter a host of objections being voiced, but they will undoubtedly raise a series of critical questions of their own.

For my part I should like to submit for consideration that sight as a sense analogue for knowing was an intrinsic feature of the ancient oral-style communication. Both Mary Carruthers[1] and Janet Coleman[2] have treated the phenomenon of interior visualization in exquisite detail in ancient communication and in medieval philosophy and theology. Sight occupied a privileged position in ancient communications theory, and around seeing a whole paradigm of sensory and cognitive perception was built.[3] Still, I wish to remind readers that Jousse did not intend his work to be a definitive solution to the problems faced by the discipline of biblical studies. Both his style and his theses were calculated to be a provocation more than a solution.

While many of the critical questions raised in this volume may well be warranted, they should not distract us from recognizing the profundity of Jousse's oral-memorial, formulaic-targumic paradigm. Context, I have suggested, illuminates his work, and in this regard the context supplied by scholarship can shed light on the relevance of many of his theories. One will recall that it was during the years of Jousse's teaching career (1931–1957) that form criticism arose to become the paradigmatic hermeneutical instrument in biblical studies. But, as mentioned before, the golden child of twentieth-century biblical criticism operated virtually without a concept of memory and seemingly at a loss to comprehend oral style as anything but ancillary to literary style. It was one of modern biblical scholarship's stark ironies that the form critics, who had made oral tradition the signature piece of biblical criticism, proved unable to adequately grasp the nature of oral style and memorial phenomenology, while two North American classicists, Parry and Lord, were documenting a thriving culture of living oral tradition at the doorstep of the form critics' home country, and subsequently proceeded to create the discipline of oral style and oral-traditional literature. It was only after Jousse's death in 1961 that biblical scholarship, haltingly and in a piecemeal fashion, began to grapple with an adequate comprehension of the pervasive power of the media, the nature of oral style, the performative character of biblical texts, and the inalienable role of memory.[4] Given this situation,

---

1. Carruthers, *The Book of Memory*.

2. Coleman, *Ancient and Medieval Memories*.

3. For a collection of essays on the thematization of sight in ancient culture, see Squire, ed., *Sight and the Ancient Senses*.

4. In New Testament studies it was Erhardt Güttgemanns who in 1970 formulated the first major analytical countermodel to form criticism in *Offene Fragen*. It is hardly accidental that he was also the first German New Testament exegete who appropriated Albert Lord's empirical findings about oral performance, striking at the heart of one of

Jousse's work seems remarkably fresh and relevant, and in many respects on the frontiers of hermeneutical perception.

The Power of the Media

Perusing Jousse's writings, one is struck by the number of comments that lament the powerful influence of "bookish grammarians,"[5] "bookish and dead philology,"[6] "bookish hypercriticism,"[7] "philologists who relied solely on writings,"[8] "bookish amnesia,"[9] "the mentality of our bookish critics,"[10] "our tame little bookish theories of rhythm,"[11] and "certain philologists" who are "not rhythmicians"[12] but who have transformed the gospel into a text that "no longer arouses the signification of this living, *purely oral* pedagogy,"[13] for example. One may regard these comments as the flip side of Jousse's exceptional insights into oral style and the role of memory, and one may appreciate them as part of his critical assessment of a philological approach that was, in his view, altogether text-based and uninformed about oral-traditional and oral-derived traditions.

In media terms, Jousse's unfavorable evaluation of how philology was practiced was premised on an acute observation of the discrepancy between the recitational, performative style of the Palestinian material on the one hand and the chirographic transformation that was generated by the written medium. Given this uncompromising criticism of a principally text-based philology, one could expect him to beware of textualization and to abstain from a transcription of oral materials into the textual medium altogether.

But once Jousse had identified himself as "a modern French ethnographer,"[14] he had unwittingly taken on the assignment of facing up

---

form criticism's basic assumptions about the existence of "the original form," a thesis programmatically articulated in Bultmann. *History*, 6.

5. Jousse, *Memory*, 330.
6. Jousse, *Memory*, 315.
7. Jousse, *Memory*, 316.
8. Jousse, *Memory*, 192.
9. Jousse, *Memory*, 138.
10. Jousse, *Memory*, 42.
11. Jousse, *The Oral Style,* 192.
12. Jousse, *Memory,* 254.
13. Jousse, *Memory,* 309 (italics original).
14. Jousse, *Memory,* 239; see also Jousse, *Memory,* 230.

to one of the most intractable conundrums ethnographers and anthropologists of oral cultures are likely to encounter. In his own words, "the omni-present and omni-potent bilateralism must be put in visual relief"[15] for the purpose of capturing and preserving the oral, performative lore as it existed both among and in the minds of hearers and speakers. Thus, in however limited or qualified a fashion, Jousse the oralist turned into a textualist, working in the manner of an ethnographic practitioner determined to construct what he referred to as a rhythmotypography.[16] What he had in mind was a form of text designed to create the impression of a *vox intexta* by means of orally discernible units, performative stanzas, indentations, the use of colors, and other facets.[17] To further his efforts at salvaging oral-style diction in the written medium, moreover, he envisioned the compilation of "concordances" that would display the sheer number and pervasiveness of oral-style patterns in Aramaic writings by means of a substantial collection of formulaic, targumic materials.[18]

In all these efforts at transcribing the rhythmic recitatives in the textual format he was consistently aware of the formidable challenges he faced. What he had set himself to undertake was no less than the representation of the living oral-style tradition "within the bounds of our awkwardly narrow pages."[19] He readily acknowledged that "the typographical lay-out poses a problem,"[20] and that "such a typographic presentation is only a skeleton which all the users must cover with their own anthropological and rhythmic flesh."[21] Such were his linguistic sensibilities and insights that he sensed the inherent media incongruity about the textualization of his oralist project: "I greatly regret being obliged to present in rhythmotypographical arrangement on inert pages as a substitute for the normal, rhythm-melodic and corporeally balanced method of revivification."[22]

15. Jousse, *Memory*, 237.
16. Jousse, *Memory*, 237.
17. For an insightful study of the ethnographic project of negotiating the shift from the polyphonic, oral performance to the silent, printed text, see Joubert, *The Power of Performance*.
18. Jousse, *Memory*, 139, 162; Jousse, *The Oral Style*, 186 and 244 n. 44.
19. Jousse, *Memory*, 140.
20. Jousse, *Memory*, 160.
21. Jousse, *Memory*, 139.
22. Jousse, *In Search of Coherence*, 274.

Although sensibility toward the power of the media was a persistent undercurrent running through Jousse's work, he was not a media critic in the mode of Marshall McLuhan, the Canadian theorist in communication and media studies. To be sure, Jousse would be in full accord with McLuhan's hypothesis about the ways the chirographic medium had superseded and had even crippled a whole civilization of oral-memorial values, aesthetics, and cognitive faculties. Unlike McLuhan, however, Jousse did not separately attend to the dynamics of the print medium, which is the subject of one of the Canadian critic's most celebrated books, *The Gutenberg Galaxy*.[23]

While refraining from pursuing a differentiated treatment of the chirographic medium versus the typographic medium, Jousse directed his attention toward the alphabetization of language and writing, and only secondarily to the printing press and the typographic medium. He did, however, frequently refer to typography, and he judged its impact as harshly as the impact of the chirographic medium. The typographic representation, he contended, "creates a physical malaise no less than the visual ill-feeling brought about by a presentation of our 'written style' without punctuation and capitalization."[24] It will, therefore, be entirely in the spirit of Jousse if I extend and sharpen Jousse's criticism of the text-based, documentary paradigm by focusing on the technologized language of typography. Print, we remember, was the very medium in which modern biblical scholarship was born and the bulk of interpretive and theological studies was conducted, and from which it acquired its formative methodological tools, exegetical conventions, and intellectual posture.

The Typographic Captivity

We are now well over five centuries into the typographic age, and for more than half a century we have also been living under the influence of the digital medium. For all intents and purposes, most academics are now working in and with the new medium. And yet, the reading, writing, and thinking habits of most humanists are still steeped in print assumptions. Irrespective of how far and deep biblical scholars may have waded into cyberspace, we are still first and foremost producers of print

---

23. McLuhan, *The Gutenberg Galaxy*.
24. Jousse, *Memory*, 237.

materials and consumers of the print Bible. This is the point: so deeply are print-induced patterns encoded in our cognitive apparatus, and so very much have they become part of our academic identity, that we have scarcely been able to raise consciousness about them.

To this day, biblical scholarship has largely failed to acknowledge, let alone analyze, print's ownership over most of our academic products. Surprisingly, there has been scarce recognition that the Gutenberg revolution from its very inception selected the Bible to be the technological showpiece and principal beneficiary of the *high tech* of the fifteenth century. Curiously, biblical hermeneutics have not sufficiently examined that it was in its typographical format that the Bible became a catalyst for modernity's scholarly dealings with biblical texts. It is only very recently, as we are rapidly moving into the new age of electronic media, that a genuinely retrospective view is feasible, and scholarship's distinctively typographical attributes and dynamics are being brought into the bright light of attention.

With the advent of the print medium, technological control over language reached a state of perfection barely imagined in chirographic culture, and nonexistent in oral-scribal civilizations. Gutenberg's accomplishment was heavily based on the production of close to three hundred identical uppercase and lowercase letters, ligatures, shorthand symbols, and diacritical marks. These were the building materials that composed the newly designed language. This newly designed language was henceforth going to be managed chiefly in typographic space, the technologically constructed media location of the printed page. Located within meticulously justified margins, the thoroughly technologized language was methodically formatted and equidistantly linearized. This newly constructed language and typographic habitat conformed to the highest standards of technical virtuosity. When viewed against the background of a millennial oral-scribal media history, the machine-made book made up of systematically organized pages conveyed an experience of fixity and stability—of permanence even—that was unprecedented and may well have seemed odd to many at the time. Instituted by Gutenberg's printing press, the *high tech* of the fifteenth century came to implement the media identity of modernity's biblical scholarship. Over the centuries, the mechanizing processes of the new medium steadily invaded scholarly thinking and writing, and they injected a drive for rationalization and systematization into the academic study of the Bible, and a passion for method, along with a far-reaching diminution of the human sensorium—all features which Jousse has chosen to define as *algebrization*[25] or *algebrosis*,[26] and which we may want to describe as the pseudomathematization of language and thought.

Owing to the duplicating powers of print technology, the communications culture, including biblical scholarship, became awash in texts. Before long the expanding quantity and seeming omnipresence of textual materials began to have an impact on how one imagined retrospectively pre-Gutenberg history. Given the rapid ascendancy of print and the growing climate of Gutenberg intellectualism, the model of Christian origins more and more took on the appearance of a textual network, with texts predominantly operating in relation to other texts, growing out of prior texts, and breeding still more texts.

Concerning this model, Jousse astutely observed that "books are created from other books, as the bee takes pollen from flowers."[27] Moreover, the concept of what constituted a text was now beginning to be different from the one that had been cultivated in ancient and far into medieval times. Leaving the world of oral multivocality and scribal fluidity behind, biblical scholarship was increasingly encountering writings in the form of printed texts, an experience that enforced the illusion of stasis, the notion that textual stability was the necessary and sole basis of the ancient communications environment. Such was the display of a typographically administered textual stasis that biblical critics were likely tempted to view print products as beacons of historical objectivity. Implicitly or explicitly, the prevailing model of Christian origins came to be viewed not merely as dominantly text based, but as essentially print based. Enmeshed in print materials, pursuing writing more and more with the aim of print publication, and reading even ancient sources in the print format, biblical scholars were inclined to operate, mostly without full awareness, on logical premises and in literary terms that were inconceivable without the controlling effects of Gutenberg's technology. Quite apart from biblical scholars, it was the Bible-reading public that "lived mainly with the illusion of the Bible produced by print technology."[28]

In the larger sense of Western philosophy and the history of media technologies, text-based, typographically grounded biblical scholarship

---

25. Jousse., *Memory*, 8.
26. Jousse, *Memory*, 364.
27. Jousse, *Memory*, 305.
28. McLuhan, *The Gutenberg Galaxy*, 135.

represented a high point in the lengthy dispute between rhetoric and dialectic that commenced in antiquity, continued through the Middle Ages, and sharply intensified in the Gutenberg era. In the broader context of that history the typographic captivity of biblical scholarship marks the decisive triumph of the dialectical, logical pole over the oral, rhetorical pole.

The Mnemonics of the Jesus Tradition

Can Jousse's bedrock thesis of the omnipresence and pervasiveness of memory have any direct bearing on our understanding of the gospel tradition? Has it not been demonstrated, abundantly and consistently, that historical, literary, and hermeneutical causalities were principally operative in shaping both tradition and gospel? This being the case, how can it conceivably be argued that memory has been the driving force in framing the dynamics and compositional structures of the gospel tradition?

The case for memorially configured frames and processes can best be made with respect to the tradition of sayings. In sampling a portion of sayings in Mark, we need to keep two points in mind. One, already the presence of sayings in the printed gospel text, and even more so their isolation apart from it, constitute an exercise in abstraction twice over. All cultural lore that is orally transmitted, one remembers, attains its performative goal contextually. Of such hermeneutical importance is social context that it can be labeled a coproducer of performance. In Joussean terms, the precious jewels are never independent but always acting in, interacting with, and reacting to their respective environments. A sampling of sayings will, therefore, amount to the kind of systematization that Jousse has labeled *algebrosis*, and that he was himself unable to escape. Two, my intention is not to disentangle authentic from inauthentic sayings. Conventionally employed in the quest of the historical Jesus, this procedure is out of character with the memory discourse. For a conceptual grasp of the performative function of sayings it is irrelevant whether recitational aphorisms were articulated by Jesus himself or by others in his name, whether they arose in tradition or assumed their place in ritual settings. The key question is, What were the enabling features allowing sayings to survive and secure places in tradition? To that end, the memory approach examines ways sayings catch the attention of hearers and accommodate their needs of remembering. Therefore, attention is focused on rhetorical features and mnemonic devices etched into the structure of the sayings.

A few examples offer glimpses into the speaking culture of the early Jesus tradition—

- Mark 2:27: τὸ σάββατον διὰ τὸν ἄνθρωπον ἐγένετο καὶ οὐχ ὁ ἄνθρωπος διὰ τὸ σάββατον: "The sabbath was made for man, and not man for the sabbath": a two-step parallelism combined with a positive-negative antithesis.

- Mark 4:9: ὃς ἔχει ὦτα ἀκούειν ἀκουέτω: "he who has ears to hear, shall hear": doubling effect of ἀκούειν and ἀκουέτω.

- Mark 4:25: ὃς γὰρ ἔχει, δοθήσεται αὐτῷ; καὶ ὃς οὐκ ἔχει, ἀρθήσεται ἀπ' αὐτοῦ: "for he who has, more will be given to him, and he who does not have, it will be taken away from him": a parallelism inverting in a second step the idea of the first step.

- Mark 7:15: οὐδέν ἐστιν ἔξωθεν τοῦ ἀνθρώπου εἰσπορευόμενον εἰς αὐτὸν ὃ δύναται κοινῶσαι αὐτόν; ἀλλὰ τὰ ἐκ τοῦ ἀνθρώπου ἐκπορευόμενά ἐστιν τὰ κοινοῦντα τὸν ἄνθρωπον: "there is nothing outside of a person that by going in can defile, but what comes out of a person that is what defiles": progressive parallelism using inside-outside antithesis.

- Mark 8:35: ὃς γὰρ ἐὰν θέλῃ τὴν ψυχὴν αὐτοῦ σῶσαι ἀπολέσει αὐτήν; ὃς δ'ἂν ἀπολέσει τὴν ψυχὴν αὐτοῦ [ἕνεκεν ἐμοῦ καὶ τοῦ εὐαγγελίου] σώσει αὐτήν: "he who wishes to save his life will lose it; he who loses his life (for my sake and for the sake of the gospel) will save it": two-step parallelism combined with saving-losing antithesis—the editorial insertion disrupting the oral structure.

- Mark 8:38: ὃς γὰρ ἐὰν ἐπαισχυνθῇ με καὶ τοὺς ἐμοὺς λόγους . . . καὶ ὁ υἱὸς τοῦ ἀνθώπου ἐπισχυνθήσεται αὐτὸν: "who is ashamed of me and my words . . . the Son of Man will also be ashamed": progressive parallelism, repeating the verbal form of being ashamed."

- Mark 9:37: ὃς ἂν ἓν τῶν τοιούτων παιδίων δέξηται ἐπὶ τῷ ὀνόματί μου, ἐμὲ δέχεται; καὶ ὃς ἂν ἐμὲ δέχηται, οὐκ ἐμὲ δέχεται ἀλλὰ τὸν ἀποστείλαντά με: "who welcomes one of these children in my name, welcomes me, and he who welcomes me, does not welcome me, but the one who sent me": progressive parallelism, the second step reversing the first one.

- Mark 9:40: ὃς γὰρ οὐκ ἔστιν καθ' ἡμῶν, ὑπὲρ ἡμῶν ἐστιν: "who is not against us, is for us": two-step construction, continuing line of thought.

- Mark 10:31: πολλοὶ δὲ ἔσονται πρῶτοι ἔσχατοι καὶ [οἱ] ἔσχατοι πρῶτοι: "many who are first will be last, and the last first": a positive-negative, negative-positive chiastic construction.

- Mark 10:39: τὸ ποτήριον ὃ ἐγὼ πίνω πίεσθε καὶ τὸ βάπτισμα ὃ ἐγὼ βαπτίζομαι βαπτισθήσεσθε: "the cup that I drink you will drink, and the baptism with which I am baptized you will be baptized": two thematic dualisms, the second one reiterating the first one in different words.

What these sayings have in common is a construction built on the mnemotechnical devices of parallelism and duality, antithesis and polarity, chiasm, and reiteration. In Jousse's terms, "the omni-present and omni-potent bilateralism"[29] here reigns supreme. Formulated around bipolar core structures, the sayings are couched in memorially usable patterns that are constitutive of what Jousse has labeled formulaic diction. They contribute an unmistakable element of stability to the tradition.

At this juncture one cannot help but recognize a touch of irony in bilateral formulism: for the purpose of securing the survival and iterability of spoken words, they will have to be solidified into stable constructions that are unlike the transitory nature of speech. For the sake of securing their existence, they will have to be frozen into still life. And yet, formulaic stability is not synonymous with immobility, and structural bipolarity is not to be equated with mechanistic memorization. It would seem appropriate to imagine the bipolar core structures in the form of instruments on which musicians play and from which musical tunes are elicited. Depending on the particularity of the instruments, they embody both constraints and liabilities, and they hold assets as well as produce benefits. What matters in oral tradition is not simply the instruments, but in a special sense the music that is being played on them. Usually, the effectiveness of a recitation depends on the skills of the performer to summon forth the tunes that are deemed fit for the audience at hand. Mnemonic structuring facilitated, and indeed thrived on, performative inventiveness in social contextuality.

---

29. Jousse, *Memory*, 237.

Owing to the formulaic structuring of Jesus' language, it was earmarked for repetition, and repetition was the prerogative of remembering. About this there can be no doubt: the mnemonic patterning of Jesus' language was designed to facilitate remembering. To be precise, remembering got underway not when the tradition carried his words but when Jesus remembered his own tradition and reiterated his own previously uttered words. To rephrase it, the tradition commenced not with recourse to archives or critical editions, not with a foundational text or a single original saying, but with processes of reiteration and remembering. Hence, from its very inception, reiterative and memorial dynamics were lodged in Jesus' proclamation. We, children of the Gutenberg galaxy, are thoroughly familiar with repetition in terms of the mechanical reproduction of fully identical copies. But repetition in this automatic sense was an experience entirely absent from the ancient oral-scribal communications culture. Jesus' reiteration, whether of others' words or his own words, was an act not of identical repetitiveness but of recurrent performativity. By remembering and reenacting his recitations, the itinerant charismatic delivered recitations considering carefully social context and circumstances.

The Oral Nature of the Early Scribal Tradition

It cannot escape the attention of the observant reader of Jousse's writings that he repeatedly refers to the early Jesus tradition in terms of "fluid texts."[30] This seems a curious label even by current standards when greater allowance is being made for the oral contextuality of ancient writings. To be sure, chirographically produced texts are rarely ever fully closed and never hermetically sealed. Yet ought one not assume that Jesus' oral proclamation, once transposed into writing, acquired the assurance of material stability that comes with the technology of writing?

With the notion of "fluid texts" (*les textes fluides*) in mind, let us review the early papyrological gospel tradition that has been assiduously collected, classified, and interpreted by text critics. As is well known, the discipline of textual criticism has conventionally been propelled by the aspiration to reconstruct the so-called original version and to secure a standard text for the New Testament. Wherever textual variants exist, the goal is to isolate what was assumed to be the original. In the words of

---

30. Jousse, *Memory*, 30–33, 101, 337–38, passim.

David Parker, when "it is assumed that there is an original text, the textual critic's task is very simple: to recover the original text."[31] Virtually up to the present, that project has been deemed to be axiomatic for textual criticism. By sorting out originals from variants, the discipline assumed responsibility for what came to be called the "critical edition" of the New Testament.

Given the customary mission of textual criticism, the unusual nature of recent initiatives taken by three prominent text critics—David Parker,[32] Eldon J. Epp,[33] and Kim Haines-Eitzen[34]—cannot be overstated. In what amounts to a Copernican revolution of textual criticism, they have abandoned the discipline's program of privileging the assumed single, fixed point in the tradition, and instead have refocused attention on the tradition made up of variants. Not the alleged original but every single scribal version had to be seriously taken into account. In the wake of this reorientation, it now seems obvious that fixation on constructing an authoritative standard text has blinded us, has kept us from seeing the early papyrological tradition for what it really was. Enlightened by new insights into the early scribal tradition, Epp, a cautious and judicious scholar, exclaimed, "Suddenly textual criticism comes alive and becomes relevant in ways that no one might have imagined," and he queried, "Why didn't we see this sooner, and how could we have missed it?"[35]

What had been missing was a full intellectual acknowledgement that the early papyrological tradition was characterized by and consisted of an extraordinary variability and multiformity of items. In light of the new direction taken by Parker, Epp, and Haines-Eitzen, there is no escaping the recognition of both the amount and the degree of variance. Significantly, scribal fluidity exists not merely between Synoptic passages in Mark, Matthew, and Luke (a feature rather well-known) but also with respect to a gospel's individual passages. Again, we should have been cognizant of this fact because unlike copies of the print medium, "it is of the essence of a manuscript tradition that every copy is different, both unique and imperfect."[36] Parker fully understands this matter: "No manuscript

---

31. Parker, *The Living Text*, 6.
32. Parker, *The Living Text*, 6.
33. Epp, "Oxyrhynchus"; Epp, "It's All about Variants."
34. Haines-Eitzen, *Guardians of Letters*.
35. Epp, "Oxyrchynchus," 8.
36. Parker, *The Living Text*, 188.

preserves the original text."[37] Comprehending these scribal facts on the ground is bound to challenge the concept of the original text. Not only is the search for the single original fraught with virtually insurmountable technical difficulties, but, far more importantly, the concept makes no sense in the oral-scribal communications world.

Broadly speaking, we are dealing with a communications complexity that must not be reduced to simplistic uniformity. The early gospel tradition, in other words, commenced not with the original saying any more than with a single, foundational text, but with oral-scribal fluidity. As Parker explains, "the written tradition was at its most fluid in the first century of its existence."[38] What we find in the initial period, therefore, is a significant degree of scribal fluidity, which is enhanced "the further back we go."[39] Or, as he has elsewhere formulated it, "initial fluidity is followed by stability."[40] Accordingly, we will have to imagine a communications culture without a single, standard text—a culture in which each version is authoritative and in a sense "original." At most, we are dealing with a plurality of "originals," and hence not with the single original at all.

There is one final inference to be drawn from this reassessment of the early papyrological tradition. When it is viewed from the angle of oral, recitational processing, one is struck by the fact that the early scribal tradition functioned in ways that were analogous to the oral tradition. Like oral-recitational cultures, so the early scribal traditions were characterized by the presence of variables and multiforms. Like the most memorable oral performances, the early scribal tradition (notwithstanding its chirographic fixity) endeavored to stay with the flux of time by remaining socially adaptable. Like oral cultures generally, the early scribal tradition did not differentiate between primary and secondary (or original and derivative) texts. All in all, it is difficult to adequately capture and define the characteristic identity of the early papyrological gospel tradition. Undoubtedly committed to scribality, it nonetheless functioned in a typically oral fashion. To say, for example, that due to its fluidity, it "lacks" textual stability, is to misjudge it from the perspective of print conventionalities. Here we come back to Jousse's label of *fluid texts,* an interesting designation so long as textual fluidity is not viewed

---

37. Parker, *The Living Text*, 120.
38. Parker, *The Living Text*, 200.
39. Parker, *The Living Text*, 188.
40. Parker, *The Living Text*, 70.

as an aberration but to the contrary as illustrative of the deepest and best instincts of the early scribal tradition. We shall return to Jousse's concept of *fluid texts*.

Tradition as Mnemo-History

Jousse was fond of imagining tradition in the form of oral units lined up like pearls on a necklace. "Pearl-lessons,"[41] he called the string of recitational segments assembled in orderly fashion. The metaphor of pearls derived from the observation that "families transmit their jewels as loose precious stones, and each generation reassembles them anew: the stones remain the same, but their ordering always differs."[42] Collecting and facilitating control over the traditional material was a way to ensure that its arrangement served mnemonic purposes. Memory, therefore, on this model, was a basic rationale of the gospel tradition. The specifics of this model aside, is there any evidence that memory, in whatever form and for whatever function, played as signal a role in the workings of the tradition as Jousse suggests? Conventional biblical scholarship widely assumes that textual hermeneutics, coupled with historical causalities, provided the decisive forces that empowered the tradition. From a Joussian perspective, a model of the tradition would have to be firmly grounded in memory and would include dynamic rather than mechanical word processing, verbal-gestural reperformance rather than verbatim reproduction, and—importantly—not merely transmissional but performative dynamics located in social contextuality.

These requirements appear to rule out sole reliance on the following four models, all of which are still currently in use. One, we cannot think of the early tradition as an assembly-line production, carrying inert items of information to be conserved for posterity. Preservation is a partial incentive, but not the primary impulse motivating the tradition. Two, the notion of tradition as a process of accretion and successive layering takes its point of departure from textuality, operates in dominantly textual terms, and fails to adequately deal with the oral-verbal arts on the ground. Three, the developmental model, still in the background of a large part of the current scholarly imagination, has not come to terms with the fact that spoken words do not exhibit any sense of directionality;

---

41. Jousse, *Memory*, 18, 20, 39, *passim*.
42. Jousse, *Memory*, 182.

they operate entirely in time without the constraints of space. Four, the trajectory model, introduced by Koester and Robinson,[43] has made development and textuality the overriding motivating forces of tradition: a forward motion in time, "moving from one document to another, from one generation to another"[44] conducts intertextual operations in an unreal distance from social realities.

How can one, with Jousse's assistance, although without following the specificities of his "pearl-lessons," understand and conceptualize the dynamics and motivations as enablers of the tradition? Manifestly, tradition is concerned with the past. But the prevailing rationale we observed in the oral and early scribal traditioning was not retention of the past in the archival interest of preservation. The key recognition was a persistent hermeneutical desire inherent in the traditioning processes to relate the past to the present. Unlike all developmental models, the dynamics we observed characterized not simply a forward thrust but both a regressive gesture (resuming or remembering the past) and a performative gesture (formulating tradition in the interest of serving present identity). In slightly more religious terms, the intent of the tradition was to keep the Jesus of the past alive in the present.

Is there a name for the model of the tradition that corresponds to the above description? The designation of this model as social memory has been introduced and developed by Halbwachs,[45] the Assmanns,[46] and Kirk and Thatcher,[47] among others. According to social memory theory, the early traditions grew out of a tension between two competing aspirations: retaining the message of Jesus and securing its existence for the present, and reperforming it with the aim of assuring its relevance for present and future circumstances. Although the specifics of the social memory model are different from Jousse's paradigm, there is agreement that tradition is appropriately conceptualized as grounded in and empowered by memory. In the words of Kirk and Thatcher, "every act of

---

43. Robinson and Koester, *Trajectories*.
44. Robinson and Koester, *Trajectories*, 16.
45. Halbwachs, *Les Cadres Sociaux*.
46. Jan Assmann, *Das kulturelle Gedächtnis*; Assmann, Aleida, *Erinnerungsräume*.
47. Kirk and Thatcher, eds., *Memory, Tradition, and Text*.

traditioning is an act of remembering,"[48] so that "'tradition' is in fact the substance of memory."[49] Jousse could not have said it better.

The So-called Synoptic Problem

What in gospel studies is conventionally referred to as the *Synoptic problem* furnishes a classic example of the hypertextual approach instituted and pursued by historical criticism. In view of the standard articulation of the problem as one that concerns "the literary relationship of the first three Gospels to one another,"[50] any possible adjudication is by that definition confined to the rubric of *Literaturkritik* conventionally understood in terms of literary sources and dependencies. If the approach to the problem is a priori an exclusively literary one, any solution will be a literary one and will preclude nonliterary (oral and memorial) considerations. Predictably, the diagrammatic representation of the well-known *two-source hypothesis*, which connects Matthew and Luke by way of straight or dotted lines with Mark and Q (and sometimes with Thomas as well), features a model of direct literary relationships without reservation or exception. Jousse explicitly rejects this model, arguing that the Gospels were "not a synoptic phenomenon in which texts are aligned with one another visually in parallel columns—texts that are in mutual written dependence."[51] Although the number of scholars unreservedly committed to the traditional model is dwindling, especially in the English-speaking world, while the number of alternative proposals is rising, the classical model continues to exercise a controlling influence both on gospel studies and on our teaching. It remains a hidden force frequently lurking behind and impacting the historical quest and the interpretation of gospel materials.

The conventional diagram has placed an extravagant premium on spatial configurations, constructing a closed-circuit system of one-to-one textual relations. When charted out in this fashion, the model represents a high point of the geometrization of logic. Epistemology has been reduced to a series of linear textual strands. From a Joussean perspective, the schematic design entails a disconcerting built-in exclusion: it leaves

---

48. Kirk and Thatcher, "Jesus Tradition as Social Memory," 39.
49. Kirk and Thatcher, "Jesus Tradition as Social Memory," 40.
50. Kümmel, *Introduction*, 35.
51. Jousse, *Memory*, 109–10.

no room for oral dynamics, memorial processes, social engagement, and the role of tradition. It cannot escape our attention, and it should long ago have alarmed us, that this classic diagrammatic representation of the Synoptic problem suppresses precisely what Jousse identifies as the very bedrock features of the gospel tradition.

When Jousse made the daring observation that "there is no Synoptic Problem,"[52] he was suggesting positively that the Gospels were no more and no less than the outworking of an orally and memorially empowered tradition. In his words, "We are dealing with recitational phenomena: *there is one prototypical formulaic recitation which is variously adapted to facilitate comprehension.*"[53] Entirely in line with oral dynamics, he viewed the Gospels as multiforms of a basic (not original) oral narration. Larsen, in his contribution to this volume, has articulated the issue with an extraordinarily astute question: "Is the Synoptic problem actually a pseudoproblem produced by our own intellectual blind spots?"[54]

It is intriguing to observe Albert Lord, indepently of Jousse, making a broadly identical argument, and it should be cause for concern that the theses advanced by both scholars have met with very little response from biblical scholars. Lord made his case in a lengthy and detailed paper presented at a 1977 conference at Trinity University in San Antonio, Texas.[55] His central thesis stated that the Gospels belonged to the category of oral traditional literature. What, in his view, distinguished such works was a composition made up of traditional mythic patterns that, in the case of the Gospels, derived from Hebraic biblical traditions, ancient Near Eastern cultures, and the biographical genre. To a significant extent the Jesus story was remembered as it resonated with ancient tradition-honored themes, figures, and stories. Additionally, Lord examined distinct narrative units, recognizing that "oral traditional composers think in term of blocks and series of blocks of tradition."[56] In examining sequential patterns, he found variable configurations and chiastic formations of building blocks that were, in his view, characteristic of oral compositional processes. Contrary to the widely held view that a preponderance of verbal correspondences between the Gospels was evidence of literary

---

52. Jousse, *Memory,* 66.
53. Jousse, *Memory,* 110 (italics original).
54. See page 254, above.
55. Lord, "The Gospels as Oral Traditional Literature."
56. Lord, "The Gospels as Oral Traditional Literature," 59.

relations, Lord detected "less verbal correspondence than I would expect in a manuscript tradition."[57] The implication was that in the interest of making textuality the yardstick for the Synoptic problem, scholars were predisposed to accentuate concurrences to the detriment of differences. As for the objection raised during the conference that all the features Lord had attributed to oral dynamics were just as evident in ancient textual documents, the objectors failed to grasp the challenge Lord had posed to the discipline: textual relations were not the only medium that made sense of the Synoptic problem.

The point is not made here that the Jousse-Lord paradigm represents the long-awaited solution to the Synoptic problem. Down the generations for approximately two hundred fifty years, biblical scholars have cut their teeth on what by now some have come to view as an intractable problem. The point is rather that a rationality that proceeds from strictly textual premises, and thus is counting on a strictly literary resolution to the Synoptic problem, belongs to a period other than to the ancient communications culture.

The Greek Model of Christian Origins

That the New Testament writings, including the Gospels, were composed in Greek and have been available to us for centuries in like manner, is indisputable and a commonplace in biblical studies. However, the implications of this fact have been consequential and extend far beyond matters of language and syntax. In broad outline, the Greek linguistic form of the New Testament was a contributing factor in the construction of a particular narrative of Western history. It was a narrative predisposed to attribute a foundational role to all things Greek. With the canonization of the New Testament, the premise that the Greek language and Greek culture were foundational for the West received a major boost. Alongside the canonical privileging of texts and of the Greek language, a whole set of values and virtues and a distinct form of rationality gained supremacy, accelerating the process through which Greek ideas became the underpinnings of Western, Christian civilization. While throughout the Western Middle Ages the Latin Bible reigned supreme, and Latin provided the controlling linguistic rationale for the professional culture of theologians, politicians, and jurists, during the Renaissance period of the fifteenth

---

57. Lord, "The Gospels as Oral Traditional Literature," 59.

and sixteenth centuries Greek experienced a revival, and the study of the Greek language and of Greek philosophy was gradually restored to the Western curriculum. In modernity, the cultivation of Greek history, the Greek language, and Greek culture reached its pinnacle in the European academic world of the nineteenth and twentieth centuries. Not only in theological faculties and biblical research, but in classical philology, history, and philosophy, as well as in the political life of Europe a strong pull and a decided bias toward Greek and Hellenistic culture was in evidence. More recently, well-known New Testament projects such as Bultmann's form criticism,[58] the trajectory model developed by Koester and Robinson,[59] and the North American Jesus Seminar under the mentorship of Robert Funk and John Dominic Crossan[60] all displayed a partially nuanced and partially pronounced advocacy for Hellenistic influences on Christian origins. This is how Shawn Kelley has critically described this Greek model: "civilization and culture originated in Greece, and moved through the increasingly oppressive and uncivilized worlds of Rome and the Middle Ages, before resting in modern Europe, which was able to revive itself by returning to its Greek roots."[61] Kelley argued that, exceptions notwithstanding, New Testament scholarship has heavily invested in this Greek model and is deeply implicated in a narrative that helped sustain a sense of Western identity, even superiority.

Greek-Hellenistic discourse was deeply deficient in that it oversimplified and distorted the ethnic-cultural complexity of the gospel traditions, and it has bequeathed to us a problematic view of early Christianity. Based on a sharp dichotomy of Hellenism versus Judaism, the model frequently ran the risk of elevating Hellenism at the cost of marginalizing or downplaying the primary importance of Jewish culture. What was being overlooked or suppressed was that the Gospels, in addition to displaying a Greek exterior linguistic form, narrate a substantial Jewish content that sustained a fundamental level of continuity with Israelite traditions. The principal storyline, most of the main characters, a plurality of images and values, scenes of communal life, characteristic features of conflicts and

---

58. Bultmann, *The History*.
59. Robinson and Koester, *Trajectories*.
60. Funk and the Jesus Seminar, *The Gospel of Jesus*.
61. Kelley, *Racializing Jesus*, 217.

deeds of power, the Passover meal, the commissioning of the Twelve, and many more facets are all deeply rooted in Jewish history and culture.[62]

By way of example, the large and thematically coherent narrative unit of Mark 4:35—8:26 is entirely cast in categories that are constitutive of Israel's identity. The two sets of five deeds of power, each set consisting of a sea crossing, three healings, and a feeding, carry motifs from Exodus and the Elijah-Elisha cycle. What merits our attention is that the narrative cycle depicts the Jesus figure as the carrier of ancient Israelite virtues and values. It is in remembrance of the venerable Jewish past that Jesus is turned into a believable figure of identity. The deep past of Jewish history functioned as his focus of identity.

Jousse was keenly aware of the Gospels' cultural ambiguity. But unlike the proponents of the Greek model, he resolutely defended the Jewish identification of the Gospels and their tradition. As he saw it, the popular oral-style, Aramaic traditions were translated into and covered up by the language and rhythms of the Gospels' final Greek form. To a large extent it was the mission of his professional life to advocate the Jewishness of Jesus and to recover the Jewish matrix of the gospel tradition. The key to the Gospels, including the key to the so-called Synoptic problem, he argued, were the targums.

The Aramaic Model of Gospel Traditions

To evaluate appropriately Jousse's thesis of the targumic genesis of the Gospels, we need to return to our discussion of the Jewish communications culture, and resume reflections on the scribal arts with a focus on the composition history of the Hebrew Bible. On these issues the work of Shem Miller and Eugene Ulrich has been of signal importance. Miller's groundbreaking *Dead Sea Media* has succeeded in effectively breaking the textual spell over Qumran scholarship.[63] The primary rationale of the Qumran Scrolls, he argues, lay in memory and performance. Objecting to the text-critical explanation of variants as derivatives of originals, he promotes concepts such as "scribal memory," "memory variants," and "scribal performance." At Qumran (and throughout the Second Temple period) "scribes are more artists than bots because they perform each

---

62. For an extensive discussion of the Israelite traditions in Mark, see Horsley, *Text and Tradition*, 264–77.

63. Miller, *Dead Sea Media*.

piece anew, like musicians authentically recreating a cover song."[64] While Qumran scholarship had been conventionally fixated on foregrounding textual stability and measuring scriptural variants against assumed textual standards, Miller views scriptural fluidity as a phenomenon that stands in its own. As he demonstrates throughout his book, Qumran scriptural tradition operated analogously to the oral register, showed little inclination towards textual finality, and refrained from promoting the one original scribal version.

Based on intimate knowledge of the Dead Sea Scrolls, Eugene Ulrich has greatly illuminated the history of the Hebraic Bible's textual traditions, and throughout his distinguished career has sounded a call for the reorientation of our comprehension of Israel's textual landscape.[65] Prior to the discovery of the Dead Sea Scrolls, the Masoretic Text (MT) served as the gold standard for purposes of textual comparison and verification. Ulrich, however, arguing on the basis of a deep engagement with the Qumran material, has advised us that "we should not begin thinking with a vision of a unified Biblia Hebraica or modern Bible."[66] As far as scriptural manuscripts and passages are concerned, the Qumran findings represent "a wide documentation of Hebrew manuscripts clearly at variance with the MT,"[67] variant text types and editions, parallel or double and multiple editions that were "intentionally different,"[68] revisions of traditional materials, and the like. It seems that at Qumran joint rituals were celebrated and communal readings were performed in the absence of a single, unifying standard text: "differing forms of the text were acceptable."[69]

Ulrich is inclined to refer to the most widely used scriptural texts of the pluriform tradition as "authoritative, sacred books."[70] But "authoritative" is not synonymous with "original." He is prepared to call the idea

---

64. Miller, *Dead Sea Media*, 153.

65. Ulrich, *The Dead Sea Scrolls*. The author was one of three general editors of the Scrolls, and chief editor of the biblical scrolls. While he is primarily a text critic with minimal interest in matters of orality and memory, his work is of inestimable value for understanding the nature of the Hebraic biblical traditions in the broader context of the early Jewish communications environment.

66. Ulrich, *The Dead Sea Scrolls*, 93.

67. Ulrich, *The Dead Sea Scrolls*, 200.

68. Ulrich, *The Dead Sea Scrolls*, 55.

69. Ulrich, *The Dead Sea Scrolls*, 93.

70. Ulrich, *The Dead Sea Scrolls*, 59–60.

of the original text "a distracting concept for the Hebrew Bible; in a real sense, there was no 'original text.'"[71] In place of "original text" he prefers the designation "base text," and suggests that we should view the Masoretic Text as the "base text, or earliest available literary edition."[72] At the same time, however, he insists that "we should not look to M [=MT] as the standard by which to judge the texts of the various books."[73] On this point Ulrich agrees with Emanuel Tov's surprising statement that the Qumran texts "have taught us no longer to posit the MT at the center of our textual thinking."[74] As far as the status of the Torah was concerned, Ulrich thinks it was viewed as the most authoritative of all deeply esteemed, sacred texts. But again, authoritative was not the same as the later developing notion of canonical, let alone the modern idea of original. From a retrospective perspective, the Torah was the leading aspirant on the path toward canonization. But even in the case of the Torah, Ulrich introduced an insightful media observation that further complexifies our understanding: "I do not know of an ancient example of all five books [of Moses] being copied together on a single scroll."[75] In large measure, therefore, the Torah was for a long time a mental, memorial (more than a materially based) scribal authority.

Miller's orally focused and Ulrich's textually oriented models, along with the studies by Chilton, Hezser, Person, and Horsley, discussed in the volume's introductory chapter, have greatly illuminated and complexified our picture of the ancient Jewish communications culture, offering informative glimpses of the emergence of the Hebraic biblical traditions. In great measure, the contributions of these six scholars have succeeded in reconstructing the appropriate communications context in which the targumic gospel tradition, as imagined by Jousse, must have functioned. Accordingly, if his thesis is to be historically assessed and appreciated, it will have to be understood in a cultural environment of textual plurality and multiformity, of scribality in an oral register, and in communicative settings that operated without a single, fixed textual standard.

Can the Jewish communications culture, as reconstructed in the manner described above, help us illuminate Jousse's targumic thesis?

71. Ulrich, *The Dead Sea Scrolls*, 115.
72. Ulrich, *The Dead Sea Scrolls*, 114.
73. Ulrich, *The Dead Sea Scrolls*, 114.
74. Ulrich, *The Dead Sea Scrolls*, 85.
75. Ulrich, *The Dead Sea Scrolls*, 90.

Knowing what we now do about a plurality of scriptural versions, what can it say about Jesus' relation to his tradition? The conventional reference to Jesus citing the Bible all too often implies the unreflective premise of his citing the "Old Testament." As is widely known, however, there was no Bible in the modern sense of a book, whether Aramaic or Hebraic, that carried the individually authored and canonically authorized texts between two covers. Moreover, as Jousse and many others have abundantly confirmed, the language Jesus was raised in was Aramaic, and the living Israelite traditions he conversed in and was feeding on were likewise Aramaic. As Jousse has repeatedly reminded us, our habitual use of the Greek text of the Gospels has resulted in covering up the tradition's Aramaic roots. In that regard, the Greek version generated forgetfulness.

Not immediately influenced by Jousse, yet very much in the Joussian tradition, Chilton has taken a fresh look at Jesus' implementation of the scriptural traditions, stating that "Jesus used the biblical interpretative tradition of his time."[76] This statement is adverting not to the "Old Testament," but to the Aramaic, targumic legacy, which he called "tradition" rather than "the Bible," and defined as being "interpretative," suggesting a living process rather than a single, fixed text. Moreover, Chilton emphasized that we must not assume that Jesus "had access to the Targum as we can read it today,"[77] an assumption that is "out of the question."[78] Undoubtedly, "a direct comparison between the theology of Jesus and that of the Targum would be anachronistic at best."[79] Therefore, the issue is not whether Jesus used the targumim, but "whether interpretative traditions later incorporated in the Targum had a formative influence on the wording of some sayings attributed to Jesus."[80] Chilton's nuanced and precisely formulated approach to the exceedingly difficult issue of Jesus and the targumim has the effect of taking readers out of the realm of sources and stable texts and into the world of traditions in motion.

If Jesus' commitment to and familiarity with the targumic tradition of his time can be inferred, the question inevitably arises whether the language of Jesus or of the Gospels furnishes any evidence of targumically colored citations. At this point, the reassessment of the composition

---

76. Chilton, *A Galilean Rabbi*, 167.
77. Chilton, *A Galilean Rabbi*, 57, 139.
78. Chilton, *A Galilean Rabbi*, 70.
79. Chilton, *A Galilean Rabbi*, 67.
80. Chilton, *A Galilean Rabbi*, 137.

history of the Hebrew Bible has implications for our understanding of the Gospels' citations from what is commonly referred to as the Old Testament. It is widely assumed that the citations show a proneness for the Septuagint, although Krister Stendahl favored the Masoretic Text in reference to the Gospel of Matthew.[81] As a rule, the understanding of citational references has until recently relied heavily on comparisons with the Masoretic Text, the Septuagint, and tangentially with the Samaritan Pentateuch. The scholarly expectation has been that each gospel's citations derive predominantly from a single textual tradition that, scholars have assumed, has existed in a relatively fixed state. With the new plurality model in mind, however, one may ask whether in a world of textual bodies in flux and variable recensions in circulation, the gospel citations are realistically imaginable as commitments to a single, fixed textual tradition.

When Eugene Ulrich suggested that both the Masoretic Text and the Septuagint were developing textual bodies that had grown out of variable traditions, he was thereby undermining the model of a static, textual universe.[82] When Chilton observed that "the correspondence between New Testament citations of the Old Testament and the Septuagint is not usually exact,"[83] he was reminding his readers that "the text of the Septuagint was itself not completely fixed in the New Testament period,"[84] and thereby weakening the image of a communications culture of textual stability. When he furthermore asserted that while many of Matthew's citations followed the Hebrew text, "many more" "agree with the Septuagint and its variants,"[85] he was suggesting that the Gospel was partaking in "an emerging tradition of Old Testament translations,"[86] rather than relying on a single textual body. These were all observations that paved the way for the plurality model.

It is precisely at this point that Jousse's targumic thesis can be seriously considered and brought into the broader discussion. As a result of the plurality of scriptural rewritings, the sizable variability of Hebrew manuscripts, the proximity of many to the oral register, and the absence

---

81. Stendahl, *The School of St. Matthew.*
82. Ulrich, *The Dead Sea Scrolls*, 146, 163, 206.
83. Chilton, *A Galilean Rabbi*, 89.
84. Chilton, *A Galilean Rabbi*, 89.
85. Chilton, *A Galilean Rabbi*, 89.
86. Chilton, *A Galilean Rabbi*, 89.

of a single textual standard, space has been created for exploring the presence of Aramaic targumic traditions. Furthermore, given the impact of the Dead Sea Scrolls on our understanding of the Jewish communications culture and the processing of Aramaic and Hebraic traditions, is it not reasonable to surmise that the targumim may have left traces in the stream of gospel traditions?

Once again, Chilton's achievement is to have decisively shaped and advanced our knowledge of the targumim, and to have explored their influence on the New Testament, paying close attention to targumic features in the gospel tradition.[87] Using Targum Isaiah as test case, Chilton proceeds to build his case for targumic affinities with gospel traditions that make use of the so-called Old Testament. To that end, he surveys all cases where Jesus made use of Isaian references, admitting as evidence citations, allusions, and imagery, and making allowance both for verbal similarities and thematic coherence. Moreover, he dismisses versions that were intelligible as redactional features of the gospel compositions. Additionally, he extends his explorations beyond citations from the so-called Old Testament by including the kingdom language of the parables. Of special importance to his targumic argument is the demonstration of evidence that differed from and was not explicable in reference to the great textual bodies of the Masoretic Text, the Septuagint, the Vulgate, and the Peshitta. Last but not least, Chilton is fully aware that in Jesus' lifetime Targum Isaiah was not a document but "an assortment of local traditions";[88] he thus steers away from a strictly textual model and allows for the popular, oral nature of targumic traditions.

Independent from Jousse, and yet fully in the spirit of his work, Chilton has developed and solidified the core of the Joussian targumic thesis. Manifestly, the argument concerning a targumic coloring of gospel traditions is based on a high degree of historical insight, methodological skills, and rhetorical subtlety. Chilton clearly understands that on the targumic issue there are no easy generalizations. One is bound to operate on the level of possibilities, not certainties. But the point to be made in the context of this book is that Chilton's work once more demonstrates

---

87. In addition to Chilton's *Galilean Rabbi*, see his contribution to this volume, in which he demonstrates the procedure of retroversion (the transfer of a Greek version into Aramaic) using the examples of the Lord's Prayer and Mark 7:15. Retroversion was initially introduced by Jousse. See also the monumental study by Flesher and Chilton, *The Targums*; as well as Chilton et al., eds., *A Comparative Handbook*.

88. Chilton, *A Galilean Rabbi*, 116.

the relevance of Jousse's work. Even on the seemingly esoteric topic of the gospel's targumic legacy, Jousse proved himself to be astoundingly prescient. To be sure, it is clearly understood that nobody will claim today that the targumim provide the key to the gospel traditions. The plurality model will look with skepticism on single-tradition solutions, including on the targumic tradition as a single solution. But on one point Jousse was quite correct: Once we concede Jesus' Aramaic vernacular and free ourselves from the notion that he was using the so-called Old Testament as his Bible, we are bound to ask deeper questions, and are inescapably confronted with the targumic issue. Irrespective of the particularities of Jousse's targumic thesis, to have made the targumim a major issue must rank among his most remarkable achievements.

Epilogue

The purpose of this book has been to provide a general introduction to the oeuvre of Marcel Jousse by explicating, critically assessing, and further developing his major ideas. It is entirely in Jousse's spirit that his thinking is making uncommon demands on its readers. Likewise, insomuch as his theses received much criticism, *The Forgotten Compass* is likely to provoke its share of critical responses. A principal point of criticism could well be that Jousse's work represents one of the earliest and most conspicuous articulations of what came to be called by its critics the Great Divide.[89] Critics saw Jousse as placing a wedge—a great divide—between orality and textuality.

When beginning in the 1970s biblical scholarship was taking the first tentative steps toward an ethnographically and media-based recognition of oral style and oral dynamics, the single most pronounced reaction was lament over the flawed conception of the Great Divide. The argument that the notion of the Great Divide was flawed asserted that a clean differentiation between the oral medium and the scribal medium missed the point that in linguistic actuality the two media operated synergistically and in coexistence. Pitting orality against textuality, it was objected, failed to come to terms with the media realities on the ground. Was it not one of the lessons of the media history of antiquity (as well as of many other periods) that oral and scribal dynamics were overlapping

---

89. Rodriguez, "Great Divide."

and interfacing realities? Do we not time and again observe media locked in conflict over claims to cultural supremacy?

A major problem with this objection to the Great Divide is that it falls short of a full understanding of the discipline of media studies, and in turn reflects a limited grasp of communications history. How realistic is the charge that orality theorists, in an exclusive focus on the Great Divide, were ignorant of or uninterested in coming to terms with the interconnectedness of communications media? I would suggest that the notion of orality studies privileging an absolute media dichotomy to the exclusion of media interactions represents a reductionist perspective on recent work on the theory and practice of media ecology. In a sense, the critics' single-minded attention to what they choose to call the Great Divide has magnified the media gap.

Consider the work of the experts who have spearheaded the fields of orality, scribality and media ecology. Such distinguished scholars as McLuhan and Ong, Parry and Lord, and Havelock and Foley, have greatly enriched the discipline of cultural history by illuminating in unprecedented fashion media interactions, fusions, and conflicts. All six of them can justly be called experts in comparative media ecology. But they were able to accomplish their work precisely by developing and operating with a conceptual model of distinctive media identities. The same can be said of Jousse. He illustrated how oral processes and bookish algebrosis were locked in a dialectical but in the end conflictual relationship, which showed again and again how the literary civilization came to override, suppress, and eclipse oral attributes and values.

To be sure, conflict is by no means the only relation that orality and scribality are involved in. But it is a defining relationship. How else can one grasp intermediality unless one has a developed sense of the noetics and psychodynamics of orality vis-à-vis that of the technology of writing and textuality? Without critically discerning which media are at work, and without precisely defining separate media, it is nearly impossible to detect media interdependencies, to explain media interactions, and, in short, to know the life of media activities. This was one of the main problems confronting the form critics: Displaying no interest in classifying differences between oral processes and scribal processes, they proceeded to derive what they called the forms of speech straight out of textuality. I suggest that Jousse's oeuvre in its integrated totality demonstrates that oral culture and the interaction of oral with chirographic/typographic media are part and parcel of a single communications paradigm. Theoretically and in media actuality, one does not exist without the other. By refusing to acknowledge specific media attributes, however, objectors to the Great Divide run the risk of taking us back to Bultmann's assumption that differentiating between the oral and the textual is irrelevant.

Jousse's thesis challenges the conventions of biblical scholarship. Readers of this volume are given ample opportunity to observe his relentless polemic vis-à-vis a scholarly approach in which written and by extension printed textuality serve as the paradigm for exegesis, hermeneutics, and biblical theology. The language Jousse employed to castigate biblical scholarship's overconfidence in words-in-space is harshly critical and so cannot escape readers' attention. Obviously, more is involved in meeting this challenge than merely modifying or correcting the conventional textual model. Matters that biblical exegetes have long assumed to be settled (therefore requiring no more critical reflection) become unsettled and are open to question when Jousse's work is taken seriously. Authorship and editorship, tradition and composition, reading and writing, memory and imagination, cognition and logic—central tropes of the Western intellectual history—are all affected by the Joussean model. Implicated also are more specific linguistic terms, such as *edition* and *recension*, *variants* and the *original* version, *publication* and *literary sources*. Whether one takes the implications of Jousse's work as broadly theoretical or more narrowly technical, on Joussean terms a whole apparatus of nomenclature appears misapplied and ill-suited to dealing with the communications realities of ancient Near Eastern cultures.

Jousse was fully cognizant that the success of his novel paradigm depended in no small measure on a pertinent nomenclature—hence his dissatisfaction with the time-honored terminology, and his preoccupation with a conceptualization of neologisms. It could be argued that even the concepts of text and textuality, foundational tropes of scholarship in the wake of Gutenberg, are problematic in light of Jousse's criticism, since they are loaded with assumptions derived from modern literary criticism and print technology. Jousse's own designation of *les textes fluids*, while insightful and inventive, is not entirely satisfactory either, because it refers to the oral disposition of scribal materials while holding on to their textual designation. Perhaps when dealing with the pre-Gutenberg history we should relinquish the designation of text altogether and instead become accustomed to using terms such as *manuscript* and *scribality*, *chirography* and *scriptography*, *scriptum* and *scripta*—all designations that denote the craft of handwriting.

Given the single-minded, driving purpose of Jousse's mode of argumentation, one may well call his paradigm *a strong thesis*. There are drawbacks to strong theses because they are susceptible to potential blind spots. They are particularly prone to screening out what is deemed unsuitable for sustaining the master thesis. And yet, strong theses are often necessary because they break new theoretical ground and create thinking space. There is no getting around the fact that Jousse has presented us with a strong alternative model that encourages us to rethink the hermeneutical landscape of biblical studies and to reset media priorities.

One cannot do full justice to Jousse's work without acknowledging his central interest in recovering lost sensibilities. The combination of a strong thesis with sensitivity to dimensions of communication that have often been overlooked or suppressed makes his work exceptionally worthy of attention. Indifference to the vast range of sensory modalities has become the norm in academic biblical scholarship to such an extent that their absence is hardly even palpable. We have lost consciousness of how reductionist and narrowly text bound the hermeneutical framework has become in which exegesis is conducted and thinking takes place. In making the human sensorium a central issue of his paradigm, Jousse reclaimed sense perceptions that had been gradually but persistently marginalized over the course of Western intellectual history. Once again, *algebrization* or *algebrosis*, the categories Jousse had singled out for special criticism, provide the necessary explanatory context. From Jousse's point of view, the invention of the alphabet, accelerated by the expansion of writing systems, and reaching a culmination with the spread of print technologies, exacted the heavy price of sensory deprivation by effecting a growing disconnect from the oral-memorial-sensory matrix of human culture.

Once the print Bible was established, interpreters were destined to derive meaning from its technologically constructed textuality, increasingly discounting the copious realm of sensibilities. Over and against a major proportion of ancient and medieval communication theories and practices, the influence of the Reformers resulted, gradually, and notwithstanding their concern for the living Word of Scripture, in reducing the threefold or fourfold sense of Scripture to the one: the literal or historical sense. In the wake of the Reformation, a large part of the human sensorium, along with memory, was marginalized and virtually eliminated from Protestant biblical exegesis, while by the twentieth century Catholic exegesis was well on the way toward very similar developments.

Indeed, the collective amnesia of biblical scholarship with respect to the work of Marcel Jousse is itself a measure of the reductionist hermeneutics in biblical interpretation. Increasingly, and dramatically so after Gutenberg, texts came to conjure up the systematically organized printed page, private-silent reading, and literary competence. Although not a media critic in the modern sense, Jousse was acutely sensitive to these cultural developments. Unlike very few in his lifetime, he succeeded in articulating the media *algebrosis,* and unlike anyone at the time, he managed to forge a substantial alternative model.

Against the backdrop of a millennial chirographic media history and five centuries of typographically enforced thinking processes, Jousse's paradigm is comprehensible as the recovery of lost sensibilities. In the face of a dominant scholarly propensity to treat texts as the one medium through which other senses must be interpreted, Jousse argued that voice and recitation, rhythm and gesture, memory and performance, sound and verbomotoric style were characteristic of the biblical traditions and provided the appropriate means for reactivating them. All these operations of verbalization and remembering were, in his view, somatically rooted, and collectively represented a whole set of sensory values. It was his lifelong conviction that there was no cognitive perception without a grounding in sensory perception. Last and not least, Jousse's sensory rehabilitation of biblical exegesis closely attached itself to the sacred. Particularly noteworthy in this regard is his oral-memorial-sensory interpretation of the ritual of Mass as an oral-memorial repristination of an ancient Palestinian mimodrama. All in all, Jousse's rediscovery of lost sensibilities is in urgent need of a theological appropriation.

If it is objected that Jousse's interests were single-mindedly focused on the oral and oral-style medium while for us biblical traditions are primarily accessible in the textual medium, I wish to alert readers to the fact that the contributors to this volume have amply demonstrated the applicability of Joussean principles to biblical and other ancient texts. But we need be mindful that in the wake of Jousse, oral-scribal priorities are being reversed. Whereas by the long-standing conventions of biblical hermeneutics, orality tends to be antecedent and subordinate to texts, in Joussean thinking, biblical texts were derived from, dependent on, and operating in the service of oral sensibilities.

Let me, at the end, return to the beginning, and bring this volume to a close by framing it with one of Jousse's favorite designs: the clampword mechanism. I conclude with his aphorism that is placed at the head of the book's first chapter: "I am teaching you to find what I have found myself to be unable to find." Accordingly, it was not Jousse's intention to create an academic school of faithful followers. Rather, his intention (and ultimately the purpose of this book) is to allow Jousse's model to impact our thinking about gospels and biblical traditions in the interest of becoming more deeply reflective about the biblical discipline, and to extend his insights, in whatever revised or modified form, to our work in the current digital media revolution.

Bibliography

Assmann, Aleida. *Erinnerungsräume: Formen und Wandlungen des kulturellen Gedächtnisses*. C. H. Beck Kulturwissenschaft. Munich: Beck, 1999.

———. *Cultural Memory and Western Civilization: Functions, Media, Archives*. New York: Cambridge University Press, 2011.

Assmann, Jan. *Das kulturelle Gedächtnis: Schrift, Erinnerung und politische Identität in frühen Hochkulturen*. C. H. Beck Kulturwissenschaft. Munich: Beck, 1992.

———. *Cultural Memory and Early Civilization: Writing, Remembrance, and Political Imagination*. New York: Cambridge University Press, 2011.

Bultmann, Rudolf. *Die Geschichte der synoptischen Tradition*. 3rd ed. Forschungen zur Religion und Literatur des Alten und Neuen Testaments 29. Göttingen: Vandenhoeck & Ruprecht, 1957.

———. *The History of the Synoptic Tradition*. Translated by John Marsh. New York: Harper & Row, 1963.

Carruthers, Mary. *The Book of Memory: A Study of Memory in Medieval Culture*. Cambridge: Cambridge University Press, 1990.

Chilton, Bruce D. *A Galilean Rabbi and His Bible: Jesus' Use of the Interpreted Scripture of His Time*. 1984. Reprint, Eugene, OR: Wipf & Stock, 2013.

Chilton, Bruce D., et al., eds. *A Comparative Handbook to the Gospel of Mark: Comparisons with Pseudepigrapha, the Qumran Scrolls, and Rabbinic Literature*. The New Testament Gospels in Their Judaic Contexts 1. Leiden: Brill, 2009.

Coleman, Janet. *Ancient and Medieval Memories: Studies in the Reconstruction of the Past*. Cambridge: Cambridge University Press, 1992.

Epp, Eldon Jay. "It's All about Variants: A Variant-Conscious Approach to New Testament Criticism." *Harvard Theological Review* 100 (2004) 275–308.

———. "The Oxyrhynchus New Testament Papyri: 'Not without Honor Except in Their Hometown'?" *Journal of Biblical Literature* 123 (2004) 5–55.

Flesher, Paul V. M., and Bruce Chilton. *The Targums: A Critical Introduction*. Studies in Aramaic Interpretation of Scripture 12. Waco: Baylor University Press, 2011.

Funk, Robert W., and the Jesus Seminar. *The Gospel of Jesus according to the Jesus Seminar*. Santa Rosa, CA: Polebridge, 1999.

Güttgemanns, Erhardt. *Candid Questions concerning Gospel Form Criticism: A Methodological Sketch of the Fundamental Problematics of Form and Redaction Criticism*. Translated by William G. Doty. Pittsburgh Theological Monograph Series 26. Pittsburgh: Pickwick Publications, 1979.

———. *Offene Fragen zur Formgeschichte des Evangeliums: Eine methodologische Skizze der Grundlagenproblematik der Form- und Redaktionsgeschichte*. Beiträge der evangelischen Theologie 54. Munich: Kaiser, 1970.

Haines-Eitzen, Kim. *Guardians of Letters: Literacy, Power, and the Transmitters of Early Christian Literature*. Oxford: Oxford University Press, 2000.

Halbwachs, Maurice. *Les cadres sociaux de la mémoire*. Travaux de l'Année sociologique. Paris: Alcán, 1925.

———. *On Collective Memory*. Edited, translated, and with an introduction by Lewis A. Coser. The Heritage of Sociology. Chicago: University of Chicago Press, 1992.

Horsley, Richard A. *Text and Tradition in Performance and Writing*. Biblical Performance Criticism Series 9. Eugene, OR: Cascade Books, 2013.

Joubert, Annekie. *The Power of Performance: Linking Past and Present in Hananwa and Lobedu Oral Literature*. Trends in Linguistics: Studies and Monographs 160. Berlin: de Gruyter, 2004.

Jousse, Marcel. *In Search of Coherence: Introducing Marcel Jousse's Anthropology of Mimism*. Edited and translated by Edgard Sienaert. Eugene, OR: Pickwick Publications, 2016.

———. *Memory, Memorization, and Memorizers: The Galilean Oral-Style Tradition and Its Traditionists*. Edited and translated by Edgard Sienaert. Biblical Performance Criticism Series 15. Eugene, OR: Cascade Books, 2018.

———. *The Oral Style*. Translated by Edgard Sienaert and Richard Whitaker. Albert Bates Lord Studies in Oral Tradition 6. New York: Garland, 1990.

———. *Le style oral et mnémotechnique chez les verbo-moteurs*. Paris: Beauchesne, 1925.

Kelley, Shawn. *Racializing Jesus: Race, Ideology and the Formation of Modern Biblical Scholarship*. Biblical Limits. London: Routledge, 2002.

Kirk, Alan, and Tom Thatcher. "Jesus Tradition as Social Memory." In *Memory, Tradition, and Text: Uses of the Past in Early Christianity*, edited by Alan Kirk and Tom Thatcher, 25–42. Semeia Studies 52. Atlanta: Society of Biblical Literature, 2005.

———, eds. *Memory, Tradition, and Text: Uses of the Past in Early Christianity*. Semeia Studies 52. Atlanta: Society of Biblical Literature, 2005.

Kümmel, Werner Georg. *Introduction to the New Testament*. Rev. ed. Translated by Howard Clark Kee. Nashville: Abingdon, 1975.

Lord, Albert B. "The Gospels as Oral Traditional Literature." In *The Relationships among the Gospels: An Interdisciplinary Dialogue*, edited by William O. Walker Jr., 33–91. Trinity University Monograph Series in Religion 5. San Antonio: Trinity University Press, 1978.

McLuhan, Marshall. *The Gutenberg Galaxy: The Making of Typographic Man*. Toronto: University of Toronto Press, 1962.

Miller, Shem. *Dead Sea Media: Orality, Textuality, and Memory in the Scrolls from the Judean Desert*. Studies on the Texts of the Desert of Judah 129. Leiden: Brill, 2019.

Parker, David C. *The Living Text of the Gospels*. Cambridge: Cambridge University Press, 1997.

Robinson, James M., and Helmut Koester. *Trajectories through Early Christianity*. 1971. Reprint, Eugene, OR: Wipf & Stock, 2005.

Rodriguez, Rafael. "Great Divide." In *The Dictionary of the Bible and Ancient Media*, edited by Tom Thatcher et al., 163–64. London: Bloomsbury, 2017.

Squire, Michael, ed. *Sight and the Ancient Senses*. The Senses in Antiquity. London: Routledge, 2016.

Stendahl, Krister. *The School of St. Matthew, and Its Use of the Old Testament*. Philadelphia: Fortress, 1968.

Ulrich, Eugene. *The Dead Sea Scrolls and the Origins of the Bible*. Studies in the Dead Sea Scrolls and Related Literature. Grand Rapids: Eerdmans, 1999.

Index

Alexander, Loveday, 45, 45nn174–79, 47
Alter, Robert, 118, 118n54, 119, 119nn59–60, 120, 120n63, 121, 121n64, 124, 145, 145n84
Aquinas, Thomas, 18
Aristotle, 29, 80, 222, 223, 224, 225, 228
Assmann, Aleida, 22, 22n54, 272, 272n46
Assmann, Jan, 22, 22n54, 45, 45n172, 128–29, 128nn6–7, 272, 272n46
Astell, Ann W., 225n40
Auerbach, Erich, 223, 223n37, 223n38, 226, 228

Baillaud, Bernard, 100n127
Bakhtin, Mikhail, 124, 124n71
Baron, Gabrielle, 78, 78n19, 211n1, 230, 230n50
Bataille, Georges, 222
Bauman, Richard, 146, 146n91
Bérard, Victor, 59, 59n11
Bergson, Henri, 21
Berlin, Adele, 139, 139nn58–59, 140, 140n64, 141n67
Bhaumik, Mani, 229n45
Black, C. Clifton, 194n42
Black, Matthew, 38, 38n139, 216, 216n14
Boman, Thorleif, 191, 191nn34–35, 215, 215n9

Boomershine, Thomas E., 189
Botha, Pieter J. J., 189, 189n25
Branch, Robin Gallaher, 122n67
Breed, Brennan W., 244n29
Broshi, Magen, 128n3
Brougham, A. E., 112n43
Bryant, John, 244, 244n30
Buffon: see Leclerc, Georges-Louis
Bultmann, Rudolf, 5, 5n13, 7, 7n14, 20n51, 182, 187, 188, 188n21, 194, 237, 237n5, 240, 259n4, 276n58
Burney, Charles F., 38, 38n137
Buzy, Denis, 60–61, 60n15, 61nn16–17, 63–64, 64nn19–20, 66, 66n21
Byrskog, Samuel, 182n4

Caillois, Roger, 222–23, 222n33, 223n35, 225
Camp, Claudia V., 107n13
Carr, David M., 136, 136n45, 243n25
Carré de Busserolle, J.-X., 213n3
Carruthers, Mary J., 17n45, 18, 18nn46–47, 259, 259n1
Casey, Maurice, 38, 38n140
Chancey, Mark A., 40n146
Chartier, Roger, 237n4
Cheng, Joyce, 222n34
Chesneau, Gabriel, 199, 199n2, 200
Chilton, Bruce D., x, 38, 38n141, 41n149, 42n151, 42n153, 50, 50n185, 50n187, 195n46,

291

211, 214n7, 216n11, 216n15,
218n19, 219n20, 223n38,
230n48, 242, 279, 280,
280nn76–80, 281, 281nn83–
86, 282–83, 282nn87–88
Chouraqui, André, 119
Churgin, Pinkhos, 216, 216n12
Clark, Herbert H., 140nn63–64
Coleman, Janet, 17n45, 259, 259n2
Craigie, Peter C., 139
Crossan, John Dominic, 276
Culley, Robert C., 139n57

Dahlmann, Britt, 244n29
Dahood, Mitchell, 139n58
Dalman, Gustaf, 57n5, 214, 214n5, 216
Darío, Rubén, 109n25
Darnton, Robert, 252n51
Dean, Margaret E., 163n56
Deese, James Earle, 140n63
Dewey, Joanna, x, 180, 189n23, 190n28, 191n33, 192n39, 194n41, 258
Dibelius, Martin, 5, 5n12, 187, 237n5, 240
Díez Macho, Alejandro, 216, 216n14
Dobbs-Allsopp, F. W., 111–12, 111nn39–40, 119, 119n61
Dostoevsky, Fyodor, 224
Draper, Jonathan A., 46n182
Dumas, Georges, 57, 201, 201n5
Durkheim, Émile, 21

Eddy, Paul Rhodes, 217n18
Eisenstein, Elizabeth L., 19, 19n50, 237n4
Elder, Nicholas A., 189n26
Epp, Eldon Jay, 269, 269n33, 269n35
Evans, Craig A., 216n15
Everett, Hugh, III, 229n46

Falasca-Zamponi, Simonetta, 222n32
Finnegan, Ruth, 146n89
Fitzmyer, Joseph A., 218, 220n25, 220nn21–23

Flesher, Paul V. M., 38, 38n141, 41n149, 42n152, 42n154, 50, 50n187, 214n7, 216n11, 216n15, 282n87
Foley, John Miles, 2, 12, 12nn20–24, 13n25, 15, 15n36, 189, 284
Follet, René, 57, 57n6, 70
Foucauld, Charles de, 206, 206n9
Fraade, Steven D., 41n150
France, Marie de, x–xi
Funk, Robert W., 220n24, 276, 276n60

Gaster, Theodor H., 142n70
Gellius, Aulus, 250–51, 251n47
Gerhardsson, Birger, 182, 182n4, 215, 215n10, 242, 242n19
Gevirtz, Stanley, 139, 139n61
Giffone, Benjamin D., 118, 118n58
Girard, René, 223–24, 223n38, 225, 225n40, 226, 228
Goguel, Maurice, 59, 77, 203n7, 214
Goodhart, Sandor, 225n40
Gottwald, Norman K., 37, 37n129
Grées du Loû, Gabrielle des, 57, 57n5
Grundmann, Walter, 34n120
Gry, Léon, 99n122
Gurd, Sean Alexander, 243n25, 244n29
Güttgemanns, Erhardt, 259n4

Haines-Eitzen, Kim, 160, 160n39, 269, 269n34
Halbwachs, Maurice, 21–22, 21n52, 23, 28, 32, 272, 272n45
Hameroff, Stuart, 230n48
Hanson, Anthony, 238n6
Harrington, Daniel J., 220n25, 220nn21–23
Harris, William V., 189n22
Hasselbalch, Trine Bjørnung, 130n18
Havelock, Eric A., 145n83, 190, 190nn29–32, 247n38, 284
Hengel, Martin, 243n24
Hezser, Catherine, 25n73, 43, 43nn160–61, 44nn162–63,

47, 156, 156n29, 243n25, 279
Hinton, David, 154–55, 154n22, 155n23
Hochschild, Paige E., 23n58
Holt, Mark Timothy Lloyd, x, 104
Homer, 4, 20, 59, 66, 68, 118, 155, 247–49
Hoover, Roy W., 220n24
Horsley, Richard A., 37, 37n130, 37n132, 40n145, 41n148, 43, 43nn158–59, 46, 46nn180–82, 47, 47n184, 277n62, 279
Hovind, Jacob, 223n37
Hughes, Julie A., 143n75, 145n86
Hurowitz, Victor Avigdor, 106n10

Isidore of Seville, 71

Janet, Pierre, 9n16, 222
Jeremias, Joachim, 218
Johnson, William A., 243n25
Joubert, Annekie, 261n17
Jullian, Camille, 210, 210n15

Kahle, Paul, 42, 42n153, 216, 216n13, 217
Kaku, Michio, 229n47
Kaufman, Steven A., 217, 217nn16–17, 220n25, 242n20
Keck, Leander E., 192n38
Keith, Chris, 35n123
Kelber, Werner H., x, 1, 5n10, 8n48, 129nn10–11, 130, 130nn15–16, 133, 133nn27–28, 137n48, 150n1, 182n4, 189, 215n8, 240n11, 242n21, 253, 253n53, 258
Kelley, Shawn, 276, 276n61
Kirk, Alan, 44–45, 44nn168–70, 45nn171–73, 47, 160–63, 160n40, 160nn37–38, 161n41, 161nn43–46, 162nn50–53, 163nn54–55, 165, 165n58, 166, 166n59, 168–69, 168n60, 169n61, 172, 172n63, 173, 173nn64–65, 175, 176–77,
243n25, 272–73, 272n47, 273nn48–49
Kittel, Bonnie, 142, 142n71, 143, 143n75, 143nn77–78, 146n88
Kivy, Peter, 247n36
Klein, Michael L., 42n151
Koester, Helmut, 272, 272nn43–44, 276, 276n59
Kraft, Charles F., 142n70
Kugel, James, 115, 115nn49–51, 116n52, 119, 119n62, 123, 123n69, 139, 139n60, 142n69
Kümmel, Werner Georg, 273n50

La Fontaine, Jean de, 206–7, 206n11
Lao Tzu, 154
Laplace, 104
Larsen, Matthew D. C., x, 234, 235n1, 240n12, 244n29, 248n39, 249nn42–43, 250nn45–46, 251nn47–48, 252n51, 274
Leclerc, Georges-Louis, 83, 83n41
Lee, Margaret E., x, 150, 158n35, 159n36, 161n49, 163n56, 172n62, 258
Leeuw, Gerardus van der, 94, 94n95
Letteney, Mark, 235n1
Licht, Jacob, 142, 142n70
Loisy, Alfred, 58–59, 58n8, 59n9, 67, 67n24
Lord, Albert B., ix, 107, 182, 184–85, 189, 192, 193, 259, 259n4, 274, 274nn55–56, 275, 275n57, 284
Lorenz, Elisabeth, 34n120
Lowth, Robert, 107, 108
Lugt, Pieter van der, 142n71

Machiela, Daniel A., 42n156
Malherbe, François, 69n25
Manson, T. W., 216, 216n15
Marion, Henri, 206, 206n10
Marxsen, Willi, 238n6
Maunoury, Auguste-Francois, 72, 72n6

McCowen, Alec, 189
McGann, Jerome J., 237n4
McGill, Scott, 252n52
McKenzie, D. F., 237n4
McLuhan, Marshall, 4, 4n6, 19n49, 187, 262, 262n23, 264n28, 284
McNamara, Martin, 216, 216n14
Metzger, Bruce M., 239n9
Miller, Shem, x, 42n155, 43n159, 127, 131n21, 136n45, 138n55, 277–78, 277n63, 278n64, 279
Morlaàs, Joseph, 57, 57n4, 63
Mroczek, Eva, 238n7, 243n25, 244n29

Nagy, Gregory, 247n35
Najman, Hindy, 244n29
Newsom, Carol, 143n75
Nietzsche, Friedrich, 239n8
Nirenberg, David, 35, 35n121
Novick, Tzvi, 121, 121n65

Ombredane, André, 201n5
Ong, Walter J., 4, 4n7, 18, 18n48, 130, 130n17, 182, 189, 190, 190n27, 191, 191n37, 258, 284

Papillault, Georges, 200, 200n3
Parker, David C., 186, 186nn17–18, 244n29, 269–70, 269n36, 269nn31–32, 270nn37–40
Parry, Milman, ix, 20, 21, 22, 23, 107, 129–30, 130n15, 136, 136n45, 182, 215, 259, 284
Pascal, Blaise, 58, 58n7
Pasternack, Carol Braun, 145–46, 146n87
Peirano, Irene, 244n29, 248n41
Penrose, Roger, 229–30, 230n48
Perrin, Norman, 238n6
Person, Raymond F., 44, 44nn164–67, 47, 137, 137n52, 243n25, 279
Petersen, Anders Klostergaard, 243n24

Plato, 190, 223, 224, 225, 226, 247, 247n37
Proust, Marcel, 224

Racine, Jean, 207n12
Rad, Gerhard von, 105, 105n4
Rebeillard, Éric, 244n29
Reed, A. W., 112n43
Ribouillaut, Claude, 212, 212n2
Richards, E. Randolph, 252n52
Robinson, James M., 272, 272nn43–44, 276, 276n59
Rodriguez, Rafael, 129n14, 283n89
Rousselot, Jean-Pierre, 60, 60n14

Sarzana, Guiseppi, 213n4
Schmidt, Karl Ludwig, 5, 5n11
Schrödinger, Erwin, 229
Schuller, Eileen M., 128n3, 130n18, 131n20, 131nn23–24, 132n25, 135, 135nn33–39, 136n44, 136nn40–41, 137nn50–51, 138, 138n54
Scott, Bernard Brandon, 158n35, 159n36, 161n49, 163n56, 172n62
Scott, James C., 37n131
Sertillanges, Antonin, 200, 200n4
Shorey, Paul, 247n37
Siegismund, Kasper, 121–22, 122n66
Sienaert, Edgard, x–xi, 2, 5, 5n9, 30, 32, 60n15, 61nn16–17, 64nn19–20, 71, 150, 152n10, 181, 222, 222n29
Siker, Jeffrey, 245n31
Spire, André, 62, 62n18, 63, 67
Squire, Michael, 259n3
Stegemann, Hartmut, 131n19, 131nn23–24, 132nn25–26, 135, 135n36, 135nn38–39, 136n44, 137nn50–51, 138, 138n54
Stendhal (Marie-Henri Beyle), 224
Stendahl, Krister, 281, 281n81
Strange, William A., 239n10

Talmon, Shemaryahu, 137, 137n52

Thatcher, Tom, 272–73, 272n47, 273nn48–49
Thiering, Barbara, 142–43, 143n73
Torrey, Charles Cutler, 38, 38n138
Tov, Emanuel, 279

Ulrich, Eugene, 245n31, 277, 278–79, 278nn65–70, 279nn71–75, 281, 281n82

Vansina, Jan, 191, 191n36
Virgil, 68–69, 248

Walsh, Robyn Faith, 241n18
Waltke, Bruce K., 107n14, 112, 112n44
Walton, Brian, 73n7
Watson, Francis, 241n17
Watson, Wilfred G. E., 115, 115n48, 129n8, 143n76

Watters, William R., 139n57
Wernberg-Møller, Preben, 217, 217n17
West, Martin L., 248n40
Whitaker, Richard, xi
Whitman, Walt, 109n25
Wire, Antoinette, 189, 189n24, 192n39
Wise, Michael Owen, 39n142, 40n143
Wolters, Al, 105, 105n7, 107, 107n12, 109nn31–34, 114, 114n46, 122, 122n68

Yoder, Christine Roy, 105–7, 105nn2–3, 105nn5–6, 106nn8–9, 107n11, 114
York, Anthony D., 217, 217n17

www.ingramcontent.com/pod-product-compliance
Lightning Source LLC
Chambersburg PA
CBHW032051220426
43664CB00008B/954